Unthinkable? Think again. Ian Easton has done a remarkable job taking the PRC at their word. Using PLA manuals and publications, this Project 2049 Institute study shows that China is prepared to invade, intimidate or interdict. This is a scholarly work which most China hands would like to overlook. No longer can they do so. Well done, Mr. Easton.

—Ambassador Richard Armitage,
former Deputy Secretary of State

Argues persuasively that the risks of conflict in the Taiwan Strait lurk on the horizon. Persuasive and in places controversial, Mr. Easton sets out the case that armed conflict has not been made irrelevant in the Western Pacific even with the closer economic ties between China and Taiwan. An unsettling but necessary read for students of Asia.

—Dr. Kurt M. Campbell,
former Assistant Secretary of State for Asian Affairs

Ian Easton has done an enormous amount of research in both Chinese and Taiwanese sources about a potential military conflict across the Taiwan Strait. While I disagree with many of his assertions ... I found myself interested in his citations and often challenged by his assertions. Whether you agree with his conclusions or not, it is worth reading this serious examination of the reality of a Chinese invasion of Taiwan.

—Admiral Dennis Blair (USN, ret.),
former Director of National Intelligence and
Commander of U.S. Pacific Command

Calls attention to threats in plain sight but overlooked by our policy makers and strategists. Taiwan, a vigorous democracy at the confluence of the contested East and South China Seas ... exists under often-declared threat. It is the most consequential political and military challenge of our times.

—Lt. General Wallace Gregson (USMC, ret.),
former Assistant Secretary of Defense and
Commander Marine Forces Pacific

A comprehensive and insightful treatment of one of the most significant geopolitical military challenges facing the United States ... a conflict over Taiwan has the potential to explode as the PRC grows in economic and military power. Ian Easton sheds light on a potential reality that we must be well prepared to handle.

—Lt. General David A. Deptula (USAF, ret.),
former Commander Pacific Command Air Component and
Chief of U.S. Air Force Intelligence

A powerful and thought-provoking study helping policy makers as well as experts reshape their perceptions and analysis ... in an ever changing and dire Taiwan Strait. It is a must-read book for those who hold power to protect Taiwan as a beacon of democracy.

—Andrew Nien Dzu Yang,
former Minister of National Defense, Taiwan (ROC)

An extremely readable and informative text describing the most dangerous, destructive, and least likely option in the Taiwan Strait ... clearly illustrates why deterrence of such an event should be Taiwan's and America's primary objective in cross-strait relations.

—Dennis J. Blasko,
author of *The Chinese Army Today*

While much of the world has forgotten the importance of Taiwan to the peace and stability of the Asia Pacific region ... Mr. Easton's well-sourced and clearly enunciated work reminds us all of the likelihood and cost of war and the price of freedom.

—Captain James Fanell (USN, ret.),
former Pacific Fleet Director of Intelligence

14 possible landing beaches, 4 weeks of permissive weather twice a year, and 1,000 individual targets for air strikes in the run-up to an invasion. These are some of the facts and figures readers will take away from this unique and indispensable trove of insights into the PLA's preparations.... This is an authoritative exposé of the PRC's offensive plans.

—Jacqueline N. Deal,
President, Long Term Strategy Group

The threat is not the threat itself. The real threat is the connection between the threats.... How to obtain a clear picture? The author crafts a detailed roadmap for the audience to discover. Bravo Zulu!
—Admiral Richard YK Chen (ROCN, ret.), former Commander of the Navy and Vice Minister of National Defense, Taiwan (ROC)

In this carefully researched and forcefully argued study, Ian Easton draws on a wide range of Chinese-language sources from both sides of the Taiwan Strait to describe how a conflict there might start, how it would likely be fought and how it might end ... explains why the outcome would matter to the United States and how, through a mix of measured diplomacy and prudent military preparations, deterrence can be maintained and peace preserved."

—Aaron Friedberg,
author of *A Contest for Supremacy*,
Professor at Princeton University

This book is a "Must Read" for China watchers and Asia strategists alike. Ian Easton's impressive research analyzes one of the most dangerous flashpoints in Asia.... It makes a powerful case for deterrence and for changes in U.S. and Taiwan force posture to deal with this looming contingency.

—Evan Medeiros,
former National Security Council Senior Director for Asian Affairs
and Special Assistant to President Obama

THE CHINESE INVASION THREAT

The Chinese Invasion Threat

Taiwan's Defense and American Strategy in Asia

Ian Easton

For Mia, Kelly, and Grace

Published by Eastbridge Books, an imprint of Camphor Press Ltd
83 Ducie Street, Manchester, M1 2JQ
United Kingdom

www.eastbridgebooks.com

ISBN   978-1-78869-176-5 (paperback)
          978-1-78869-177-2 (cloth)

The moral right of the author has been asserted.

Set in 11 pt Linux Libertine

Contents

Maps

Abbreviations

CCP	Chinese Communist Party
CMC	Central Military Commission
DPP	Democratic Progressive Party
KMT	Kuomintang, or Nationalist Party
MAAG	Military Assistance Advisory Group
MND	Ministry of National Defense
PLA	People's Liberation Army
PRC	People's Republic of China
ROC	Republic of China
TRA	Taiwan Relations Act
USSR	Union of Soviet Socialist Republics

Note on Terms

THE following book will not use the military term "D-Day" to refer to the notional day on which a Chinese invasion operation was launched against Taiwan. Any practice of making allusions to Operation Overlord and the June 6, 1944, Normandy landings would almost certainly be detrimental to the person reading. Americans and other English-speaking peoples view D-Day as a glorious and magnificent moment in human history. The term D-Day, while sometimes used more broadly by military experts, is associated with strong positive emotions and would be inappropriate for discussing the subject at hand.

This book will instead refer to the date of a future Chinese invasion of Taiwan as "Zero Day" (or Z-Day). This term will designate the day of the invasion operation, since it has not yet been determined by Chinese war planners, or is secret. Z-Day will be used in combination with numbers and plus and minus signs to indicate points of time before or after operations are initiated. For example, Z-Day minus five (Z-5) would mean five days before Zero Day, and Z-Day plus five (Z+5) would mean five days after Zero Day. This term, Z-Day, was used by Winston Churchill when discussing the date of a potential Nazi invasion of England, an operation Adolf Hitler planned to launch in 1940 but aborted after the Battle of Britain resulted in a decisive English victory.

Foreword

Two decades have passed since the 1995–1996 Taiwan Strait Crisis, and senior American policymakers and strategists have drifted away from the cross-Strait flashpoint. Their time and attention have been consumed by events elsewhere. There has been a pressing need to respond to terrorist attacks, global economic recession, cyber infiltration, nuclear proliferation, and simmering tensions all over the world. In Washington, a chronic sense of crisis has set in, and the space for long-term strategic thinking has diminished.

One consequence of this phenomenon is that our nation's policy toward the People's Republic of China and Taiwan still remains largely frozen in a framework developed in the late 1970s, a time when the United States confronted a very different set of foreign policy challenges than it does today. To be effective, policies must evolve over time and adapt to current realities and new facts on the ground. Much has changed in Asia, especially across the Taiwan Strait.

Taiwan has become a flourishing democracy and a beacon of good governance and human rights in a region that still suffers from too many revanchist and authoritarian regimes. Taiwan's success story is an American success story. Our two governments stood shoulder to shoulder in World War Two and during the Cold War. More recently, Taiwan has been a major contributor to reconstruction in Afghanistan, a first responder to global humanitarian crises ranging from earthquakes in Haiti to Ebola in Africa, and a close partner on regional security affairs. Unfortunately,

Taiwan's important role in the world has largely gone unnoticed and its efforts unacknowledged.

At the same time, the PRC has emerged as a near-peer strategic competitor. China is rapidly expanding its military power, with the principal aim of resolving cross-Strait sovereignty disputes by force, while deterring or defeating U.S. power projection capabilities. China is developing and fielding large numbers of offensive weapons systems, including ballistic missiles, drones, space interceptors, amphibious assault ships, stealth submarines, and cyber and electronic attack platforms. These armaments serve to undermine the confidence of our Asian allies that the United States will be able to guarantee their security in a worst-case scenario. This, in turn, erodes the American-led regional security architecture and fosters a growing sense of instability. Taken to its logical conclusion, China's military buildup across from Taiwan could tempt tragedy.

The Taiwan Relations Act (U.S. Law 96-8) states that our national policy is: "to provide Taiwan with arms of a defensive character; and to maintain the capacity of the United States to resist any resort to force or other forms of coercion that would jeopardize the security, or the social or economic system, of the people of Taiwan." As Americans, we are duty bound by both our lofty principles and our pragmatic national interests to support Taiwan's efforts to maintain a credible self-defense.

Going forward, it will be imperative for the Department of Defense to explore innovative approaches for advancing the U.S.–Taiwan defense and security relationship. High-impact arms sales should be conducted in a regular and predictable fashion. But arms sales alone can hardly be expected to preserve the peace. We should seek ways to integrate Taiwan's capable military into our regional security architecture, especially in the areas of maritime domain awareness, ballistic missile defense, and humanitarian assistance and disaster relief operations. In addition, ship visits, senior level contacts, and joint training and exercise programs are sorely needed.

Taiwan's armed forces deserve to be treated with respect and dignity, and our men and women in uniform deserve to be as prepared as possible for known contingencies. The risks facing the United States, Taiwan, and other democracies in Asia are very real. Ensuring long-term peace and prosperity in this vital region demands that we face our problems and act with alacrity to overcome them. In that vein, this volume will serve to advance public education and fuel much-needed policy debate.

Randall G. Schriver

President and CEO

Project 2049 Institute

Author's Note

I FIRST started thinking about the threat facing Taiwan in the late summer of 2005, just a few weeks after arriving in Taipei to study Chinese. Classes had let out, and I was strolling down Heping (Peace) Road on my way to the metro station when the piercing wail of an emergency alert siren cut through the sticky thick air.

I looked up into the sky, my eyes scanning for trouble. Having spent my formative years in rural Illinois, surrounded by cornfields, my brain was programmed to automatically assume that sirens meant tornados were coming. Take cover! But on this particular day the skies were dazzlingly blue, without a threatening cloud mass anywhere in sight.

Armed police officers and soldiers suddenly materialized on the streets around me, seemingly out of nowhere. I grew up in a family of cops, but had never seen so many law enforcement personnel deployed to one place before. It was like the prelude to the St. Patrick's Day parade in Chicago, only bigger, badder, and without the bagpipes.

They briskly halted traffic and sternly motioned for those of us on foot to get clear of the sidewalks. I ducked into one of Taipei's ubiquitous 7-Eleven convenience stores and watched through the windows as the bustling city streets emptied into an eerie silence, broken only by the ominous wail of sirens and the roar of black government sedans zooming past, presumably on their way to emergency evacuation sites.

The scene was surreal. Uniforms were posted at every intersection. Vehicles sat motionless on the curbs. Crowds of nervous-looking pedestrians filed out of buses, families poured out of cars, and mothers jumped off mopeds to rush their children into the nearest building, getting them off the open streets. People huddled under any structure that offered some form of cover.

It dawned on me that everyone seemed to be preparing for an air raid. I looked up again, now half expecting to see fighter jets screaming overhead. Could it be real? Was Taiwan really about to be bombed? I knew that tensions across the Taiwan Strait were high, but it had never occurred to me that a Chinese sneak attack might be coming.

I spotted a familiar face in the crowd milling around the store. It was a classmate of mine, a Japanese exchange student who had lived in Taiwan long enough to know what was up. I waved and stepped over to ask her what was going on. She told me with a worried grin that this was all part of an annual defense exercise that tested emergency procedures for an enemy air strike.

It seemed awfully intense and realistic for a routine drill, but sure enough, thirty minutes later an "all clear" siren sounded, signaling that the test was over. The police re-opened the streets to civilian traffic, and people rushed out of hiding. Hundreds of thousands of engines were fired up in unison, the rumble echoing across downtown Taipei. Traffic was an instant gridlock. Avenues that had been absolutely still and silent moments before were suddenly alive with noise and life and movement. Everything had returned to normal.

But was *this* really normal? It certainly didn't seem normal to me. I had just witnessed something that seemed extraordinary. To my mind, air raid drills belonged in documentary films about the Second World War, not the present day. I knew, of course, that China's communist government took a dim view of Taiwan's democracy and de facto independence. Yet I also knew that regional economic growth was surging to an all-time high, and life was getting better for China's 1.3 billion people. Trade across the Taiwan Strait was accelerating at a remarkably fast clip, too. It was a phenomenon our teachers called "cold politics, hot economics." Could China really afford to initiate conflict with its most important trading partner over an old, half-dormant political dispute? It seemed impossible.

"This air raid drill must be a leftover from the nineties, when things really were tense," I concluded to my friend, remembering the 1995–1996 Taiwan Strait Missile Crisis. China would never attack Taiwan today. There was no threat of war and Chinese invasion. Or was there?

That evening I kept thinking about the day's events, remembering the sight of families scattering off the streets and imagining what parents must have told their children about why they needed to seek shelter. The street scene played itself out in my mind over and over again like a movie reel in a darkened theater. I wondered what war in the Taiwan Strait would look like if it actually occurred and began to worry that one day the sirens might sound for real.

The next day, I started asking my Taiwanese teachers and friends about whether or not they thought China posed an actual threat to Taiwan. Many regarded me as *qiguai*, weird, for asking such an uncomfortable question. They evidently thought it was not something people discussed in polite conversation and changed the subject straight away. A few responded differently. They shrugged tragically, as if Taiwan had already been defeated, and told me it was probably inevitable. In their minds, China was so big that it could invade Taiwan any time it wanted. Sooner or later, they told me, the Chinese would come and take the island over, and they would flee and go live with relatives in California, or Canada, or New Zealand.

Nearly everyone that would talk to me had some kind of escape plan, but no one seemed to have invested any time working out the details. No one seemed to have any clue as to how a war might develop or how an escape, in practice, might work. No one knew the warning signs of invasion, when they should start packing their things and purchase plane tickets out. I pressed them with more questions but got no answers. They were far more concerned about their daily lives and viewed the possibility of war as minimal. As a newcomer to Taiwan, I was astounded. How could so many people live unencumbered by fear with the shadow of an enemy invasion hanging over their heads?

I ended up staying in Taiwan for the next four and a half years. My concerns about the threat of a Chinese attack waxed and waned. Over time, the air defense drills became a regular part of life. Eventually, they even started to feel normal. Other events still served as reminders of the stark possibilities the island nation faced. On October 10, 2007, Taiwan's government held a military parade to celebrate national day. Columns of tanks and missile launchers rolled down the streets just a few blocks from my apartment, and fighter jets and helicopters soared past my rooftop balcony as I looked on.

There was a war scare not long after the parade, just before Taiwan's 2008 presidential elections. In the absence of good information, wild rumors were passed around Taipei's expat community. One rumor held that three American aircraft carrier battle groups had secretly deployed to the Pacific to support Taiwan's free elections.

I went up to a cafe on the northern coast, sat outside and looked at the cold gray sea, sipping coffee and wondering what was going on over the horizon in China and if there really were U.S. Navy ships somewhere out there on patrol. Finally, not seeing anything other than container ships and fishing boats, I concluded that the stories were probably false and there was nothing to worry about. The waters looked too placid to be roiling with geopolitical tensions.

It turned out that I was completely wrong. Years later, I learned from a couple of friends that the rumors had actually been more or less true. One of my buddies was an intelligence officer posted aboard a ship in the Philippine Sea that was patrolling to the east of Taiwan at the time of the 2008 tensions, right when I was sitting on shore drinking coffee.

"The gun was cocked," he told me grimly. "No one realizes how close we came to a shooting war with China that spring."

Another friend, who was working in government security circles at the time, confirmed the sense of anxiety. According to him, the Chinese military had been moving troops and ramping up its activities across from Taiwan in a way that signaled, at least to some analysts, that it might be preparing for an attack. He repeated the line: "The gun was cocked."

* * *

During my time on the "forbidden island," I visited dozens of interesting places, including many of Taiwan's surrounding island atolls. These were often like fortresses. The Kinmen Islands, just off the coast of China, left the deepest impression. Back in the 1950s, the main island, then known as Quemoy, was a household name in America. When the Communists had tried to invade it in 1949, their landing parties were crushed on the beaches. Ten thousand PLA soldiers were wiped out by Chiang Kai-shek's Nationalist Army in a much-needed victory for "Free China."

This, however, did little to stop the "Reds" from shelling the island relentlessly for decades afterwards, and attacking it with ships, fighter planes, and frogmen. At one point in 1958, the fighting over Kinmen became so intense that the American military deployed atomic bombs to an airbase in southern Taiwan, where they reportedly stayed until 1974, just in case the Chinese Communists ever tried to invade and nothing else could stop their human-wave tactics.

On my visit, I learned that the island's granite rock was honeycombed with bunkers from which Taiwan's army could fire long-range missiles, rockets, and artillery shells at the mainland. We went into some of the older, now defunct, tunnels. They were fascinating museum exhibits of a time past. The underground warrens still used by the military were strictly off limits to the public. When our bus driver learned that I could speak Chinese and was interested in military history, he winked and pointed to one of Kinmen's highest mountains.

"It's full of tanks," he said with a mischievous smile. "They're all inside caves. I used to work inside there, right in that mountain. Yes, indeed! There are so many tunnels under this island I could probably drive my bus clear across her underground. Not much traffic down there. Probably get you to the airport in record time!" He belly laughed at the thought.

Initially Taiwan had struck me, as it does most foreign visitors, as exceedingly peaceful and safe. Violent crime was rare. The people were mild-mannered and polite, and compared to Shanghai, where I had previously lived, Taipei seemed modern, clean, and refined. Soft even. Yet as I got below the surface (sometimes literally), a different picture began to emerge.

After that trip to Kinmen I began to notice hidden pillboxes, electronic eavesdropping arrays, and other telltale signs of defensive infrastructure everywhere I looked. I began to see Taiwan as an island nation under siege, and one that had been under siege for so long that most people were numb. That was apparently why nobody I met lost any sleep over the threat.

In 2009, I began working at a Taiwanese software company as a translator. My co-workers were all geeky computer programmers, but they turned out to be hardcore defense hawks as well. In response to my occasional questions, they would proudly tell me stories about their previous military service defending Taiwan against the "Commie Thugs," as they often referred to the Chinese, using the slangy Taiwanese dialect.

I was shocked by their attitude. There was a stereotype of Taiwanese kids not liking their nation's compulsory military service. Many well-off families tried to get their sons out of it. Two of my Taiwanese friends, a lovely couple who had terrible memories of growing up in the martial law era, encouraged their eldest son to maintain a strict diet during his senior year of high school so he would be below the army's minimum weight requirements by the time graduation rolled around. He did and it worked (although it probably cost him some dating opportunities, given how emaciated he looked). This family, from what I could gather, was fairly typical.

Yet here I was in this trendy downtown office with these guys who were reminiscing about "the good old days" when they were patrolling the beaches at night or driving tanks in the stifling heat. Clearly not all young, well-educated Taiwanese abhorred military service as much as I had thought. My co-workers saw it as a rite of passage, a manly act of toughness that no one enjoyed but everyone valued. The really strange part was that after "war stories" around the water cooler, we would go hold a teleconference with the company's Shanghai or Xi'an branches. Not a word was ever said to the Chinese on the other end of the line about the simmering political tensions, but the problems were real. Even these computer nerds were pissed off!

Over the coming months, everyone at the company, from the management on down, made it clear to me that they didn't like working with the "Commie Thugs," who were constantly trying to skirt the rules, cheat them, and weaken their country ... or worse. My co-workers did, of course, value China's large pool of cheap computer programming talent, and they had no problem hiring and managing workers there. Taiwanese businessmen and businesswomen are pragmatic like that. But there was no doubt in anyone's mind that our chain-smoking office director, a fierce Taiwanese lady in her forties, would immediately stop paying all the Chinese on the payroll if Beijing ever attacked.

Economic warfare, as it turned out, was considered an area of relative strength for Taiwan. A retired national security official, whom I met with alongside my boss, told us that the military's cyber warfare branch had contingency plans to disable all communications traffic across the Strait in the event of war. Tens of millions of urban workers across China could be laid off in a digital instant, many of them middle-class employees who worked for Taiwanese technology companies.

"After all," he said with a confident grin, "their salaries all travel electronically via bank wires, and the money originates in Taiwan. So ... it'd be easy." When I heard that, I thought he was crazy. It sounded more like financial suicide than military strategy. A couple of years later a Taiwanese scholar explained the logic to me in a way that made a bit more sense.

"If China even threatens to attack Taiwan, it could greatly damage our economy. Investors will flee. That happened to us in 1996, and we haven't forgotten it. We are now in a position to cripple Shanghai's economy in return—but only if we really have to. An economic blockade would really hurt us too! Nonetheless, our businessmen are some of the most flexible in the world. They would move on to other markets and recover in a few years. China, on the other hand, would be devastated. The pain would be unbearable for the Communists."

Taiwan's national security, it seemed, was about more than air raid drills, military parades, and bunkers. There was a financial and above all human element involved that none of my graduate school books on cross-Strait relations ever captured. Geostrategic interests mattered too. Indeed, I was soon to learn that some of the most interesting aspects of the Taiwan Strait security game are played out a very long away.

* * *

I moved back home in 2010, and after a lengthy application process, landed a job at the CNA Corporation's Center for Naval Analyses, which is a federally funded think tank for the Navy and Marine Corps. I was hired as an entry-level China analyst. It was not a glamorous job, but there were some very exciting perks. As a new analyst, I got to tour naval ships based in Norfolk, Virginia. Even better, I got to fire machine guns with Marines on the training range at Quantico, just south of Washington, D.C.

Sadly, those field trips were not the norm. I passed most days in isolation, clipping and evaluating Chinese military articles. It was interesting and meaningful work, but also a bit tedious. So when there was an opportunity to get away from my desk and socialize, I always jumped at it. As a result, I got to meet quite a few of China's "barbarian handlers," the English-speaking generals, intelligence officers, and state scholars Beijing uses to shape elite opinion around the world.

At the time, Chinese delegations visited Washington regularly for military-to-military dialogues, some of which CNA hosted. These were supposed to be trust-building exercises. However, as far as I could tell, not much trust was ever built. Quite the opposite. Those Chinese generals I met seemed to regard Americans with a coldness bordering on hatred. It was startling, but I wasn't there to make friends. My mission was to learn more about how they saw the world. As an analyst, I viewed it as my job to figure out what made them tick. It was one thing to read what they wrote, quite another to meet them in person and hear what they had to say and watch how they acted.

The delegations were always vehement on Taiwan. It was more than apparent that China, or at least the cadres in the Chinese Communist Party, had an obsession. After watching one Chinese official after another argue full-throatily about his nation's "core interest" in subjugating Taiwan, I began to see why the island's government thought it prudent to hold yearly air raid drills.

One of these exchanges was particularly unpleasant. We threw a banquet-style dinner, and I found myself sitting at a table with three Chinese generals, who evidently spoke no English, and a friendly American naval officer, who spoke German, but not Chinese. Very little of substance was said during the course of the meal, and it was awkward. The American naval officer kept trying to make polite conversation with the Chinese generals, using me as the interpreter, but he was getting nowhere. They were rude and hostile.

Finally, in desperation, the officer said, "You know, I was in the Pentagon on 9/11, and lost friends that day. If nothing else, our two militaries can agree that terrorism is a common threat to us both. We can cooperate and work together to prevent similar tragedies from happening in the future." I translated this for the Chinese.

In reply, a scrawny political officer, who the other two generals were visibly afraid of, said that the United States deserved to be attacked by terrorists on 9/11. Why? For the grave sin of interfering in others' internal affairs. "That's what you get," he sneered.

I couldn't believe what had just been said about the murder of three thousand innocent Americans and didn't know what to tell the friendly naval officer. I paused for a long moment, thinking carefully about the words the general had used. Finally, I huddled in with the officer and whispered, "Sir, he just said...."

He was a power lifter, and the veins on his thick neck began to bulge out. Luckily for the Chinese, it was announced just then that the banquet was over. The general, no doubt sensing he had gone too far, abruptly stood up and scurried away. Before another word could be said, he joined others at the door and rushed out to board an awaiting bus. Few words were exchanged between us Americans as we got up and left the table. It felt like we had just extended an olive branch only to have seen it spit on.

I would never see Sino-American relations quite the same way after that. I was not the only one. I ran into that friendly officer several years later at a Naval War College conference, and he recalled the story. He then told me that other Chinese officers had acted even more disrespectfully at events he had attended more recently in Hawaii. He concluded soberly there was probably little "trust building" could achieve in the absence of shared values and goodwill.

In 2013, I took a job with more responsibility at the Project 2049 Institute, a think tank focused on Asian security issues. I had previously worked there, starting as a non-resident research affiliate my last year in Taiwan. It was great to be back. I soon had the opportunity to live in Tokyo, representing my home institute as a visiting scholar at the Japan Institute of International Affairs, the research arm of Japan's foreign ministry.

The exchange program involved field trips to several American and Japanese military bases. On these trips, I learned that many allied officers were concerned about tensions in the Taiwan Strait and confused as to why Washington was bending to Chinese pressure and freezing arms sales Taiwan had been requesting. In their eyes, this would only embolden the Chinese and encourage them to undertake more destabilizing behavior in the region, like what they were then doing in the East China Sea over the Senkaku Islands.

Many of those I met viewed cross-Strait conflict as an unlikely, but extremely dangerous, possibility. Some offered that it might be the toughest of all the Pentagon's war plans. Many were horrified by the thought and were glad that the situation, for the moment, seemed to be on a relatively even keel. Nonetheless, they felt duty-bound to prepare for the worst-case scenario, especially because American military bases in Japan would be on the frontline.

The air force guys were concerned that if the balloon ever went up China would launch its missiles at American forces concentrated on Okinawa. Target number one would probably be Kadena, the largest U.S. Air Force base on foreign soil, with potentially devastating results. One straight-talking fighter pilot told me that he hoped to be airborne when the Chinese attack happened because his hardened aircraft shelter was not designed to withstand their missiles, and he would want the chance to exact revenge on the aggressors.

Naval officers had a different concern. They worried that Chinese submarines might sink American aircraft carriers like the USS *George Washington*, or the USS *Blue Ridge*, the Pacific Fleet's only command ship. One destroyer captain in Tokyo quietly told me over sushi and sake that he was confident he could shield his boss (Admiral Thomas, then 7th Fleet Commander) from China's anti-ship ballistic missiles. It was the thought of enemy torpedoes slipping past his picket line that kept him awake at night.

No one seemed clear on exactly what might happen, but all were sure a future Chinese surprise attack would be worse than Pearl Harbor and

9/11 combined. Some even worried that a relatively limited conflict over Taiwan might rapidly escalate and spiral out of control, pulling the world's two most powerful countries into a horrendous nuclear exchange. One State Department official, an outspoken Foreign Service officer who I met on Ishigaki Island, argued that the Taiwan Strait was a terrible war trap that could lead to the death of huge numbers of Americans.

At these encounters, one question kept nagging me. If a war between America and China over Taiwan is such a disquieting possibility, why is so little written on it? By all appearances, no one in the American or Japanese research communities had been doing any serious work on the topic since 2008, when Ma Ying-jeou, a China-friendly politician, had been elected president in Taiwan. Many scholars had lost interest in Taiwan, viewing the island nation's eventual absorption into China as a foregone conclusion. Many others had come to believe that talking about war publically might actually lead to it occurring. They felt it was unnecessary and unwise to provoke a rising dragon whose power seemed limitless on the horizon. Congressman Randy Forbes, who served on the House Armed Services Committee, called this the "Voldemort effect."

Some scholars had no problem discussing conflict with China. They just concluded that the South China Sea was Beijing's preferred future battlefield, not the Taiwan Strait. In their eyes, it was maritime disputes that were the important issue, and Taiwan no longer mattered all that much. It seemed like almost everyone I met wanted to examine China's naval expansion and PLA missions other than Taiwan. I was unable to associate myself with their views. The more research I did, the more I felt that Taiwan was front and center in the PLA's thinking, and we were remiss to be sanguine about it and concern ourselves only with the popular issues of the moment.

The question of how China might attempt to invade Taiwan has intrigued me ever since that first air raid drill in Taipei. As I discovered over a decade of inquiry, the publically available information on this topic is woefully inadequate. For Americans, much hinges on solving the strategic problems associated with China's emergence as a rival center of power. In that regard, the Taiwan Strait, with its extreme perils, is the best place to start. The American approach to Asia will only bear fruit when it takes the gravest of threats into account. Worst-case scenarios are often where the essence of things can be found, and the fearful scene is rarely as dark as what might be imagined in the absence of knowledge.

My hope is that this book will shine new light and inject new questions into the American research agenda. If we are not asking ourselves what the Chinese military really thinks about the invasion of Taiwan and where they see their shortcomings and how they are trying to solve their operational problems, then we are completely missing one of the most consequential political and military challenges of our time. Of course, a single book cannot tell the whole story, and large parts of the puzzle remain unsolved. This is just the start of what I hope will be a much longer journey of discovery.

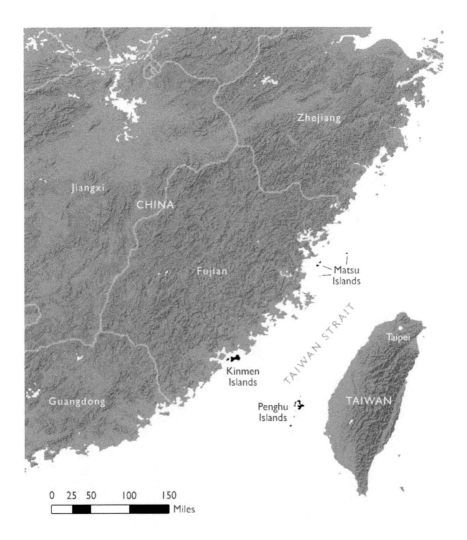

The Taiwan Strait area

THE CHINESE INVASION THREAT

Chapter One
Why Invade Taiwan?

We will not succumb to pressure from China.... Taiwan is a sovereign, independent country.

—ROC President Tsai Ing-wen

Taiwan stands to lose more from the emergence of the People's Republic of China (PRC) as a twenty-first-century superpower than any other country in the world. China's rise to become the world's second largest political, economic, and military power threatens the interests of many nations, but only Taiwan has its life at stake. Only Taiwan is held at risk of seeing its trade lines severed, its cities bombed, and its shores invaded. Only Taiwan faces the possibility of having its president assassinated and its democracy destroyed. Only Taiwan could be transformed into an Orwellian police state. The PRC is actively planning and preparing for these scenarios. China's authoritarian government challenges many countries in many ways, but it appears to only have plans for the invasion and occupation of Taiwan.

Authorities in the Chinese Communist Party (CCP) are funneling massive national-level resources into the creation of a powerful military machine. Their buildup is principally focused on acquiring the capabilities needed to annex or conquer Taiwan, something Chinese publications euphemistically call "achieving national unification." The rapid expansion of China's military power does not necessarily mean war is imminent, or even likely. CCP elites would very much prefer that the president of the Republic of China (ROC), the official name of Taiwan, signs away her nation's sovereignty under the pressure and weight of intimidation. Nonetheless, they are preparing to settle the matter through force of arms.

Since the fall of the Soviet Union, China's military has been driven by the perceived need to get ready for a future war in the Taiwan Strait. China's interests have expanded over the past decades as its economy has surged forward, but the primacy of this mission remains unchanged.[1] Invading Taiwan is at the heart of the armed wing of the CCP, which is known as the People's Liberation Army (PLA). The war plan for fighting a Taiwan "liberation" campaign is tattooed onto the PLA's corporate memory. It is something that has been indoctrinated and encoded into the minds of all top-level officers. This offensive operation shapes their lives and institutions. It defines them and gives their military service purpose and meaning. For them, the interests of the regime, not the people of China, are paramount and their "main strategic direction" (supreme objective) is to take Taiwan, ending its life as a de facto independent country.[2]

The Chinese military almost certainly could not prosecute a full-scale invasion of Taiwan today and succeed. Nor would any sane chairman of the CCP want to make the attempt. Even if a few hawkish generals were prepared to roll the dice, the costs and risks entailed by the war would be enormous and potentially fatal for the regime. PLA strategists know they still have a way to go before they will be able to achieve their objective. Little comfort, however, should be drawn from this reality. China's leaders recognize the roadblocks in their path and will continue to invest heavily in strategic deception, intelligence collection, psychological warfare, joint training, and advanced weapons. Barring countervailing efforts, their investments could result in a world-shaking conflict and an immense human tragedy.

War Plans and Politics

Worrying about the infinite uncertainties associated with the future is a basic part of the human experience. It is a fear as old as the first societies and civilization itself. War planning is essential for any nation to be prepared, and it is the responsibility of military officers and defense analysts to think through the what ifs that could lead to their country's violent demise. Whenever possible, it is also their responsibility to find out what the plans of potential enemies are. After all, what better way to avoid surprise and destruction at the hands of an enemy than to know his malicious intentions in advance?

Defense strategies, military doctrines, and operational plans are like national insurance policies, although they are hardly developed the same way. Insurance policies are based on hard data points, interpreted by actuaries. War plans are based on assumptions made by generals, admirals, and civilian officials, combining their professional judgments regarding what would be reasonable for a potential adversary to do if he ever turned into an enemy. However, if history teaches us anything, it is that countries and their leaders often do things that defy our reason and logic. Attempting to understand an adversary's perceptions therefore matters a great deal since his perceptions will influence his actions far more than objective reality as we understand it.

While it may seem unbelievable to most foreigners, officers in the Chinese military are constantly studying and practicing plans for the invasion of Taiwan. On any given day, military units from Beijing to Hainan are war-gaming various aspects of the operation out on tabletops, or via computer simulations, or on the beaches along China's seaboard. PLA officers study their assigned roles at military schoolhouses. Young lieutenants attend military academies, mid-career captains and majors go to command schools, and high-ranking senior colonels and generals study at the National Defense University in Beijing. These men (the PLA is an extraordinarily male-dominated organization) have many missions to learn to perform over the course of their careers. Their primary one, according to their professional literature, is to prepare for an all-out war against Taiwan.[3]

Any conflict between China and Taiwan will almost certainly involve America. The United States has an enduring interest in a peaceful, prosperous, and stable East Asia, and the emergence of an openly hostile China would represent a grave challenge to American interests. The U.S. government does not recognize PRC sovereignty over Taiwan and regards the island's sovereign status as unresolved. Moreover, the White House is legally obligated by the Taiwan Relations Act (TRA) to provide defensive arms and services to Taiwan, and to maintain the U.S. military's capacity to respond to any Chinese use of force against the island. Should China seek to blockade, bomb, and invade Taiwan, the United States would be compelled to help its democratic ally. Although not as binding as a mutual defense treaty, the TRA (U.S. Public Law 96-8) makes it clear that Washington is likely to intervene if China uses force. For both legal and moral reasons, the United States would be compelled to side with this island nation, even if it meant risking war with the world's second most powerful country.

In addition to being a matter of principle and honor, the United States supports Taiwan for geostrategic reasons. It has become increasingly clear to American strategists that China has embarked on a long and intense competition for dominance over the Western Pacific. Taiwan is at the geographic and political heart of this competition.[4] Maritime tensions in the East China Sea and the South China Sea, while serious, pale in comparison to this flashpoint. The possibility of conflict here, at the central gateway to the Pacific, demands close scrutiny.

Fundamental political differences over cross-Strait sovereignty between Taiwan's government and the government in Beijing began in earnest in December 1949, when Chiang Kai-shek formally moved the seat of the ROC from the war-ravaged Chinese mainland to Taipei.[5] Political differences across the Strait continue to be a major friction point in the Asia-Pacific region to this day. Despite the remarkable growth in bilateral trade and investment over the past two decades, prospects of the two governments peacefully resolving their differences are vanishingly small.

Separated by the Taiwan Strait for seven decades and counting, China (PRC) and Taiwan (ROC) each exercise authority only over the territory under their respective control. Neither side is subordinate to the other, and neither side recognizes the legality of the other. From the perspective of Beijing, the Chinese Civil War never ended. As a result, the two governments have no official relationship and are still ideologically and militarily hostile.[6] China's desire to annex Taiwan keeps cross-Strait relations perpetually strained, with the possibility of a Chinese attack on the island factoring into decisions made by presidents and prime ministers from Taipei to Tokyo and from Washington to Canberra.[7]

The PRC has long sought the annexation of Taiwan under its "one China" principle. In Beijing's view, Taiwan's de facto independence and democratic system of government pose existential threats to the CCP's right to rule China. Taiwan is thus portrayed in Chinese propaganda as a "splittist regime." If it cannot be forced back under central control, the people of China are told that they must fight for it.[8] Legitimacy across the Taiwan Strait is viewed as something political scientists typically refer to as a "zero-sum game" because only one side can win, and that will necessarily mean the other side must be vanquished. China's stated goal is cross-Strait unification under a formula called "One Country, Two Systems." This approach envisions the ROC government in Taiwan surrendering sovereignty to the PRC authorities, allowing them to transform the island nation into an occupied, authoritarian administrative territory like Hong Kong.[9]

Taiwanese Identity and Changing Dynamics

For the proud and patriotic citizens of Taiwan, any leader who agreed to unification would be a traitor and sell-out. The people of Taiwan overwhelmingly identify themselves as citizens of an independent country that is not, and should never become, controlled by the regime in China. Polling data from 2015, for example, indicates that only 9.1 percent of the population supports some type of eventual unification of the two sides. The same poll discovered that the number identifying themselves as "Chinese" has reached a new low of 3.3 percent.[10] An earlier poll found that more than 80 percent of respondents—well over a supermajority—think Taiwan and China are different countries. The same number of people told researchers they would like to secure permanent separation, if it would not trigger war.[11] Even more telling, 43 percent of young people (those under 40) would support *de jure* independence even if it resulted in a Chinese attack.[12]

The challenge facing every president of Taiwan has been to ensure their country's continued survival. From May 2008 to May 2016, Taiwan's then-president, Ma Ying-jeou, of the Nationalist or Kuomintang (KMT) party, dedicated his time in high office to the pursuit of peace with Beijing. The ambiguous framework he employed in the attempt is called the "1992 Consensus," which holds that both sides recognize some form of "one China," but each has different interpretations as to what that actually means. President Ma maintained that, for Taiwan, it means the ROC. In contrast, Taiwan's Democratic Progressive Party (DPP) and former KMT President Lee Teng-hui, who was Taiwan's leader in 1992, have repeatedly stated that no actual consensus was ever reached.[13] Further undermining prospects for popular support in Taiwan, China refused to acknowledge Ma's "respective interpretations." Beijing claims the PRC is the sole representative of China, and Taiwan is part of China. According to this false narrative, the ROC has not existed since 1949, when it lost the war and ceased to represent a sovereign state.

President Ma, in spite of the challenges, made it clear that the improvement of Taiwan's relationship with the PRC was his top priority. At first, his policies were relatively popular. Taiwan and China signed over twenty non-binding trade deals and pacts. While impossible to enforce, these agreements nonetheless allowed for an unprecedented level of economic and cultural exchange across the Taiwan Strait. The old flashpoint temporarily seemed to go quiet. With new air routes facilitating connectivity and millions of people suddenly able to flow back and forth across the stormy waters that had long separated them, many experts in the United States worried Taiwan was falling into China's orbit.[14]

Beijing, dismissive of the opportunity before it, did not respond to Ma's accommodating policies in a manner that might have secured a lasting peace. Finding a way to harmoniously maintain the status quo was not China's objective; its aim was annexing Taiwan. The Chinese leadership revealed this by continuing to rely on heavy-handed tactics, refusing to remove offensive missiles aimed at Taiwan, and investing further in a military buildup. Intimidation, not accommodation, remained the hallmark of China's cross-Strait policy.[15]

Over time many Taiwanese observers began to believe that the more their government sought to reduce tensions, the more it emboldened authorities in Beijing to press demands that Taipei move toward subjugation under the PRC's framework. Having closely watched Hong Kong's political autonomy steadily eroded over the past twenty years and its freedoms and human rights evaporate, the people of Taiwan lost faith that China might one day recognize the legitimacy of their government and respect their right of self-determination.

Negative experiences in dealing with Chinese visitors further solidified Taiwanese public opinion against the notion of "one China." Prior to 2008, the majority of Taiwan's citizens knew surprisingly little about the PRC. After 2008, a flood of Chinese tourists and business delegations poured into Taiwan, almost always leaving bad impressions in their wake. According to one of President Ma's top advisors, "The more people in Taiwan learned what it meant to be Chinese, the more they hated the idea."[16]

A consensus coalesced among the citizens of Taiwan that it was unendurable to imagine their nation falling deeper into the orbit and influence of China, and their future existence and freedom dependent upon the CCP's goodwill. In March 2014, students and civic group protesters occupied Taiwan's parliament, and the Sunflower Movement sprang to life. This three-week-long protest movement had the effect of freezing future trade deals that would have increased hostile Chinese influence over the island.[17] Although these events appear to have been mostly driven by growing public dissatisfaction generated by the administration's oversold cross-Strait economic policies, they were also affected by national security considerations.

Just prior to the Sunflower Movement, ROC defense officials received intelligence that spooked them so much that they decided to unveil it publically, even at the price of showing President Ma's peace policies were failing. In late 2013, Taiwan's Ministry of National Defense (MND) openly reported that China had developed a plan to invade Taiwan by 2020. They revealed a secret pact had been made in Beijing at the 18th National Congress of the Communist Party, when Mr. Xi Jinping replaced Mr. Hu Jintao as general secretary of the CCP. At this meeting, the new Chinese leadership committed to complete their 2020 Plan for building and deploying a comprehensive operational capability to use force against Taiwan by that year.[18] Instead of peace, the CCP and PLA, four years into cross-Strait détente, still thought it necessary to put down on planning documents the need to invade Taiwan.[19]

In response to this and other Chinese provocations, the Taiwanese identity grew, and a deepened dislike of the PRC developed.[20] In January 2016, the opposition DPP won both the presidency and the parliament in a landslide victory. On May 20, 2016, Taiwan's new leader, Dr. Tsai Ing-wen, was sworn into office, becoming Taiwan's first female president. During the transition period and early days of her administration, Beijing attempted to pressure her to accept the notion of "one China." Multiple forms of intimidation were employed. The flow of Chinese tourist groups visiting Taiwan was reduced, cross-Strait communication links were severed, amphibious war games were held, and bombers and naval flotillas were sent to circle around the island.[21] The effects of these acts of coercion were negligible. President Tsai refused to move away from the democratically expressed will of the Taiwanese people. The Chinese could only continue to make seemingly empty threats, vainly suggesting that the worst was yet to come.[22]

China's Anti-Taiwan Campaign

Taiwan's rise as one of Asia's most vibrant democracies and an alternative to China's repressive authoritarian model is viewed with extreme concern in Beijing's halls of power. From China's perspective, the existence of Taiwan as a democracy is a grave challenge to its political legitimacy. The CCP views Taiwan as its most dangerous external national security threat, and the PLA, as the armed wing of the party and guarantor of the regime's fragile legitimacy, has been tasked with the mission of preparing for an assault on the island as its principal war planning scenario. The overarching plan is referred to in restricted-access Chinese military writings as the "Joint Island Attack Campaign." The campaign includes operations that span the entire spectrum of the modern battlefield, including the air, land, sea, space, and cyber space domains. Even media outlets are a target.[23]

The fundamentally political nature of the dispute means that the Chinese government conducts an ongoing, clandestine campaign of diplomatic, economic, and psychological warfare around the globe. This includes operations to spin the news and manipulate international law to delegitimize and demoralize Taiwan. The Chinese military refers to this as "political warfare."[24] To better prepare the future battlefield, China's undercover agents of influence blanket Asia, and especially Taiwan, with disinformation. They use state media outlets, business enterprises, and cross-Strait educational exchanges as platforms for covert actions.[25] Their mission is to poison the powers of resolve and weaken resistance to eventual takeover.[26]

The American public has little visibility on China's anti-Taiwan campaign, which is being waged primarily in Mandarin on the far side of the Pacific. Many Americans experience the effects of it only indirectly. There are reportedly a considerable number of Chinese agents in the United States, who pose as diplomats, reporters, scholars, language instructors, lobbyists, and entrepreneurs. Their job, in part, is to shape foreign perceptions about China and Taiwan, and to undercut arms sales and other forms of support for the island. These hostile influence operations are particularly noticeable in Washington and on university campuses across the country.[27]

The result is that an increasing number of everyday Americans have been unconsciously gripped by the hand of Chinese propaganda and treat false information as if it were the truth. Making matters worse, an astonishing number of American companies and colleges have their financial futures anchored in China, making them vulnerable to being subjected to pressures and situations that may run against their moral and ethical principles. The CCP has worked hard to create opportunities for obtaining leverage over those it wants to manipulate or control, and few issues are more important to them than defeating Taiwan.[28]

When viewed from the perspective of Beijing, the risks associated with Taiwan are growing. With thousands of students from China now studying on the island, it may only be a matter of time before greater demand for good governance on the mainland overwhelms its oppressive authoritarian system. In theory, time favors Taiwan because it is on the right side of history. Militarily, however, it is not clear that the ROC's self-defense forces can continue to resist China's buildup. There is a growing chorus of voices that argue the island's military will soon become too weak to defend against the world's second most powerful country.[29]

The PRC's growing national strength has enabled it to advance efforts to politically marginalize Taiwan in the international community. The main focus of Chinese efforts has been Washington, where Beijing has had some remarkable successes over the past decade. Under both the George W. Bush and Barack Obama administrations, China secured long freezes or delays in new notifications of arms sales to Taiwan, and especially important sales were canceled, including new F-16 fighters, diesel-electric submarines, Aegis destroyers, and Abrams tanks.[30] At the same time, a string of influential Americans have published articles arguing that Washington should abandon or reinterpret its legal obligations to help defend Taiwan under the TRA, the law of the land.[31]

China's successes have been only partial. Attempts at driving a deeper wedge between Taiwan and the international community have served to embitter and repulse the island's electorate. As has been the case with Japan and many other nations, Taiwan's greater involvement in the Chinese economy not only failed to cement greater political cooperation, it actually fostered a growing sense of vulnerability and confrontation.[32] In light of demographic trend lines, polling data, and election results, it has become increasingly clear that the people of Taiwan want to be treated as citizens of a country recognized around the world for what it actually already is: independent, free, and sovereign.

This sentiment has not gone unnoticed in China, where the military has been planning for the worst all along. Internal PLA writings have recently emerged that confirm China plans to use force when it believes that other means are not achieving its strategic objective, and especially when there is a good chance that the United States can be kept out of the fight. These writings state that once China has "exhausted" all non-lethal options to ensure the annexation and occupation of Taiwan, a large-scale amphibious attack will be launched against the island.[33]

According to Chinese military documents, there are scenarios other than invasion. The PLA could prosecute coercive operations against Taiwan, including long-duration, but intermittent and low intensity, naval blockades and air campaigns. However, they make clear that these are sub-optimal solutions that cannot be expected to get at the root problem. Intimidation will fail if the Taiwanese government and the people are impervious to it and unwilling to submit to Beijing's authority under pressure.[34] For this reason, the PLA is focused on the employment of an all-out invasion campaign.[35]

The chilling official narrative seen in the PLA's internal literature is that a future invasion of Taiwan is probably inevitable. The exact timing is uncertain, but attacking and conquering the island is a "historic mission" that will not be put off indefinitely. The problem is cast in remarkably simple terms: Taiwan is a "splittist regime," and China's national territorial integrity remains under severe threat until it is returned to the ancestral "Fatherland."[36] The following lines crystallize the pro-invasion PLA view:

> In the end, only by directly conquering and controlling the island can we realize national unification ... otherwise "separatist" forces, even if they momentarily compromise under pressure, can reignite like dormant ashes under the right conditions.[37]

Internal documents show that the Chinese military refers to all Taiwanese government and military personnel as "separatist enemies," with no distinction made for political party affiliation or self-identity. All those who want to maintain the status quo are painted as China's enemies.[38] Yet despite the bellicosity of PLA writings, it would be a mistake to think the Chinese military establishment is overly eager for the fight. One PLA field manual, for example, warns its readers (Chinese military officers) that, "The island has complex geography, and its defensive systems are rock-solid around critical targets."[39] PLA officers are told that only through a massive and masterful military campaign could they take Taiwan. The operation would be an extremely challenging undertaking, the likes of which China has never conducted before, and the sacrifices required would be tremendous.[40]

Rationalizing Aggression

While acknowledging the huge risks entailed, Chinese military writings use many arguments to justify the invasion of Taiwan. They point out that critical geostrategic issues are at stake. Internal PLA materials argue that Taiwan sits in a controlling position along China's eastern seaboard, making it a gateway to the Western Pacific and the Indian Ocean. They assert that since the great majority of China's shipping traffic passes through the Strait, it is a vital area affecting the security of their coastline, national economic growth, and future prosperity.[41]

The *Course Book on the Taiwan Strait's Military Geography* is a restricted-access PLA manual, used to teach senior officer seminars in Beijing. It warns readers that an external military might one day use Taiwan to cut off China's trade lines, hinting that the island could be used as a military base by the United States to blockade China and undermine its rapid rise to great power status. On this basis, the manual argues that physical control over the island is vital for safeguarding against foreign blockades. China's seaborne oil imports, which pass through the Strait, are highly vulnerable, "so protecting the security of this strategic maritime passageway is not just a military activity alone, but rather an act of national strategy."[42]

This source then goes a step further, telling readers that Taiwan is a chokepoint of great utility for blockading Japan. The Taiwan Strait, it notes, is a Japanese maritime lifeline that runs from Europe and the Middle East, and based on PLA studies, Japan receives 90 percent of its oil imports, 99 percent of its mineral resources, and 100 percent of its nuclear fuel needs from ships that travel across these sea lanes. In total, 500 million tons of

Japanese imports pass by Taiwanese waters each year, with 80 percent of all Japan's container ships traveling right through the Strait, the equivalent of one Japanese cargo ship every ten minutes. Consequently, these waters will, "directly affect Japan's life or death, its survival or demise."[43]

PLA intentions and plans for a conquered Taiwan are made plain in another internal document, *The Japanese Air Self Defense Force*, a handbook studied by mid-career officers at the PLA Air Force Command College in Beijing. The stated purpose of the text is to help Chinese pilots and staff officers understand the strengths and weaknesses of their Japanese adversaries. Buried amidst hundreds of pages of detailed maps, target coordinates, organizational charts, weapons data, and jet fighter images are the following lines:

> As soon as Taiwan is reunified with Mainland China, Japan's maritime lines of communication will fall completely within the striking ranges of China's fighters and bombers.... Our analysis shows that, by using blockades, if we can reduce Japan's raw imports by 15–20%, it will be a heavy blow to Japan's economy. After imports have been reduced by 30%, Japan's economic activity and war-making potential will be basically destroyed. After imports have been reduced by 50%, even if they use rationing to limit consumption, Japan's national economy and war-making potential will collapse entirely ... blockades can cause sea shipments to decrease and can even create a famine within the Japanese islands.[44]

These writings illustrate the immense value placed upon Taiwan by the PLA, and they clearly articulate strategic rationales for invading the island and turning it into an "unsinkable aircraft carrier." They are quick to point out that Taiwan's location in the center of the First Island Chain means that once it falls under Chinese control, the PLA Navy will have assured access to the Pacific and tremendous leverage over neighboring states, giving them command over the world's most important waters.[45]

The PRC, then, has compelling political, economic, and military reasons to want to control Taiwan. In the eyes of Chinese strategists, this island's importance is unparalleled. For historical and practical reasons, the PLA assumes that it will have the leading role in the campaign. Military theorists in the PLA write that, sooner or later, the attack will be ordered and the island invaded and turned into a giant base for projecting China's strength and prestige across the region. They envision a world in which Chinese troops, planes, and ships stand watch over this chokepoint, controlling all its activities. They contemplate a future where China is the regional hegemon.

To reach this future vision, PLA writings assert the Chinese military must master all domains of warfare. Books such as the *Science of Military Strategy* and *Science of Campaigns* indicate that units assaulting Taiwan will have to be capable of amphibious assault, maneuver, indirect fires, urban warfare, and mountain warfare.[46] The field manual, *Informatized Army Operations*, written by a team of officers at the PLA Nanjing Army Command Academy, indicates that it would be an ugly, brutal, and bloody fight. Surprise attacks would first have to be executed to clear the way for the army to cross the Strait. Operations would include everything from ballistic missile attacks to drone strikes, from cyber infiltration to space warfare, and from commando raids to psychological operations. However, at its core, the invasion of Taiwan would be about putting boots on the ground and tanks in the streets. In the words of the PLA field manual, "We must annihilate our (Taiwanese) enemies in large numbers, then conquer and control the entire island."[47]

Research Challenges and Prospects

Given the gravity of the threat facing Taiwan, it is important that the international community understands China's intentions and plans. Americans need to understand why their country might one day find itself locked in a deadly embrace with China over this island nation, and allies need to know what parts they might be asked to play. If a war breaks out between the United States and the PRC over Taiwan, it will change the course of history and produce aftereffects that reverberate for generations to come. No one can know with any certainty how such a war would start, how it would play out, and what would follow it. But we can and should do more to understand the drivers of conflict and the assumptions that underpin military plans and preparations for it. No other flashpoint is as potentially dangerous to the national security of the United States.[48]

While conflict over Taiwan has been the subject of many political science studies, enormous research gaps remain. The available English-language database on Taiwan's defense against amphibious invasion is a primitive one, and nothing has been written on Chinese views of the campaign. There is an acute need for studies which attempt to look at each side's strategies, war plans, and capabilities, and then make some overall judgment regarding the cross-Strait balance and what it all means. It is in the United States' interest to develop a nuanced understanding of the threat China poses to Taiwan, and to cultivate an Asia strategy that takes this into account.

It is often the case that only by thinking tragically can tragedy be avoided. It is also true that in the absence of understanding many will assume China has only strengths and no weaknesses. As a result of this tendency, it has become conventional wisdom that the Taiwanese are hopelessly outgunned. There is a long-standing debate in Washington about reducing American commitments and assistance to Asian allies and security partners, with a particular focus on Taiwan. Doing so would have tragic consequences, making World War III more likely, not less. We need to better understand China's strategy, Taiwan's defense, and the cross-Strait balance. But where to start?

China has long placed strict controls on information related to Taiwan scenarios, making sure that all its publications serve a propaganda and psychological warfare purpose. As a result, it has been difficult, if not impossible, for American specialists to use open source materials to understand how the Chinese military really thinks about Taiwan. The most readily available Chinese sources are intended to spread misinformation. They take great pains to assure audiences that victory is inevitable no matter what Taiwanese and American forces might do to defend the island. Their message is simple, enduring, and (at least for some) quite powerful: "Taiwan is a lost cause. Resistance is futile."[49]

Foreign analysts can mistakenly buy into hostile propaganda, forgetting that the PLA is the armed wing of the CCP and a fundamentally political, not professional, military. Chinese materials, and especially the writings and public statements of PLA officers, must always be taken with a large grain of salt. Unwary readers who take their writings and statements at face value will draw false conclusions for the simple reason that they are being fed false information.[50]

Internal and restricted-access PLA writings, on the other hand, can be more candid and objective. These materials are designed to allow Chinese officers to soberly evaluate the challenges they face, including the strengths of Taiwan's military and their own relative weaknesses. Like sensitive and confidential military documents everywhere, they provide a level of detail not seen in publically available materials. They are intended to be read only by a limited number of trusted officers, so they can afford to be pessimistic.

Even highly detailed and relatively candid PLA sources do not tell the whole story. Restricted materials produced by China's military system are still consensus documents that must pass through a rigorous screening process to make sure they are politically correct reflections of the party's position. More often than not, facts and objective analysis get lost in this rigid process. Sometimes, as we will see, entire areas of study are off-limits to Chinese officers. Some questions are just too sensitive to ask, even privately.

For a more complete picture, it is important to turn to Taiwan, where writings generated by intelligence analysts and defense experts often provide insights. The ROC military's research community has exhaustively studied the threat facing Taiwan. Of available sources, professional military journals are the most useful. They offer a unique window into the minds of Taiwanese officers, who use journal articles to share information on the PLA, explore new ideas, and debate means for defending their country.

As the armed forces of a democracy, the Taiwanese military is subject to public scrutiny and faces a highly critical cable news media and a notoriously contrarian parliament. ROC military officers have to be far more open than their PLA adversaries. This is a positive, but often painful, constraint on them. No general enjoys having his every move scrutinized by media pundits and civilian politicians. They recognize, however, that transparency and oversight are essential for helping build a professional national army, and intellectual sparring between officers brings out new and innovative ideas, some of which might one day save lives.

Unfortunately, Taiwanese military studies often go unread in the West. Relatively few Americans can read Mandarin in Taiwan's traditional, complex-form Chinese characters. Fewer still understand the specialized vocabulary that is unique to the ROC military. The Chinese characters for cruise missile, for example, are entirely different in Taiwan than in China.[51] The lack of Taiwan experts in the PLA studies community compounds the problems created by Chinese disinformation operations, leaving many American China-watchers befuddled.

In an attempt to avoid potential pitfalls, this book draws from professional ROC military studies and internal PLA materials. It also draws from discussions with subject matter experts to confirm that concepts which appear in Chinese materials are real and PLA writings are not themselves part of disinformation operations. The appendix has a section where the interested reader can learn more about the methodology underpinning this book and some of the key sources.

Specific question sets that will be explored in the following chapters include the following:

1. How do internal Chinese military writings depict the campaign to conquer Taiwan, and what capabilities do they feel are necessary for executing it? How do PLA writings portray their adversary? Where do they see Taiwanese strengths and where do they see weaknesses?
2. How does Taiwan's military plan to defend the island against Chinese invasion? What capabilities do Taiwanese officers feel are necessary to execute their defense plans? In the worst case, how long could they be expected to hold out before direct American assistance was required?
3. What are the implications for American strategy in Asia? How might policymakers in Washington strengthen Taiwan and prevent China

from precipitating a crisis? What might the United States do to better contribute to future peace and stability in this region?

To answer these questions, we first need to know when the Taiwan Strait flashpoint was born and how it developed. The next chapter will examine the history behind the PRC's quest to dominate Taiwan. It will uncover a previously unknown war plan and lay bare a spy case that helped save the island from communist subversion. It will give us the backstory on why the PLA has not yet been able to invade Taiwan, and help explain why it is not going to give up on the mission.

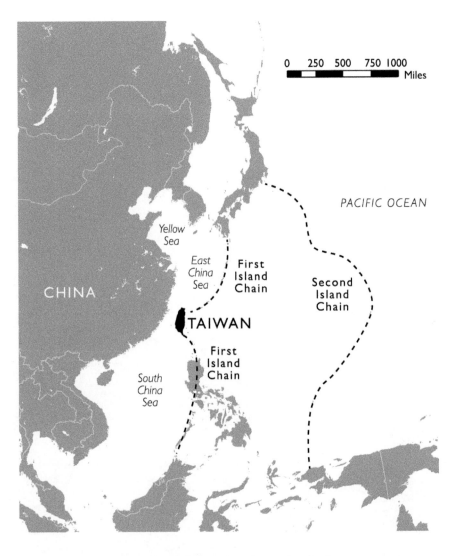

Taiwan's location in the First Island Chain

Chapter Two
An Evolving Flashpoint

Taiwan must be liberated! We must liberate Taiwan.
—CCP Propaganda Slogan

Our story of an emerging threat begins in the past, where the thorny problem first took root. The PLA's early strategy for conquering Taiwan was developed over a one-year period. From June 1949 to June 1950, generals under Mao Zedong undertook intensive battle planning and preparations for what was to become the PRC's formative strategic challenge. An unexpected turn of history kept Mao and his generals from putting their Taiwan invasion plan into action. On June 25, 1950, North Korea invaded South Korea, and President Truman swiftly decided to save South Korea's friendly government, while also ordering the U.S. Seventh Fleet to prevent a possible Chinese invasion across the Taiwan Strait.

As a consequence, the PRC aborted the Taiwan invasion, and many of the forces that had been training for the mission were subsequently redeployed to the Sino-Korean border area. In October 1950, China intervened on the side of North Korea, sending a flood of "volunteers" equipped with jungle warfare kits into frigid battles against the United Nations forces led by America. This intervention resulted in what was to become a drawn-out stalemate, both on the Korean Peninsula and across the Taiwan Strait.

Operations to conquer Taiwan and end the Chinese Civil War were post-poned, but not forgotten.

The knowledge and experience gained in 1949 and 1950 continue inform-ing Chinese war planning to this day. PLA generals still face many of the same basic operational problems that confronted their fathers and grandfathers. They view these past experiences, though forgotten by most in the West, as both relevant and inspirational. Like serious military plan-ners everywhere, they hope that by looking into the past they might find lessons for the future. The director of the Chinese Academy of Military Science's Historical Research Institute, Senior Colonel Zhao Yiping, has put it the following way:

> The entire nation and all the military, especially the units responsible for the mission of conducting Taiwan attack operations, gained and accumulated practical experiences in preparing (from June 1949 to June 1950) and they still get important guidance and workable ideas from that experience that are relevant for preparing for the military struggle against Taiwan in this new period of history.[52]

What were the origins of the Taiwan invasion plan? Who was responsible for its production and execution? Which units were assigned, equipped, and trained for the mission? How did the plan develop over time, and why was it not put into action sooner? Theoretically, what might have happened if there had been no Korean War and this operation had been launched instead? What happened to the PLA after the Korean War,? Why has China's military yet to prosecute its long cherished battle plan?

Origins of the Invasion Plan

The Battle of Taiwan was intended to be the final chapter in the Chinese Civil War, a conflict that had ravaged China from 1927 to 1949, interrupted by the Japanese invasion and occupation of Manchuria and Eastern China during the Second World War. Mao and his communist forces were essen-tially on the defensive throughout the first two decades of their insurgency.

They lurched from one battlefield defeat to the next, husbanding their strength and avoiding any decisive losses. The scene suddenly changed in late 1948 and early 1949, when they took the upper hand against the ROC Army, winning a series of crushing campaigns across northern and central China.

Their victories were unexpected, and like other unforeseen windfalls, served to make them more ambitious. In March 1949, Mao ordered his generals to add Taiwan to the list of strategic objectives to be captured. Previously, the strategy for 1949 had been to seek the "liberation" of nine provinces in China. After the dramatic series of battlefield victories, the list of provinces to seize by the end of the year was expanded to seventeen, including Taiwan. The propaganda slogan: "Taiwan must be liberated! We must liberate Taiwan," was first published by the Communist Party mouth-piece, Xinhua News, on March 15, 1949.[53]

Events developed rapidly. Within just a few months of the policy shift, PLA troops had captured Nanjing and Shanghai and were marching down the eastern seaboard of China on their way to Fujian Province, across from Taiwan. At this moment, Mao decided to reach out to the star commander of 3rd Field Army, General Su Yu, and his chief of staff, General Zhang Zhen.[54] On June 14, 1949, Mao directed them via telegram to find out whether Taiwan could be taken in a short timeframe and told them to plan a large-scale military operation to capture the island.

In his message, Mao alluded to the possibility of using covert actions to get Nationalist forces to defect at the key moment—something his undercover intelligence officers in Taiwan were already preparing. A week later, Mao sent his war architects another telegram, in which he expounded on the strategic importance of quickly occupying Taiwan. He asserted that if the island was not taken, the ROC military would have a permanent base for its navy and air force, which it would use to hold Shanghai at risk. He told his generals that by capturing Taiwan, they could break free of foreign blockades and gain hundreds of thousands of tons of commercial shipping assets.[55]

General Su and his staff officers wasted little time. They soon acquired maps of the Taiwan Strait and began battle planning. They first looked into the geographical layout and logistical realities of the area. They discovered to their chagrin that the straight-line distance between mainland China and Taiwan was approximately 80 miles at the nearest point, and the locations of ports and other staging areas meant that army groups would have to be transported and supplied across 90 to 140 miles of seawater. The PLA, having almost no navy to speak of, was totally unprepared to execute this type of operation.

Making matters worse, Su discovered that the Nationalists were fortifying a chain of island groups running down the mainland coast. These islands controlled the shipping channels into and out of southeastern China's natural harbors, bays, and ports—the very places where the assault troops would need to assemble and embark aboard ships. Su concluded that these offshore islands represented a dagger at the throat of his invasion plans. As long as the Nationalists held these islands, they could launch devastating surprise attacks on any armadas he assembled, sinking his ships and drowning his troops before they even had a chance to get underway. The offshore islands represented a formidable defensive perimeter, giving the Nationalists abundant warning time, tactical flexibility, and strategic depth. Su knew he would have to break through. But how to proceed?

Two competing approaches were explored by Su and his top lieutenants for dealing with the offshore islands. The first option called for storming and seizing each in turn. Once they were "liberated," he could concentrate his main forces on the big island of Taiwan and launch ships across from all the opened staging areas. The second option was to utilize American island-hopping or "leap-frog" tactics developed during World War II. This strategy envisioned units storming Xiamen (then known as Amoy) and Kinmen Island (then known as Quemoy), breaking the center of the offshore island chain. With these critical islands in hand, Su could launch his attack from one central staging area. Troops along the coast could use artillery bombardments and feints to pin down the Nationalist forces garrisoning the other island groups.

In this way, the archipelagos of Zhoushan, Tachen, Matsu, Penghu, and Hainan, could all be circumvented at low cost. This option was founded on the logic that frontal assaults on each of the island citadels would cause unnecessary force attrition and weaken and exhaust offensive units. By attacking Taiwan from Xiamen and Kinmen, the Communists could better concentrate an overwhelming force on the enemy's center of gravity. Once Taiwan fell, the remaining island garrisons would be isolated and could be expected to collapse in piecemeal fashion, without much of a fight.[56]

Mao and his advisors on the Central Military Commission in Beijing weighed both options and, despite the promised efficacy of island hopping, decided in favor of the strategy to capture each offshore island group. There were several compelling reasons why the more conservative of the two approaches was selected. First, the Nationalists had air superiority and sea control throughout the entire region. This meant that Su's amphibious ships could be discovered and destroyed in detail as they concentrated on Xiamen. Without an air defense umbrella protecting vulnerable troops as they embarked and sailed, there was simply no way to move an organized force against the prime target. In addition, they worried that, once the invasion campaign began, garrisons on the offshore islands could evacuate their forward positions to reinforce the defense of Taiwan, or they might instead fling themselves against vulnerable mainland ports nearby, cutting frontline PLA troops off from their rear area supply lines. In either event, there would be no way to stop them.

Chiang Kai-shek's strong air and naval advantage meant that his Nationalist forces could move freely throughout the theater. It would have been impossible to pin them down. Moreover, Su's officers had zero experience conducting modern amphibious warfare and no dedicated ships for the mission. They could use motorized sailboats and wooden Chinese junks to assault offshore islands close to the mainland, with the dark of night as cover, but small boats were incapable of crossing the notoriously rough waters of the Taiwan Strait. They would need time to build a real navy. In the interim, Mao reasoned that Su and his men could accumulate valuable amphibious combat experience assaulting small island groups.[57]

Once the overall strategy had been decided upon, Su began striking his designated targets. From August to October 1949, elements of the 3rd Field Army stormed Pingtan Island, Xiamen Island, and several smaller islands along the Chinese coast across from Taiwan. Initially, the strategy appeared to be working. Chiang's forces seemed to be crumbling all over southeastern China. However, in late October, an amphibious attack on the vital stepping-stone of Kinmen was decisively defeated. Nearly ten thousand PLA troops were lost.[58]

Mao, buoyed by victories elsewhere, took the loss in stride and concluded that the local commander had simply underestimated the resolve of the island's defenders and attacked too hastily to gain the initiative. He advised Su and his generals to be more cautious in the future.[59] Soon thereafter, an assault on Dengbu Island in the Zhoushan Island group was also repulsed, resulting in another heavy loss for the PLA. Stunned by his second major defeat in a matter of weeks, Mao halted further amphibious operations. The early winter months of 1949 were a sobering time for the would-be invaders of Taiwan. They would try again the next year, once the final plan was hammered out.[60]

Evolution of the Plan

In the summer of 1949, the blueprint for assaulting Taiwan began to take shape. The first version of the invasion plan was entitled, "Draft Plan for Operations to Liberate Taiwan." According to official PLA accounts, the plan was comprised of seven sections:

1. Taiwan's Geography.
2. Enemy Force Assessment.
3. Strategic Direction.
4. Guiding Principles.
5. Overview of Troop Deployments and Maneuver.
6. Communications, Logistics, Air and Chemical Defense.
7. Operational Preparations.[61]

On September 21, 1949, the draft plan was sent to all 3rd Field Army commanders at the division level and above.[62] It envisioned a force of eight corps-level units, totaling between 320,000 and 400,000 soldiers, who would carry out the attack. The 3rd Field Army's subordinate 9th Army

Group, made up of four corps-level units, was to spearhead the amphibious assault. The second wave of the attack was envisioned to include four army corps held in reserve until beachheads had been secured and ports opened for their use. Toward the end of 1949, the number of troops allotted to the campaign was increased. The PLA's 24th Corps was added to first wave, and an additional three corps added to the second wave, for a total of twelve army corps. The invasion of Taiwan now had approximately 500,000 troops assigned to it.[63]

After the failed attempts to capture Kinmen and Dengbu, Su realized that he had a considerable challenge ahead of him. From mid-December 1949 to mid-January 1950, he assembled his generals in Nanjing for a major war planning conference. Their mission was to study and solve the problems associated with the coming operations. During the conference, they shared their respective lessons learned from the island landings so far undertaken. Seminars were held on sea-to-land operations and amphibious training, the naval and air balance, and airborne (parachute) assaults.

Su had ten years of meteorological data collected and analyzed. He emphasized to his officers the need to familiarize themselves with the tactical layout of the area, the local weather, and the island's geography. He told them to study public sentiment in Taiwan and look for ways to exploit it to their advantage. He pressed ship captains to study the tides, winds, currents, and clouds, and the locations of fog banks and hidden reefs. He exhorted them to train their crews in navigating the open sea, repairing ships, sailing in formations, and loading and unloading troops for amphibious landings. After the lectures and seminars were over, Su organized exercises on the nearby Yangtze River to experiment with beach obstacle clearing and amphibious landing techniques.[64]

By the end of the Nanjing Conference, the 3rd Field Army's supreme commander and his staff had developed four basic tenants for the campaign. The first was to focus on the importance of time. The enemy had significantly reduced their defensive lines, making them more concentrated than before. While they were thought to be "hanging by their necks" on the one hand, on the other hand their powers of resistance were believed to have grown. Su told his generals they were not to be rushed in equipping and training their men, since time was on their side. In recent campaigns, lightning-quick strikes had been emphasized to take the initiative and keep the Nationalists off balance. This time they would unfold operations in a deliberate fashion, delaying the invasion as needed in order to make sure assault forces were adequately prepared.[65]

The second tenant was the importance of sufficient amphibious strength. Their overall naval fleet had to be larger than that of the enemy, and the first wave of troops to land on Taiwan had to be sufficiently well equipped to fight for at least three days on their beachheads. The envisioned transport fleet supporting them would be slow given the protracted logistical turn-around times across the Strait, and ships would be exposed to enemy naval and air attacks during daylight hours. The first wave of troops to storm ashore thus had to be able to quickly secure their assigned beachheads without the support of covering fires. If the first wave got mauled and pinned into small pockets along the coast, it would only be a matter of time before enemy counteroffensives drove them back into the sea. Complications were expected to deny the initial landing forces air support and slow reinforcements, so the first wave needed to land a powerful and decisive blow.[66]

The third tenant dealt with problems associated with actually crossing the Strait. Su knew it would take ships a long time to cross, unload on Taiwan, and then turn around and sail back to Chinese ports. He worried that vulnerable transports might suffer grievous losses during the first wave of the assault. It was thus agreed, in principle, not to recycle transports. If at all possible, the second wave of the attack would be equipped with its own seaworthy vessels and not rely upon those used by forces spearheading the offensive.[67]

The fourth tenant was to emphasize modern combined operations, with army, navy, and air force units working together in a coordinated fashion as one team. The 3rd Field Army's strategists believed the invasion of Taiwan would be an operation the likes of which they had never attempted before. They viewed coordination and centralized command to be particularly important for achieving victory. At the end of the Nanjing Conference, they staged a simple combined operations drill that failed to inspire any confidence. After it was over, Su warned, "If we can't learn to do this (combined operations) right, it will greatly weaken the power of our every tactic and weapon."[68]

The problem of command and control for combined amphibious operations continued to be a key issue that they struggled with in the months that followed. On January 17, 1950, at the close of the Nanjing Conference, the chief of staff, General Zhang, summarized the five critical command challenges facing them. These were the difficulty of: (1) leaving the Chinese mainland at high tide and arriving in time to attack Taiwan's beaches at low tide; (2) sailing across the Strait at maximum possible speeds without disrupting ship formations; (3) landing along a wide front at multiple points and then joining up and concentrating forces to push inland; (4) conducting simultaneous attacks with dispersed forces operating in multiple waves; and (5) using ultra shortwave radio communication channels that could result in each command post unintentionally jamming the others' radios.[69]

Su and his generals had their work cut out for them, but there was cause for optimism. A critically important political development had occurred during the Nanjing Conference. In January 1950, President Truman's secretary of state, Dean Acheson, publically announced that Taiwan, like South Korea, was now to be considered outside America's defense perimeter in Asia. Official Washington, and especially the State Department, had lost faith in America's old ally, Chiang Kai-shek, after he had retreated off the mainland of China. By all appearances, the U.S. government had decided to throw its erstwhile allies to the wolves. This sudden policy shift electrified Chinese strategists working on the Taiwan invasion campaign.[70]

Mao had previously predicted that the United States would probably not intervene on Chiang's behalf once it was clear that the Communists were going to be victorious on the mainland. His logic was that the more powerful his forces became, the more likely it would be that America's leaders would abandon their support for a Nationalist government they saw as hopeless. Nonetheless, Mao had told Su to plan for the worst-case scenario: American military intervention. This caveat had made plans for the invasion of Taiwan more academic than practical because there was no possible way the PLA could realistically operate in the Strait once the Seventh Fleet juggernaut arrived from its homeport in the nearby Philippines.[71]

After the American policy shift, however, the Chinese leadership approached the campaign to "liberate" Taiwan with new energy and optimism. This moved Mao and his top advisors to allocate financial resources needed for conquering Taiwan. They intended to grasp the potentially fleeting opportunity and were willing to adjust the national budget radically, if necessary. Su zealously wrote, "In spite of the costs, the center is determined that expenses will not get in the way. So if we have to fight on empty stomachs, we will still fight. Only then can the revolution be completed."[72]

The Big Buildup

It was widely accepted in Beijing's leadership circles that the Taiwan landing campaign would be their most expensive undertaking yet and require them to commit massive national resources. On February 7, 1950, Su reported to Beijing that, "Victory or defeat in modern warfare is not only about political factors, it ultimately hinges upon the overall competition in manpower, equipment, wealth, and weapons ... whoever has the advantage in all will achieve victory."[73]

Mao, who was in Moscow visiting Stalin, then made a radical move, offering his ally 10 percent of China's grain harvest in return for armaments needed to conquer Taiwan. In addition to grain shipments, Mao negotiated for an additional loan of US$300 million. As a result, the newly established People's Republic of China sank deeper into debt and hunger. Cost estimates took into account what was needed for hauling troops, equipment, weapons, vehicles, and horses across the Taiwan Strait. They initially assumed that 500,000 soldiers would have to be transported by ship, with each man occupying a claustrophobic 6.5 square feet of space. They assumed troops would need some 130,540 tons of equipment to sustain them. Based on these logistical realities, they calculated the PLA would need 575 ships, each displacing 1,000 tons or more, and 2,000 small landing craft, which would take the first wave of 60,000 troops ashore.[74] These numbers, already colossal, would continue to grow as plans firmed up.

On April 23, 1949, the precursor to the PLA Navy's East Sea Fleet was founded. Within a few months, Su initiated emergency measures across southeastern China to build the fleet up as fast as possible and, in August, the fleet was given to his direct command. When Guangzhou fell to communist forces that November, it became the fleet's temporary homeport until ships could move north to Shanghai. At that time, the fleet was made up of a mere seven captured ROC frigates, nine gunboats, and a ragtag force of 600 landing craft, mostly local fishing boats that had been impounded by the Communists. This tiny fleet was a mere fraction of what was needed.

The Central Military Commission ordered that all civilian fishing boats from the coastal provinces of Shandong, Jiangsu, Zhejiang, and Fujian be confiscated, and their crews forcibly pressed into military service. In addition, local shipbuilding was mobilized and large numbers of Soviet vessels were purchased. To avoid being detected and attacked by Chiang's patrols along the mainland coast, landing craft were loaded onto trains and transported to Hangzhou and Shanghai, where the invasion armadas were forming up.[75]

By March 1950, a total of some 1,300 landing craft of all types had been brought together, but the PLA was still far from reaching its goals. In Moscow, Mao had attempted to convince Stalin to send Soviet naval and air force "volunteers" to China to help invade Taiwan. The Chinese had a battle-tested ground force, but little in the way of sea or air capabilities. Mao proposed a joint PRC-USSR campaign, with China providing the army and Russia the ships and aircraft. Both nations, according to his proposal, would go into combat shoulder-to-shoulder.

Stalin, fearing that direct Soviet involvement would draw his country into World War III with America, rebuffed Mao and instead offered huge arms contracts to keep his Chinese friend placated. These deals included most of the ships and advisors the PLA so desperately needed. However, the promised naval deliveries were slow to arrive. By April 1950, the PLA had met only a sliver of its naval requirements. A meager 38,000 sailors and 92 vessels were in service, and only 52 of the ships were seagoing.

Moreover, Su and his staff had increased total operational requirements to nearly 2,300 landing craft, and debates were underway about pushing the number even higher.[76]

Su was keenly aware that Chiang's forces on Taiwan would have a significant advantage over him in terms of air power. As early as July 1949, PLA intelligence analysts estimated that the Nationalists had 200 to 250 combat aircraft to defend against invasion. To gain local air superiority, the PLA armaments plan called for a flying force of 300 to 350 combat planes. This air fleet was to be divided between fighters and bombers in a two-to-one ratio. In August 1949, the Chinese Communists asked the Soviet Union to sell them the aircraft. At first, Moscow only tentatively agreed. It was not until February 1950, that Mao and Stalin signed a final deal, increasing the total number of aircraft to 586, including 280 fighters and 198 bombers.[77]

The Soviet-built air force, like the navy, was slow to arrive. In May 1950, the PLA Air Force, with the help of Soviet advisors, graduated its first class of flying professionals, a paltry 89 pilots, 20 navigators, and 107 ground support personnel. The 4th Composite Air Brigade was subsequently established in Nanjing with the objective of supporting the coming operation. This flying force was comprised of 30 fighter planes, 30 fighter-bombers, and 20 bombers. Shortly thereafter, the PLA established an airborne unit in Shanghai which was intended to be developed over time into a crack brigade of 5,000 paratroopers, armed with specialized equipment including light fighting vehicles, mortars, artillery, machine guns, and sniper rifles.[78]

Mao and his supreme commander, General Su, had initially hoped to invade Taiwan before the end of 1950, but the tremendous financial pressure associated with the buildup and the need to acquire giant fleets of ships and planes from the Soviets contributed to a decision in the spring of 1950 to push the invasion date back to July 1951. There were other factors at play as well. While the buildup was an important factor, it seems likely that nothing did more to delay the Battle of Taiwan than the Cai Xiaoqian spy case.

Spy Games in Taiwan

The PLA needed more than ships, planes, and troops to conquer Taiwan. For the plan to work, the army needed a large network of secret agents buried in Taiwan's society, whose cardinal mission was to recruit ROC military commanders, convincing them to defect (preferably with their entire units intact) to support communist operations when the landings began. Beyond enticing Nationalist officers to betray their cause, secret agents were needed for fomenting social unrest, organizing riots, and engaging in acts of sabotage all across the island. The effort dated back to April 1946, when the top secret "Taiwan Works Committee" was established in China. Over time, this covert action group developed an extensive web of undercover operatives, who were spun across Taiwan and poised to strike at the key moment.[79]

At the dark heart of these operations was Cai Xiaoqian, the spymaster who served as the PLA's station chief in Taipei. Born in 1908, Cai was a Taiwanese native who had grown up under Japanese colonial rule. In the 1920s, he left Taiwan as a teenager to attend school in Shanghai, apparently because tuition was cheaper there. On campus, far from home, Cai was lonely and confused, making him easy prey for communist recruiting efforts. After a long period of cultivation, Cai joined Mao's insurgency against the Republic of China government.

Cai's intellectual potential was readily apparent, and like all the best and the brightest he was assigned to the Red Army's political department. He excelled at writing and was given a coveted position as a propaganda officer. Eventually he became the only Taiwanese native to survive the Long March. During the Second Sino-Japanese War (World War II), Cai became an expert in interrogating and reprogramming Japanese prisoners and translating and analyzing their documents. Born a Taiwanese subject of Imperial Japan, he was a fluent speaker of Japanese. Over time, Cai's skills became so renowned that he was asked to write teaching materials to guide other spies who would follow in his footsteps.[80]

In early 1946, just months after the Empire of Japan surrendered to the Allies, Cai arrived in Shanghai and began preparing for his next mission.

He had been hand-picked to lead a group of secret operatives against Nationalist forces in Taiwan. In July 1946, he adopted a new identity and infiltrated back into his native island. It took him and his team little time to blend in and establish themselves. Reports indicate that they developed and recruited nearly 70 local agents within their first six months, and by 1948 they controlled an estimated 285 agents.

In 1949, Nationalists forces began a mass exodus to Taiwan, and Cai's spy network surged in the depressing tumult. In December 1949, undercover operatives under his control reportedly numbered up to 1,300 agents. Additionally, Cai estimated that up to 50,000 civilian assets, almost all of them unwitting, could be mobilized for factory strikes, protest marches, and campus riots. He told his 3rd Field Army superiors that his covert forces would be ready to play their part in eroding support for Chiang's regime just before the landings started. He recommended that the invasion be launched in April 1950, when the weather would be most favorable for amphibious operations.[81]

In late 1949, Cai had good reason to be optimistic. He had a prize agent, a two-star ROC general, Wu Shi, who had retreated to Taipei from Nanjing. General Wu had been assigned to the MND General Staff Department, a position which gave him access to war plans and other highly sensitive strategic information. Wu met repeatedly with Cai, handing over top secret documents, including military maps showing the locations of landing beaches, troop dispositions, and military bases on Taiwan. Wu also purloined documents on troop deployments and artillery emplacements on the Kinmen and Zhoushan islands. These documents were subsequently smuggled into mainland China through a trusted female officer named Zhu Fengzhi. It is not clear whether or not these intelligence jewels arrived in Nanjing in time for General Su's winter planning conference. Nonetheless, great damage had been done to the defense of Taiwan.[82]

Unbeknownst to Cai or Wu, a net was slowly closing around them both. In the fall of 1949, Chiang Kai-shek began to consolidate his retreating forces on Taiwan. Having experienced a fatal hemorrhaging of intelligence and the defection of key military units in mainland China, he was determined to eradicate undercover spies who had infested Taiwan. It was a race against time. Chiang needed to clean up his ranks before communist agents could lure away his displaced and demoralized officers. Recognizing the perils facing him, he made counterintelligence and counterespionage operations his emergency government's top priority, placing the MND Counterintelligence Bureau in charge of the dragnet.

The first breakthrough for Chiang's spy catchers came in September 1949, when they uncovered a spy ring and underground printing press in the port city of Keelung. As a consequence, they were able to track down the official in charge of PLA underground intelligence work in southern Taiwan. They arrested him in Kaohsiung that November. Cai's long-cultivated spy network then quickly came unglued, as one secret agent after the next was apprehended and compromised.

By January 1950, Taiwan's men in black had closed in on Cai himself. Counterintelligence officers discovered his home address in Taipei and quickly moved to arrest him. The arrest came as a surprise to Cai, but did little to knock the wind out of his sails. Cai, himself a seasoned interrogator, knew exactly what to do in jail to turn the tables on his captors. It didn't take long. After a brief period of interrogation, Cai convinced MND officers that he had defected and would help them. They allowed him to visit a certain phone booth in downtown Taipei, where he promised to take a call luring in his commanding officer. Despite being escorted through the streets by a large contingent of plainclothes officers, Cai was able to make a successful escape and vanish into the city nightlife.

A manhunt ensued over the following weeks, with counterintelligence officers spending their Chinese New Year holidays tracking down Cai. It was the year of the tiger, and they were hunting. The trail led them to his rural hometown of Changhua, in central Taiwan, where they finally found him. After being on the run for weeks, Cai was cold, destitute, filthy, and homeless. His spy ring was broken and he had lost all his friends. As dusk drew across the land, he was surrounded in a rice paddy. Armed counterintelligence officers circled and closed in. Seeing no way to escape, Cai's last reserves of courage evaporated and he gave himself up without a fight. Although he could have committed suicide, Cai still had too much to live for. He was desperately in love with a young girl who had been captured by counterintelligence officers.[83]

March 1, 1950, was a pivotal date in the history of cross-Strait relations. That evening, after a long interrogation session, Mao's spymaster in Taiwan cracked under pressure and defected. He became a ROC military officer and, in return, gained his girlfriend's freedom, a huge sum of gold, and a high-ranking position in the military. To earn his generous reward, Cai fingered General Wu Shi and Agent Zhu Fengzhi, and revealed the identities of his other collaborators, exposing every major communist officer on the island. Cai's information allowed MND officers to make a clean sweep, clearing out enemy spy rings and underground cells across Taiwan. Life-shaking dramas played out quietly. In Taiwan and on the outer islands, PLA operatives were arrested as they filled out forms in government offices, lounged in military barracks, or attempted to cross military checkpoints.

Chairman Mao and General Su Yu were oblivious to the tectonic shifts taking place underneath their feet. They found out in early June 1950, when the Republic of China government went public with the round up, publishing front page newspaper pictures of Wu Shi, Zhu Fengzhi, and two other subordinate collaborators, both before and after they were executed in downtown Taipei by firing squad. In total, 80 separate communist operations were neutralized and over 400 secret agents were arrested. The survivors fled the island and made desperate escapes back to China.[84] Cai's once formidable intelligence apparatus on Taiwan had been thoroughly decimated, its demise guided by the hands of its own maker.[85]

The 1951 Battle Plan

News of the Cai Xiaoqian spy case, with all its bleak military implications, shook Su, who was in Beijing meeting with Mao and the other party elders when word arrived. He attempted to resign his command, claiming the overriding strategic importance of the Taiwan campaign meant that Mao himself should now serve as supreme commander. Too savvy to take direct ownership of such a high-stakes operation, Mao refused the position. Su then attempted to haggle for an additional four army corps and several paratrooper divisions, something that would have brought the planned invasion force up to 16 total corps, or around 675,000 men.[86] Sources vary on whether or not his request for more troops was granted.[87]

According to its official history, the final weeks of planning for Taiwan "liberation" operations saw the PLA leadership make some critically important changes to their battle plan. Beijing decided to increase the size of the first wave and reduce the size of the reserve force. The Communists had recently wrested Hainan and the Zhoushan Islands from ROC control, but neither operation had resulted in a decisive victory. More than 100,000 Nationalist troops had retreated to Taiwan, giving the island a defense force of over 300,000 ground troops. They were supported by an estimated 250 combat aircraft, 200 navy ships, and many additional troops on Kinmen and Penghu, making the overall defense force 500,000 strong.

Su now knew he would have no deep cover agents in Taiwan to crumble Chiang's army from within and worried he would also lack numerical superiority. In the face of these unfavorable facts, he pinned his diminishing hopes on the ability of his first wave assault force to punch through Taiwan's coastal defenses. Su added an option for doubling the number of first wave attackers to the plan, subject to the availability of landing ships, and planned rigorous pre-invasion training as a means of giving the PLA Third Field Army some qualitative advantage.[88]

His final timetable called for nine months of basic amphibious training before the invasion. From July 1950 to March 1951, individual units would practice their roles. Next, they were to undertake two months of combined exercises, where land, sea, and air units would learn to operate as one team. These drills were set for April and May 1951. Su planned to use captured equipment and facilities on Zhoushan to conduct the tri-service exercises. In July 1951, once his force's skills were sufficiently sharp, they were to marshal in Fujian and make the plunge across the Strait.[89]

As of June 1950, the campaign reportedly envisioned a large-scale invasion of Kinmen in August 1950, followed by a grueling series of battles against the offshore island chain, and then a final mass attack on Taiwan's northwestern coast. The battle plan had options for assaulting four Taiwanese beaches with 200,000 troops, or eight beaches with 360,000 troops. In either case, a large reserve force would have followed. Second echelon forces were tasked with capitalizing upon whatever beachheads and ports had been secured by the first wave. In addition, some 25,000 paratroopers were to conduct airborne assaults behind enemy lines to catch defenders by surprise, and a small mountain warfare detachment was to be inserted on the east coast of Taiwan to encircle the capital from the rear.

The plan anticipated that the operation would take approximately fifteen days to complete and cost the PLA an estimated 100,000 casualties.[90] However, these planning assumptions were highly optimistic, and the operation was recognized as a high-risk affair. In the afterlight, it is far from clear that the landings, had they occurred, would have borne fruit. It is quite possible that the invasion would have instead turned into a humiliating fiasco, even if the United States had not ultimately intervened to protect the ROC government on Taiwan.

Could It Have Worked?

It is unknowable whether or not China could have successfully invaded Taiwan in the summer of 1951 as planned. There exists no means of proving that an event which never occurred would have gone one way or another had it hypothetically occurred. The generally accepted narrative promoted after the fact by Chinese propagandists was that Taiwan's demoralized and corrupt defenders would have fallen without much of a fight. This narrative claims that if it were not for the outbreak of the Korean War and American intervention, Taiwan would have been decisively defeated and China would be a unified country today. Anything is possible, of course, but this alternate history is questionable in light of information that has emerged in recent years.

Sources indicate that the Taiwan "liberation" plan was more a product of radical ideology than professional military thought. Many of the assumptions used by the Communists, when viewed in hindsight, appear fundamentally unsound. It seems doubtful that the invasion would have resulted in victory if it had been launched as planned. The operation was more likely to have proven to be an enormous disaster, even if the United States had stood by and done nothing. While any assessment of a non-event must be considered highly speculative, there is another Taiwan invasion plan contemporary to the PLA's that can be used for the purposes of comparison.

During World War II, the United States military conducted intensive planning for the invasion of Taiwan (then called Formosa). In 1943 and 1944, Pentagon war planners considered its capture essential to their long-term plan to invade the Japanese home islands and bring the conflict to a close. On August 19, 1943, the tentative American plan for the invasion of Formosa was briefed to Winston Churchill and the British government at the First Quebec Conference.[91] By early 1944, the planned attack had become the central feature of American strategy in the Pacific. General Douglas MacArthur's return to the Philippines was considered a secondary and supporting campaign.[92]

The plan for the assault on Formosa was code-named "Operation Causeway." It envisioned an attack force of approximately 300,000 soldiers and 100,000 marines, augmented by 4,000 ships and thousands of planes. It would have been a massive combined assault on Taiwan's southwestern coast, centered on the large beachfront at what is today Fangliao Township. The total estimated number of American forces engaged would have been half a million.[93]

The basic rule of thumb Pentagon planners used was to ensure that American forces always outnumbered the Imperial Japanese by a minimum three-to-one ratio. However, the dense cities and mountainous geography of Formosa were so highly advantageous to the defender that planners concluded that they would need a five-to-one superiority to secure a victory. American intelligence assessed that Japan could have had up to 100,000 ground forces defending Taiwan by the spring of 1945, when the operation was scheduled. These might have been supported by significant numbers of air force and naval units based on the Japanese home islands and Okinawa. As a result, Operation Causeway was expected to require an assault force of at least 500,000 men. Moreover, it was anticipated that the battle could rage for as long as three months before American control was effected over the island.[94]

The American plan was straight-forward. After the initial landings on southern Formosa, marines and soldiers would fight a long hard slog up the urbanized western coast, slowly working their way up to Taipei and the port of Keelung. Meanwhile, tactical fighter squadrons and bombers would install themselves on captured airfields in the south, around what is today Pingtung and Kaohsiung, and support ground operations. Once the island fell, it would serve as a staging area and springboard for the invasion of Japan. Using data collected from the Battle of Saipan, the Pentagon estimated that the bloody house-to-house, jungle, and mountain fighting on Formosa would take a horrific toll: 150,000 American casualties.[95]

In late 1944, a number of considerations ultimately resulted in the decision to abort Operation Causeway. One of the most important was that American forces in the Pacific lacked needed manpower. Anywhere from 77,000 to 200,000 of the troops needed for the envisioned campaign (depending on the timetables and assumptions one used) were still fighting Germans in Europe. Early versions of the Operation Causeway plan hinged on a swift collapse of the Nazi regime, something that did not materialize nearly as fast as the Pentagon expected. Only after the war in Europe had ended would enough army divisions have been available to fight on Formosa. The extreme violence of the envisioned battle and high casualty estimates also argued against it. As a result of these and other considerations, Taiwan was not invaded. Instead, the United States blockaded the island with ships and submarines, neutralized its airfields and ports with bombers, and executed a "leap-frog" move around it to attack Okinawa.[96]

In light of the historical record, it seems fair to ask: if 500,000 Americans were required to overcome 100,000 defenders on Taiwan in 1945 at a projected cost of three months and 150,000 casualties, how could 500,000 PLA troops have defeated 500,000 defenders in 15 days with only 100,000 casualties in 1951? The American plan had the advantage of being informed by hard-earned amphibious experience, the likes of which the PLA lacked. American forces had vastly superior equipment and training over their foes. Most importantly, American ground forces would have been supported heavily from sea and air. By late 1944, there was no question in any planner's mind about whether or not the United States had total sea control and air supremacy in the Western Pacific.

In contrast, PLA units in the early 1950s were plagued by shortcomings across the board, including shoddy equipment, food shortages, poor training, morale problems, and an officer illiteracy rate that stood at 67.4 percent.[97] We also now know that communist war planners assumed they would not be able to secure unchallenged control over the Strait in the face of a superior ROC navy and air force. Even more striking, the Communists planned to launch invasion operations during the month of July, right when Taiwan's annual typhoon season starts. PLA strategists reportedly had good meteorological intelligence in hand, but chose to ignore it, possibly under pressure from Beijing. This case may be considered an example of how radical ideology undermines military professionalism and encourages incompetence, with potentially catastrophic results.

Today there is no way to know what might have occurred if one of the two invasion plans was put into action. However, new information available indicates that China's planning assumptions were deeply flawed and maybe even suicidal. The PLA's problems appear especially pronounced when their Taiwan plan is contrasted with the American plan, designed just six years prior. Having evaluated both, it seems likely that the long-running narrative is wrong and Chiang Kai-shek's army would have repulsed the Chinese Communists if they attacked Taiwan in the early 1950s.

From Past to Present

When North Korea attacked South Korea, President Truman ordered the Seventh Fleet, then based at Subic Bay in the Philippines, to sortie and neutralize the Taiwan Strait, keeping the PLA from attacking Taiwan. His official statement included the following lines:

> The attack upon Korea makes it plain beyond all doubt that Communism has passed beyond the use of subversion to conquer in-

dependent nations and will now use armed invasion and war ... in these circumstances the occupation of Formosa by Communist forces would be a direct threat to the security of the Pacific area and to United States forces.[98]

On June 29, 1950, the aircraft carrier *Valley Forge*, the heavy cruiser *Rochester*, and eight destroyers steamed into the Taiwan Strait, conducting a show of force within sight of the Chinese coast. Closely following this, armed American seaplanes deployed to the Penghu Islands, where they began to patrol the area in search of hostile movements toward Taiwan. American submarines sailed from Japan on secret intelligence-gathering missions, approaching the major Chinese ports of Shantou and Xiamen to confirm that no invasion was imminent. In late July 1950, two American cruisers and three destroyers made another show of force. A week later, in August, four destroyers deployed to the port of Keelung. These destroyers, backed up by planes and submarines, were ordered to patrol 16–20 miles off the Chinese coastline, with at least two ships in the Strait at all times to watch for signs of an invasion buildup. This mission was to continue for nearly three decades to come.[99]

The Military Assistance Advisory Group (MAAG) began taking shape. On May 1, 1951, Major General William Chase arrived to head the MAAG. This organization had the mission of providing American training, logistics, and weapons to the ROC military, transforming it into a well-equipped, modern fighting force. In the decades that were to follow, the MAAG's advisory teams modernized Taiwan's entire military establishment. At one point, up to 2,347 American personnel were assigned to the mission. Air Force teams built and manned airbases and communications sites in Taipei, Linkou, Taichung, Chiayi, Tainan, and Kangshan. American ships and aircraft were stationed at refitted naval stations in Keelung, Kaohsiung, and Zuoying. U.S. Army and Marine Corps advisors established large training bases in Kaohsiung and Pingtung and organized joint training exercises, including amphibious landing drills on the beaches around Fangliao, the very place they would have assaulted in 1945 if things had gone differently in World War II.[100]

Chiang Kai-shek, safe from any immediate attack on Taiwan, refitted his tattered forces, preparing them to continue the war against his hated communist adversaries. His long-term goal was to defeat Mao Zedong and retake the mainland, but for the moment he was content to settle for fighting up and down the offshore islands. This made Washington nervous; U.S. policy was to contain the communists, not roll them back. In April and October 1952, respectively, Chiang launched two minor raids against Nanri Island in the Taiwan Strait. The PLA retaliated by attacking and seizing Nanpeng Island, breaking the blockade of Shantou harbor. Many American opinion leaders, outraged by Mao's intervention in Korea, liked what Chiang was trying to do and urged him to light up the entire seaboard.

In February 1953, President Eisenhower made good on his campaign pledge to "unleash Chiang," and lifted orders that restricted ROC forces from heavy attacks on the Chinese Communists. Chiang responded by ordering another raid, this time with 3,000 troops, who briefly stormed Meizhou Island.[101] Following this operation, Nationalist forces attacked Dongshan Island in July 1953, with a combination of 6,500 marines, paratroopers, and "sea guerillas," who staged out of Kinmen. Chiang's amphibious logistics capabilities were still weak and, after an initial breakthrough, the assault lost momentum and turned into a tactical failure. Despite his inability to hold Dongshan, his raiders had nonetheless achieved America's strategic objective. The landings, in addition to other factors, helped put pressure on Beijing to come to terms on the Korean Peninsula.[102]

On July 27, 1953, PLA representatives signed an armistice in Korea. Soon thereafter, Mao began deploying enormous numbers of troops in southern China across from Taiwan, heightening cross-Strait tensions. To balance against the hostile buildup, Chiang sent an additional 58,000 troops to reinforce Kinmen and placed 15,000 more on Matsu. Mao apparently interpreted the buildup as preparations for an attempt to retake the Chinese mainland and sent even more soldiers to stand guard across from Taiwan. By August 1954, the balance had tipped toward the PLA. Buoyed by a groundswell of troops in Fujian, Mao's top lieutenant, Zhou Enlai, publically declared that China must invade Taiwan and destroy the Nationalists. A few weeks later, the PLA began shelling Kinmen and Matsu, igniting the First Taiwan Strait Crisis. Not long after, they launched concurrent air and sea attacks on the Dachen Islands, 200 miles north of Taiwan. The objective of the attacks was to break free of the naval blockade the ROC Navy had been enforcing since 1950 in tandem with a tough American trade embargo.[103]

In November 1954, Mao initiated the heavy bombing of the Dachen group. He then concentrated amphibious forces on the northernmost ROC-held island base of Yijiangshan, located nearby. Using new Soviet equipment and tactics, the PLA executed an overwhelming assault on the island, which fell on January 18, 1955. In response, Chiang pressed for American naval and air support for his troops on the Dachens. Reinforcements arrived, but the islands were far from Taiwan, making them vulnerable and strategically unimportant. The United States was reluctant to commit the large naval forces that were needed for defending them over the long term. Facing Mao's giant invasion force which had assembled close by, Chiang reluctantly agreed to retreat and abandon the entire coast of Zhejiang Province, where he had grown up, to his archenemy.

On February 8, 1955, Operation King Kong, the evacuation of the Dachens, was launched. American marines landed on the islands and helped ROC commanders organize an evacuation effort, safely transporting over 15,000 civilians, 11,000 troops, 125 vehicles, and 165 artillery pieces off the remote islands with no casualties. The Seventh Fleet supported Operation King Kong with an enormous task force of 70 warships, centered on seven aircraft carriers. Mao had hoped attacks on the Dachens would drive Washington and Taipei apart. Instead, the crisis and successful evacuation operation strengthened the relationship.

Washington signed a mutual defense treaty with Taipei in December 1954, and the Senate ratified the alliance in February. On March 3, 1955, the final ratification documents were formally exchanged. President Eisenhower concurrently requested permission from Congress to exercise special powers in the defense of Taiwan. This was granted in the form of the Formosa Resolution. Beijing, under mounting pressure from Moscow, began deescalating the fiery standoff. On May 1, 1955, the PLA stopped shelling Kinmen. Three months later, Mao released eleven captured American airmen, ending the 1954–1955 Taiwan Strait Crisis.[104]

Tensions remained high across the Strait. The PLA stationed an estimated 750,000 troops across from Taiwan, but its weak naval arm could do little to break free of the blockade, which continued to restrict China's ability to trade with countries other than the Soviet Union. As a result of Taiwan's siege warfare, port operations all along China's seaboard were paralyzed. ROC Navy patrols used Kinmen and Matsu as bases from which they went out to sink communist vessels whenever they found them nearby and detained foreign trade ships on their way to or from China. In addition, the offshore islands were used to stage commando raids and to insert intelligence operatives into the mainland. Beijing worried these joint U.S.-ROC operations could be a precursor to a Nationalist-led invasion of Fujian, with Kinmen and Matsu being used as the stepping stones.[105]

On August 23, 1958, the simmering waters boiled over again. The PLA launched a surprise attack, ferociously shelling Kinmen with an enormous barrage of forty thousand shells during the opening phase of bombardment alone. Mao intended to test America's bottom line, seeing if the threat of all-out war could get Washington to split with its new Cold War ally. He also hoped that by first softening up and then seizing Kinmen, the PLA could demoralize Nationalist forces stationed in Taiwan. The plan backfired. Chiang's forces had already turned Kinmen into a rabbit warren of tunnels and bunkers, and his troops were able to weather the onslaught of shells with surprisingly few casualties. The PLA's amphibious landing attempt on the tiny nearby island of Dongding failed, and artillery firepower directed against Matsu proved similarly ineffectual.[106]

The Seventh Fleet arrived on the scene of battle with four imposing aircraft carriers and a formidable host of cruisers, destroyers, submarines, and amphibious ships. In a remarkable move, the fleet was equipped with tactical nuclear bombs, intended to be released in the event of a human-wave invasion of Kinmen, a tactic previously seen in Korea. Not only had Mao completely misjudged the resolve of the Americans, he also shocked his Soviet allies. Moscow was horrified by Mao's provocative attacks and put pressure on him to back down.

Mao ignored the changing facts on the ground and continued shelling. Escalating the crisis, he ordered torpedo boats and artillery to attack Chiang's resupply ships going to Kinmen. To get payback, Chiang ordered the ROC Air Force to draw up plans for large-scale strikes against targets on the mainland. On September 7, 1958, the U.S. Navy began to escort Nationalist convoy ships to Kinmen, protecting them with cruisers and destroyers. This obviated the immediate need for air strikes which could have escalated the conflict. From September 18th to 20th, the Americans clandestinely rolled ashore six giant 8-inch artillery guns capable of firing tactical nuclear rounds that could flatten any invading fleet. The nuclear shells were kept aboard nearby ships under control of American forces. But even with conventional rounds, the new mega artillery gave the frontline garrison a much needed boost in terms of both firepower and morale.

Five days later, a formation of American-made F-86 Sabres, flown by ROC fighter pilots, mauled a flight of PLA MiG-17 jets, splashing four of them into the ocean with the revolutionary new Sidewinder missile. Over the coming days, Nationalist pilots tallied up 33 enemy kills in return for the loss of four of their own. Mao finally began to realize his bluff had been called. On October 6, he directed his forces to back down and announced a cease-fire. To save face, the PLA continued to shell Kinmen on odd-numbered days for the next twenty years. The 1958 Taiwan Strait Crisis was over, and Taiwan's offshore island bases remained undefeated.

Mao's Taiwan Strait gambits produced a series of tactical setbacks and resulted in unrequited strategic losses. He failed to drive a wedge between Washington and Taipei and instead pushed them closer together. The United States extended its nuclear umbrella over Taiwan, built up Chiang's backward force into a high-caliber professional military machine, and gave his government a powerful seat at the United Nations. In the years and decades ahead, the United States nurtured Taiwan, helping it grow from a devastated wartime base of emergency operations into a stable and increasingly responsible world player. Taiwan flourished economically and then politically, becoming a miracle of the modern, post-war world.[107]

While Mao inadvertently strengthened his old nemesis on Taiwan, he also bit hard into the Soviet hand that had long fed him. The Sino-Soviet split, worsened in part by Beijing's frightfully provocative behavior in the Taiwan Strait, began as a series of small ideological fissures in the mid-1950s. Over time, these fissures grew and developed into ever larger cracks. Finally, in 1960, the USSR angrily withdrew all its technicians and experts from China. Despite the growing spiral of deterioration, Mao indulged in radical tirades against the Soviets and channeled his unbridled hubris into aggressive and irrational acts against his former benefactor. In 1962, the two communist powers broke diplomatic relations and became openly hostile. The dark shadow of nuclear war and possible Soviet invasion spread over China. Facing this strategic peril, the PLA began to focus on protecting China's long northern border. The Taiwan Strait standoff continued, but as a secondary theater of less consequence.

Mao's failures at home and abroad prevented the PLA from posing a serious threat to Taiwan. His policies resulted in a horrific famine, lasting from 1958 to 1962, with the starvation compounded by domestic terror tactics and systematic violence in the collective farms he had masterminded. The outcome was tens of millions of innocent deaths. From 1966 to 1976, Mao purged and persecuted enormous numbers of CCP officials and systematically turned social groups against each other, all while cultivating a fanatical cult of personality around himself. The chaos and violence Mao orchestrated up until his death in 1976 represented an economic and above all human disaster that has no easy parallel in history.[108]

Taiwan's security was bolstered by Beijing's distraction and dysfunction. The PLA remained a low-quality military opponent centered on illiterate peasants whose main focus was the USSR, against whom they planned to fight a ghastly war of attrition. Consequently, the PLA developed little in the way of amphibious capability and had no way of taking control of the air and seas around Taiwan. In 1979, when President Jimmy Carter played the "China Card" against the USSR and switched diplomatic recognition from Taipei to Beijing, Taiwan suffered an earth-shaking strategic loss. From a purely military perspective, however, the balance was still unquestionably favorable to Taiwan and would remain that way for a long time to come. The PLA continued to focus on the danger of war with the Soviet Union, and events at home and abroad shook the Chinese military establishment, including the June 4, 1989, Tiananmen Square Massacre, and the startling success of the American-led Operation Desert Storm.[109]

In the early 1990s, Taiwan found itself in China's gun sights again. When the Soviet Union collapsed, the PRC's main strategic objective once more became to liberate its "wayward province." After Taiwan's 1992 parliamentary elections, this mission appeared especially urgent to Beijing. Taiwan was transitioning to a democracy and becoming what might naturally be perceived by the post Cold War world as a legitimate, independent country. Taiwan's president, Lee Teng-hui, broke with the long-held KMT position and declared that his government no longer claimed to represent all of China. In his view, the Chinese Civil War was over and Taiwan was now the ROC, and the ROC was Taiwan. The communist regime in Beijing was still illegitimate, but Taiwan no longer had any ambition to claim sovereignty over the mainland.[110]

President Lee's position, basically an indirect declaration of independence, infuriated China's leaders. Making matters worse for them, Taiwan planned to hold its first free and fair presidential elections under American tutelage. In June 1995, President Lee went to his alma mater, Cornell University, to give a speech and share Taiwan's democracy plans with his friends. In reaction, the Chinese conducted a series of ballistic missile tests in July, angrily firing rockets into the waters north of Keelung. The PLA also mobilized army units in Fujian Province and conducted live-fire naval exercises in August, accompanied by further missile firings. In November, the PLA followed through by carrying out a highly publicized amphibious assault drill.[111]

These military acts were all part of a psychological warfare operation whose objective appears to have been to pressure President Lee to call off the American-style election. If that failed, the secondary objective seems to have been to ensure that a pro-China candidate was elected instead of Lee. In March 1996, just before Taiwan's elections, the PLA fired ballistic missiles into Taiwan's territorial waters off the ports of Keelung and Kaohsiung, and implicitly threatened to turn a planned drill into a real invasion.[112]

President Lee knew that China's threats were completely empty. While human-wave attacks could have been conducted against Kinmen and Matsu, the Chinese military had no actual ability to cross the Strait and land on Taiwan. Its amphibious lift situation was abysmal, and its units were poorly led, trained, and equipped. Lee, thanks to his spies in Chinese military circles, had superb intelligence on what was going on inside China and knew that Taiwan fielded a far superior ground force, air force, and navy.[113]

The United States played a pivotal role throughout the crisis. President Bill Clinton responded to Chinese provocations with alacrity, staging a show of American military might in the form of two carrier battle groups that were sent to international waters near Taiwan. The American demonstration of resolve and commitment to democracy was decisive. China deescalated the crisis, and Taiwan's elections went ahead as planned. President Lee, bolstered by public support for his courageous policies, saw a surge at the polls and won the elections decisively. The 1995–1996 Taiwan Strait Crisis ended on a high note, but peace and stability were far from secure.[114]

In the following years, China began to sharply ramp up military spending on equipment and training. New advanced weapons systems and technologies poured in from Russia. The PLA was downsized and restructured to make it more lethal and light. Units staged increasingly large and sophisticated military exercises. Previously decrepit and blunt, the PLA grew more muscular and sharp, narrowing the gap with the ROC military.[115] Two decades after the missile crisis, the amphibious threat facing Taiwan now appears increasingly credible. Although the PLA continues to have many endemic weaknesses and probably still cannot execute a major landing operation, it is already a dangerous fighting force.[116]

The probability appears to be growing that at some point in the 2020s China's military could be ready to launch a cross-Strait invasion. How might we know if that was about to happen?

Chapter Three
Warning Signs

The issue of political disagreements that exist between the two sides must reach a final resolution ... these issues cannot be passed on from generation to generation.

—Xi Jinping

TODAY it is sometimes assumed that China could mount a surprise attack on Taiwan and invade the island with little or no warning. In this hypothetical scenario, Taiwan's leaders might find themselves astonished and overwhelmed by a numerically superior enemy, who would suddenly present them with a torrent of life and death problems. They would presumably struggle to mount an effective defense in these circumstances, and organized resistance could conceivably crumble within days. Taiwan's democratic government, having fallen prey to China's well-orchestrated strategic deception operations, might quickly cease to exist. Communist collaborators would take over and turn Taiwan into an Orwellian police state.

The assumption that China has the capacity to catch Taiwan off-guard is foundational to most negative assessments regarding Taiwan's defensibility.[117] Surprise is viewed by those who embrace pessimistic judgments as not only possible, but probable. From their perspective, the analytical problems of early warning repeatedly seen throughout history, from Pearl

Harbor to September 11, 2001, make the anticipation of a Chinese attack on Taiwan nearly impossible, especially since the intentions animating the CCP (and by extension the PLA) are often so opaque. However, such leaps in analytical logic deserve close scrutiny in light of what is known about indications and warning, which is the art of avoiding surprise and judging when an attack is coming.

The process of indications and warning in the Taiwan Strait begins with indications, evidence that China is preparing to attack. Indications are generally comprised of some developments, or some uncertain signs or information that provide grounds for a belief that hostilities might be looming ahead. According to a seminal work on the subject, *Anticipating Surprise*, written by an American intelligence expert, Cynthia Grabo, an indication can be "an absence of something, a fragment of information, an observation, a photograph, a propaganda broadcast, a diplomatic note, a call-up of reservists, a deployment of forces, an agent report, or anything else. The sole provision is that it provide some insight ... into the enemy's likely course of action."[118] An indicator is something the adversary (in this case China) is known or expected to have to do in preparation for hostilities. Lists of things to be monitored that are anticipated might occur prior to conflict are known as watch lists or indicator lists.[119]

Strategic warning, according to Grabo, is more long-term in nature and can be issued well in advance of attack. Strategic warning would come "if a large-scale deployment of forces is under way, or the adversary has made known his political commitment to some course of action involving the use of force." This type of warning "may be possible only when enemy action is imminent, but it also may be possible long before that."[120] Strategic warnings are generally issued to national-level leaders such as presidents and prime ministers. Tactical warning, on the other hand, is more of an operational concern, and something available to generals with access to radar pictures and other sensor networks that provide timely indications that an enemy attack in under way.[121]

The elected officials leading the Taiwanese government probably spend very little of their time worrying about the possibility of an enemy surprise attack. That is the job of intelligence officers, who view the collection and dissemination of indications and warning information as vital to the life of their country. According to the website of the National Security Bureau (Taiwan's counterpart to the CIA), providing advanced warning of Chinese preparations for an attack on Taiwan is the highest priority of the island's intelligence services.[122] This mission is essential during peacetime to prevent China from achieving the advantage of surprise, and it is especially critical during periods of limited conflict to provide strategic warning of war escalation. In a crisis, Taiwan's government will need to know if China intends to add fuel to the fire, inflaming pre-existing tensions into a mass conflagration.[123]

Timely and accurate warning is important for enabling Taiwan's government to select the right moment to put contingency plans into action and mobilize the country for war. Taiwan maintains a professional military of around 200,000 personnel, almost all of whom are volunteers. To bolster these professional warriors, Taiwan also maintains a conscript-heavy reserve force of over 2.5 million men, giving it the ability to mobilize a giant army of citizen-soldiers.[124] Taiwan can further augment its military by mobilizing nearly one million civil defense reservists, who are registered to provide war support.[125] Early warning of a Chinese attack is needed for activating this tremendous, but latent, military and civilian power. Strategic warning is vital for helping Taiwan's president to judge when best to order the military to increase the readiness levels of fielded troops.

The main challenges to strategic early warning are Chinese espionage and deception. Taiwan faces a well-documented spy threat, which has resulted in a considerable number of espionage cases. If unchecked, Chinese agents could undermine the discernments made by Taiwan's elected officials. However, while the threat of enemy infiltration is very real, Taiwan's counterintelligence community has established a solid track record of identifying and stopping leaks. In many cases, Taiwan's spy-catchers have discovered and arrested traitors soon after China has recruited them, ensuring that security breaches were short-lived.

Spy scandals have done great damage to Taiwan's reputation, but most foreign experts assess that appearances are worse than reality when it comes to Chinese penetration of Taiwan, and there is little justification for assuming that Taiwan's ranks are riddled with Chinese spies.[126] Even more important, experts point out that Taiwan has done an extraordinary job recruiting well-placed agents in China who can provide early warning information to the Presidential Office (and the White House).[127]

Taiwan has long had a close relationship with the American military and intelligence communities, giving Taipei access to world-class arrays of early warning sensors, including radars, satellites, and electronic eavesdropping stations. These capabilities greatly reduce the risk that Taiwan's president might be caught off guard by a Chinese surprise attack.[128] Internal PLA publications evince concern that Japan would also send warning to Taiwan. One excerpt states that Japan shadows and tracks Chinese forces with its aircraft, ships, submarines, and satellites, and uses reconnaissance and early warning networks on its southwestern islands to monitor PLA activities. According to Chinese military assessments, Tokyo has excellent early-warning intelligence on the Taiwan Strait area.[129]

It is impossible to accurately assess matters that by their very nature are secret, but the information available strongly suggests Taiwan is well prepared to avoid the threat of strategic surprise. Studies produced by experts in both China and Taiwan have closely examined indications and warning specific to a cross-Strait invasion scenario. They conclude that, while any Chinese attack on Taiwan would place a premium on deception, the PLA is unlikely to have the element of surprise on its side. It is not foreordained that events would follow exactly as anticipated, and errors in judgment are always possible. Yet according to analyses conducted on both sides of the Strait, PLA preparations for an attack on Taiwan could not be hidden from view because at least five categories of indicators exist and are routinely monitored by Taiwan, America, and Japan, and information in these categories, once collected and studied, would provide a sound basis upon which to make judgments regarding the potential for Chinese invasion.[130]

Category 1: Readiness Indicators

Chinese military operations to invade and capture a large and well-defended island nation like Taiwan would be fundamentally different from other smaller and less challenging operations, such as bombing it from the air or harassing it from the sea. Preparing for an all-out invasion is far more demanding and difficult to hide, since a vast number of people must be involved for the operation to have any serious chance of success. According to Chinese writings, the invasion of Taiwan would be a fantastically complex endeavor, directly affecting the lives and well-being of millions of people who would participate. The operation would require the PRC's military units, civilian bureaucracies, and corporate organizations to become tightly knit. They would each have to surrender their own selfish interests to a larger cause, overcoming the conflicting dynamics known to organized groups of people everywhere.

Chinese analysts make clear that it would be a fool's errand to try to completely eradicate office politics, competing departmental sub-cultures, and divisive factions, especially in a society as bureaucratic as China's. Instead, national efforts would focus on smoothing over major splits and divergences. To prepare for the coming war, organizational structuring, planning, and coordination arrangements would have to be hammered out. This means that important people in China, whose daily activities are routinely monitored, will have to meet with each other in person to discuss what is going on and what the plan is, then they will have to negotiate and agree on who is going to do what in support of the plan, and when they are going to do it.

It is anticipated that the leaders of the party and the military would begin covertly convening several months prior to the onset of hostilities. In addition to a flurry of CCP Politburo meetings in Beijing, at least one major war planning and coordination conference is likely to be held in the Eastern Theater Command. This hypothetical conference would be attended by executive-level representatives from the army, navy, air force, rocket forces, space forces, intelligence services, public security forces, militia, and provincial and city governments. Each member present at the war conference would represent an organization with an important role to play in the coming operation. A smaller circle of trusted super-elites would likely be selected and appointed to a Joint Taiwan Attack Leading Small Group and/or Joint Taiwan Attack Command Center, responsible for finalizing details of the war plan, refereeing inter-agency disputes, and distributing copies of committee decisions throughout their respective military and civilian chains-of-command.[131]

Any one of the elite group members could be a foreign spy, or they could have a trusted confidant who was. Chinese organizations typically make judgments about loyalty based on personal ties and family connections. Relatives of high-ranking Communist Party heroes are routinely favored over their peers, no matter how incompetent they might be, or how questionable their personal behavior. The system has few checks and balances and is opaque and ridden with corruption. As such, leaks are probably inevitable. Even assuming for perfect security, the mere fact of certain leaders meeting in a non-routine fashion should indicate to Taiwanese (and American) intelligence analysts that trouble could be brewing, especially during periods when cross-Strait relations were deteriorating and tensions were running abnormally high.

As Z-Day drew closer, the PLA's Rocket Force would move ballistic missiles and cruise missiles out of their peacetime garrisons. Traveling on highways and rail lines deep within the mountainous interior of China, missile brigades would rumble toward their launch sites. Once arrived, they would begin conducting pre-launch inspections, warhead mating drills, and tests. Once deployments began in full, thousands of missile launchers, communications vans, security trucks, and logistics support vehicles would be moving. They would carry with them an army of personnel, each with hometowns full of friends and family and neighbors, some whom might be garrulous or indiscrete.[132] The associated chatter would probably alert Taiwan's undercover agents on the ground, who would report anything unusual. The movement of large numbers of strategic missiles would also be noticed by eavesdropping satellites, aircraft, and other surveillance assets who are tasked with watching them from afar. Alarm lights would start flashing and secure phones would start ringing in Taipei and Washington.

Along with the sudden and alarming uptick in missile movements, many other elements of the military, dormant in peacetime, would begin coming to life. Chinese air defense units would leave their peacetime garrisons and move in large numbers to Fujian Province, where their surface-to-air missile batteries would be established in prepared sites to bolster the defense of vulnerable airspace around command bunkers, airbases, and port facilities. Elite army groups specializing in amphibious assault would cancel all vacation leave, mobilize to full strength, and ready their equipment for deployment. Reserve and militia units would be called up for service. These radical departures from routine activity, no matter how well coordinated and concealed, would place immense strain on China's communications and transportation infrastructure, which would be noticeable.[133] Train stations, bus depots, and airports across China would be crowded with troops, and islands and other staging areas along the Taiwan Strait would be teaming with uniformed military personnel, visible for anyone to see.[134]

It is highly probable that the PLA would conduct a series of rehearsal exercises and amphibious drills to improve the readiness levels of forces soon to be engaged in deadly combat. Army groups in southeastern China are expected to conduct full-strength landing exercises, with entire brigades and divisions simulating beach assaults. With war approaching, Chinese generals would focus on neglected and expensive aspects of training for their troops. In the Chinese military, political officers generally make all the key decisions, and they tend to be cautious, cheap, and risk-adverse. If peacetime expedients were ever to be cast aside, now would be the time. It is anticipated that political officers would unchain combat commanders and allow them to organize intensive live-fire exercises, night fighting drills, and field maneuvers. In addition, large-scale combined operations involving land, sea, air, and rocket forces would likely be conducted. Soldiers participating in these exercises would not return to their home bases after the drills. Instead, they would deploy to coastal areas at or near known points of embarkation, concentrating on the ports and bays along the coast.

Intelligence would indicate that large and menacing troop movements were underway. Electro-optical satellites, their telescopic eyes staring down from space, would capture shots of Chinese tanks, rocket launchers, artillery pieces, and armored vehicles, lined up in long rows aboard flatbed train cars, some in transit, others arrived and waiting to unload at the major rail yards. Imagery would show sprawling coastal camps being established, and troops marshaling not far from transport ships loitering offshore. Helicopter activity would spike as army aviation units from all over China flocked in and landed on Fujian's fields. On digital map screens around the world, intelligence officers would track a giant red army moving toward Taiwan like ball bearings drawn to a magnet.

Air activity would also tip China's hand. There are around twenty military airfields in China's southeast that lie close enough to Taiwan to place the island within the extended combat radius of a fighter jet.[135] Large numbers of fighters and fighter-bombers would relocate from their distant inland bases to these airfields ahead of any notional Z-Day. It is believed that, once established at frontline bases, they would engage in intensive training drills. Exercises would likely focus heavily on improving capabilities for night operations, air-to-air combat, bombing, and electronic jamming. In addition to unusually rigorous combat training, air squadrons would likely practice dispersing to and operating from alternative bases in case their airstrips were destroyed. When moving to backup locations, each unit's maintenance and logistics support crews would go with them. In addition, drone fleets would cluster in frontline bases, and Chinese paratroopers would rehearse airborne operations, simulating the seizure of airfields.

At a certain point, PLA ships and submarines would put to sea and sail out to operating areas in the Yellow Sea, the East China Sea, and the South China Sea. The grey-hulled vessels of the PLA Navy would join up with vast numbers of mobilized civilian vessels to practice maneuvers in formation. Naval jets and helicopters would probably join these maritime exercises, practicing their roles providing overhead fleet air defense. After naval exercises were over, it seems probable that many of the participating ship groups would not return to their home bases. They would instead seek shelter inside the warm ports and natural harbors along the coast facing Taiwan.

Civil air traffic could slow to a crawl as the number of flights in and out of major cities was reduced to free up additional airspace for military maneuvers.[136] In cities like Shanghai, fighter jets and other aircraft operating from local airports might be seen flying low in great formations as they rehearsed their roles in the invasion. Another unmistakable and ominous sign would be the presence of massed fleets of maritime militia boats gathering and clogging up ports and anchorages in the provinces of Jiangsu, Zhejiang, Fujian, and Guangdong.

It is sometimes assumed that China plans to invade Taiwan with two separate amphibious groups, each of which would target a different section of Taiwan's coastline. One group would presumably assault Taiwan's northwest coast, launching its attacks from bases around Pingtan Island and Nanri Island. The other amphibious fleet would presumably assault Taiwan's southwest coast from amphibious bases around Dongshan Island and Nan'ao Island. The ports of Wenzhou, Fuzhou, Xiamen, Meizhou, and Shantou would be heavily involved. Extraordinary ship concentrations in these sensitive areas along China's coast could indicate an attack was about to begin.[137]

One of the most provocative and destabilizing steps China could take prior to Z-Day would be to engage in nuclear testing. There is a precedent for this. In the summer of 1995, during the 1995–1996 Taiwan Strait Crisis, Beijing exploded two atomic bombs, each one ignited at a politically sensitive moment.[138] Internal PLA writings state that nuclear weapons could be tested in an invasion scenario to deter American intervention.[139] Regardless of whether or not atomic experiments were actually conducted, it can be speculated that China might seek to raise the readiness levels of its nuclear forces by ordering nuclear ballistic missile submarines to sortie from their underground bases on Hainan Island. In addition, Beijing might deploy nuclear missile launchers from their garrisons and disperse them into the mountain wilderness of central China.[140]

Category 2: Logistics Indicators

Early warning experts know that logistics is the oxygen of battle. So they monitor stockpiling, which is an early and obvious sign that a country is preparing itself for war. Long before the final attack orders were sent out, China would begin purchasing and storing vast lakes of oil and gas. Fuel depots across from Taiwan would be topped off, and new tank farms quickly built and filled. Mountains of coal would be piled up. Chinese factories producing weapons, ammunition, and equipment would rapidly expand production.

Trains and trucks, groaning under the weight of their heavy loads, would motor into staging areas with war supplies of all kinds. Food, water, uniforms, medicine, and batteries would all be stockpiled. Blood banks would be filled. Farm animals, especially pigs, would be gathered in huge herds to feed the troops. As one consequence of China's stockpiling surge, the price of commodities like petroleum, copper, rice, soybeans, and wheat would likely bubble up on the world markets, driven by a seemingly insatiable Chinese demand.

Stockpiling would be accompanied by a spike in infrastructure projects, providing another indication that an invasion attempt was imminent. Every large and medium-sized port from Jiangsu in the north to Hainan in the south could see a colossal increase in their manpower and heavy equipment numbers. To support the immense number of transport ships required by the invasion, infrastructure expansion activities would likely include the construction of new warehouses, docks, workshops, and cranes. Roads and railroads serving the ports would be expanded to accommodate the greatly increased traffic volume. Air defense and armed security patrols, probably both regular army and armed police, would take up station in and around port facilities. Maritime militia units would guard the harbor approaches. Merchant marines from around the world who use these ports would take notice of the engineering projects and the tightening of security, which would restrict their activities.

Shipyards across China would begin the mass production of flat-bottomed landing ships and amphibious assault vehicles. It is envisioned that fishing fleets would be called in for refitting. The great shipyards at Shanghai, Zhoushan, Guangzhou, Wuhan, and Dalian would be clogged with commercial transport ships, roll-on/roll-off ships, ferries, and barges—all lined up to be refitted with military-grade communications systems and other equipment to improve their utility in combat.[141] Shipyards would probably be operating at breakneck speeds for at least three months before the invasion, working on 24-hour shifts and brightly lit up at night.[142] Light and noise travel great distances over water, making them easy to pick up with submarines and surveillance ships. Overhead imagery, provided by passing satellites and aircraft, would give additional proof that preparations were underway for an invasion.

Many of the Chinese airstrips near Taiwan are already fortified in preparation for combat operations, but many others are not. To support the influx of aircraft, there is expected to be a significant uptick in construction activity at airbases. This would presumably include the building of new hangars, hardened aircraft shelters, concrete revetments, back-up control towers, ammunition storage bunkers, fuel dumps, workshops, and other structures. Construction projects would likely include runway and parking ramp extensions, and efforts to make current structures more durable. Army and militia units armed with air defense guns would dig in around their perimeters. Elsewhere, new command bunkers would be tunneled into the earth. Closer to Z-Day, land mines would be sown along the Fujian coast, obstacles erected, and razor wire spooled out across endless miles of shore to keep potential infiltrators out of restricted areas. China would turn its entire southeastern coast into a well-stocked war camp.

Category 3: Reconnaissance Indicators

Good information is important in peace, but it is a matter of life and death in war. Chinese writings describe some of the unusual information-gathering activities that might be expected off the coast of Taiwan prior to an invasion. PLA intelligence ships, disguised as fishing trawlers, would be equipped in large numbers with specialized suites of electronic intelligence gear to operate as listening posts at sea. Such ships are expected to be manned by crews of up to thirty men, some of whom had specialized technical training and some of whom would be armed with machine guns and assault rifles for security. Outfitted with nets and other fishing tackle as camouflage, these ships would sail near some of Taiwan's most sensitive coastal waters to collect information on the beaches and sea bottom conditions. They would attempt to linger offshore to watch as coastal fortifications were erected, naval activities spiked, and troop movements began.

PLA writings state that China's space launch centers would drastically ramp up the tempo of their operations in the weeks before conflict to launch emergency satellites into orbit.[143] The Chinese public would most likely be told these additional space assets were remote sensing payloads for helping agriculture, fishing, and traffic control. Chinese satellites that had long flown in fixed orbits would suddenly conduct orbital maneuvering to provide increased coverage of Taiwan and the Western Pacific.[144] One Chinese military text writes that at least four imagery satellites would be needed for daily passes over Taiwan to provide intelligence analysts with an updated reconnaissance picture of the entire island. Additional satellites would be needed to monitor Taiwanese military exercises and American aircraft carrier strike group movements within 3,000 kilometers (1,620 nautical miles) of the Chinese mainland.[145]

Chinese intelligence-gathering aircraft would likely prowl the skies around Taiwan, skirting the edge of Taiwan's airspace to glean whatever bits of information they could. Some could orchestrate fake attack operations, charging jets past the Taiwan Strait centerline to test Taiwanese reaction speeds. Intelligence planes would loiter nearby, vacuuming up valuable data on Taiwan's tactics, techniques, and procedures.[146] Far away from these airborne scenes of brinksmanship, China's human intelligence activities would likely surge. However, the more agents were pressed to produce quick results, the more likely it would become that Chinese spies would have their covers blown.[147]

Category 4: Propaganda Indicators

War begins and ends not just on the battlefield, but in the minds of the women and men involved. One component of the invasion, according to internal Chinese military books, would be using internet and television media outlets as weapons of psychological warfare to weaken Taiwan's powers of resistance before the main attack. PLA writings describe a number of factors as being advantageous for such operations, including the broad appeal of China's economic miracle, the large number of expatriate Taiwanese businessmen in China, the influence of politicians who frequently visit Beijing, cross-Strait tourism and cultural exchanges, and economic entanglements. Psychological warfare operations are often combined with something they call "legal warfare" and "public opinion warfare." All fall under the broad umbrella of political warfare operations.[148]

One internal document offers the following guidance to Chinese officers undertaking such operations against Taiwan:

Utilize legal warfare and public opinion warfare together with psychological warfare to divide and erode the island's solid willpower and lower the island's combat strength. Of these, utilize legal warfare against the enemy's political groups and their so-called "allies" as a form of psychological attack. Clearly make the case that a joint attack campaign against the main island is legally justifiable and based on a continued, and internal, war of liberation ... utilize public opinion warfare against the enemy's military groups as a form of psychological attack. Point out the benefits of giving up their support for "independence" with effective messaging themes.... Use the Internet media heavily against non-governmental groups on the island and the masses as a form of psychological attack. Proactively spread propaganda regarding the benefits of unification for the nation and the people, and erode the social foundation of the "separatist" forces on the island.[149]

As part of the effort, propaganda campaigns would ignite war fever across China. Party mouthpieces would excoriate "Taiwan independence forces," and saturate the airwaves with jingoistic articles using canned catchphrases like, "Better one thousand troops dead than one inch of territory lost!" "Rebuild Taiwan! (after obliterating it)," and, "Annihilate the Taiwan splitist forces!" Stories would likely be run and re-run glorifying past PLA heroes and model soldiers, and media reports would breathlessly tell Chinese troops that they inherited just and courageous traditions. Troops would be told that the sacrifices made by past heroes were worthy of emulation in the days ahead.

Radical pro-unification media outlets on Taiwan would parrot the messaging themes of China. In Washington, D.C. and other American cities, Chinese United Front workers would probably organize conferences and hold public events targeting foreign policy elites. PRC embassies and consular offices would do everything in their power to convince foreigners to stay out of "China's internal business" and to abandon Taiwan in its hour of need. Some might dole out extravagant contracts and business deals to foreign agents of influence in return for them writing editorials espousing Beijing's position.[150] Others would issue threats to American government officials using diplomatic notes and unofficial backchannels, hinting that any conflict could rapidly escalate into a nuclear exchange.[151] PLA writings indicate that while Japan and other American allies are considered secondary targets of intimidation, they would, too, be subjected to extremist threats in an effort to undermine their support for Taiwan.[152]

Category 5: Subversion Indicators

As the Western Pacific approached boiling point, things are expected to happen in Taiwan to make people there feel deeply insecure. It is widely assumed that significant increases in subversive activities would occur prior to the onset of war, with legions of spies infiltrating into Taiwan, Penghu, and the outer islands to conduct sabotage missions. Saboteurs are likely to poison water supplies, blow up bridges and tunnels, and attack the power grid and oil depots. Taiwanese security authorities expect a

THE CHINESE INVASION THREAT

sharp rise in human smuggling, associated with discoveries of weapons caches and clandestine communications equipment.[153]

Organized crime syndicates with pro-unification agendas are expected to become highly active, seeking to rapidly recruit new teenage manpower. Violence would presumably break out at nightclubs and other nightlife establishments as pro-CCP gangs began expanding into the territory of local Taiwanese gangs. Police would confront the possibility of gangsters being armed with weapons previously unthinkable in Taiwan, such as assault rifles and explosives. Gangs and other underground elements could organize anti-government demonstrations in Taipei and engage in bloody battles with the police. In addition, Chinese intelligence agents would reportedly attempt to foster financial chaos, rioting, campus protests, and labor strikes.[154] They would also make efforts to manipulate politicians and military generals, turning them against each other.[155]

Acts of crime and espionage, designed to weaken social order and under-cut feelings of national confidence, would presumably squeeze the country from every side. Based on internal PLA writings, the Taiwanese president and other high officials, and their families, could become the victims of assassination or abduction attempts.[156] Taiwan's legal code anticipates this threat and authorizes greatly expanded security measures to ensure stability. At a certain undefined point, the mounting threat would become impossible to ignore, and Taiwan's president and her cabinet would be forced to declare a state of emergency and mobilize the country for war.[157]

Invasion Watch List*

1. Readiness
- Suspicious leadership meetings (CCP Politburo, CMC, and Eastern Theater Command)
- Establishment of leading small group/joint command for Taiwan (Beijing, Nanjing, and/or Fuzhou areas)

---

*   Note that this list is notional and does not include every indicator of potential invasion.

- Field deployments: theater missiles (Fujian, Guangdong, Jiangxi, Zhejiang)
- Field deployments: strategic air defense batteries (Fujian, Greater Shanghai, Greater Guangzhou (S-400, S-300, HQ-9))
- Field deployments: army amphibious and airborne units (elements of the 1st, 31st, 12th, and 42nd group armies)
- Field deployments: fighter groups (20 major airbases near Taiwan)
- Mobilization of reserves and militia (Eastern, Southern, Northern, Central theater commands)
- Amphibious assault drills (Zhoushan, Pingtan, Dongshan)
- Ship and submarine sorties (East Sea Fleet at Ningbo, South Sea Fleet at Zhanjiang)
- Air and sea traffic restrictions (major cities including Shanghai, Hong Kong, Guangzhou, etc.)
- Maritime militia fleet drills (ports of Zhejiang, Fujian, Guangdong)
- Nuclear testing (Lop Nur nuclear test site)

2. Logistics
- Stockpiling (oil, gas, coal, food, water, medicine, weapons, animals, etc.)
- Blood drives (Fujian and major PLA hospitals across China)
- Defense industrial surge (weapons, munitions, vehicles, aircraft, radios, parachutes, etc.)
- Port expansion surge (from Jiangsu to Hainan)
- Road and rail expansion surge (Zhejiang, Fujian, and Guangdong)
- Airport hardening and resiliency surge (military and civil airfields within 500 miles of Taiwan)
- Shipyard production surge (amphibious assault ships, landing craft, mine sweepers, etc.)
- Fishing fleets and other commercial ships refitted (military radios, gun riveting, fire-fighting equipment)
- Coastal fortification projects (Fujian's offshore islands)

3. Recon

- Intelligence ships and aircraft activities (Taiwan Strait area)
- Emergency satellite launches (Xichang, Sichuan, etc.)
- Orbital changes (for increased PLA coverage of Taiwan Strait area)
- Human intelligence operations (worldwide, with special focus on Taiwan and the United States)

4. Propaganda

- Propaganda campaign (strident themes)
- Influence operations (worldwide, with special focus on Taiwan and the United States)
- Diplomatic messaging operations (worldwide, with special focus on the United States and Japan)
- Nuclear blackmail (media and personal contacts)

5. Subversion

- Sabotage (financial, transportation/electric grid, water/fuel supplies)
- Abduction or assassination attempts (president of Taiwan and other key leaders and their families)
- Gang-related violence (Taiwanese night clubs, prison breaks, police station attacks)
- Violent protests, rioting, strikes (near Presidential Office Building in Taipei)
- Smuggling and infiltration (gun-running, intelligence agents in Taiwan)

Chinese Deception and Operational Surprise

Chinese analysts have produced a large body of work on the art of military deception. Some of this work discusses the application of deception in a Taiwan landing campaign.[158] Relevant military studies highlight the critical importance of shock in paralyzing Taiwanese decision making at every level of command. Only this could allow the PLA to rapidly overrun Taiwan's beach defenses, seize Taipei, and decisively bring combat operations to an end before the United States could intervene.[159] The challenge facing the Chinese military is that hiding preparations for a massive over water attack is next to impossible.

According to Dennis Blasko, an American PLA expert, "Army units would be required to move significant distances using land (road and rail), air, and water (sea or river) means of transport ... in the era of satellite reconnaissance and social media, such movements are unlikely to be made in secret, reducing the chances of ground forces attaining strategic surprise to close to zero."[160] The mobilization of civilian forces to support a military campaign would further compromise strategic surprise, and the sum total of the indicators available would provide Taiwan's government with sufficient and solid grounds upon which to base strategic warnings and begin mobilizing the country for invasion.

China's leaders have good reason to assume their intentions will be discovered by Taipei well in advance of the attack. If so, the military would lose its ability to execute a "bolt out of the blue" assault. Based on Chinese writings, this would represent a strategic setback, but it is not viewed as a showstopper so long as the PLA still has tactical surprise on its side. It is one thing for an enemy to know you are planning an attack against him at some point in the near future, it is quite another for him to know exactly when, where, and how you will do it. Strategic deception is viewed by the Chinese military as desirable, but probably not attainable. Tactical deception, on the other hand, is seen as vital.

Tactical deception is described by PLA writings as an essential part of a landing campaign for a number of reasons. Perhaps most important, it is critical to the success of political assassinations, or "decapitation operations," to eliminate Taiwan's president and other top leaders at the outset of war. To prosecute such operations, Chinese writings envision launching surprise missile raids to destroy the Presidential Office Building in Taiwan. They also imagine surprise attacks on other buildings with important political significance.[161] One PLA text offers the following guidance to operational commanders:

It is important for you to emphasize the requirement to uncover the (Taiwan) Enemy's head organizations, and especially their head person's location, and the defensive measures protecting them. Then you should use high-tech weapons that have a strong capability to penetrate their airspace with precision and destructiveness to execute fierce strikes against their head person(s). Assure they are successfully knocked out with one punch.[162]

Another text indicates that during invasion operations Chinese special forces will try to abduct or kill many of Taiwan's most important political and military leaders, weapons experts, and scientists using a combination of clandestine means and direct attacks.[163] Early-warning intelligence networks are therefore critical not only for providing strategic warning that an attack is being planned, they are important for tactical warning to ensure top leaders, including the president, are not caught by surprise and killed in the first hours of war.

According to PLA writings, Taiwan has a highly sophisticated network of intelligence, reconnaissance, and surveillance capabilities for monitoring Chinese activities which could indicate preparations for an attack. Taiwan's frontline radar networks on the outer islands are viewed as considerable obstacles to surprise and dangerous because they are linked with missile units capable of suppressing Chinese air operations. Additionally, there are large air force and naval radar stations on the main island of Taiwan that are capable of seeing well across the Taiwan Strait. These land-based radars are further backed up by naval ships, patrol aircraft, and satellites that provide early warning information.[164]

Taken as a whole, Taiwan's early warning network is judged as survivable, in-depth, and able to provide three-dimensional pictures of the cross-Strait battle space. From the Chinese military's perspective, this network reduces the likelihood of achieving surprise. According to PLA texts, this network allows the ROC military to monitor, track, and intercept enemy targets approaching Taiwan, and it provides the president of Taiwan and other government leaders with time to escape air strikes and missile raids. One internal source states: "(Taiwan's) quite dense air defense system not only reduces the shock of our joint 'decapitation' operations, it also reduces the effectiveness of using fire-power raids."[165]

PLA writings describe their anticipated pre-invasion situation as follows:

> The enemy scrutinizes and monitors our coastal areas, which makes plans for the movements of army amphibious landing troops and their assembly difficult to hide. The enemy on the island has recon-naissance capabilities ... and electronic warfare capabilities that are constantly improving. Their long-distance, high fidelity, overlapping reconnaissance methods turn dark nights into bright days. Our tra-ditional camouflage for "staying unseen from the air and hard to discover on the ground" has lost its value. Large-scale troop move-ments would struggle to escape "field sightings." Large-scale troop movements are easily exposed through leaked secrets as well. These make plans to clandestinely move and assemble army amphibious landing troops ever more difficult.[166]

PLA writings tell officers that it is essential to hide their operational plans to invade Taiwan, and to minimize the damaging effects of security leaks. They exhort commanders to be flexible in choosing the time and place of attack. Once the decision had been made, commanders are expected to undertake deception operations employing decoys, feints, and camouflage to cover up their plans. The overriding objective would be to confuse Tai-wanese military generals and convince them the attack would come at a false time and place. The PLA could then strike suddenly to catch defenders off-guard and keep them unbalanced throughout the ensuing battle.[167]

Deception operations for achieving tactical surprise on a notional Z-Day would rely heavily on disinformation. In the minds of Chinese military analysts, the key to success would be to employ deception oper-ations just before an invasion attempt, and make them good enough to convince Taiwan's defenders. They envision deception operations coming in a number of different forms, each intended to strengthen the overall effect. The operation would begin with military communications traffic simulating the buildup of forces in places where there existed little actual activity. At the same time, media outlets in Taiwan or America would be fed false information that would be disseminated by credible news shows, newspaper reports, and radio broadcasts. Chinese cyber warfare units would help the effort by smothering truthful reporting, leaving viewers with a distorted picture of the situation. The overriding goal would be to get Taiwanese leaders to make bad decisions in the tense days and weeks prior to invasion, and then catch them completely by surprise on Z-Day.[168]

To make deception operations appear more believable, PLA writings advise military commanders to use actual units for the mission. Using real units and actual physical attacks as decoys makes them more convincing. Just prior to Z-day, a missile battery could rain fire down on a target to make it appear that the Chinese military was softening it up for attack. Once Taiwanese forces had shifted strength to reinforce the affected area, the PLA could then attack its real targets elsewhere. Shifting missile strikes between real and false targets is seen as an important method of gaining surprise. If everything is getting pummeled, seemingly at random, it is more difficult to know what the attacker is getting at. Another envisioned deception operation would involve maneuvering forces at sea to draw Taiwanese attention away from the intended points of attack.

Notional operations might entail an armada moving north as a decoy, while helicopters swept south to land troops behind Taiwanese lines. Then the armada could suddenly reverse course and land in the south to reinforce the airborne raiders.[169] In addition, amphibious ships could feint toward one beach and then land on another, or a decoy invasion armada could sit off one beach while the actual landing forces arrived on another or intelligence could be leaked through available channels, suggesting that a certain beach was going to be stormed.[170] Any known and com-promised Taiwanese (or American) agents in China would be at risk of manipulation. Perhaps the most resource intensive and costly deception operation envisioned would be to conduct mine sweeping and obstacle clearing operations at numerous beaches at the same time to keep defend-ers guessing as to which was the intended landing point. If successful, it is thought that deception operations could get Taiwanese defenders to apply reserve stocks of men, mines, and beach obstacles on the wrong areas and leave the intended points of attack more lightly defended.[171]

There are, however, serious limits as to what tactical deception operations could offer. One technical study published by a PLA institute that specializes in amphibious warfare shows the results of computer simulations run on Taiwan's potential susceptibility to tactical deception on a notional Z-Day. The study mathematically accounts for risks, including Taiwan's intelligence capabilities, its disruptive counterstrike capabilities, the timing errors associated with planting false information, the distances over which forces would have to move, and the chance that large units would be exposed on land or at sea. The study results showed an exceptionally high degree of pessimism regarding each of the examined risk factors. For example, the modeling showed Taiwan's intelligence capabilities were 70 to 80 percent likely to prove "extremely dangerous" or "very dangerous" to a camouflaged landing campaign, and there was a 50 to 60 percent chance the PLA would accidentally time leaks wrong and blow its own cover.[172]

The View from Taiwan

For their own reasons, military authorities in Taiwan have a strong degree of confidence they would know Beijing's malicious intentions in advance and have adequate, if not abundant, time to prepare for invasion. This assumption appears to stem from their deep understanding of PLA plans, their knowledge of what to look for, and their agent networks in China. Their confidence has been further boosted in recent years by the American-built Surveillance Radar Program, which is reportedly the most powerful intelligence-gathering radar in the world. Sitting high on a mountain in the north of Taiwan, the mega radar complex is designed to withstand the most intense barrage of jamming conceivable while it surveys military activity within striking range of Taiwan. When combined with information gleaned from indigenous capabilities and external intelligence sharing channels, Taiwan's surveillance radar network is anticipated to provide a tremendous early-warning advantage.

In the worst-case scenario Taiwanese military planners assume they would have around 60 days ambiguous warning, followed by 30 days unambiguous warning. Strategic warning times could be weeks longer than that in practice, but the unexpected can happen, and it is always prudent to prepare for the worst possible outcome when one's life is at stake. Indeed, defense officials in Taiwan make cautious judgments and have designed illustrative scenarios to help civilians imagine what the days before a Chinese invasion could look like.[173] One of the favorite storylines is seen in standardized textbooks issued to high schools and universities across the island.

The make-believe scenario begins in the early July of some future year, when the PLA suddenly moves amphibious combat units to southeastern China for training exercises which simulate joint attack operations on Dajin Island (off the coast of Guangdong Province). In August, amphibious combat units then gather in training areas near Xiangshan (in Zhejiang Province), and Shanwei (in Guangdong Province). Here they run war games and drills to certify their ability to blockade and capture offshore islands, bomb Taiwan, and finally invade in two major waves of amphibious landings.

By early September, naval and air training activity spikes all across southeastern China, and the ports of Fuzhou, Hui'an, Xiamen, Dongshan, and Shantou are overrun with large concentrations of troops. Next there is a surge in intelligence operations aimed at Taiwan's coastal areas and beaches, and Chinese fighter aircraft begin regularly crossing the Taiwan Strait centerline, seeking to provoke a response. In the middle of September, the PLA cancels all leave and begin 24-7 operations. The Central Military Committee (CMC) establishes a Joint Theater Command to direct the overall campaign, activates emergency logistics procedures for supporting amphibious operations, and orders the mobilization of reserve units. Large-scale amphibious exercises involving land, air, and sea forces are then announced—alongside warnings for ships and aircraft to avoid waters near the Zhoushan Islands, and international shipping traffic in the area is restricted.

According to the scenario, authoritative tactical warning information comes from American intelligence authorities, who confirm that Taipei's worst nightmare is about to come true. The coming exercises are actually a cover story, and China's real intention is to invade Taiwan. Within hours of Washington's message, Taiwan's president orders the military to go to its highest state of alert. All reservists are activated, fully mobilizing millions of men in Taiwan and the outer islands. A nationwide alarm goes out, warning every citizen to prepare for an impending invasion. At this point in the scenario, Taiwan's police and fire departments, public ministries, schools, and businesses all institute their emergency action plans. A lethal hail of Chinese ballistic missiles begins raining down on the island shortly thereafter, causing power outages, communications disruptions, traffic jams, building destruction, fires, and mass civilian causalities. The textbook scenario then ends with a brief message to Taiwanese students, reminding them that they too can help defend against the Chinese invasion threat, and all able-bodied citizens must be prepared to help save their country.

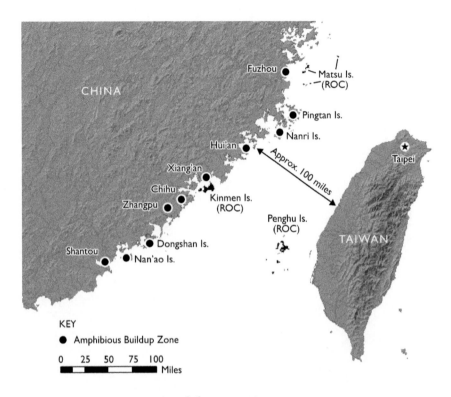

Amphibious staging areas

Chapter Four
China's War Plan

Only by militarily occupying The Island can we fundamentally conquer the "separatist" force's natural living space, and totally end the long military standoff across the Strait.

—PLA Field Manual

BEIJING has made no secret of its intention to conquer Taiwan. As we have seen, the Chinese military has had plans for invading Taiwan since the autumn of 1949, when the PRC was first established. However, the PLA was not capable of invading Taiwan from 1949 to 1978, especially once the U.S.-ROC alliance solidified. From 1979 to the 2000s, the PLA was still far too weak to make the operation militarily feasible. China's recent military buildup has made the invasion of Taiwan seem like an actual possibility, albeit perhaps a still distant one.

The PLA has placed a great emphasis on training and equipment associated with this future campaign, but by its own admission has a long way to go to get ready for it. Contrary to the Chinese propaganda line, the PLA hardly expects to be able to run over Taiwan's defenders and capture the island in a few days' time. A prolonged and bloody fight is expected which could easily result in stalemate or defeat. To avoid this fate, China's top military strategists have invested heavily in sophisticated operational planning.

Newly emerged sources of information offer us details on the scale and form of China's likely war plan. Based on these sources, the formal plan for wartime operations outlines the roles which would be played by Chinese military and civilian units before, during, and after the future invasion. The objectives of the plan would be to: (1) rapidly capture Taipei and destroy the government; (2) capture other major cities and clear out the surviving defenders; and (3) occupy the entire country. To do this, the plan apparently calls for overwhelming the ROC military's coastal defenses and forcing surrender before the United States could deploy sufficient forces to the area. PLA writings indicate that China has developed additional contingency plans for fighting against American and coalition forces in the Pacific to prevent them from helping to defend Taiwan.

The conceptual plan, which is referred to in internal PLA writings as the Joint Island Attack Campaign, appears to be highly centralized and updated regularly based on the latest intelligence, weapons production, and lessons learned from exercises and training. It is a highly classified document, or more likely a series of documents. Unfortunately, these are not available. What are available are internal military manuals and technical studies that have recently leaked from within the PLA. These provide an extraordinarily detailed look into Chinese thinking on this campaign. Additionally, Taiwanese officers have scrutinized the threat facing them, and they have made many of their intelligence findings public. Armed with these new documents, it is now possible to form a rough picture of China's Top Secret invasion plan.

This chapter will use Chinese language sources to shed light on a topic that has been cloaked in darkness. The illumination, however, must remain imperfect. Chinese war planning can be addressed only to the extent that sources allow, and some details remain unclear, classified, or are altogether unknowable at the moment. It must also be accepted that even plans which are highly centralized and rigidly adhered to can still be subjected to last minute changes. PLA writings may envision prosecuting operations a certain way, but that does not mean things would actually play out as such in the heat of battle. Most sources speak in terms of aspirations, describing capabilities the PLA does not have at the current time but hopes to build in the next five to ten years. The following pages look at China's plans as described by those solid sources we currently have available. It is an analysis of what is imagined might happen in the future, not a prediction of what would really happen if the attack was ordered today.

Overview

Restricted-access PLA writings reveal that Chinese war planners approach the invasion of Taiwan as a step-by-step process. Based on extensive passages found in leaked military documents and technical studies, the campaign can be divided into three major operational phases.[174] The first phase is blockade and bombing operations. The second phase is amphibious landing operations. The third phase is combat operations on the island. Each of these operational phases is comprised of numerous individual missions that would have to be carried out successfully for that phase to be completed. Only when one part of the plan was finished could the campaign move on to the next because the invasion is designed to be carried out in a sequential fashion. This means that a delay, disruption, or defeat in any major battle could risk delaying or halting the overall operation, preventing it from moving ahead.

The plan for conquering Taiwan might be thought of as analogous to a life-and-death relay race held at night on a gigantic obstacle course primarily consisting of saltwater pools, urban jungle, and row after row of mountains. If an individual athlete fell or dropped the baton at any point in the race, the whole team would suffer. Each member of the team would play a critical role, and victory would only be possible when everyone performed their very best. If anyone failed in any significant way, they could drag the entire team down.

What makes PLA planning especially difficult in this scenario is that the Chinese relay team is huge and unwieldy. Most of the athletes are poorly trained conscripts, and many officers are strangers or rivals. The racecourse is full of concealed and deadly traps, and the Taiwanese team is trained and equipped by the world champions, who may at anytime decide to join the games on their side, totally changing the rules of play. It's a complicated situation to say the least.

China's plan requires its "team" to prosecute joint operations on the land, on the sea, in the air, in outer space, across the airwaves, and throughout cyberspace. Army groups, naval fleets, air force divisions, and missile brigades would all have critical roles to play. If one of them performed badly, the whole campaign could be seriously impacted. Participating in key supporting roles would be a considerable number of intelligence assets, space forces, electronic and cyber warfare units, reservists, state security offices, propaganda outlets, militias, and state-owned industries. Each would be assigned a variety of individual missions tailored to their particular strengths. Each would be asked to operate as seamlessly as possible with the others. Given the mindboggling array of actors involved, coordination would be vital.

The following pages will describe what each of the major phases of operations envisioned by PLA writings would look like in the broad sweep—assuming of course that the United States and others stayed on the sidelines and everything went according to plan. Having established an overall picture of what assumptions the Chinese campaign plan is based on, later chapters will explore the vital question of how it might actually unfold if put into practice.

Phase One: Blockade and Bombing Operations

Internal PLA sources make it clear that Chinese experts regard the Taiwan-ese military with professional respect and see it as a dangerous opponent capable of fierce resistance. They posit that it would therefore be imperative for them to execute a concentrated opening attack to blockade or "quarantine" Taiwan's armed forces at the outset of hostilities. Electronic jamming, cyber attacks, and missiles strikes would first cut the island off from the rest of the world. Once Taiwan was sufficiently isolated, the Chinese could launch strikes with bombers and fighter-bombers. These two operations, blockade and bombing, overlap to a significant degree. Although they are sometimes presented as distinct operational types and given separate chapters in military texts, in reality, they share similar operational objectives and are mutually supporting. In the event of invasion, it would be nearly impossible to cleanly separate them into distinct operational phases.[175] The reason is simple: China cannot effectively blockade Taiwan without bombarding it, and Taiwan cannot be bombed until it has been blockaded.

The Crisis and War of Nerves

The Chinese objective at the outset of war would be to gain localized control over the airwaves, airspace, and seascapes surrounding Taiwan. The most likely approach could be to create a crisis situation and constrict the Taiwanese government's freedom of action before first strikes were launched. In this scenario, PLA writings envision conducting military operations to harass aircraft and ships leaving or approaching Taiwan. As an island trading nation, Taiwan is reliant upon the seas for transporting its export goods and supplying its domestic consumption needs. The bulk of the trade goods Taiwanese people make and use, the fuel they burn, and the food they eat passes over vast tracts of saltwater to reach them.

The PLA views the application of combined sea blockades and air strikes to be essential for weakening Taiwan's war fighting capabilities and political willpower to resist invasion and occupation. In addition to coercive military operations on the sea and in the air, the Chinese would attempt to disrupt or temporarily sever Taiwan's internet and communications traffic. If successful, such operations would temporarily black out one of the most wired countries on Earth, crippling its vibrant economy (and global supply chains).[176]

The first military targets for digital attackers would be the early-warning surveillance radars that ring Taiwan. According to PLA writings, aircraft equipped with jamming devices would scramble Taiwan's air defense intelligence picture and reduce coverage. Active jamming would be accompanied by passive jamming from transport planes, which would dump large volumes of chaff into the air to create electronic smokescreens. At the same time, intelligence-gathering aircraft would loiter across the

Strait, collecting electronic data samples used to assess radar performance and vulnerabilities. It is anticipated that once radar signals had been captured, they could be electronically fingerprinted, making them more easily recognized and jammed in the future. A special emphasis would reportedly be placed on collecting intelligence on short-range air defense radar systems, so that they could be knocked out on Z-Day.[177]

PLA texts indicate that electronic warfare units in China would likely attack American strategic warning satellites on station high over the Pacific.[178] With these space assets jammed or degraded, Taipei and Washington would have less advanced notice of Chinese ballistic missile launches. The PLA would use planes, ships, and trucks to send out dummy radio chatter, designed to mimic large-scale troop and ship movements along the mainland coast. These electronic feints would be intended to trick Taiwan into thinking that enemy forces were assembling in areas where they were not, for attacks along lines of approach they did not intend to take. The aim would be to lure military commanders into deploying troops to the wrong places, while keeping Taiwan's president and her cabinet confused and off balance.[179] Available sources do not offer us information on planned timetables, but it seems likely that the war of nerves could go on for many weeks or months before the crisis reached boiling point.

Missile Attack

Once Beijing judged that conditions were ripe, orders could go out, and the countdown to all-out war would begin. At a certain undefined moment, alarms would sound, and strategic rocket brigades would begin launching missiles at pre-planned Taiwanese targets. Tense minutes would pass. Then everything would erupt in violent action as ballistic missiles rained down on the island. Given their supersonic speeds, no one watching on the ground would see or hear their fiery fall. Targets would start exploding in sudden crunching impacts, with concrete and earth kicked up in giant plumes of destruction.

Slow flying drones and cruise missiles with small guided warheads, designed to home in on radar signals, would arrive and strike their targets.

Radar stations that were not knocked out or damaged by the first wave would be forced to turn off their emitters and go dark to avoid the second. Chinese planes and ships would close in on Taiwan, blasting the island's networks with electronic energy and overwhelming digital defense systems. Electronic attacks are expected to pave the way for salvos of follow-on missile raids, which would pepper Taiwan's air defense infrastructure.[180]

To ground the ROC Air Force, the Chinese would strike airbase runways, aircraft shelters, air traffic and control towers, and communications stations. It is also expected that missiles would strike surface-to-air missile batteries, command posts, and supply depots. Few if any Taiwanese warplanes are expected to be caught sitting out on open tarmacs. The principal objective of the first strike would be to degrade Taiwan's air defenses with a series of strong blows against critical infrastructure like early-warning radars and airbase runways.[181]

PLA writings indicate that, after the first strikes had sown sufficient destruction, operations would shift gears. Heavy, but ragged and less coordinated, missile barrages and air raids would come streaking across the Strait.[182] Chinese writings anticipate that once Taiwan's air defenses were sufficiently degraded by missile attacks, slender pathways over the Strait would be secured by fighter jets, and the army could begin covertly landing special operations forces by helicopter or parachute. The most frequently emphasized special mission seen in PLA writings is to provide target designation, painting targets with laser beams to guide smart bombs down. In addition, commandos are expected to make murderous raids on airbases, radar stations, command posts, oil reserves, and ammunition dumps. While missiles plummeted down from above, they would spark firefights below.[183]

It is anticipated by PLA field manuals that Taiwan might rapidly recover and launch fighter jets screaming into the fray. To shoot them down, the PLA Air Force would launch jets from forward bases, sending them out to meet their archrivals for the long-awaited contest of strength. Chinese fighter jets are expected to dogfight with advanced air-to-air missiles and target Taiwan's "Hawkeye" airborne early-warning and control aircraft. A ferocious dogfight for air superiority across the skies would be joined.

At the same time, Chinese surface-to-air missile batteries would also be alerted and assigned the mission of defending against Taiwanese counterattacks in case the dogfights went the "wrong" way.[184]

It is not clear from PLA writings how long the bloody air war would rage across the skies. The expected end result, however, seems to be that the Chinese would have at least temporary mastery overhead. With Taiwanese airbases and highway runways cratered, some severely, and many air defense assets shot-up and ruined completely or damaged but fixable, the PLA would have a significant advantage—especially given its preponderance in numbers. The opening acts of war, concentrated lightning operations to master Taiwan's airwaves and airspace, would be complete.[185] The Chinese high command, having established a grip on the skies, would now shift its attention and malice to the waters surrounding Taiwan.

Naval Blockade

It is almost impossible for any military to execute an effective sea blockade without at least localized control over the air. This is especially the case in the Taiwan Strait because Chinese ships and submarines are vulnerable to Taiwanese jets, torpedo-carrying patrol planes, and submarine-hunting helicopters. As such, PLA writings place a strong emphasis on gaining control over the air first. The fight for the seascapes would come next. Having reduced Taiwan's air defenses, the PLA would start attacking the island from the sea, while at the same time moving its invasion armadas into position along the Chinese coast.

PLA writings embrace the view that the ideal way of blockading Taiwan's potent naval fleet would be to mine the approaches to its harbors and then bomb its ships at their docks. However, they acknowledge that the majority of Taiwan's fleet will have put to sea before the onset of hostilities. To defeat the ROC Navy, Chinese sources anticipate combined sea and air offensives against Taiwanese battle groups. Taiwan's large guided missile destroyers are targets of special interest. What is less clear is how they would be attacked and how the encounters are planned to go.

The sources currently available to us gloss over tactical naval engagements. The sparse writings we do have are also contradictory. For example, one passage blithely assures readers that battles at sea would result in Taiwanese ships being sunk, scattered, or left floating in crippled clusters, and those able to steam under their own power would find themselves unable to return home, since their ports would have been sown with sea mines. Yet the same source later goes on to express concern that naval offensives might not be able to find and deal with Taiwan's warships. In such an event, it indicates that the PLA Navy would quickly master localized approaches to Taiwan's invasion beaches and mine and harass everything else until Z-Day.[186]

PLA writings focus on the use of sea mines. First, they anticipate that submarines would release drifting contact mines at the openings of Taiwan's major ports. Next, bombers would sow belts of bottom contact mines two or three nautical miles farther out. Finally, mines would be moored in the deeper waters six to eight nautical miles beyond that. One source asserts that it is important to lay many different types of mines at various depths, making the job of minesweepers more difficult and dangerous. If everything went to plan, the waters within ten nautical miles of Taiwan's major ports would be heavily mined—assuming, of course, that strike operations had already suppressed the defender's ability to attack and drive minelayers away.[187]

The envisioned goal of offensive mining operations would be to limit Taiwan's cargo shipping capacity, not to stop it completely. To erode Taiwan's ability to break through the watery quarantine, it is anticipated that fighter jets would sink ships approaching or leaving Taiwan's major ports, and bombers would blast apart the transportation lines connecting port cities with the rest of the country. In addition to harbor infrastructure, bombing operations are expected to flatten major rail yards, bridges, tunnels, and highway nodes.[188]

If the invasion was launched within a few days to maximize shock, China's blockades would be strong and intense. On the other hand, if the plan called for softening Taiwan up for a couple weeks or more to improve odds on Z-Day, the PLA Navy could fully institute its planned operations, gradually establishing an ever more elaborate series of naval siege works around Taiwan. This plan contemplates the establishment of a three-ringed blockade. The innermost ring would consist of minefield belts extending from the mouths of commercial ports. The next ring outwards would be a zone patrolled by surface warfare ships, and perhaps submarines, who would stalk the waters well off the coast. The outer ring would cover a vast swath of sea stretching out as far as 50 nautical miles. This area would be patrolled by naval aircraft. Chinese sources evince concern that serious coverage gaps could develop east of Taiwan due to the wide open spaces and China's relatively limited naval capabilities. To plug potential gaps, they would reportedly rely on the threat of extended range anti-ship missiles to deter blockade runners.[189]

Like all extended blockades, this one would mostly rely on intimidation because the sea is far too vast to be blanketed with ships, submarines, planes, and mines. It is imagined that China would permit international shipping through the outer patrol zone around Taiwan, provided that foreign ships agreed to be escorted by warships and occasionally boarded for inspection. If a foreign ship was found to be carrying "illegal" materials to Taiwan, or conducting a mission that violated strict international neutrality, or resisting inspection, they would have their cargos seized and impounded. If a ship or convoy of ships was found trying to run the blockade, the navy would intercept them and order them to immediately change course. They would then be taken to controlled areas for boarding and inspection. When necessary, international ships would be fired upon, and even damaged, as a warning. But only in extreme cases would they be sunk.[190]

To maintain the quarantine for more than just a few days, the PLA would need to establish a robust network of reconnaissance and surveillance assets for monitoring the sea approaches to Taiwan. The imagined network would be fed data from patrol planes and ships, coastal radars, listening stations, and ocean surveillance satellites. The aim would be to provide early-warning if Taiwanese vessels broke the maritime blockade. Once "illegal" shipping had been identified, the surveillance network would guide Chinese forces on interception missions, ensuring suspect vessels could not escape into international waters outside the quarantine zone. To reduce the significant risks entailed, professional writings indicate the PLA Navy would put strict rules in place so that submarines and ships would not venture out of their assigned patrol zones. They would attempt to patrol along unpredictable routes and regularly exchange classified identification signals according to set procedures so that each vessel could identify their counterparts in the fog of war. When moving into or out of their patrol zones, they would follow strict timing schedules and take pre-planned routes. Maintaining close coordination and secrecy is viewed as critical for avoiding "red-on-red" fire and ambushes.[191]

PLA writings anticipate the possible discovery of large convoys anchored off of Taiwan's coast looking to run the blockade, and advise campaign commanders on how to execute large-scale raids to sink them. In planning their missions, Chinese officers are told to use reconnaissance satellites, spy planes, and undercover agents to collect detailed intelligence on the numbers, locations, and makeup of convoys. They should then send combined air and sea strike groups to quietly approach them, using radio silence, jamming, and the cover of night to gain the element of surprise, then slam them with a combination of jet-launched missiles, ship gun fire, and torpedoes.

Restricted-access Chinese military writings envision subsequent attacks on the radar stations around ports to reduce Taiwan's eyes and ears. Nearby docks, cranes, and other infrastructure would reportedly be destroyed as secondary targets. According to our sources, the overall objective would be to weaken Taiwan's coastal defenses and port infrastructure as fast as possible to provide protection for minelayers and patrol craft to operate freely off the coast. Even more important, these operations would help protect amphibious assault ships from attacks as the armadas concentrated in the Taiwan Strait area.[192]

Air Blockade

In support of the blockades, PLA writings call for establishing an aerial keep-out zone around the island. The plan reportedly includes options to put an air defense identification zone and/or a no-fly zone in place above Taiwan. In this scenario, China would use its fighters and surface-to-air missile batteries to confront any Taiwanese military aircraft that took to the skies. All foreign aircraft that approached or entered the no-fly zone would be intercepted, identified, and addressed on international radio frequencies. Chinese jets would flash lights and make threatening aerial maneuvers to force them to immediately leave the area. Civilian aircraft or "illegal" third-party aircraft (for example American or Japanese recon-naissance planes) would be forced to land at pre-selected Chinese airbases where they could be held captive and inspected in detail.[193] In cases where civilian planes or third-party aircraft did not respond to warning signals, fighter jets would fire their cannons in the air around them. It is believed these actions could ensure that aircraft of non-PRC origin would not dare to break or interfere with the air blockade.[194]

Meanwhile, Beijing's rocket troops would continue striking Taiwan's airbases, air defense batteries, command nets, ammunition dumps, and fuel storage depots. Each would be stricken, first with ballistic and cruise missiles, then with a variety of air dropped bombs. Keeping the ROC Air Force grounded for an extended period of time is viewed as vital to estab-lishing the conditions necessary to invade. The PLA assumes that many Taiwanese fighter squadrons could survive its attacks. It is surmised that these would most likely form up for counterattacks on Chinese airbases to disrupt the no-fly zone, or strike at seaports to sink invasion ships. PLA texts call for relying heavily on surface-to-air batteries to defend against the threat. In case they failed, the PLA's top-tier aircraft would be parked inside mountainside bunkers, or hidden in concrete shelters to minimize their vulnerability. Less important planes would rely on camouflage, dis-persal, and decoy targets to weather potential counterattacks.[195]

Space Operations

PLA studies have paid close attention to the role China's national space program would theoretically play before and during blockade and bombing operations. They assert the Taiwan Strait area is simply too expansive to see and communicate across without satellites. Commanders from the navy, air force, and rocket troops are therefore expected to work together at joint command centers where they could directly access information provided by space assets, including imagery, signals intelligence, early-warning, guidance and positioning, communications, mapping, and weather forecasting. It is envisioned that space intelligence cells would be formed of experts and embedded within the joint command centers. They would be tasked with giving high-ranking theater commanders a coherent picture of maritime activities surrounding Taiwan and updates on the weather.[196]

Just prior to the onset of hostilities, sources anticipate that satellites would be used to gather intelligence on Taiwan's military movements, with special attention paid to the locations of navy and air force units. Chinese intelligence analysts would study the numbers and types of surface ships in port and forecast how long they might stay before their next sortie. They would watch Taiwan's submarine force to learn deployment locations and activities, and air force bases to find out how many aircraft, and what types, were deployed to each. The ultimate objective of these intelligence-gathering operations would be to provide campaign planners with detailed target lists, including precise coordinates where missiles could be aimed. Reconnaissance satellites would also be used to produce images and maps for those planning mine-laying operations.[197]

Once the blockade and bombing operations were launched, intelligence satellites would peer at and listen to scenes of battle, dispassionately collecting information on the status of targets. They would play a key role in helping Chinese generals assess whether or not they had gained enough localized control to cross the Strait and land on Taiwan. Satellites would also search for suspicious ship convoys and alert tactical units to possible blockade runners. But most importantly, they would provide warning of American carrier group movements. The high command in Beijing would need satellites to decide if American military forces intended to provide, or were already providing, Taiwan with indirect support (intelligence, minesweeping, convoy escorts), or if they were heading toward "direct intervention." This phrase is a common Chinese euphemism for

U.S. Navy and Air Force combat operations to defend Taiwan before or during invasion.[198]

In addition to spy satellites, SATCOM (satellite communications) would be used by joint command centers to stay in touch with task force commanders at sea. Satellites would also be used to set up wide area communications networks, connecting command posts with air force, rocket troop, and army groups in the field. According to PLA materials, China's theater command centers already have direct fiber optic cable links with the CMC and each of the PLA service headquarters in the national capital region. Strategic SATCOM networks would serve as an important backup, in case buried cable links were severed.[199]

China's version of GPS, the Beidou navigation satellite system, would have a key role to play as well. It would provide combat forces with precise positioning and timing data, helping them identify their positions relative to each other. This would be especially important when thousands of ships and aircraft were operating together in the low-visibility conditions common to the Taiwan Strait. Ensuring friendly naval forces did not crash into each other would be but one of many challenges Beidou satellites are intended to help overcome. Rocket troops would rely on satellite guidance to make sure their ballistic and cruise missiles hit intended targets, and pilots would use them for airborne navigation and, when shot down, to guide rescue teams to their locations.[200]

Bombing Operations

Chinese military writings state that Taiwan must be bombed heavily to soften it up for invasion.[201] Referred to as "firepower strike operations," these focus on maximizing the strategic effects of finite munitions stockpiles to quickly take the initiative and isolate Taiwan in the first days of war.[202] PLA writings refer to the first round of firepower strikes as "initial strikes." These would be comprised of massed surprise attacks on Taiwan's most important command and control centers, early-warning radars, airstrips, and air defense batteries. In addition to missile attacks, China's war plan reportedly calls for using high-powered microwave and laser weapons to damage vulnerable computer hardware and electronic systems to loosen Taiwan's grasp on information dominance and situational awareness.[203]

The first wave of bombardment would be quickly followed by what Chinese military theorists call "key point strikes." Its objective would be to bomb Taiwan's government ministries and military headquarters, demolishing critical parts of the ROC government.[204] The Presidential Office Building would likely be the first to be hit. China reportedly plans to attack it with cruise missiles and ballistic missiles during the first hours of hostilities to blow up an important symbol of political sovereignty.[205] Other targets in the heart of Taipei would likely include the nation's leading political and economic affairs bureaucracies, the cabinet building (Executive Yuan), parliament (Legislative Yuan), Ministry of Foreign Affairs, Ministry of Economic Affairs, and others.[206]

Taiwanese government ministries and offices, though large, unmoving, and easily identifiable from the air, would be well protected. To make sure their attacks were effective, it is envisioned that Chinese agents could collect first-person intelligence on the locations of key government leaders, seeing whether they were in their offices or not. Spies could further be tasked with providing information on building structures, camouflage usage, and potential weak points in the bunkers below them.[207] To ensure redundancy in case undercover agents were captured, reconnaissance satellites would be tasked with the same intelligence collection missions.[208] PLA writings express hope Taiwan's key decision makers could be assassinated with powerful surprise attacks from the air. If successful, decapitation strikes could have a considerable impact on the final outcome of the war.[209]

After the central government district, the most heavily bombed part of Taipei is likely to be Dazhi, near the Grand Hotel, the Dominican International School, and the Miramar Entertainment Park. While not mentioning specific locations by name, PLA sources strongly indicate that missiles would pound Taiwan's joint command complex in Hengshan Mountain, the Ministry of National Defense Headquarters, the Navy Command, the Air Force Command, and other key facilities in this strategic neighborhood. Outside Taipei, the ROC Army Command Headquarters in Longtan, the Sixth Army Headquarters in Zhongli, the 10th Army headquarters near

Taichung, and the Eight Army Headquarters in Qishan would be targeted for missile strikes as well. The stated objective of these strikes would be to cut theater commanders off from one another, reducing their ability to conduct coordinated defense operations.[210]

During wartime, it is anticipated that Taiwanese generals would work in underground bunker complexes which are deeply buried. PLA writings judge these bunkers to be tough targets as they are protected by strong hardened structures and made up of complicated tunnel system networks, often concealed by large office buildings on the surface. As such, they emphasize the importance of collecting detailed intelligence on each site, with every possible method of spy craft used. It is envisioned that commanders would launch missile and air attacks against them using precision guided warheads and penetrating "bunker buster" bombs.[211]

The next targets of key point strikes would reportedly be fuel supplies and the power grid. Like island nations everywhere, Taiwan is almost totally dependent upon imported oil and natural gas. There are large emergency stockpiles for war, but these are hardly bottomless. The PLA plans to fire missiles and drop bombs on Taiwan's oil refineries, tank farms, and pipelines. During this phase of the bombing, we are told that hydro-electrical power plants, thermal power stations, and electrical transformers would also be stricken and burned. Command nodes in the power grid would be targeted by cyber attacks. The stated objective of such attacks is to place a strain on the civilian populace.[212]

The only element of Taiwan's power grid that might not be targeted is the country's nuclear power plants. One Chinese field manual takes pains to remind the intended readers (PLA officers) not to bomb nuclear power plants, because the radioactive fallout could poison the broader political situation and turn world opinion against China.[213] Another PLA field manual, however, contradicts this guidance, specifically urging attack helicopter pilots to hit Taiwan's nuclear plants. This passage confidently states that air-to-ground missiles would be accurate enough and small enough to only temporarily black out power generators, leaving reactors stable and intact for China to use after Taiwan was conquered.[214]

THE CHINESE INVASION THREAT

If the invasion timetables allowed, key point strikes would notionally be followed by what the PLA refers to as "continuing strikes." Their purpose would be to bomb Taiwan on a broad scale, slowly eroding the foundation of the nation's military strength and political resolve. While initial attacks would hinge primarily upon the effects of missiles, it is anticipated that continuing strikes would be executed by bombers and attack fighters, which would now be more or less free to fly close over their victim's heads when dropping their payloads. Targets of special interest would include fighter squadrons and mobile missile batteries that had survived the first days of war. In this phase, drone decoys are expected to play an important role in exhausting Taiwan's stocks of air defense munitions so that surviving targets might be overwhelmed and flattened.[215]

As Z-Day closed in, Chinese bombers, we are told, would repeatedly raid Taiwanese bases to confirm attacks had neutralized all coastal defense missile batteries, especially those responsible for defending key routes across the Strait.[216] PLA Rocket Force missiles would hit surviving targets that could not be safely reached any other way, and bombers would carry out mop-up raids. As munitions began to run low, reserve stockpiles would be called up to make sure the air campaign did not lose its momentum just before invasion.[217]

The last wave of bombing is referred to as "final strikes." Its goal would be to weaken Taiwan's ability and willingness to resist attack and, ideally, force the government to surrender and submit to early occupation. This is portrayed as a two-step process: first, annihilate the island's combat power; second, demonstrate that further resistance is futile. The former requires an intensive bombing campaign against all military targets; the latter calls for aiming at the civilian population.[218] According to one PLA source, Taiwan's water, electric, gas, and transportation infrastructure could all be obliterated to "terrorize the island into submission."[219] At the same time, strategic psychological attack operations would reach their high point. In the final days of bombardment, it is contemplated that China would broadcast offers of humanitarian aid packages and offer rewards to those in Taiwan willing to surrender or defect. This is perceived as an operation that could, if successful, "shake the foundation of the enemy's control, and force the enemy to abandon their will to resist."[220]

Before invasion, the PLA would demolish the island's bridges, tunnels, communications infrastructure, and defense industries. Supply depots and logistics distribution centers could be hit, along with the major highways and railways that entwine Taiwan's cities together. Airports would be bombed to ensure passenger and cargo planes did not escape to the outside world. It is even imagined that radio stations and television studios could be bombed. Starved of information and war material, and the ability to travel from one city to the next, the national life of Taiwan is expected to cease existing in any recognizable form. Chinese military writings argue that blockade and bombing operations could, at least in theory, erode the defender's morale and reduce their president's resolve to resist the coming invasion.[221]

Political Factors and Timing

Despite the joint firepower PLA texts envision bringing to bear, Chinese writings do not at all appear comfortable with the idea of blockading and bombing Taiwan for an extended period of time. The decision is one with enormous strategic and political gravity because the longer China blockaded and bombed Taiwan, the more likely it would be that the United States and other democracies would decide to enter the war.[222] Chinese writings warn that the military is unlikely to be strong enough across the board to carry out extended operations of this nature while also quelling the domestic unrest that is anticipated at home.[223] Since operations would be every bit as political as they were military, they make clear that Beijing, not local commanders, would decide the scope and duration of operations, and would likely select the targets to be hit. The plan to attack Taiwan, readers are told, must be flexible enough for the CCP Politburo and CMC to interject and make changes at any time in the course of the war.[224]

Although PLA writings theorize that protracted blockade and bombing operations might possibly force Taiwan to surrender, they also note that the domestic and international repercussions would likely become too painful to bear well before that time came.[225] Indeed, serious concerns apparently exist that pro-independence sentiment on Taiwan would only be strengthened by a bloody war of siege and starvation. Rather than give up, Taiwan's beleaguered citizens are viewed as far more likely to become enraged and resolved to fight to the bitter end.[226] With these factors in mind, Chinese doctrine calls for short but intense strikes on Taiwan to secure localized control over the airwaves, airspace, and seascapes. Once these were in hand, it is anticipated that the campaign would shift gears to focus on surprise landings.[227]

Summing Up

As a final summary to this phase of operations, it may be helpful for the reader to imagine, as Chinese military officers are taught to do, that Taiwan is an organic defense system. Pre-invasion operations make more sense when viewed this way. Chinese strategists portray Taiwan's early-warning networks as the nation's eyes and ears. Command and control bunkers are the central nervous system, and communications lines the nerves that wire everything together. Top leaders (the president, vice president, premier, etc.) play the role of the brain. Taipei, the capital city, is the beating heart, connected to everything else by transportation infrastructure. Ports, airfields, roads, railways, bridges, and tunnels are the arteries and veins of the system. They allow the lifeblood of war, the fuel, ammunition, equipment, and supplies, to flow wherever needed. The armed forces are the arms, legs, and muscles. Electricity and fuel are oxygen. They keep everything powered up and running, and their consumption spikes when stress is placed on the system.

Chinese military writings envision first blinding the country's eyes and muffling its ears, and then shocking its nervous system to paralyze it. Taiwan might next have its head chopped off. But here the metaphor falls short because, unlike most organic systems, Taiwan is still expected to survive and fight on after decapitation. Two reasons may account for this. First, the skull and neck could be too thick to cut through, and the "brain" (the president and cabinet) could survive. Second, even if the brain was lost, the system allows for some decentralized action. The arms and legs might shutter and flail without perfect coordination, but they could still land devastating blows on the attackers. New leaders might emerge and establish themselves within the system, and communications links, command posts, and critical infrastructure can always be repaired. Taiwan's defense system is capable of restoration, as long as it is allowed enough time.

China's war plan is reportedly to make sure the Taiwanese government is not provided with the time it needs to recover from the astonishment and trauma of a sudden attack. The Chinese high command would weigh their information and judge the first moment when they had won victory in the invisible electro-magnetic domain, in the air, and on the sea. An enormous army would be waiting on the southeast coast, ready to sail across the Strait. A fearful decision might then be made in Beijing, and orders transmitted, the dice cast out onto the table of destiny and fate, with glory and agony suspended in the balance. On one side of the scale would hang the lives of China's CCP elites and millions of their subjects, on the other, the future of Taiwan's 23 million defiant citizens.

Phase Two: Amphibious Landing Operations

How might a future invasion of Taiwan unfold? Based on internal Chinese military writings, it would most likely begin with attacks on Taiwan's small island fortresses. PLA writings portray it as essential to rapidly storm Kinmen and Matsu, paving the road to Z-Day. These islands are a key to success because they sit within range of the ports and airstrips where China would likely assemble its invasion armadas. Unless completely neutralized, Taiwan's defenders could use their frontline island perimeter to mount missile strikes, commando raids, and helicopter assaults on the mainland. Perceiving a serious threat from these otherwise modest islands, the PLA has conducted extensive studies on surrounding and seizing them in the opening days of war.[228]

Invasion of Kinmen and Matsu

According to PLA studies, early and fast operations to neutralize Taiwan's outer islands are made imperative by the local geography. Kinmen is a group of some fifteen granite islands, including Greater Kinmen (Chin-men, or Quemoy), Lesser Kinmen, Dadan, Erdan, Tungting, and ten other tiny rocks. These form a natural barrier, controlling the approaches to Xiamen harbor, one of China's major ports. Artillery guns on Lesser Kinmen sit just six miles from the sprawling dockyards of Xiamen. Other tiny islands in the group are as close as two miles from Chinese territory. Located 141 miles west of Taiwan, the Kinmen island group has a total size of 94 square miles, with 97 percent of the land being made up of Greater Kinmen and Lesser Kinmen.[229] Kinmen also administers the tiny fortress of Wu-Chiu (Wu-qiu). Remote and rugged, Wu-Chiu is garrisoned by Taiwanese marines, who stand watch on two rocks 83 miles to the northeast of Kinmen and 14 miles south of an important Chinese staging base, Nanri Island.[230]

The Matsu group, located 175 miles northeast of Kinmen, consists of 28 islands which are in another strategic position off the Chinese coastline. Like Kinmen, these are heavily fortified, solid-granite islands. The largest of them are Nangan, Dongju, Xiju, Beigan, and Dongyin, which form a long arc across the maritime approaches to Fuzhou City, the capital of Fujian Province. Fuzhou is an important port city and home to numerous frontline military bases that would be critical to the invasion of Taiwan.[231]

The outer islands form Taiwan's first line of defense. They serve as a strategic trip-wire, alerting Taipei to Chinese military activities. Their mission is to buy time for their brother units (and families) on Taiwan to prepare for invasion. The following excerpt captures the official PLA view on this long belt of islands:

> The enemy occupies offshore islands in the waters near the mainland coast. These pose a serious threat to the assembly of landing troops in the coastal area, and to their crossing during the opening phases of operations. As such, if we can blockade the waters and occupy the islands the enemy has near our crossing routes, this will remove

the serious threat that offshore islands pose to our landing troops as they load aboard ships, cross the sea, and assault the main island. This will ensure we can smoothly launch our offensive against the main island.[232]

PLA writings indicate the Chinese military would likely initiate offshore island attacks with a sudden barrage of fire, pounding them with heavy artillery, long-range rockets, and tactical ballistic missiles. The outer islands are protected by air defense screens and linked to arrays of radars and listening posts. These networks would be the first targets of bombardment. Only after they had been silenced would fighter-bombers and attack helicopters approach overhead. At that point, any radar turned on and emitting energy into the atmosphere would become like a homing beacon, guiding missiles into their targets.[233]

PLA sources advocate using drones to draw out local air defenses, making them targets for strikes. Early warning computer networks would be hit with cyber attacks, and penetrated systems paralyzed by malicious codes. Radios would be jammed, and satellite ground stations which reportedly provide the isolated rocks with access to American early warning information, would be disrupted with cyber attacks and then destroyed with drone strikes.[234]

The Chinese military would next direct its firepower against the airstrips, ports, and logistical lines that tether the islands back to Taiwan. Anti-ship and ground attack missile batteries would be bombed and knocked out. It is anticipated that frogmen would sever seabed communications cables, cutting the umbilical cords providing Taipei with intelligence updates on frontline events. Wherever possible, the PLA would clandestinely insert special reconnaissance units onto the islands to provide target designation for laser-guided missiles. In some cases, local agents could be activated to carry out sabotage missions, demolishing bridges, roads, and tunnels. Submarines, fishing boats, and naval aircraft would sow minefields in the sea, laying ambush sites to sink resupply convoys. Long-range air defense systems would further tighten the net, sealing the islands off from air delivered assistance that might be sent.[235]

Once Taiwanese garrisons had been marooned, cut off from outside support and made unable to communicate even locally, PLA generals would decide which of the islands to capture and which to keep alive but isolated. This is a surprisingly big question. Chinese military writings agonize over this issue at length, weighing and re-weighing what would be best to do. PLA manuals offer repetitive and vague guidance, evincing a greater sense of uncertainty about this question than nearly any other in the invasion campaign.[236]

Here is the perceived dilemma: Taiwan controls so many tiny island citadels that China might risk exhausting precious amphibious resources if it conquered them all. Storming the Kinmen and Matsu archipelagos might be done quickly. But if things went wrong, the main invasion of Taiwan could be delayed past the point of no return. On the other hand, any island left unconquered might be a ticking time bomb. Bunkers, tunnels, and cave networks could be hiding forces who were waiting for an opportune time to emerge and strike. If not neutralized, they could turn out be a lethal threat. It is next to impossible to know for sure that an island has been rendered safe by airstrikes and shelling alone. Only a boots-on-the-ground effort, with troops and marines physically landing and clearing them, could ensure that each had been rid of danger.[237]

Chinese writings briefly address the possibility of not landing on any of the offshore islands until after Taiwan had been conquered. Advocates of this approach describe it as akin to cutting off a giant octopus head and then dealing with the tentacles later. However, this approach apparently would be unrealistic, even dangerous, to most military thinkers. PLA manuals appear determined to make officers realize they must ensure that Taiwan will not have the ability to attack critical amphibious staging areas. The tentative solution they offer is to capture those offshore islands that are the most likely to pose a real threat, while suppressing the others with protracted and intense artillery bombardment.[238]

The idea, in essence, is to conduct a small-scale island hopping campaign. The metric proposed for selecting amphibious targets is fairly straight-forward: the bigger an island is, the more dangerous it will likely be to the Joint Island Attack Campaign and the more imperative it is seized. Of course, some islands are more difficult to storm than others, and often it is the biggest and most challenging of them which would be used as staging bases for launching strikes against the mainland. As a general rule, military writings assert it is far better to land against weakly defended islands and to keep the others pinned down. They nonetheless seem to believe that this is not likely to be possible in this particular case.[239]

The PLA has generated detailed studies on operations against the outer islands. Data has been collected and analyzed on their military geography, including their weather patterns, tides, coastal water depths, sizes, and beach compositions. Analysts have carefully examined the locations of hidden reefs, scalable cliffs, potential helicopter landing zones, and open areas that could accommodate parachute drops.[240] The official textbook used to train Chinese helicopter commanders, for example, dedicates an entire lengthy chapter to a discussion on conducting air assaults on them.[241] These writings provide an uncommonly clear picture of how Chinese planners imagine operations to take Kinmen and Matsu.

In theory, what would an invasion of Taiwan's outer islands look like? According to our sources, it would entail two major combat forces, who would land and fight in tandem. The first force would be mostly air assault units (light infantry delivered by helicopters) and paratroopers, who would land behind frontline defenses along the shore. The second would be army amphibious troops and marines, who would storm the beaches. Operations are described as likely to begin in the dark of night, with special operations forces clandestinely inserted by helicopters or small boats for the purpose of securing landing zones ahead of the main assaults. Demolition teams would also land, their mission to clear pathways through minefields, obstacles, tank traps, trenches, barbed wire, and pillboxes. Special operators would strive to neutralize many of the garrisons, helping to secure landing zones for incoming troops.

It is thought that large helicopter groups, flying low across the sea to avoid detection, would swoop in on rear area targets around daybreak. They would attempt to seize each island's command posts and missile bases, which are viewed as centers of gravity. Early warning sites that were thought to have survived shelling and air strikes, most likely hardened radars stations and listening posts, would be assailed. In addition, air assault groups would be tasked with capturing strategic hilltops, ports, and airstrips. Once key targets were in hand, fresh troops could land to support the main invasion, attacking beach defenders from behind, flanking or enveloping their lines and cutting them off from reinforcements. Finally, massed amphibious troops would storm ashore, landed by small boats or barges, and supported by air and sea fires, trapping Taiwan's frontline defenders between the seaward hammer and the inland anvil.[242]

Once ashore, amphibious troops and/or marines would attempt to blast through defense lines, seize key points, and clear out the defenders, one pillbox and tunnel at a time. The following excerpt indicates how officers are advised to take these islands:

> When attacking each base's rather long lines of underground military works, first use troops and artillery and obstacles to block up the exits and entrances, while you clear out enemy defenders nearby. Then use at least two assault teams, attacking into the tunnels from different directions and working toward the core (of the bunker). Apply marksmen, flamethrowers, and grenade throwers, and other methods.... If the enemy's works are resolute and solid, or if our attacking troops are inadequate for the job, the mouths of the tunnels can be dynamited to seal them up. The enemy will have entombed himself. Or you can actively use political attacks (psychological warfare) to erode his will to fight, and force him to surrender.[243]

This same source provides guidance for dealing with the defenders that are expected to hold out from inside bunker networks long after their islands had been invaded. It states the following: "Hunt down, shoot, blow up, bury, burn, and smoke them to death. Gradually clean out their nests."[244] Internal PLA writings envision fierce and brutal struggles to neutralize Taiwan's island citadels along the mainland coast. The mission is portrayed as a tough but necessary prelude to the main amphibious operation.

Invasion of the Penghu Islands

Chinese military writings present the Penghu Islands (or Pescadores) as of great importance to the invasion of Taiwan, second only to the capture of Kinmen and Matsu in terms of priority. They describe this island group as a critical target for assault immediately following, or perhaps even concurrent with, operations against the outer islands. Penghu is an archipelago of 64 islands located some 35 miles off the coast of central Taiwan. It features one of the region's best natural harbors: Magong. During World War II, the Imperial Japanese Navy used Magong as a key base and a springboard for attacks against General Douglas MacArthur's forces in the Philippines. Today, the ROC military uses Penghu as a fortress capable of cutting into the flanks of invasion fleets that might be launched along the northern or southern approaches to Taiwan. Bristling with long-range missiles for sinking ships, intercepting aircraft, and striking targets in China, these islands are apparently viewed by Chinese strategists as a formidable obstacle. If captured, however, they could become an indispensable staging area supporting the invasion of Taiwan.[245]

The Penghu Islands are probably too numerous and dispersed to be rapidly assaulted one by one. For the PLA, the key target is Magong, which is considered a central hub.[246] Attack operations would be prosecuted by amphibious forces supported by navy, air force, and conventional ballistic missile units. It is envisioned that attacks would begin with electronic warfare and missile strikes, paralyzing the islands' defense nets. The island would then be bombarded by naval warships, hit with airstrikes, and raked with gunfire from attack helicopters. Ordinance would rain down on beach fortifications, coastal obstacle networks, minefields, and ports facilities. Bombing operations would focus on cutting apart roads, preventing Taiwanese tank columns and mechanized forces from maneuvering and counterattacking landing zones.[247]

It is contemplated that a naval task force would establish control over at least two lines of approach, allowing troop transport ships to sail across the Strait under an umbrella of protection. This sea guard would include escort ships equipped for countering anti-ship missiles, submarines, fighter

THE CHINESE INVASION THREAT

jets, and electronic jammers. Once everything was in place, Chinese amphibious troops would storm to shore under the cover of concentrated naval gunfire, with amphibious tanks, small landing vehicles, and fishing boats making landfall in waves. Attack helicopters would be overhead, guarding them from above. Air assault units would alight inland from their transport helicopters, and paratroopers would drop onto pre-surveyed landing zones.[248]

While the major battles were taking place on the beaches, special operations forces would scale seaside cliffs and execute assaults in rear areas. Their mission would be to help overwhelm defenders with sneak attacks from unexpected directions. The aggressors would scramble to occupy key high ground, seize control over port facilities and waterways, and gain secure footholds before local garrisons could mount effective counterattacks to repel them. Once the main island of Penghu was overrun, the PLA would shift its aim to the other islands in the archipelago. Some amphibious units could be tasked with seizing a few of them, but only after they had been softened up by bombing.[249]

Troops and engineers would then begin digging in to defend their positions in case Taiwan mounted a counterattack. Reconstruction teams would arrive to establish a new local government and to root out "splitist" opposition. We are told that once Magong had been secured, it would be quickly transformed into a forward operating base, supporting attacks on the main island of Taiwan. Wherever possible, transportation infrastructure would be rapidly repaired, especially vital airstrips, seaports, bridges, and roads. Efforts would be made to restore basic communications, water, electricity, and gas services. If battle damage rendered critical infrastructure inoperable for an extended period of time, engineering teams would work to quickly construct makeshift airstrips and docks.[250] Next would come the supreme battle.

Zero Day Approaches

Internal PLA writings and technical studies offer Chinese military officers detailed discussions and guidance on the invasion of Taiwan. This is something they describe as the pinnacle of future conflict and the most difficult and bloody mission facing the Chinese military.[251] Amphibious landing operations are part of a much larger joint campaign plan, but they are viewed as the most consequential component of the overall enterprise. Nothing else in the campaign would matter if the army could not successfully seize hold of Taiwan's shore and quickly grind into the heart of the island. Everything in the war plan is designed to enable and support the ground forces during this furious trial of strength.[252]

The invasion of Taiwan would begin for PLA ground forces with orders to deploy to China's southeast coast. It is forecast that troop movements would mostly occur at night or under the cover of rain, fog, or smog. Most soldiers would load up their gear and take long train rides to coastal towns in the provinces of Zhejiang, Fujian, and Guangdong. A few would board airplanes and fly to their rally points, which would be hives of urgent activity. Once they arrived, the ground forces would marshal at campsites. Rank and file army officers would get to know local officials in charge of ship loading, air transport, and logistics, while high ranking generals and admirals attended planning sessions with amphibious task force commanders to work out final planning details.[253]

PLA writings indicate that the ground forces would erect localized air defense networks, buildup coastal perimeters, organize patrols, and camouflage their camps. No one could know for sure whether an attack would be ultimately ordered, or if the whole thing would turn out to be a drill, or a bluff, or a political negotiation tactic to put pressure on Taipei. Rumors would likely run rampant and troops would be told to stay on edge, alert to the possibility of Taiwanese agents infiltrating their ranks.[254]

The space forces are expected to play a crucial role collecting eleventh hour intelligence. Imagery analysts supporting joint command centers would be ordered to scrutinize Taiwan's coastline and beaches, tides and currents, and track the status of Taiwan's command posts, group armies, and air defenses. Satellites are expected to provide communications, enabling theater commanders to tightly coordinate far-flung units for the crossing down to the level of individual ships, aircraft, and army companies. Weather satellites would have the role of feeding commanders meteorological intelligence, assisting them in selecting the best moment to launch.[255]

Once final attack orders came, the army assault forces would hurriedly begin loading up on buses and trucks for the drives to their loading areas. Navy ships and confiscated civilian boats would be waiting for them in vast fleets strung out along the coastal harbors and bays. Frenzied ship loading operations would take place, troops loading aboard ships according to tightly coordinated loading plans and procedures, making sure they were able to quickly offload in an orderly fashion once they neared their respective invasion beach. Dock space, cranes, and roll-on roll-off ships would be at a premium. Chinese military manuals call for loading basic supplies aboard ships first, followed by heavy weapons, and then more valuable equipment. Troops are supposed to be the last to climb aboard, in case ships were attacked and sunk before they could get underway.[256]

PLA writings advise unit commanders to load as strictly and rapidly as possible, preferably at night, or during foggy or inclement weather to avoid detection. An army at sea is viewed as an exposed target and highly vulnerable. Early warning systems and reconnaissance patrols along the sea would be on high alert, ready to vector fighter jets, attack helicopters, and ships to any intruders. Meanwhile, air assault troops and paratroopers would load onto their helicopters and planes. Second echelon and reserve troops would maintain positions further inland, waiting to flow into the coastal areas once the first wave had departed.[257] To confuse Taiwanese intelligence, the army would create decoy amphibious staging areas and conduct feints with non-essential ship groups to draw attention away from assembly operations.[258]

With the clock ticking down, troop transport ships that had been fully loaded would steam out of their harbors and bays, sailing to pre-arranged waiting areas offshore, seeking to remain as dispersed as possible until orders came to assemble for the crossing. Once it was time, ships would fall into formation. According to PLA writings, small and medium-sized transport ships would form wide lines across the sea. They would likely sail in a giant V-shape with the tip of the spear pointed at Taiwan. It is anticipated that the bulk of troop transports would be civilian ships, pressed into wartime service for "non-traditional" landing operations.[259]

Each amphibious assault group would theoretically carry waves of storm troops, who would go shore one after the next. PLA professional writings indicate that waves (or echelons) would probably add up to a division-sized unit or more hitting each major landing zone.[260] Chinese divisions vary in size, but are believed to consist of approximately 10,000 men and 1,000 vehicles.[261] Each amphibious division would be led by minesweepers and obstacle clearing boats, as well as gunboats to shell the shore. It is imagined that escort ships (destroyers, frigates, and fast missile boats) would place themselves in between troop transports and potential threats. Large deck amphibious assault ships, homes to hovercraft and helicopters, would sail farther to the rear.[262]

According to one Taiwanese military assessment, the PLA's invasion armadas would likely appear over the horizon in box-like formations. It is believed that their front would be made up of four lines of ships: mine-sweeping craft, naval gunboats, civilian ships armed with army artillery, and small boats for clearing beach obstacles. The long sweeping edges and back end would likely be made up of escort ships for air defense and protection against surface threats. At the front, just behind obstacle clearing boats, would be the first wave assault force, tasked with storming the beaches. They would be followed by second wave assault forces tasked with driving inland to seize key terrain, used to protect beachheads from counterattacks.

Behind the amphibious assault forces would come ships full of artillery and supporting forces to build up the beachheads—engineers, communications specialists, electronic warfare experts, and staff officers. Toward the back of formations would be supply ships, oilers, repair ships, and hospital ships. Ships full of main battle tanks and other heavy vehicles would come last. They could only be landed when the coast was secure and docks were in place. In the center of armadas would be their flag-ships, large amphibious assault ships carrying top-ranking generals and admirals. Forward command post afloat would notionally be followed, at a significant distance, by the joint command post, the reserve command post, and the rear area command post. Each would be surrounded by the forces under their purview, with major ship groups spaced some 4–5 nautical miles apart.[263]

PLA writings anticipate that amphibious assault groups would follow a tightly coordinated plan during the crossing. We are told that they would be ordered to follow strict radio silence and, to the extent possible, keep their lights extinguished. As they crossed the mid-point of the Taiwan Strait, fighter aircraft would take off from frontline bases in China and rapidly climb their way into the skies, where they would fly tactical patterns above the troops below, screening them from incoming attackers. Naval helicopters would be launched to further strengthen the protective air umbrella.[264]

Pushing large numbers of aircraft into the middle of the Taiwan Strait could alert defenders to the approaching danger, but PLA planners seem to view this as a risk worth running, especially since Taiwan's surveillance networks can easily range these waters anyway. It is assumed that escort ships would have to fight off wave after wave of Taiwanese air attacks. Rescue and repair ships would deal with those that had been hit and crippled, but were not yet sunk. Ships would approach their assigned anchorages off Taiwan and position themselves for the long-awaited assault.[265]

Zero Day

Before first light, airports and helicopter bases across China's darkened seaboard would be flooded with paratroopers and air cavalry, who would pile aboard their planes and helicopters. Once airborne, it is contemplated that transport aircraft would form up in large formations, flying low over the seawater to stay under Taiwan's radars. Escorts would fly out in front to provide reconnaissance, covering fire, and guidance, helping each squadron make it to their drop sites and landing zones. Electronic warfare aircraft would jam the defender's radars and communications nets on the ground. After crossing the Strait, transport planes would pop up at the last minute, climbing to the altitudes required for safely disgorging paratroopers.[266]

Before the invaders began landing along Taiwan's coast, the PLA would launch waves of missiles, rockets, bombs, and artillery shells, pounding shoreline defenses, while electronic jammers scrambled communications. Their objective would be to destroy Taiwan's major coastal defenses, while paralyzing and isolating defenders, decimating their ranks and rendering them unable to coordinate. If the PLA Rocket Force had not already exhausted its stockpiles, important coastal targets would be subjected to tactical ballistic missile strikes.[267]

Minesweepers and obstacle clearing teams would be the first to approach from the sea. They would attempt to clear disembarkation zones free of sea mines before the transport ships arrived to drop anchor. Only after staging areas were free of danger could the minesweepers proceed toward the beaches. It is envisioned that military engineers and underwater demolition teams would help secure long lanes, stretching from disembarkation zones to beaches. Pre-invasion bombing runs would likely have knocked out some of the lethal traps, but no one could know what the situation looked like for sure until teams were onsite. Once mines and obstacles had either been blown up or towed away, the lanes that were cleared of danger would be marked with flags or buoys.[268]

The armadas, now anchored across sprawling staging areas 10–30 miles offshore, would begin disembarkation operations. In the early morning hours, troops would climb into amphibious tanks, hovercraft, and small landing craft. They would then motor to shore in groups, one after the other. As they approached, the beaches would be fired on with naval guns. Army artillery pieces bolted to the decks of civilian ships and strike fighters would join in the fiery spectacle.

Covering fire for the assault groups could not continue indefinitely without risking fratricide. Once landing craft had gotten within around one half mile of the shore, airstrikes would notionally be re-directed to targets inland. It is anticipated that major sea-to-shore bombardment would cease once troops were within a few hundred yards of the beaches. At that point, the only firepower available to them would come from small boats nearby, armed with small-caliber guns and short-range rockets or mortars, firing at point-blank ranges.[269]

PLA writings indicate that the invasion beaches are probably divided into sectors, each generally large enough to accommodate a battalion-sized landing force of some 500 men. These beach sectors, once stormed and secured, would be melded together to form division-sized landing zones. Although the exact mix of forces which would first hit the beaches is unknown, technical studies indicate that they would likely be infantry in small landing craft, amphibious tanks, air defense teams, and anti-tank specialists. Four helicopters would notionally provide overhead covering fire for each battalion as they landed.[270]

Internal writings indicate that amphibious units would probably start landing on the beaches as high tide approached. Around Zero Hour, paratroopers and helicopter-borne forces would assault areas near the landing beaches. Some sites might already be in the hands of special operations forces that had infiltrated ashore during the night. Wherever possible, road junctions and bridges that could be used by Taiwanese forces would be taken and blown up, as necessary, to stop the defender from counterattacking.[271]

Chinese writings call for multi-directional, multi-dimensional landings at various levels of depth into Taiwan, with non-traditional flanking maneuvers covering the main frontal attacks. In practice, this means that PLA commandos would scale the cliffs surrounding the main invasion beaches or come ashore at nearby fishing harbors to encircle defenders. Amphibious troops would then storm ashore, pinching beach defenders into isolated pockets of resistance. If successful, Taiwan's frontline troops would be cut off from reinforcements. PLA field manuals emphasize that each main landing zone must include ports, docks, and airstrips in addition to beaches. All would have to be within a few miles of each other so that landing forces could link up and join hands quickly after Zero Hour.[272]

To capture port facilities, PLA writings suggest that Chinese frogmen would infiltrate in to cut underwater electricity, gas, and water supply lines—and cables connecting underwater surveillance nets. Electronic attacks would ensure local communications were blacked out, and obstacles and mines at harbor mouths would be pushed aside. Then amphibious forces would storm ashore, flanking and enveloping the area, while helicopters ferried in commandos to seize key targets. The mission would be to overmatch local defenders and capture targeted port facilities with their docks intact, ready for offloading cargo ships supporting the invasion effort. Once ports were seized, Chinese forces could quickly fan out to take up defensive positions in the surrounding area. A special emphasis would be placed on ensuring control over high ground and traffic intersections in the vicinity. Once these were in hand, the attackers would dig in, set up roadblocks, and wait for possible counterattacks.[273]

The overall campaign objective on Z-Day would be to capture and reinforce multiple bridgeheads that could quickly be augmented by second echelon forces in the days that followed. Chinese forces would strive to maintain total control over the battle, making sure that Taiwan's defenders could not mount effective counterattacks to disrupt shipping and repel them from the island. Chinese military sources view it as highly likely that counterattacks would begin almost immediately after the first wave made it to shore. To avoid having their newly won beaches overrun, amphibious forces reportedly plan to move a few miles inland to stand together with paratroopers and commandos. Once pockets of localized control were consolidated, they would then begin expanding beachheads.[274]

PLA writings envision a series of intense battles raging along the coast as Chinese landing forces met with Taiwanese defenders. Each side would struggle to master local fortifications—the tunnels and bunkers that run through the hills along the coast—and hold whatever high ground and road junctures where available to them. Taiwan's coastal fishing villages, airport tarmacs, and golf courses would be scenes of desperate action. Wave after wave of Chinese forces would come ashore to bolster the offensive front. Wave after wave of Taiwanese would push them back. For a stretch of time, the PLA's lightly armed units would have to radio in requests for air and naval support. Heavy covering fires would be needed whenever they ran into concentrations of tanks, armored fighting vehicles, and infantry. Chinese tanks and self-propelled artillery are expected to take a painfully long time unloading from their ships and moving forward to join the battle.[275]

Chinese military writings state that Taiwanese counterattacks would probably be too strong for the first echelon to hold off alone. It is surmised that the PLA vanguard would already be weakened and drained by fierce battles to capture footholds along the coast. Getting large numbers of fresh troops and supplies ashore as fast as possible is viewed as imperative for maintaining momentum. Infantry units armed with mortars and bazookas would form outer perimeters and fight off counterattacks. Many would be engaged in house-to-house fighting across the front. Fresh forces would join the battle in ever greater numbers to augment areas that had been seized.[276]

Chinese generals would work to establish defensive bubbles around their landing zones. It is imagined that air defense nets would be needed to fight off Taiwanese attack helicopters, fighter jets, and drones. Chinese electronic warfare teams and snipers would climb to the tops of whatever high outcroppings were available, playing their respective roles of jamming enemy radios and eliminating officers. Military engineers would land their equipment and begin to clear obstacles and debris away from captured terrain, opening the shore up to receive fresh troops and tanks. Logistics experts would work under great strain to maximize the speeds ships with which could be disgorged. Everything that followed in the battle of Taiwan would hinge on the establishment of an unending river of supplies. Everything would be hanging in the balance.[277]

From Beijing to Fuzhou, and from flagships in the Strait to command posts on Taiwan's invasion beaches, information would be received, orders sent and acted on. It is imagined that satellites would monitor the entire battle, sending down streams of data to be processed into actionable intelligence and channeled to forces in the field. Once the first waves of amphibious troops, paratroopers, and commandos had landed and formed up, the most critical mission of the space forces would be to give theater commanders situational awareness and early warning of Taiwanese air or naval movements indicating possible counterattacks against the fleets offshore or troops on the beach.

Reconnaissance assets would focus heavily on tracking the movements of Taiwan's armor brigades and strategic reserve forces. If not stopped, they could launch themselves against the beachheads and drive the invaders into the sea. Chinese military sources emphasize that officers should be prepared for a fierce and potentially drawn-out fight, with pitched battles. Once landing zones were firmly in hand, plans call for concentrating forces for what is expected to be a hard slog into Taiwan's interior.[278]

Amphibious Assault Plan, Z-2 to Z+2

Step 1: Load Amphibious Assault Ships
Location: PRC coast (Fujian, Zhejiang, and Guangdong)
Duration: 1–2 nights
Gather ships at loading areas in advance and wait offshore in dispersed groups
Dock (or anchor) and load at night
Gather for the crossing

Step 2: Make the Crossing
Location: Taiwan Strait
Duration: 1 night (approx. 10 hours)
Steam two or more armadas across 70–225 miles of water
Gather at anchorages

Step 3: Disembark and Form Up Assault Groups
Location: 12–37 miles offshore
Duration: 2+ hours*
Anchor and unload large amphibious assault ships 25–37 miles offshore
Anchor and unload traditional landing ships 12–18 miles offshore

Step 4: Bombard Coastline
Location: 1–12 miles offshore
Duration: 2+ hours*

*   Note that Step 3 through Step 5 could occur at the same time or overlap each other, depending on circumstances.

Shell coastline and surf zones with destroyers, frigates, and civilian ships carrying artillery pieces
Strike coast with helicopters, fighters, and bombers in coordinated raids**

Step 5: Sweep Mines and Clear Obstacles
Location: From anchorages to beaches
Duration: 1–3 hours *
Remove minefields and beach obstacles
Clear 2–3 lanes to get each battalion's landing craft ashore and 4–6 safe pathways across each beach

Step 6: Storm Beaches
Location: Taiwan's shoreline
Duration: 1–4 hours
Land special forces groups to secure beach pathways for the assault group
Land beach assault groups to secure sectors for reinforcements
Seize nearby airstrips and ports with airborne assaults

Step 7: Consolidate and Strengthen Landing Zones
Location: Taiwan coastline, average zone size: 3–6 miles across, 3–5 miles inland
Duration: 1–3 days
Capture key terrain and fight off counterattacks
Establish forward command posts and air defenses
Link beaches, airports, and harbors into consolidated landing zones
Construct artificial harbors, repair transportation, unload deep-draft ships

---

**   PLA would likely subject coast to 1–15 days of attacks prior to Z-Day with ballistic missiles, rockets, bombers, and fighters. Source: Tsai Ho-Hsun, "Research on the Communist Military's Joint Landing Campaign," pp. 35–49.

Phase Three: Combat Operations on the Island

Chinese military writings describe the invasion of Taiwan as a campaign that would be extremely risky and costly, but not necessarily impossible. If landings were successful and troops made it to shore and captured their objectives along the coast, everything would next depend on the battle to drive inland, take Taipei, and conquer the rest of the island. Combat operations on the island would decide the final outcome of the war. Perhaps as an indication of China's increasing willingness to actually consider the invasion of Taiwan, this phase of operations appears to be receiving more attention. PLA professional writings produced nearly a decade ago offered almost no discussion on the post Z-Day conflict. More recent publications cover it in detail.[279]

There are at least three possible explanations for this. The first is that Chinese strategists previously assumed that once they got footholds on Taiwan the rest of the invasion would be relatively easy. Presumably no Taiwanese army that still had fight left in it would allow the invaders to establish stable beachheads in the first place. The second explanation could be that landing operations appeared so daunting to them that they dedicated little time to thinking about what might follow. They decided, in effect, to cross that bridge in the war plan when they got to it—and now they have. The third possible explanation is that Chinese strategists have been working on developing doctrine and plans for combat operations on Taiwan all along, but their studies were classified or written in books not currently available to us. Whatever the case may be, recently published internal writings offer insights into how they envision the closing weeks and months of the war.

The first theoretical question planners appear to ask themselves is where the PLA should draw the line between amphibious landing operations and the final fight to conquer the entire island. At what point would one phase of operations transition to the next? According to our sources, the invasion of Taiwan would reach this important milestone only after amphibious forces had first met a number of critical mission objectives. The most important is that at least one major landing zone was firmly in hand, and the invaders had successfully weathered the ROC Army's opening counterattacks.

A major landing zone would include a large beach, a harbor (possibly prefabricated and towed across), a dockyard, and an airport. All nearby towns along the coast would have to be occupied, cleared of defenders, and made ready to support an enormous flow of incoming men and material. Control over the local electromagnetic, air, and sea domains would have to be secured and maintained. Only after these missions were completed could the campaign officially transition from landing operations to combat operations on the island. Then the final push into Taiwan's rugged depths could begin.[280]

The writings available to us do not provide any timetables or estimates regarding how long the battle along the coast might have to rage before one or more landing zones could be firmly established and built up. The PLA's goal would be to offload a massive army onto Taiwan as quickly as possible, but offloading takes time in the chaos of war, and no one can know what might happen to delay or accelerate events. Based on Chinese accounts, the Taiwan Strait after Z-day would be an ominous scene. Shipping convoys would be shuttling back-and-forth in great numbers, moving troops, tanks, artillery guns, ammunition, fuel, food, and water from the mainland to the front.

The skies above would be choked with smoke and the ground darkened with the shadows of planes and helicopters as they passed overhead. Electronic warfare units perched on high ground near the frontlines would search for invisible targets, seeking to blast Taiwan's interior with energy shot across the frequency spectrum to jam the defender's radio nets. Tactical missiles and rockets that remained in the arsenal would be used to flatten Taiwanese mobile command posts wherever they were discovered. Naval guns and army artillery would spit fire along the coast, softening defenders up for the swelling forces in the landing zones, paving the way for them to fight into the island's interior.[281]

The Blitz Inland

It is anticipated that Taiwan's fate in the days after Zero would be decided on the highways and roads that connect landing zones to the major cities nearby. Once harbors and docks were secure, main battle tanks would be offloaded from deep-draft ships and made ready to grind inland. Chinese units specializing in military deception would also land and work their way to the front, creating a phantom army with false radio chatter, decoys, and fake troop movements. Selected roadways would be assaulted with lightning attacks along traditional and nontraditional lines of approach.

PLA field manuals recommend mimicking the tactics used by the U.S. military during the 2003 invasion of Iraq.[282] Frontline commanders would keep their attack groups lean, enabling them to maneuver quickly and adroitly as they pushed their way into Taiwan's dense urban interior. Large tank columns could easily clog up war-torn roads. To avoid this, Chinese officers are advised to forego frontal assaults against heavily defended urban strongholds. Instead, they would try to pin the Taiwanese down with helicopter gunships and artillery, allowing tanks and mechanized infantry to wheel around flanks and encircle positions.[283]

Special operations forces, we are told, would be carried behind Taiwanese lines by transport helicopters. Small teams would be dropped near residential neighborhoods and office parks, areas where they could gain access to high towers. Here they would perch, providing covering fire to support armored units as they fought their way down labyrinthine road networks. Military engineers would use the cover of night to dismantle roadblocks and repair severed traffic arteries, allowing invaders to flow into the breach and overpower Taiwan's defenders. The envisioned fighting would be intense, as troops struggled to gain control over key traffic nodes and cleared out surrounding pockets of resistance in the urban jungles. PLA intelligence officers would assess weak points and evaluate whether traps and ambushes were lurking down those roads that appeared the most inviting. Chinese generals would work to keep the flow of fresh forces moving forward in a well-orchestrated concert of violence. If too many units were sent inland all at once, they could gridlock the available roads.

If not enough, offensive thrusts could lose momentum and crumble in the face of resolute defense.[284]

It is expected that Chinese mechanized forces pushing down Taiwanese roadways would encounter heavy debris, military-grade obstacles, anti-personnel mines, anti-tank mines, and ambush sites. Engineering efforts would be vital for clearing viable pathways forward, something that would require rebuilding bridges, removing obstacles from tunnels, and clearing urban minefields—all while withstanding potentially withering attacks. The literature advises Chinese officers on the ground to call in helicopter gunships when they need covering fire, and to turn the Taiwanese obstacles and bunkers against the defenders during their counterattacks.

PLA sappers would resurrect roads and bridges and ports, fill in cratered airstrips, sweep minefields and clear obstacles, and dispose of unexploded ordinance. As they established pathways forward, large numbers of tanks and infantry would flow in behind them. Special operations forces would already be scattered ahead, providing intelligence. Maintaining the traffic flow of logistic support, including fresh ammunition and supplies needed at the front, is deemed as vitally important for keeping advancing forces from getting exhausted and mired in urban deathtraps. It is described as essential that Chinese ground forces operate in dispersed groups, moving inland under cover of overwhelming fire support and air defense screens. They could otherwise be caught out on open roads and slaughtered by Taiwanese jets or helicopters held in reserve for final defensive action.[285]

There is another, far more nightmarish, reason why Chinese military officers are told to avoid exposed positions. Restricted-access PLA writings state, in an oddly detached manner, that large concentrations of troops could be hit with weapons of mass destruction. According to them, once the Taiwanese are convinced the life of their country is in mortal peril, they could quickly develop and unleash makeshift atomic weapons, poison gas, and biological agents on the coastal landing zones.[286] What is left unsaid is that the battlefield could instead be contaminated by the Chinese destruction of nearby infrastructure; nuclear power plants, petrochemical facilities, and pharmaceutical labs are located near some of the largest landing beaches. PLA writings, glossing over their own culpability, claim without citing evidence that Taiwan's coastal defense plan includes engineering efforts to create "contamination zones" to deny coastal areas to the invader.[287] Whatever the case may be, Chinese military texts advise combat commanders to organize rapid decontamination and cleanup operations when needed, making sure not to lose offensive momentum.[288]

After pushing through imagined swamps of horror along the coast, the PLA would fight for the inland high grounds. Hills overlooking key cities, in particular those around Taipei, would be taken and occupied. It is envisioned that tank groups, working in tandem with helicopters and commandos, would bear the brunt of the uphill battles. China's electronic warriors are expected to play an important role as well. They would attempt to triangulate and target ROC Army command posts, jamming their radios and disabling their weapon systems as they retreated into city centers. Once surrounded, cities would be subjected to shelling and psychological warfare attacks aimed at eroding the will to resist. PLA writings portray the battle of Taiwan as the final act in an unresolved civil war and place great emphasis on winning (or at least weakening) hearts and minds. To do that, the PLA would struggle to convince Taiwan's defenders they are in a hopeless situation.[289]

To support thrusts into Taiwan's cities, Chinese writings anticipate using a preponderance of artillery to soften targets up, a series of airborne paratrooper assaults to capture key points, and a stream of special force infiltrations to fight behind Taiwanese lines. Chinese officers would notionally keep their battle plans as elastic as possible and pin down and maneuver around neighborhood strongholds, using overlapping covering fires to boldly exploit any open streets. They would blitz into areas where they could break apart Taiwanese transportation infrastructure, especially the highways linking large defense units. The main PLA targets appear to be the ROC military's joint theater command centers, each of which controls one of the island's major defense zones. To reach these interior command complexes, the PLA would first smash through surrounding army bases. It is envisioned that Chinese officers would execute both frontal and oblique attacks, fighting their way forward, burning and rolling over everything in their way, while trapping and burying alive defenders who were inside tunnel networks underneath.[290]

It is imagined that Taipei would be encircled and pummeled from the land, air, and sea. Whenever possible, Taiwan's armies would be drawn out into the suburbs and attacked in fierce, close-up fighting, saving the city centers from complete destruction. The outer defensive works ringing the city would then be shattered. Chinese troops and tanks would roll in, fighting down the main avenues, splitting urban districts apart from one another. Government buildings and military headquarters would be seized in pitched firefights. Next, telecommunications centers, train stations, and major intersections would be attacked. Finally, radio stations and television studios would be stormed and taken over.[291]

Absent from Chinese writings is the effect that attacks on major population centers would have on the millions of people who lived there. PLA materials fail to discuss the mass civilian casualties that would almost certainly result from their envisioned operations, leaving tactical commanders with no guidance whatsoever on this issue. It is simply stated that Chinese troops would occupy buildings overlooking major city streets and should anticipate that some stout-hearted Taiwanese would barricade themselves into maze-like residential neighborhoods, shopping complexes, and office buildings. They further advise that some Taiwanese forces would hide out in subterranean parking garages and use metro line tunnels to move and fight across the city. To crush the resistance, PLA officers are recommended to encircle and clear out their "nests and dens" one at a time, slowly and methodically annihilating them. Their methods are expected to be targeted strikes mixed with negotiation. Chinese psychological warfare officers are experts at persuasion. It is expected that they could get some ROC troops to surrender. The diehards would be attacked one street at a time.[292]

Taiwan's central mountain range and rugged east coast are expected to be the last to fall. PLA texts evince a considerable sense of concern that once Taiwanese army groups were broken up along the coastal plains, they would retreat and regroup in the high hinterlands. Taiwan's military engineers have long maintained roads across the mountains, to be used only in wartime. These are exceedingly rough going. To cross all the way over the mountains requires weeks of harrowing foot travel through dense jungle, long tunnels and deep ravines. These secret mountain trails are reportedly well prepared, well stocked, and designed to maximize the favorable defensive terrain.

Chinese officers are given relatively vague guidance on mountain warfare. The professional literature exhorts combat commanders to make rapid advances, cutting Taiwanese forces off before they could retreat back to the hills. Officers are told to use air assaults, dropping units by helicopter to maximize surprise. Their missions would be to get to the top of favorable terrain before the defender could and to take hold of mountain roads. As a final resort, the PLA apparently plans on occupying the lowland plains and isolating the defenders in the mountains. The "liberators" could then attack into the highlands at the times and places of their own choosing, clearing out defense works in grueling operations.

In the event the war ever reached this point in China's military plan, something would have gone terribly wrong for the defender. The Americans presumably never showed up, and the Taiwanese army was defeated along the shores and in the suburbs. One chapter in the story of Taiwan would end, and another would begin. The lights of freedom, democracy, and social justice would be extinguished. The shadows would deepen across the island, as the last rays of hope faded into a long night of terror.

Occupation

How do PLA writings depict a post-war Taiwan? In theory, what would follow the invasion if Taiwan's army collapsed and the island was actually conquered? Internal Chinese military writings anticipate that Taiwan would be turned into a garrison state. After Taipei and the other major cities had fallen, Chinese officers would quickly make the transition to post-conflict stability operations. Such operations would mean first declaring martial law to institutionalize military control over Taiwan's largest cities. Next, they would tighten control over the towns, farmlands, and mountains.[293]

The victors would then begin their purges. PLA sources envision Taiwan being cleansed of resistance, with army and police units going from neighborhood to neighborhood and house to house to hunt for remaining fighters. To manage the civilian populace, Chinese officers are told they would need to establish tight control over each city's traffic junctions, local television studios, and radio stations. To dampen hostile public sentiment, which is expected to be deeply embittered, PLA writings state that military authorities would run post-war radio programs, television shows, the Internet, print media, and the postal services. The theme of social stability and a new social order would be pervasive.[294] The ground forces would patrol the mountains, drawing out guerillas who were still hiding inside bunkers, or organizing resistance in secret camps. Roads leading into the mountains would be manned by heavy guard groups. Elsewhere, ordinance disposal teams would clear unexploded munitions and defuse mines emplaced by retreating forces.[295]

It is contemplated that fragments of Taiwan's navy, potentially along with large numbers of civilian refugees, would need to be swept up near the coast. In some cases they would be fished out of the water in life-threatening conditions. The major harbors would need to be cleared of mines and debris, and coastal areas would need to have their defensive obstacles dismantled. The internal literature urges officers to recycle war materials, as the PLA would have to erect new defenses, protecting potential targets from sabotage. The new government's political bodies, economic centers, and cultural heritage sites would all require protection. Experience in Tibet and Xinjiang suggests the occupation forces would be quick to set up monuments and exhibits celebrating the "glorious liberation" of Taiwan. Military manuals caution their readers that such facilities could be bombed or raided by "terrorists."[296]

Chinese army units would be tasked with protecting factories and industrial zones, and patrolling basic social infrastructure like schools, hospitals, airports, and fishing harbors. Troops would stand watch and fight off attacks organized by former ROC military personnel who had evaded death or capture at the hands of the invader. PLA writings conclude somberly that after they win, the Taiwanese, having suffered terrible hardships and grievous "collateral damage," will almost certainly not embrace them. Many are expected to become plainclothes insurgents, fighting street-to-street, shooting the "liberator" in the back or bombing him in the dark. The rest of the civilian populace will simply be passive, silently harboring grudges. One source warns: "They will watch us with cold eyes, not lifting a finger to help."[297]

It is imagined that Taiwan would have a new provisional government established for it, which would fall directly under Beijing's rule and be enforced by the army. The puppet government, peopled with CCP collaborators, would be responsible for rebuilding the war-torn island into a submissive province. Jobs would be created at refurbished manufacturing centers and commercial districts. The military would help restore oil, gas, water, and electric services, and make every attempt to transform the Taiwanese into an "orderly and stable" populace, while erasing memory of democracy and self-rule. The old order would be vilified by the propaganda machine and replaced by something alien and oppressive.[298]

Distracting attention from domestic matters, the threat of another war might loom. The PLA literature states that military officers would rapidly build up Taiwan into a base of forward operations and fortify the coastline against foreign (read: American) invasion from the sea and air.[299] They appear to assume that the United States might lead an international coalition to free Taiwan from PLA rule, expelling them in a manner similar to the way the Iraqis were removed from Kuwait in 1991.[300] The invasion and occupation of Taiwan would be the PLA's ultimate test, the very mission it has been focused on for decades. But it would not necessarily be the end of war. Rather, it could mark a turning point in a much longer saga of violence, signaling China's ascendance as the hegemon of Asia, and eventually, perhaps, beyond.[301]

Here it must be emphasized that all of the PLA's internal materials on the invasion of Taiwan are theoretical, and its campaign plan is based on imagined conditions and assumptions. In reality, the operation would be far more complex and far less forgiving than what is depicted in the "ideal" textbook scenario presented in this chapter. The PLA is cognizant of this and anticipates that any attempt to land on Taiwan would be beset by a multitude of problems, some of its own making, some the result of bad luck, many more the result of Taiwanese and American ingenuity. As the following chapter will show, the costs of aggression are expected to be crippling, even if the Chinese military of tomorrow is far more capable and resilient than it is today. The PLA, in full recognition of the magnitude of its operational challenges, is investing heavily in building up for this mission.

Joint Island Attack Campaign

Phase 1. Blockade and Bombing
Main objectives: Obtain uncontested control over the airwaves, airspace, and seascapes across Taiwan Strait
Missions:
- Execute massed missile raids behind screen of electronic and cyber attacks
- Secure air superiority
- Battle Taiwanese naval fleet
- Blockade major ports
- Bomb Taiwan

Phase 2. Amphibious Landing
Main objectives: Capture beaches, ports, and airfields near Taipei and other targeted cities
Missions:
- Gather invasion forces
- Attack Kinmen, Matsu, and Penghu
- Embark amphibious troops
- Sail armadas across the Strait
- Clear mines and beach obstacles
- Anchor and disembark troops
- Conduct surprise assaults on targeted beaches, sea ports, and airstrips
- Land multiple amphibious divisions in two major waves of attack

Phase 3. Combat on the Island (Urban and Mountain Warfare)
Main objectives: Occupy Taiwan and impose will on the survivors
Missions:

- Secure footholds on Taiwan
- Build up major landing zones and offload massive army
- Capture strategic terrain and military bases inland
- Capture Taipei and other major cities
- Institute martial law
- Clear defenders out of mountains

Chapter Five
Planning Problems

No plan of operations extends with any certainty beyond first contact with the main hostile force.

—Field Marshall Moltke the Elder

Iꜰ China is ever going to put its war plan into action, generals tasked with the invasion will have to squarely face a large number of problems that have no easy solutions. The first problem is deciding where amphibious landing operations could be best made. There are several options that are open, each of which has its own strengths and weaknesses. These would have to be weighed, and many of the factors are uncertain, dynamic, and subject to variation. The principal factors are the locations of suitable beaches and nearby airfields and ports that could be captured. Proximity to the capital city, which is the main prize, length of voyage across the Strait, and the nature of inland areas for subsequent operations are further points of consideration. PLA generals must also evaluate defending force deployments (where each Taiwanese brigade would be waiting to meet them), and coastal minefields and fortifications.

Locations are important to consider because everything the plan envisioned would be limited by the constraints of surrounding geography. The land, water, and air characteristics of the Taiwan theater are all dramatic and different than those of other places around the world. What works somewhere else could fail here, and what might be unthinkable in other places could be a common sense approach locally. As we will see, locations that could be involved in the conflict are well known and have been exhaustively studied.

The second problem they face is deciding when to attack. It is sometimes assumed that China could invade Taiwan whenever it wanted. Nothing could be farther from the truth. In reality, the complexity of natural conditions in the area means that it's difficult to find a good Z-Day. The main factors in choosing the right time to attack are the seasons, which influence the weather, winds, waves, currents, and tides. Mother Nature is always a factor, and her moods fluctuate wildly.

Given the many variables identified by our sources, which time windows, in theory, give the PLA greatest hope? Which are the most suitable by some measures, but unsound when the overall picture is seen? When would Z-Day be? Time matters in war almost above all else, but it is the most unpredictable element. Plans always have to estimate how long things take to get done and account for the many things that could happen before they do that could accelerate, delay, disrupt, or change the course of events.

When would the pre-invasion missile and air strikes begin? How long might they go on? How long would the amphibious assault groups take to load up and assemble? How long would it take them to get across the Strait? How long might it take them to clear pathways through the off-shore mines and beach obstacles? When might Taiwan's counterstrikes against them arrive? At what stage should the plan assume the Americans are most likely to intervene? Would there be preemptive PLA strikes on U.S. forces? If so, at what point relative to Z-Day? How long might the Americans be knocked out of the main fight? When it comes to questions of time, the answers are less clear across the board and more unpredictable.

The third planning problem facing them is who would spearhead the attack and who would follow. How many units and what type of units would be needed? How should the invasion force be structured? Organizations are of utmost importance for any military and any war plan. They are particularly important for a Leninist military obsessed by ranks, grades, protocol orders, and party structures. The bureaucratic system in China is a tool of social control and, when needed, mass mobilization. It is elaborate and rigid, but often powerful when applied against Beijing's problems.

Military considerations would include things like the number of men, ships, and aircraft in each notional amphibious assault group. On Z-Day, how many divisions and brigades could they deliver across? Which units would they be? Who and how many would follow? Who and how many would be held in reserve? What would the command and control arrangements look like? Who would be responsible for what? How many missile launchers, bombers, destroyers, submarines, satellites, and cyberspace assets could be available to support the invasion? How many might be needed for other missions? If the "Strong Enemy" intervened, which American (and Japanese) combat forces would the PLA have to face? How many Chinese units could be dedicated to deterring or destroying them?[302]

The fourth problem is getting good intelligence for making operational and tactical decisions during the tumult of dynamic and fast-changing events. Additional problems involve overcoming the PLA's shortcomings in equipment, personnel, and logistics. Domestic political problems and the impact this campaign would have on the PRC's external security situation are further points of worry.

PLA writings on a Taiwan landing campaign dedicate an extraordinary amount of attention to planning problems. They make it clear that China has a unified plan for fighting an all-out war of conquest against Taiwan, and this plan is being worked on and refined over time with the objective of rectifying known shortcomings. It is equally clear that Chinese war planners continue to have many serious concerns. According to the military's internal assessments, some of the fundamental challenges facing them are only getting worse.

Restricted-access PLA writings describe a situation where the realities facing officers on the ground simply do not comport with the desires of their political masters in Beijing. From the military perspective, having good strategies, doctrines, and war plans is only the starting point. The PLA must be better equipped and trained, so that it can become a professional and competent fighting force. It must be better organized, structured, and coordinated so that cadres at every level of command can learn to work together as one team. Soldiers, sailors, and airmen must be given ever-increasing degrees of responsibility, making them flexible enough and resourceful enough to overcome the unforeseen problems that would inevitably crop up along the way.[303] At the current time, the Chinese military is not a finely honed instrument of war. For the invasion of Taiwan to become militarily feasible, it would have to get in much better shape.

If the invasion was attempted today, it would probably turn into a debacle. PLA studies assume that tactical commanders would destroy too many "incorrect" targets in the run-up to invasion, souring world opinion and inviting American intervention. They assume the Rocket Force and Air Force would be unable to completely knock out Taiwan's military in the first days of conflict, leaving the PLA vulnerable to counterstrikes launched to devastate the amphibious assault groups.

On Z-day, PLA experts worry that troops could get tangled in obstacle nets offshore or landed at the wrong places. Soldiers might panic and freeze up on the beaches, and be decimated. After Z-day, Chinese military experts seem convinced that their supply lines would almost certainly break down, leaving the ground forces unable to punch through Taiwan's urban defenses. Without fresh supplies, the invasion force could lose momentum and collapse. These are but a few of the recorded problems that keep Chinese war planners awake at night. For them, the agonizing possibilities are endless.

From the Chinese political perspective, the practical military problems associated with attacking Taiwan are relatively unimportant. What matters most is the CCP's ability to be seen as uniting China, thereby burnishing its legitimacy. The PLA's mission is to defend the Party's continued rule and all that it requires. The PLA must deliver whatever the civilian bureaucrats in the Politburo demand, even if their demands are unreasonable and based on unsound logic or incomplete information. If an invasion operation seems impossible, the armed wing of the CCP must prepare for doing it anyway. Their job is not an enviable one.

Chinese war planners must face a large number of hard questions relating to the invasion of Taiwan. Not all of these questions will be, or can be, addressed here, but some of the most important ones are. The following pages will examine the many challenges confronting PLA officers who work on the blueprint to conquer Taiwan.

Invasion Beaches

In the event of an all-out amphibious attack, where would the Chinese land on Taiwan? To answer this question, Taiwan's geography has been subjected to exhaustive military study over the past seven decades, with experts on both sides collecting and scrutinizing information on every aspect of the potential battlefield. Their secret studies are frequently updated and provided to strategists and war planners, making this area quite possibly the most carefully studied place on the globe. PLA thinking can be pieced together using internal materials. Many further details can be found in Taiwanese military publications that are available to anyone with internet access.[304]

The PLA's internal professional literature is quite frank on the question of where best to land on Taiwan. The ideal landing ground, readers are told, would include a place with beaches that are relatively close to mainland China, with only open water in between the two sides. The longer an invasion force had to transit the Strait, the more likely it could be detected and attacked. The ideal location would have port facilities and airfields close at hand that could be assaulted by airborne units and special operations forces. The site chosen should be close to a strategic node, like Taipei, but relatively far from defending armor and mechanized brigades. The location must be lightly defended and offer the element of surprise, and it should provide enough open space for troops to quickly build up their beachhead and drive inland.[305]

Unfortunately for Chinese generals, there are only a limited number of beach options to choose from, and not a single one of them meets all of the above criteria. Taiwan's 770-mile-long coastline is remarkably unsuited for amphibious operations. Nearly 75 percent of the island is covered in mountains, and the rest is mostly heavily urbanized or inhosptible terrain.[306] Taiwan's east coast is principally made up of cliffs, blades of mountain rock slicing straight down from the central mountain range into the Pacific's dark depths. It would be a dangerous place to land in force. There are three small coastal flats, but they are penned in by East Asia's highest mountains and connected to the rest of the island by roads and rail lines that pass through long tunnels and gorges. The ROC military has plans in place for quickly demolishing these vulnerable transportation channels. Any attacker that landed on the beaches here would almost certainly find himself encircled by a wall of rock that could not be climbed over or passed under.[307]

Taiwan's west coast, which faces China, is far more forgiving. Here there are workable landing beaches that could be captured to facilitate the invasion. The problem is that few of them are large enough to support landing operations by major units and all are enveloped by some kind of unfavorable terrain. There is no location with miles of unbroken sand for an army to land. Most of the western coastline is comprised of densely populated cities and towns. Coastal areas that can be inhabited have been inhabited. People live in steel-reinforced concrete block structures, which in rural areas are dotted around rice paddies, fish farms, and irrigation ponds. Sprawling mudflats are a feature of this area, forming a natural barrier to landing operations.[308] During the dry season, Taiwan's mudflats are fed by thin streams that flow through steep gullies made of loose, sandy soil that can barely support foot traffic, let alone tanks and trucks. These gullies are filled with violent white water that plummets down from the mountains each time it rains.

Chinese military writings state that the primary mission of invading forces will be the swift capture of Taipei. They hope that by seizing the political nerve center of Taiwan, operations might be concluded decisively before they are caught up in an exhausting war of attrition that could rapidly weaken CCP unity, perhaps fatally.[309] Specific areas that have been identified as having potential for landing operations include Taoyuan in northwestern Taiwan, the Chuoshui River delta in central Taiwan, and the Chianan Plain in southwestern Taiwan.[310] These coastal stretches are thought to offer possible beachheads and convenient access to roads that could be used to mount operations to push into the depths of the island.

PLA books note that, as a consequence of having decades to prepare, the Taiwanese are very clear about their defense situation and have put measures into place to ensure that the few semi-favorable landing areas are a planning nightmare. These obstacles are expected to make landing, lodgment, and break-out operations very difficult. PLA texts state that Taiwan has conducted engineering projects to alter many of the landing beaches by building seawalls and breakwater structures and planting thick vegetation to stop coastal winds. In addition, networks of coastal ponds have been dug in low-lying areas for irrigation and fish farming. The result of these projects has been to create manmade obstacles that negatively impact upon offensive military operations.[311]

Supporting Taiwan's coastal engineering efforts, the ROC Marines, experts in amphibious warfare, survey the entire shoreline every year. Their studies are sent to the Ministry of National Defense headquarters, where they are integrated into Taiwan's defense plan. From their perspective, the more suitable beaches are for invasion, the more vulnerable they might be to attack and the more defensive investments and preparations are required to protect them.[312]

The metrics Taiwanese marines use to measure beach suitability are unknown, but it seems probable that they take into account information like offshore water depths, sea bottom conditions, gradients (the slope of the bottom), surf conditions, tidal conditions, beach frontage and size, beach composition, beach exits and off ramps.[313] The details of their studies, of course, are not publically available. However, it is known that they categorize beaches by color. Red beaches are considered the most suitable for landing operations in force. Yellow beaches are of medium suitability. Green beaches are of low suitability and are not concerning except for their potential to be used in small-scale, irregular landing raids using hovercraft, hydrofoils, and ground effect vehicles (sea skimmers).[314]

The color of a beach does not necessarily relate to probability it would be attacked. Yellow beaches near Taipei would certainly be more tempting for PLA commanders than red beaches in the middle of nowhere. The ROC Marines do not take a comprehensive view of all the factors that would determine which beaches might be stormed. Their job is to focus on the shoreline, without regard to the inland terrain. It is the responsibility of defense planners at headquarters to account for other strategic factors that have less to do with the beaches themselves.

The color assigned to a given beach can change from one year to the next, depending on the impact of weather and erosion. Natural geography is not the only factor. Coastal engineering projects in peacetime can work wonders in altering beach suitability for wartime. Environmental protection and commercial developments have reportedly had a particularly favorable effect for the defender. Coastal wind farms, breakwaters, artificial reefs, and aquaculture sites have been established in large numbers. These serve the purpose of generating renewable energy, reducing coastal erosion, creating safe harbors, promoting marine life, and harvesting aquatic organisms. More importantly, they improve coastal defense and reduce susceptibility to invasion. The result has been a clear reduction over time in the number of red and yellow beaches, and an increase in the number of green beaches.[315] These developments present Chinese war planners with a worrisome trend line.

Recently published ROC military studies indicate there are only 14 beaches left which are suitable for major enemy landing operations. Two of them are red beaches, while the rest are yellow beaches. Nine are concentrated in northern Taiwan, with two northwest of Taipei, four nearby Keelung, and three on the Yilan Plain, to the southeast. The remaining five are concentrated in southwestern Taiwan, three near Tainan, one in Kaohsiung. The final beach, which is the largest, is located at a military training area in the rural township of Fangliao. Taiwan's fourteen invasion beaches can be seen in the following map (overleaf).

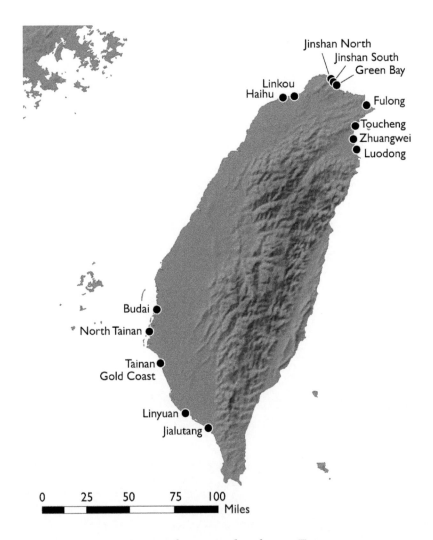

Potential invasion beaches on Taiwan

List of Taiwan's Fourteen Invasion Beaches

Red Beaches:

- **Jialutang Beach**, southwest Taiwan, in Pingtung County's Fangliao Township

- **Jinshan South Beach**, northeast Taiwan, in New Taipei City's Jinshan District

Yellow Beaches:
- **Linkou Beach**, northwest Taiwan, in New Taipei City's Linkou District, near the Port of Taipei
- **Haihu Beach**, northwest Taiwan, in Taoyuan County's Luzhu District, directly adjacent Taoyuan International Airport
- **Jinshan North Beach**, northeast Taiwan, in New Taipei City's Jinshan District
- **Green Bay Beach**, northeast Taiwan, in New Taipei City's Wanli District
- **Fulong Beach**, northeast Taiwan, in New Taipei City's Gongliao District
- **Toucheng Beach**, northeast Taiwan, in Yilan County's Toucheng Township
- **Zhuangwei Beach**, northeast Taiwan, in Yilan County's Zhuangwei Township
- **Luodong Beach**, northeast Taiwan, in Yilan County's Wujie Township
- **Budai Beach**, southwest Taiwan, in Chiayi County's Budai Township
- **North Tainan Beach**, southwest Taiwan, in Tainan City's Jiangjun and Qigu Districts
- **Tainan Gold Coast**, southwest Taiwan, in Tainan City's South District, near Tainan Airport
- **Linyuan Beach**, southwest Taiwan, close to Kaohsiung International Airport

Source: Wu Qi-yu, "Research on Executing Surf Zone Mining Operations with Combat Engineer Units (工兵部隊執行激浪區布雷作業之研究)," *ROC Army Combat Engineer Journal*, No. 147, 2015, pp. 24–27.

After beach suitability, the next most important thing that would be considered is the potential Z-Day battlefield's proximity to airborne landing zones. As we have seen, the invasion force would include large numbers of paratroopers and helicopter assault troops who would need flat open spaces to land. Airborne units are comprised of light infantry with little in the way of heavy weaponry, let alone armored transportation. If cutoff from the main force during an invasion, their supplies would be exhausted in hours, not days. They rely on heavy divisions landed on the beaches to sustain them once their initial objectives have been seized.

Airports near the invasion beaches are ideal targets for airborne assaults because they are easy to identify from the air and offer purpose-built landing zones, close to the main scenes of action. In addition to accommodating airdrops during the initial attack, their runways could allow for the inflow of reinforcements. Once seized and repaired, airports might be turned in to airheads where transport planes and helicopters could land in great flocks. Beachheads and airheads are mutually reinforcing, but capturing runways far from landing beaches does little good. If paratroopers cannot quickly make contact with regular army troops pushing inland from the beaches, they will be in peril of being surrounded and defeated in detail.

According to PLA studies, during the invasion, Chinese airborne units will be landed in battalion sized groups (approximately 500 men). As a general rule, they would assault targets between one and three miles from the invasion beaches and avoid operating far away from the main army. Close proximity to the beaches is vital because it is assumed that they could only carry on independent combat operations for three to four hours. After that, it is expected that they would have exhausted all their ammunition, making them extremely vulnerable to being overpowered by local defenders. To avoid that fate, they would have to rapidly break out of their isolated pockets to join up with those on the beaches, while staying under the protective umbrella of firepower provided by warships parked offshore.[316]

In addition to airports, the selected invasion beaches will necessarily be close to harbors, needed because offloading heavy equipment onto beaches from transport ships is impractical when large volumes are required and speed is essential to sustain momentum. Weather and sea conditions are ever changing, and Taiwan's narrow beaches would be highly limited in throughput capacity. Prefabricated portable piers and docks might be moved into place by engineers to facilitate the rapid offloading of men, vehicles, and supplies. However, artificial harbors would take a long time to tow across, and they would be tough to establish in choppy waters. It would be a monumental feat of engineering to set them up, and the manmade harbors could not be brought online until large coastal fronts had been secured. Counterattacks would first have to be dealt with, and the area swept clear of mines, obstacles, and debris.

Pre-existing port facilities, on the other hand, could be brought into action much sooner, providing they were captured intact, which is deemed unlikely, or at least readily repairable. When combined with beachheads and airheads, serviceable ports would greatly ease the PLA's immense logistical burdens. The estimated tonnages required by operational planners are unknown, but they are depicted as vast. PLA writings strongly indicate that major amphibious landing zones would be designed to include beaches, airports, and harbors, and obtaining this transportation trinity would be the main objective of Z-Day attacks. Without it, the entire operation is likely to stall out, and the landing forces driven back into the sea.[317]

Internal Chinese military writings judge close proximity to Taipei as a critical factor to consider when planning the invasion. Landing close to the island's capital city, readers are told, could help alleviate much of the risk of being bogged down in a long war of attrition. Landing in the center of the western coastline and then fighting north under a hailstorm of defensive fire, with the potential of being pinned down in every city street and mountain pass, would be impractical. The rugged geography of Taiwan provides ample opportunity for the defender to drop bridges and explode tunnels to block the invader's path. The PLA's professional literature assumes most Taiwanese will fight to the death for their homeland, destroying whatever they must to prevent it from falling into their hands.[318]

The rapid seizure of Taiwan's seat of government is viewed as something that could have a sizable shock factor, shaking the confidence of ROC military personnel all over the island. It might also shock American decision makers so much they could give up on their ally and call off intervention operations.[319] The beaches northwest of Taipei are the closest suitable points to China. Landing here would greatly reduce the length of the voyage and the amount of time troops had to spend aboard vulnerable ships as they crossed the sea. Close proximity would have other advantages. Rocket artillery could reach across the Strait to provide covering fire. Fighter jets, bombers, and helicopters could arrive faster and stay on station longer. Supply ships could deliver fresh reinforcements more swiftly.

In addition to other factors, PLA texts advise commanders to consider each beach's proximity to highways and their distance from major defense units that could counterattack to repel the landings. The closer beaches were to accessible roads the better. Transportation infrastructure would be critical for lightning attacks inland once the main landing zones were secured. Chinese officers are told, however, not to land in the teeth of the defender. Taiwanese units armed with tanks, self-propelled artillery, rocket launchers, air defenses, and helicopters are to be avoided. This poses an unavoidable dilemma. According to PLA assessments, those locations most suitable for amphibious landing operations have been built up, with large concentrations of defenders dug-in nearby. Moreover, roads and bridges spared by pre-invasion bombing runs could facilitate the movements of invading forces inland, but they could just as easily allow defenders to mount overwhelming counterattacks.[320]

According to both Chinese and Taiwanese military writings, Taoyuan is where the PLA is expected to establish the prime landing zone. [321] Taoyuan is a special municipality at the outer edge of greater Taipei. Located approximately 30 miles from the capital, Taoyuan is a satellite city and the fourth largest metropolitan area on the island. It hosts Taiwan's largest international airport and features a huge number of residential buildings and hotel blocks. In addition, Taoyuan is home to aerospace industrial parks, tech companies, logistical hubs, and oil refineries. Hemmed in by the Taiwan Strait and surrounded by mountains, Taoyuan's flatlands feature hundreds of irrigation ponds, fed by heavy rains and highland runoff.

Numerous PLA and ROC military writings, which appear to be indicative of doctrine, agree that this is by far the most likely spot to be targeted for invasion.[322] The landing beaches around Taoyuan are appealing to Chinese generals because they are the only workable locations close to Taipei with the needed trinity of beaches, airfields, and ports. A notional landing zone here could stretch from the mouth of the Tamsui River and the Port of Taipei at Bali in the north down to the Yong'an Fishing Harbor. At its heart would be Haihu Beach, Taoyuan International Airport, and the Zhuwei . After it was built up, strategic terrain that would be attacked early on in breakout operations include the plateaus at Linkou, Zhongli, and Hukou.[323] These are where the highways meet and cluster together and where key military bases are located. According to PLA writings, these vital crossroads would have to be taken as soon as possible.[324]

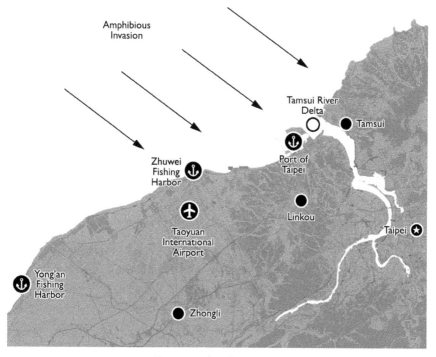

Taoyuan landing zone

In war, there are always several courses of action that are credible and many more that are possible. Alternative landing zones might be considered by the PLA if Taoyuan was judged too heavily defended to smash into with frontal attacks. Taoyuan is where the bulk of the ROC Army is concentrated. It bristles with tanks, missiles, rockets, and artillery guns. It houses special forces units and infantry brigades, backed up by attack helicopters, including the world's most advanced variant of the Apache helicopter gunship. The hills are lined with tunnels and bunker systems. Along the coast are low laying fields and wetlands that could be flooded to trap enemy forces as they landed. The Taoyuan area has been well prepared for battle.

An hour's drive down the coast sits an unlikely, but possible, alternative landing site at Hsinchu. With a giant science and technology park and over 360 high-tech companies involved in computer and information technology products, Hsinchu is Taiwan's Silicon Valley and the island's most prosperous economic hub. It is relatively close to the capital and the nearest point from Taiwan to China. The local air force base could become a target of airborne assaults. Close at hand are the Hsinchu Fishing harbor and a slender stretch of beaches.

Hsinchu's coastal area, however, is muddy and uneven, and the beaches are dominated by large artillery positions on overlooking hilltops. Weather patterns keep the area foggy, windy, and soaking wet. Widespread urban sprawl leaves little space for establishing lodgments ashore. Two ROC Army tank brigades sit in a blocking position just to the north, holding a strategic chokepoint between the mountains. After Taoyuan (and of course Taipei), Hsinchu is probably Taiwan's most heavily militarized and well-protected area. On balance, this area is highly favorable to the defense and ill-suited for landing a massive army.

Another hour farther south takes one to Taichung, Taiwan's large central city. Like Hsinchu, this area appears more favorable for nontraditional amphibious operations and paratrooper drops. Taichung has two elements of the transportation trinity Chinese generals will be looking for. It lacks suitable beaches, but the airport and seaport are large. Taichung is surrounded by high plateaus and mountains, making it a strategic bottleneck through which all north-south traffic must pass. Seizing the city would mean splitting Taiwan in half, isolating major defensive units in the north from those in the south. By virtue of its infrastructure and location, Taichung offers an attacker tremendous logistical benefits. The beaches are not suitable for landing thousands of troops, but there is a chance that the nearby river deltas might be used as a rough substitute.[325]

Two hours further south by car takes one down to Tainan. This mid-sized city has the transportation trinity. Tainan's sprawling seafront, Golden Beach, is near an airport and seaport, both logistical hubs. While farther away from the Chinese mainland than other possible landing zones, PLA writings note that Tainan has served as an entry point in the past for both Dutch and Chinese colonialists.[326] It is anticipated that by seizing Tainan and swinging southeast, the PLA could threaten the command post at Qishan, the ROC Army's southern nerve center.[327]

In spite of the operational advantages that may accrue from landing at Tainan, any campaign anchored here could risk becoming bogged down in a long war of attrition. Tainan's beaches lay in close proximity to dense areas of urban sprawl and are boxed in by salt flats, hills, and jungle. Tainan should be regarded as a likely, but still challenging, point of attack. Linyuan Beach, which is located south of the large port city of Kaohsiung, is another option. Although close to Kaohsiung International Airport and the island's largest harbor, the enormous petro-chemical complexes near Linyuan would make it a hellish place to land and fight.

Perhaps even less likely would be attacks on the far southern tip of Taiwan's western plain, at the rural town of Fangliao. This is where Taiwanese marines train. It has the tactically splendid Jialutang Beach, but there are no large airfields or ports nearby that could be stormed. Troops landed here would have to fight up through the sprawling Kaohsiung suburbs with no prospect of cutting off any major defensive formations along the way. Fangliao is simply too far away from high value targets to be considered a strategic place to land in force.

On the northeastern coast of Taiwan, the sparkling beaches outside Keelung could easily accommodate amphibious landings. They are relatively lightly defended and near a mega port. On the other hand, Keelung lacks an airport and the rugged natural geography surrounding the area is a defender's dream. The sandy bays at Jinshan, Wanli, and Fulong are surrounded by hills. The terrain would not allow for building up a major landing zone and blitzing inland, except perhaps with light forces, easily halted and crushed outside Taipei.

To the south of Keelung lays the Yilan plain, coastal flats famous for their hot springs and single malt whiskey. The port of Su'ao is close at hand, featuring a naval base nestled inside a dramatic and well-protected harbor. Yilan's geography would make it an excellent place to land but an awful place to establish a major landing zone. The entire area is locked in by imposing mountains, and the serviceable highways into Taipei wind over fragile bridges, across cliffs, and through long tunnel systems. These routes would become deathtraps for any attacking army moving through them. The roads from Yilan to the Taipei could be defended, or fatally severed, with very few troops much like the "Hot Gates" of Thermopylae.[328]

From the perspective of Chinese military experts, there are simply no good places to land on Taiwan with a large enough force to quickly steamroll into Taipei.[329] Overall, Taiwan's 770-mile-long coastline is remarkably unsuitable for amphibious operations. The number of invasion beaches is shrinking. There are fourteen left. The shores of Taoyuan and Tainan are almost certainly the best options open to PLA generals, but they each have many dangers associated with them. These are heavily populated lowland areas, overlooked by hills. They have each been well studied and well fortified. Taiwan's military has all manner of mines and obstacles piled up in bunkers nearby, ready to deploy on short notice. Mobile tank brigades and massed infantry could overwhelm and obliterate Chinese skirmishers as they approached and landed. The beaches, airports, and harbors along Taiwan's west coast would be formidable targets to attack, but they would still be better than alternative east coast landing sites. The PLA's architects of war must choose the best of their bad options.

THE CHINESE INVASION THREAT

Potential landing zones, with pros and cons for amphibious operations*

Jinshan
25 miles to Taipei*, 120 miles to Pingtan, PRC****
Pro: Excellent beaches and harbor facilities and best proximity to Taipei
Con: No airfield, local roads can be easily severed, and terrain unsuited for building up and maneuvering forces inland

Taoyuan
30 miles to Taipei, 100 miles to Pingtan, PRC
Pro: Suitable beaches and harbor facilities, and island's largest airport, with ample room to build up and maneuver forces inland and close proximity to PRC staging areas and best access to Taipei
Con: Extremely well defended

Yilan
40 miles to Taipei, 135 miles to Pingtan, PRC
Pro: Suitable beaches and harbor, lightly defended, with ample room to build up forces; however,
Con: No airfield and extremely poor wartime access to Taipei and other cities

---

*   This list does not represent every possible landing zone on Taiwan. Others might be considered by the PLA, but these are the most likely

**   All distances measured along major roads using Google Maps and approximate. Actual travel distance in Taiwan during war would be circuitous and far longer due to traffic gridlock, obstacle emplacements, military checkpoints, and demolition of certain sections of the transportation infrastructure.

*** All distances measured point-to-point using Google Maps and approximate. Actual distances across the Taiwan Strait would be longer because ships would not take direct routes. They would have to maneuver around islands, sandbars, minefields, reefs, and other obstacles.

Hsinchu
53 miles to Taipei, 85 miles to Pingtan, PRC
Pro: Good airfield, fair harbor facilities, and closest proximity to PRC staging areas
Con: Unsuitable beaches, limited room to build up and maneuver forces inland, and very well defended

Taichung
105 miles to Taipei, 100 miles to Pingtan, PRC
Pro: Large airfield and harbor, with ample room to build up and maneuver forces inland, and close proximity to PRC
Con: Unsuitable beaches, large urban sprawl, and well defended

Chuoshui Delta
135 miles to Taipei, 120 miles to Pingtan, PRC
Pro: Ample room to build up and maneuver forces inland, and lightly defended
Con: Unsuitable beaches, no airfield and no harbor, and surrounded by mud flats

Tainan
195 miles to Taipei, 180 miles to Dongshan, PRC
Pro: Suitable beaches, large airfield, good harbor facilities, and some room to build up and maneuver forces inland
Con: Well defended and far from PRC staging areas

Kaohsiung (Linyuan)
225 miles to Taipei, 190 miles to Xiamen, PRC
Pro: Semi-suitable beaches, nearby island's best seaport and second best airport
Con: Little room to build up and maneuver forces inland, well defended, and far from PRC

Fangliao

250 miles to Taipei, 215 miles to Xiamen, PRC

Pro: Best beaches, with ample room to build up and maneuver inland

Con: No airport or harbor, and far from island's main cities and PRC staging areas

Timing the Attack

The next big question to consider is when Z-Day might be. There are many important factors influencing when amphibious assaults would be scheduled. Of these, weather is the most important. Taiwan would be difficult to invade for a number of naturally occurring reasons that have been identified by PLA analysts, who have spent decades monitoring the patterns of local winds, waves, currents, tides, rains, and fog. Their internal writings express what they see as a forlorn conclusion: Mother Nature is on Taiwan's side of the fight.[330]

The Taiwan Strait is 80 miles across at its narrowest point, from Fujian Province's Pingtan Island to Taiwan's Hsinchu Harbor, and 255 miles across at its widest opening. From north to south, the Strait is around 230 miles long.[331] The island of Taiwan features 258 mountains that are over 9,800 feet in elevation.[332] These are knitted together on an island that is 245 miles long and 90 miles across at its widest point.[333] Nowhere in East Asia are mountains so tall and so close to a large body of water.[334] This concentration of extraordinarily high peaks in a relatively small area creates a wind tunnel through the Taiwan Strait that exacerbates other weather effects.

During the sweltering summer months, powerful wind currents channel an explosive mixture of tropical air up from the Philippine Sea. Storms are born and fed, getting bigger and more powerful until they make landfall on Taiwan, often in the form of typhoons. In an average year, six typhoons will strike Taiwan, but some years see as many as nine.[335] In winter, the air currents around Taiwan reverse course, and cold air masses blow down from Siberia, crossing Mongolia and China before arriving. Squalls rip across the Taiwan Strait, winds screaming. From late October until the middle of March, weather in the Strait is so foul it regularly grounds civil air traffic and delays passenger ships.

The trees that manage to grow on the Penghu Islands in the middle of the Strait are an indicator of operational risk. While most trees grow upwards, these grow outwards. Over time they become extraordinarily low and wide, having evolved this way to survive. The winds are so strong that any tree that grows too tall is quickly uprooted. Farming is difficult because topsoil blows away as soon as the land is tilled.[336] Most of these islands are barren, having had most of their foliage stripped away. Sparse vegetation clings to exposed rocks. The winds affect the waves too, sometimes making them gigantic.

The waves in the Taiwan Strait are so high that Chinese military studies advise their readers that amphibious landing craft would be completely unable to operate for much of the year. PLA writings assess that the Strait has militarily significant waves 97 percent of the year, with average sea states between level four and level seven. Level four waves means that waves are between four and eight feet high. The implication of this is that weapons aboard Chinese landing ships and torpedo boats would be unlikely to hit their targets, if not completely useless. Level seven waves are between 20 and 30 feet high, conditions that make even the operation of large warships like destroyers difficult. In winter, the waves are the worst, but summer brings only temporary periods of improvement. In August and September, typhoons can generate sea states as bad as they can possibly get, up to level nine (waves 46 feet and higher).[337]

As the seasons change and the weather turns, freak waves can roll past that could easily flip heavily loaded invasion ships.[338] During the spring and fall, it would be relatively smooth sailing, but often still just choppy enough to make it difficult for groups of landing craft to maintain a steady heading for beach assaults. There are concerns that as troops disembarked from their larger ships to board small landing craft, seasickness would sap them of their ability to fight. According to one PLA study, "Sailors and boarding personnel could easily suffer from seasickness. This will reduce and weaken their combat power."[339] The rocking of vessels would have additional consequences, greatly reducing the precision of naval gunnery. As such, the study assesses that, "It could be difficult to effectively support landing units (with naval gunfire) as they fought to beaches and moved ashore."[340]

Other dangers are present for the PLA that go well beyond the weather. High tide and low tide along China's side of the Strait are regular and predicable, but uneven. Tides change three hours earlier in the north than in the south, and the average surface difference between high and low tide is 15 feet. According to Chinese military writings, this means that troops are best loaded aboard ships at the high-water mark, and vessels must generally enter and exit their ports at the low-water mark to make this happen in an orderly fashion. Organizing, assembling, and loading amphibious ships is therefore complicated by the tides.

The tides along Taiwan's coast can be powerful and erratic. PLA writings note that northwestern Taiwan has semi-diurnal tides. In other words, they have a cyclical period of 12 hours and 25 minutes, half a lunar day (the time it takes the earth to rotate once relative to the moon). A typical lunar day of 24 hours and 50 minutes will see two high tides and two low tides. In stark contrast, southwestern Taiwan has either diurnal tides or irregular tides. Areas with diurnal tidal cycles will experience one high tide and one low tide per lunar day, and irregular tides, as their name suggests, tend to be erratic and difficult to predict. The tidal ranges along the west coast of Taiwan can be over 14 feet, or as little as little as one foot. The average surface difference between high tide and low tide is eight feet, but it varies greatly depending on the exact location.[341]

Chinese military writings state that the tides would be one of the main considerations taken into account when selecting Z-Day. The textbook approach they offer is to schedule an invasion on a date when the tides along Taiwan's coast would be at their monthly peak, making beaches smaller so that troops could surge out of their landing craft closer to beach exits and the distances they would have to cross over open sand would be reduced. This way, it is anticipated fewer would be mowed down by machine gun fire as they dashed inland.[342] Pre-invasion obstacle clearing operations are expected to take place at the low tide mark, when most of the traps were exposed and sticking out of the water. Zero Hour would be several hours later, during the rising tide so that landing craft could beach themselves ashore to unload troops and later get back into the water.[343] However, researchers at Chinese National Key Laboratories note it is difficult to accurately model local tidal behavior.[344] If their predictions were off, the invasion could end up being scheduled for an inopportune time, with potentially disastrous results. Even assuming the PLA's estimates proved accurate, north-south variations along Taiwan's coast make it improbable that a time could be found when conditions were optimal for landing at multiple points on the island simultaneously.

Water currents flowing through the Strait represent another serious problem that Chinese war planners must face. Like the tidal cycles, the currents around Taiwan are complex and erratic. While not all observed phenomenon can be scientifically understood, there are two good explanations for why the currents here are so peculiar. The winds and tidal forces powerfully affect the currents, and the unusual topography of the sea bottom has an additional impact. Nonetheless, much mystery continues to surround the Taiwan Strait's currents, and less rational explanations are sometimes given for their strange behavior. According to local legend, the Strait is a "Black Ditch" haunted by the multitudes who have drowned over the centuries trying to sail to Taiwan from China. Superstitious believers claim that local currents are not currents at all, but rather the hands of sea demons, who malevolently drag their victims down into the afterlife.[345]

While no evidence exists for such claims, they may one day ring true for Chinese amphibious troops ordered to storm Taiwan. PLA studies express concern that erratic currents could wreak havoc on Z-Day landings. They state that currents may push small landing craft off course at speeds up to five knots, sending them either northward or southward along the coast, depending on the water conditions. As a result, troop ships may find it difficult to get to their assigned rally points offshore. It is anticipated that the first wave to go in for assaults might drift outside of safe lanes and crash into each other. Tangled and struggling to maneuver, hapless vessels could touch off sea mines or get ripped apart by obstacles. Disabled boats could create hazardous roadblocks to attackers lined up behind them. Those who made it to shore could find themselves on the wrong beach sector, something that might throw off carefully laid landing plans and invite confusion and defeat.[346]

One PLA source succinctly summarizes the challenges Mother Nature poses to invasion in the following words:

> It is difficult to grasp the right time for landing operations. The tides inside the (Taiwan Strait) area, the direction of the currents, the size of the waves, and the strength of the winds would all have a complex and ever-changing impact on the situation; so too would the shape of the coast, its composition, height, and steepness. Factors such as strong winds, large waves, thick fog, torrential rains, low clouds, and other unfavorable weather conditions would make it extremely difficult to fire, break through obstacles, and capture beaches during the landing phase. All these considerations would affect the time chosen to make landings. They would even impact our overall success or failure.[347]

To cope with this situation, PLA writings call for invasion fleets to use rain, fog, and low clouds to hide their movements along China's coast, and for commanders to select a number of possible Z-Days and maintain flexible plans, keeping the Taiwanese guessing at the invasion date for as long as possible.[348]

According to PLA studies, weather conditions on an ideal Z-Day would be clear. The sea states would be at level five (8 to 13 foot waves) or less. The best time to begin landing on Taiwan would be a few hours before high tide, preferably on a weekend or national holiday to catch ROC Army generals with their guard down. In theory, the PLA could attempt landing during foul weather to maximize surprise, but this would be a dangerous path to take. Effective air and naval support in such conditions would be virtually nonexistent, and the landing forces would have to make do without covering fire. An even worse problem is that amphibious tanks and landing craft could easily be swamped or capsized.[349]

Invasion armadas would almost certainly be supported by large numbers of submarines. One feature of the Strait that does work for the PLA is that the level of background noise is much higher than in the open ocean depths, greatly improving the odds that Chinese submarines could avoid sonar detection as they sneaked up on Taiwan. According to one PLA study, "Conditions here, tactically speaking, are good for making surprise attacks ... and near Kaohsiung waters get deep, with many underwater canyons. This is beneficial for our submarine operations."[350] On the other hand, the same study notes that underwater operations may be perilous because the waters are too shallow and the sea bottom is littered with ship wrecks, sandbars, and hidden reefs. As such, it would be all too easy to run submarines aground on the bottom and difficult to remain concealed. Moreover, Taiwan is believed to be fully capable of laying defensive mine perimeters that could make it dangerous to operate in the deeper waters near its coast.[351]

When no storms are present, the winds and waves in the Strait are relatively mild from late March to late October, and much more suitable for amphibious operations. However, heavy seasonal rain storms called "Plum Rains" fall from May to late June. Tropical storms and typhoons begin to arrive on a regular basis in July, and they don't typically die down until the end of September.[352] Given these limitations, PLA materials express a belief that there are only two realistic time windows open for invading Taiwan. The first is from late March to the end of April. The second is from late September to the end of October.[353] During these two periods, winds are usually light, and waves low.

The weather situation is regarded as far from ideal. April tends to be very foggy and rainy, with only a small number of clear days, and October could be marred by a late season typhoon. To be successful, a cross-Strait campaign would take a considerable amount of time to carry out. The PLA would have to move an enormous army across water, including hundreds of thousands (if not millions) of troops, thousands of tanks, artillery guns, and armored vehicles, and mountains of food, water, ammunition, and supplies. Time would not be on their side, especially if the Strait got completely fogged in or an unseasonably late storm arrived and ruined plans.[354] Each spring and fall has approximately four weeks of suitable weather. According to PLA assessments, these time windows are when Chinese authorities would probably have to plan the invasion.[355]

Weather Factors and Suitability for Amphibious Operations

January
Gales, high winds/waves, low clouds.
Poor suitability.

February
Gales, high winds/waves, heavy fog.*
Poor suitability.

March
High winds/waves early in the month, subsiding later, heavy fog throughout.
Variable suitability.

April
Heavy fog.
Good suitability.

May
Plum rains, heavy fog.
Variable suitability.

June
Plum rains, fog, strong currents.**
Poor suitability.

July
Typhoons, variable waves, strong currents.

---

* Fog is a major operational factor from February 15 to June 15, with the worst fog in morning hours of April and May. Overall, average visibility is 2km in spring, 4km in winter, and 10km in summer.

** Currents in the Strait tend to be strong in summer and weak in winter.

Poor suitability.

August
Typhoons, variable waves, strong currents.
Poor suitability.

September
Typhoons, variable waves, strong currents.
Variable suitability.

October
High winds/waves later in the month.
Good suitability.

November
Gales, high winds/waves, low clouds.
Poor suitability.

December
Gales, high winds/waves, low clouds.
Poor suitability.

Sources: PLA's Course Book on Taiwan Strait Military Geography, Research on Port Landing Operations, and Research on Joint Tactical Thought.

Participating Units

Long before China's high command had decided where and when to attack, they would decide the question of who (which units) would join the attack. According to PLA writings, the invasion of Taiwan would require an all-hands-on-deck approach, with each service and branch involved. The military would be greatly aided by mobilized civilians, pressed into action by the authorities. The ground forces would have the leading role, taking and holding Taiwan's territory. The key operational headquarters would likely be those at Nanjing, where the Eastern Theater Command is located, and Fuzhou, where the Army Headquarters, under theater command, has recently been moved. The Eastern Theater Command, while prime, would be heavily augmented by the Southern Theater Command, in Guangzhou. The army's technical reconnaissance bureaus in Nanjing, Fuzhou, and Guangzhou would provide intelligence support.[356]

It is generally assumed that the Joint Island Attack Campaign would have two major waves. On Z-Day, the first wave would storm the coast and seize lodgments ashore. The second wave would build up the landing zones and slog into the island interior. It is anticipated that the PLA would seek to ferry around a million total combat troops across, but could opt to send as few as 300,000 to 400,000, depending on the circumstances. In any event, China would commit all of its best-trained and most capable forces to the offensive. The bulk of the PLA, with the exception of units held back for border defense and internal security missions, would cross the Taiwan Strait. The first wave across would be limited in size and scale. The second would be massive.[357]

Chinese army units are currently divided into group armies (30,000 to 60,000 men), divisions (5,000 to 10,000), brigades (3,000 to 6,000), and regiments (1,000 to 2,800). The total number of personnel in each unit varies widely depending on whether they are infantry, artillery, armor, or anti-aircraft artillery (air defense) units, and depending on whether or not they are manned at full-strength.[358] Units that specialize in amphibious assault, helicopter assault, and special operations would be the first to cross the Strait.

Unconfirmed media reporting suggests that the PLA is in the process of establishing new army amphibious units.[359] Evidence is lacking, but if true, that could greatly increase the number of troops potentially available for the first wave. Although each unit's combat strength and transport needs are unknown, we might estimate the total army contribution, as it currently exists for this mission, might be anywhere from 20,000 to 68,000 troops, depending on the assumptions one used.[360] In any event, numbers that are low today are likely to grow in the coming years.

Army units would be joined by paratroopers who fall under the command of the PLA Air Force, and marines who are commanded by the PLA Navy. The 15th Airborne Corps in Xiaogan has three airborne divisions: the 43rd in Kaifeng, the 44th in Guangshui, and the 45th in Wuhan. Each division has around 10,000 personnel, for a total of around 30,000 men. The PLA Air Force's airborne units utilize some helicopters in addition to planes for delivering paratroopers.[361] At least one or two of these divisions would probably be selected for parachute and helicopter assaults against Taiwanese airbases and ports on Z-Day. Others would follow close behind. The PLA Navy commands two marine brigades, the 1st Marine Brigade and the 164th Marine Brigade in Zhanjiang, for a total of around 12,000 marines.[362]

While speculative, the first wave to hit the outer islands and Taiwan's beaches, ports, and airbases would most likely be comprised of the units seen in in the table below, many of whom have long been specially trained for this operation.[363]

First Wave of Taiwan Assault Force and Probable Missions*

1st Amphibious Mechanized Inf. Division
Garrison: Hangzhou, Zhejiang
Amphibious assault against northern Taiwan.

5th Army Aviation Regiment
Garrison: Nanjing, Jiangsu
Air assault against northern Taiwan.

12th Group Army's SOF Brigade
Garrison: Somewhere in Jiangsu Province
Air assault against northern Taiwan.

---

* Note that unit designations are current as of 2016, but undergoing changes as part of PLA reorganization.

31st Group Army's Amphibious Armor Brigade
Garrison: Zhangzhou, Fujian
Amphibious assault against outer islands and/or northern Taiwan.

10th Army Aviation Regiment
Garrison: Hui'an, Fujian
Helicopter assault against outer islands and/or northern Taiwan.

31st Group Army's SOF Brigade
Garrison: Quanzhou, Fujian
Helicopter assault against outer islands and/or northern Taiwan.

26th Group Army's SOF Brigade
Garrison: Tai'an, Shandong
Helicopter assault against northern Taiwan.

7th Army Aviation Regiment
Garrison: Liaocheng, Shandong
Air assault against northern Taiwan.

124th Amphibious Mechanized Inf. Division
Garrison: Boluo, Guangdong
Amphibious assault against southern Taiwan.

6th Army Aviation Regiment
Garrison: Foshan, Guangdong
Helicopter assault against southern Taiwan.

42nd Group Army's SOF Brigade
Garrison: Guangzhou, Guangdong
Helicopter assault against southern Taiwan.

1st Marine Brigade
Garrison: Zhanjiang, Guangdong

Amphibious assault against outer islands and/or Taiwan.

164th Marine Brigade
Garrison: Zhanjiang, Guangdong
Amphibious assault against outer islands and/or Taiwan.

43rd Airborne Division
Garrison: Kaifeng, Henan
Parachute assault against outer islands and/or Taiwan.

44th Airborne Division
Garrison: Guangshui, Henan
Parachute assault against outer islands and/or Taiwan.

45th Airborne Division
Garrison: Wuhan, Hubei
Parachute assault against outer islands and/or Taiwan.

The above list is based on Taiwanese assessments. Unit data from Dennis J. Blasko, *The Chinese Army Today*, pp. 97–103; and *The PLA as an Organization: Reference Volume v2.0* (Fairfax, VA: Defense Group Inc. 2015), pp. 244 & 322.

The critical limiting factor would be the number of available planes, helicopters, and ships. Given their leading role in a Taiwan invasion scenario, Chinese amphibious units (and their lift capabilities) will likely grow as the PLA continues to reorganize for the purpose of improving its joint operational capabilities. China would not attack Taiwan with the force it currently fields, but rather a much stronger future one.[364]

Numerous artillery units would be selected for shelling Taiwan's outer islands, while others would embark aboard ships to supplement naval gunfire. Those most likely to be chosen for the mission appear to be the 1st Group Army's 9th Artillery Division in Wuxi, the 31st Group Army's 3rd Artillery Brigade in Quanzhou, and the 42nd Group Army's 1st Artillery

Division in Qujiang. Aside from traditional artillery guns, some of these units are equipped with long-range rocket launchers capable of firing across the Taiwan Strait. They would be further augmented by artillery units from all over China.

The PLA maintains a number of subordinate logistical units that would be involved in the transport of troops and equipment, moving them first to staging areas, and, in some cases, across the Taiwan Strait. These include the ship transport groups in Shanghai, Nanjing, Zhuhai, Qiongshan, Dongshan, and Xiamen, and the reserve ship transport group in Zhangzhou.[365] Others that would probably be selected for early action would be the chemical defense regiment in Nanjing and the reserve chemical defense regiment in Shenzhen, in addition to a large number of air defense and coastal defense brigades.

Infantry and tank divisions, most likely under the 1st, 31st, 42nd, 12th, 41st, and 26th group armies would be landed once beachheads, airheads, and ports had been seized. Depending on the size of the envisioned invasion force, the PLA could draw from the 54th Group Army in Henan, the 65th Group Army in Hebei, the 39th Group Army in Liaoning, and possibly others even farther afield. There are many army divisions and brigades across China that specialize in urban, mountain, and jungle warfare, but which could only arrive on Taiwan after landing zones were secured. Engineers would be essential to the success of the campaign. Elements of the 31st Pontoon Bridge Brigade in Jiangsu, and the 32nd Pontoon Bridge Brigade in Hubei, might be sent across just after Z-Day. They would be critical for moving units across rivers in Taiwan since most (if not all) bridges would probably be destroyed.[366]

The ground forces would rely on the navy for clearing and maintaining safe lines of communication across the Strait. Naval task forces would attempt to decisively engage Taiwan's navy before the invasion, or hold it at bay during the course of operations. On Z-Day, specialized fleets would have to clear dangerous sea mines and obstacles. Others would have the unenviable mission of deterring or attacking U.S. and Japanese naval forces. The bulk of the Chinese navy, however, would be allocated for transportation, escort, and naval gunfire support duties.

The East Sea Fleet, whose headquarters is in Ningbo, would have the leading naval role. Major bases under its purview include those at Shanghai, Zhoushan, and Fuzhou. Other important bases are located at Wenzhou and Xiamen. The East Sea Fleet commands the 5th Landing Ship Flotilla in Shanghai, the 22nd Submarine Flotilla in Ningbo, the 42nd Submarine Flotilla in Xiangshan, and the 3rd and 6th destroyer flotillas in Zhoushan.[367] There is an important landing craft unit in Ningbo, and escort ship units in Wenzhou, Pingtan, and Ningde.[368] Fleet aviation bases that would support air operations against Taiwan's fleet, and possibly the U.S. 7th Fleet, are at Ningbo, Shanghai, Taizhou, Feidong, Ningbo, Changzhou, and Yiwu.[369]

The East Sea Fleet would be supported by the South Sea Fleet, headquartered at Zhanjiang and home to major amphibious assault vessels, landing craft groups, and two marine brigades. Other important naval bases of the South Sea Fleet include those at Guangzhou, Shantou, Hong Kong, Yulin, and Sanya. In addition, Hong Kong houses a small number of landing craft, escort ships, and transport ships.[370] The South Sea Fleet's aviation units are headquartered at Haikou, with major bases at Jialai, Guiping (bomber), Lingshui, Ledong, and Sanya.[371]

China's third naval fleet, the North Sea Fleet, based in Qingdao, would probably keep most of its assets in defensive positions afloat, protecting the sea approaches to Beijing. Nonetheless, it seems very possible that the North Sea Fleet could contribute some units to the Taiwan invasion campaign. This might include H-6 bombers from Dalian; Y-8 early warning and reconnaissance planes from Laiyang; submarines, minesweepers, and minelayers from Lushun; and landing craft, logistics ships, and submarines from Qingdao.[372]

The army and navy would rely on the air force for air defense. The PLA Air Force would have two cardinal missions: to protect coastal bases and staging areas from Taiwanese and American missile strikes and air raids, and to carry out bombing operations against Taiwan, softening it up for amphibious assaults. PLA Air Force assets could also be allocated for offensive operations against American and Japanese bases in the Western Pacific. Major air force command posts that would almost certainly be involved include those at Fuzhou, Shanghai,

Zhangzhou, Wuhan, and Nanning.[373] Each of these five command posts would probably oversee at least one radar brigade, one surface-to-air missile and/or anti-aircraft artillery division (or brigade), and one fighter division.[374] The East Theater Command appears to have two fighter divisions, one ground attack division, one bomber division, and one special aviation division (airborne). The South Theater Command appears to have three fighter divisions, one bomber division, and one transport division.[375] These would be further augmented by air force units from elsewhere in China.

Fighter interceptors and air defense batteries would rely heavily on China's coastal radar surveillance infrastructure for conducting air defense operations. From north to south, critical PLA air surveillance units in theater are the Third Radar Brigade in Shanghai, the Second Radar Brigade in Ningbo (Navy), the Fourth Radar Brigade in Fuzhou, the 12th Radar Brigade in Zhangzhou, the 19th Radar Regiment in Shantou, the 20th Radar Regiment in Foshan, the First Radar Brigade in Nanning, and the Third Radar Brigade in Haikou (Navy).[376]

The PLA Rocket Force would be responsible for striking Taiwan's most critical targets with conventional theater missiles, suppressing air defense networks and paralyzing the island's communications. Although the capability exists, there are no indications that would suggest Beijing might consider launching any of its nuclear weapons at Taiwan. The PLA Rocket Force's 52 Base, headquartered in Huangshan, oversees at least six conventionally armed ballistic missile brigades, located throughout southeast China. The 52 Base would notionally be augmented by the 53 Base and 55 Base, headquartered in Kunming and Huaihua, respectively. These command both ground launched cruise missile brigades and ballistic missile brigades.[377]

Military police units would have important roles to play supporting the invasion campaign. It is standard practice in the PRC to deploy internal security forces in the event of an emergency to ensure regime stability and local control. The People's Armed Police has mobile divisions for rapidly responding to major incidents and unrest. At least three such units in southeast China would be directly involved in a Taiwan contingency.

They are the 8690 Unit in Yixing, the 8710 Unit in Putian, and the 8720 Unit in Wuxi.[378] Each province maintains its own People's Armed Police unit, approximately the size of a light infantry division, to support PLA operations. In wartime, it can be expected that provincial units in southeast China would be bolstered by rapid reaction divisions arriving from all over the country. These units would provide local security, traffic management, and population control, allowing main force PLA units to focus on their principal missions.[379]

Military police units would be greatly augmented by the militia. The paramilitary militia, different than the PLA and the People's Armed Police, is the third arm of the CCP's armed forces. The militia provides wartime support to the PLA and police operations. Personnel strength is uncertain, but the militia may number up to eight million total personnel, over half of whom appear to be tasked with air defense, engineering, chemical defense, communications, and network security. The militia has additional units that specialize in camouflage, concealment, and deception, as well as electronic and cyber warfare. PLA units rely heavily on the militia for transportation and logistics support when away from their home garrisons.[380]

The maritime militia would directly support military operations against Taiwan. Civilian vessels that would be mobilized vary widely, from fishing boats to ferries and from cargo container ships to oilers. They would greatly assist the PLA Navy transport and succor the invasion forces. All vessels in major ports across Taiwan that are over 50 tons must register for wartime service with city defense authorities. China's ocean going fishing fleets double as militia units, trained to transport troops during amphibious operations. Other maritime militia units specialize in wartime support operations including reconnaissance, mine laying, minesweeping, sabotage, rescue, and emergency repair. They are further used for replenishing forward positions, and transporting fresh troops, equipment, ammunition, fuel, water, and other supplies.[381]

There are many possible staging areas for units participating in the invasion of Taiwan. Some are directly across the Strait on large offshore islands and inside wide coastal bays. Others are the PRC's major port cities. Potential amphibious staging areas, from north to south, might include

Wenzhou, Ningde, Fuzhou, Haitan/Pingtan Island, Quanzhou, Dongshan, Shantou, and Shanwei. Locations even farther away might also be considered. The following list outlines current port capacities.

Chinese Ports in Theater

Fuzhou
155 miles to Taipei*
35 million tons of foreign trade cargo per year**
3,657 registered transport ships**

Putian
160 miles to Taipei
7 million tons of foreign trade cargo per year
258 registered transport ships

Ningde
170 miles to Taipei
11 million tons of foreign trade cargo per year
926 registered transport ships

Xiaocuo (Meizhou Bay)
175 miles to Taipei
20 million tons of foreign trade cargo per year
549 registered transport ships

---

* Google's mapping tools were used to measure all distances. They are approximate and measured in terms of direct point-to-point travel. They do not represent actual or practical sea lines of communication, which would be longer. To calculate distances from each port to landing beaches near Taipei, subtract 15 miles. No subtraction is needed for Tainan because it sits directly on the coast.

** Source: *China Port Authority Yearbook 2014* [中国口岸年鉴2014] (Beijing: China Port Authority Press, 2014), pp. 38–40.

Quanzhou

185 miles to Taipei
5 million tons of foreign trade cargo per year
4,000 registered transport ships

Wenzhou

210 miles to Taipei
5 million tons of foreign trade cargo per year
262 registered transport ships

Xiamen

220 miles to Taipei (170 miles to Tainan)
68 million tons of foreign trade cargo per year
23,725 registered transport ships

Zhangzhou

250 miles to Taipei (195 miles to Tainan)
11 million tons of foreign trade cargo per year
859 registered transport ships

Shantou

330 miles to Taipei (225 miles to Tainan)
6 million tons of foreign trade cargo per year
3,016 registered transport ships

Ningbo

335 miles to Taipei
198 million tons of foreign trade cargo per year
7,651 registered transport ships

Zhoushan

345 miles to Taipei
108 million tons of foreign trade cargo per year
4,690 registered transport ships

Shanwei

420 miles to Taipei (310 miles to Tainan)

1.5 million tons of foreign trade cargo per year

532 registered transport ships

Shanghai

430 miles to Taipei

273 million tons of foreign trade cargo per year

25,113 registered transport ships

Source: *China Port Authority Yearbook 2014* 中国口岸年鉴2014 (Beijing: China Port Authority Press, 2014), pp. 38–40.

As a general matter, groups of transport ships and their naval escorts would arrive in theater from the PLA Navy's major bases north and the south of Taiwan, the two most important of which are Ningbo and Zhanjiang. Vessels would notionally steam to rendezvous points directly across from Taiwan, hugging the coastline to stay under the protective umbrella of shore based air defenses. They would load troops and their equipment just before Z-Day to minimizing the time large army units were at sea and vulnerable. Once ready, they would gather into great armadas for the plunge across the Taiwan Strait.

An alternative approach might see assault forces embarked at greater distances from Taiwan, and, after steaming to rally points, form up for more direct lines of attack. This would increase the time forces spent afloat, and therefore raise their risk of being intercepted and sunk in transit. But it might be judged safer than operating in ports within range of Taiwan's missiles and rocket artillery. Operating from greater distance could also lend itself to greater tactical surprise. Gathering first wave forces and launching them from Wenzhou, for example, might be deemed to be safer than attempting operations from Fuzhou. Once Taiwan's outer islands were seized or suppressed, and lodgments were secured on Taiwan, staging areas closer to the fight could spring into action in support of the second wave.

Intelligence Problems

Good intelligence would be vital for deciding who should attack, where they should attack, and when the attacks should begin. But getting quality intelligence sources, correctly analyzing what they say or mean, and getting the final product to the right decision maker at the right time is exceedingly hard. As a result, military officers the world over complain about the intelligence they receive on the enemy and the overall situation. They feel they never get enough intelligence, and the quality of what they do get is never satisfactory. Their appetite for perfect intelligence is understandable. In war, decisions might have to be made by them that, if wrong, could result in their own death or the death of those they are responsible for leading.

In the case of generals responsible for war planning in authoritarian states like the PRC, the very survival of their regime, their families, and their way of life may be at stake. Many of their decisions rely on intelligence, which can be defined as an organized and honest presentation of what is known for a fact, what is thought to be known with some level of certainty, and what is known to be unknown. The last of the three, though naturally undesirable, is just as important as the others. A competent military will strive to identify what it does not know, and then keep that knowledge secret in order to hide its weakness while it seeks to remedy the problem.

It is sometimes wrongly assumed that China has flawless intelligence and knows all of Taiwan's secrets. If true, the PLA would have a great advantage and a much easier time planning the invasion of Taiwan. The reality is that Chinese officers do not feel they have adequate intelligence, let alone perfect intelligence, on Taiwan. This sentiment is expressed in internal publications which offer their readers impressive levels of detail and demonstrate the diligent efforts Chinese military analysts have paid to studying their target. In spite of the vast time and money spent on exhaustive research, they are evidently distressed by how much they still do not know, or by how much they think they might know but cannot confirm, or by what they know today that could change tomorrow.

The strategic, operational, and tactical intelligence problems associated with preparations for the invasion of Taiwan are significant. PLA writings shed light on some of the intelligence problems that confront war planners. The first problem is finding targets to hit and deciding which of them are the most important since munitions stocks are finite. Chinese planners have assembled a master list of military and civilian targets on Taiwan which would have to be neutralized by precision bombing before amphibious landings could be considered a viable option. The target list was reportedly still incomplete as of 2008, but it already included "over ten target categories and 1,000 individual targets," making it dangerously bloated.[382]

By way of comparison, internal PLA materials note that in Operation Desert Storm the U.S. military's target list "proposed around 600 individual targets, of which, around 50 were ultimately selected for heavy strikes."[383] The excessively large number of targets on Taiwan is apparently a serious concern, since it took America 42 consecutive days and nights of intensive bombardment to achieve its objectives against Iraq. In the PLA's war planning circles, this appears to have begged the question: How could we possibly eliminate nearly twice as many targets on Taiwan, in far less time, and with far less effective weapons, especially when the Taiwanese are far better prepared than the Iraqis ever were?

Their answer seems to have been to whittle down the target list, finding and focusing only on centers of gravity. However, PLA sources express concern that Taiwan has invested heavily in camouflage, concealment, and deception operations to protect its most important facilities and military units from being targeted. Taiwanese camouflage reportedly helps fixed targets blend into surrounding environments, with living foliage and mountainous terrain used to cover them up and conceal their locations from overhead imagery. When effective, they may keep Chinese planners unsure of where they are located. The following lines illustrate and summarize the PLA's problem:

Although maps, aerial photography, and top-level intelligence reports can be used for assessing the enemy's defense deployments, terrain, and movements ... getting intelligence on the enemy will be a serious problem before the war. During the war, time will be pressing, and the enemy's concealment and camouflage will be limiting factors. It is not easy to find and expose the enemy's defensive deployments in the mountains.... The enemy has the ability to get information from the sea and the air, and has supporting firepower, so there is no way for us to conduct close-in aerial reconnaissance operations to study the terrain. It is difficult to completely grasp the actual situation regarding the terrain. It is difficult to assess in detail and judge the details of the enemy's situation inside the island's interior.[384]

A related problem is that Taiwanese combat engineers have spent decades digging tunnels, constructing and reinforcing elaborate underground facilities whose exact details and dimensions appear unknown. This system of defense works is reportedly vast and especially dense around potential landing zones along the coast. It is notable for long tunnels that connect defensive bunkers and firing positions. These defensive works are blended into the surrounding environment through the use of natural and synthetic camouflage, enabling the ROC Army to hide stores of pre-positioned weapons, ammunition, mines, obstacles, and supplies. Chinese military analysts expect that these concealed defense works could create "kill boxes" (ambush sites) for mowing down attackers.[385]

Taiwan's coastal defenses are considered the foremost targeting challenge facing the PLA. Prior to an amphibious assault, Chinese officers would need to know where to strike along Taiwan's coast and where not to. It is anticipated that theater-level headquarters and tactical landing units would demand a complete intelligence picture of Taiwanese army movements and their positions along the coast. They would want details on coastal bases and defense works, including the exact locations of missile batteries, artillery guns, beach obstacles, and minefields.[386] However, the PLA's reconnaissance capabilities are limited, and many of those it does have could fall victim to Taiwanese electronic jamming.[387] The following lines overview the problem:

It is difficult for the Army's traditional optical reconnaissance methods to reach across the sea because of the distance. Radio technical reconnaissance, radar reconnaissance, and surface sensors can easily meet with electronic jamming, making it difficult for them to provide detailed battlefield intelligence. Before the assault, when army landing groups are about to spring into action, time will be extremely tight. It is difficult for the Army's traditional reconnaissance methods to execute complete and detailed battlefield reconnaissance operations against enemy coastal defenses in an extremely short period of time.[388]

Space assets provide the PLA with an alternative means of collecting intelligence on coastal battlefields. But satellites are reportedly tasked with serving the needs of theater commanders, not tactical planners on the front lines, and they are inherently vulnerable to jamming. Moreover, an entire ghost army reportedly exists on Taiwan. Its mission is to confuse and deceive Chinese satellites, convincing attackers to waste finite resources tracking false targets in peacetime and attacking them in wartime. It is believed that Taiwan has built decoy command posts and communications stations for its ghost army, complete with radio arrays designed to realistically mimic real military signal traffic. Key early warning radars are similarly protected by decoys designed to confuse observers and lure attacking missile seekers away from true targets. Dummy tanks, missile launchers, and other mock equipment are believed to be stockpiled across Taiwan and the outer islands.[389]

The ROC Air Force is believed to employ various means to defeat the PLA's intelligence and operational planning communities. Examples include smoke screens that can interfere with targeting systems and high fidelity decoys that mimic runway craters and debris. These assets would reportedly maximize the chance that a targeted airbase runway, once hit and cratered by missiles, could avoid being re-targeted for additional strikes, allowing rapid runway repair teams to return bases to working order. Decoys also exist for tricking bombers. These include defunct fighter planes and air defense guns that can be parked on airbase ramps or in revetments to serve as false targets.[390]

Equipment and Personnel Problems

In addition to flawed intelligence, internal Chinese military writings portray inadequate equipment and weak personnel as reducing their odds of success. According to professional assessments, giant fleets of specialized military transport aircraft and amphibious ships would be ideal for projecting an invasion force of overwhelming size across the Taiwan Strait. Such armadas do not currently exist in China. The PLA's doctrine calls for supplementing the relatively modest military transportation fleet with enormous numbers of civilian aircraft and sea-going vessels.[391] China would reportedly attempt to convert container ships, merchant oiler ships, ferry boats, cargo boats, fishing boats, maritime rescue ships, and even motorized lifeboats for the mission. Wherever possible, PLA planners hope to place artillery guns aboard civilian craft to increase inadequate naval gunfire.[392]

The problem facing the PLA is that civilian vessels are not made for amphibious operations, which are specialized and require specialized equipment. Civilian ships would be difficult to load and unload, and very difficult to coordinate. They could slow military ships down and blow their cover by getting in the way, talking on open radio frequencies, causing accidents, setting off mines, and running into beach obstacles. Poorly trained merchant marines and fishermen could end up unloading crack troops at the wrong spot on the beach or in waters so deep that they drown. Civilian ships are expected to be vulnerable to Taiwanese strikes. Once hit, they would sink quickly because they lack protective armor plating and watertight compartments. In the considered opinion of PLA experts, civilian vessels in China are not suitable for amphibious operations.[393]

Chinese planners foresee difficult challenges in using *ad hoc* jumbles of civilian vessels. One challenge would be communicating in an electronic environment that is expected to be perilous for radios that are not resistant to jamming. Civilian vessels operate on different standard frequencies than the navy, using a wide variety of radios.[394] The PLA could install a large number of military radios at the eleventh hour and offer operator training. However, such activities would almost certainly require more time and communications equipment than are anticipated would be available. Military writings express a belief that shipyards would not be able not produce enough landing craft and convert enough civilian ships in time for the mission. Emergency production and refitting work would be attempted to prepare as many as possible, but capacity bottlenecks are expected.[395]

Civilian ships are slower than naval ships and most would not be accustomed to the sea conditions common to the Taiwan Strait. It is judged that civilian ship captains, as a general rule, would probably be unsuited to the task. In the bureaucratic parlance of the PLA: "Civilian ship crews lack rigorous standardized training. Sailors have low combat quality. It would be difficult for them to satisfy the demands of large fleet formations."[396] The problems associated with moving an entire army across the Strait are so severe PLA planners apparently think that the mission is a hopeless one until they can get an enormous infusion of amphibious vessels and better training. According to one officially sanctioned view, "An (amphibious) army without ships is not an army at all."[397] Another excerpt states the following:

> If we cannot do a better job in solving our operational problem of "getting across," then it is not even worth talking about our landing operation against the main island, let alone our campaign on the main island. If we cannot get the amphibious support problem right in crossing the Strait, then the PLA will have no reliable ability to conduct protracted operations.[398]

For the PLA, the situation is far from an entirely bleak one. Although the quantity and quality of China's amphibious lift platforms are low, the number of planes and helicopters at the military's disposal is anticipated to grow rapidly over time. Aviation has been identified as a potential game-changer for the PLA ground forces. Planners appear to see good prospects for China's dual-use aircraft fleets to help compensate for the lack of suitable landing ships and professional sailors. It is contemplated that militia pilots could land some paratroopers and helicopter assault troops on Taiwan, helping to augment the main ground forces.[399] Nonetheless, for reasons that are not well understood, the PLA continues to under-invest in operational transportation capabilities. Serious gaps exist across the board, including in amphibious landing ship tanks, hovercraft, planes, and helicopters.

Another operational problem is more mental than material. PLA subject matter experts have medically assessed the negative impacts the Taiwan invasion scenario could have on Chinese military personnel. Their research is recorded in an internal study, *Informatized Warfare and Psychological Protection*, written for officers specializing in military medicine and political warfare. It describes the anticipated mental effects of combat on Taiwan, offering a rare glimpse into some of the human factors that are expected to plague the operation.

The first recorded problem is the savage nature of the expected amphibious battlefield. It is anticipated that Chinese troops could suffer seasickness while crossing "bitterly heavy seas" and be exposed to accurate strikes from Taiwanese ships, planes, coastal batteries, and submarines. These are judged as likely to give seaborne troops "extraordinary physical and psychological burdens ... and lead to a lowering of their will to fight."[400] The battlefield ashore is expected to be even more difficult for them. Once they landed on Taiwan, it is anticipated troops would face "the life and death test of ferocious bombing, excessive explosions, and bloody killing ... from start to finish, every moment and throughout the entire landing operation."[401] The authors summarize their assessment regarding the impact the battlefield will have in the following words:

These (battlefield) factors will all quite naturally place an extraordinary set of physical and psychological burdens on our officers and men, who have either not participated in war for many years, or never before. These will create feelings of anxiety, terror, disappointment, and despair, which will lower unit reaction times and the ability to coordinate. Overall psychological problems expected to lower the will to fight include the dissipation or sinking of willpower, fear of combat, combat avoidance, and combat fatigue.[402]

In addition, PLA medical professionals express concern that the sudden and urgent nature of surprise landing operations could create widespread psychological problems for participating units. They write that the average Chinese army outfit, after a long period of training and preparation, will suddenly find itself mobilized for action, transported from home base to an unfamiliar coastal area, then loaded aboard ships, sailed across the Taiwan Strait, landed on beaches, and ordered to quickly fight inland. These units will be exposed to "horrific scenes of carnage, earsplitting shelling, and extraordinarily ferocious combat." Moreover, they will have no chance to rest and recover in the midst of the chaos.[403]

According to the study, conditions such as these have historically caused combat units to experience widespread nervous breakdowns. One example given is a World War II American Army unit on Sicily that opened fire on friendly paratroopers who they mistook to be Germans. Soldiers in the offending unit were later found to have suffered mass hysteria after a long and grueling series of battles which ultimately led them to hallucinate and ignore the paratroopers' friendly uniforms and their other identifying markers. PLA doctors worry that similar tragedies could occur during the invasion of Taiwan.[404]

A further concern relates to the psychological effects of modern precision weaponry. The study anticipates that Taiwan's usage of guided weapons against Chinese forces could lead to mass casualties, and cause those who survived to suffer extreme mental pressure. Losses could be so stunning that Chinese soldiers could "lose their ability to think and express themselves normally and rationally, and lose self control ... participating officers and troops could have mental breakdowns, and abnormal behavior."[405]

Making matters worse, troops could be overwhelmed by a flood of information during the course of operations or experience communication blackouts. Too much information might cause the receiver to experience, "an inability to concentrate, a reduction in good judgment, which if continued could create misunderstandings and lapses." On the other hand, if units had their information systems denied to them by enemy jamming or technical failure, they could "feel an unsettling sense of not knowing who is in charge, and where they fit in, and what they should be doing."[406]

Informatized Warfare and Psychological Protection catalogues other envisioned problems that could reduce PLA combat capabilities during the invasion, summarizing them in the following words:

> During the war, missions could be switched around or changed to meet emergencies that arise. This will make officers and men feel like they are not ready and cannot easily adapt. Operational setbacks, or large numbers of manpower casualties, will make them moody and demoralized. Subordinates and superiors will harbor grudges against each other. Logistics support is not optimal. Officers and men will suffer from extreme hunger, fatigue, and sleeplessness. Their wounds may not receive timely treatment. As a result, their reaction times will be slowed down. They will feel without initiative. This could even generate feelings of despair or isolation.[407]

The study concludes with a warning for readers to watch out for Taiwanese psychological warfare operations. The authors write that both sides will try to destroy the other's morale and reduce their combat power. Both will make countless attempts against the other to shake his resolve and sense of purpose. Both have detailed plans to destroy the other side's "thinking, relationships, and morale," and there is certainly no guarantee that the PLA can win this battle. "During future landing operations, if we do not emphasize the containment of the enemy's 'soft power kill,' our officers and men will be seriously affected psychologically, making the officers and men in some units have ... lapses during action."[408]

Political Problems

Despite the negative effects associated with attempting rapid amphibious operations, there are a number of political reasons why time would be of the essence and the PLA would have to rush. "Outside interference" is regarded as the most important. Internal Chinese military writings make it clear that an invasion campaign would have to be swift and decisively occupy Taiwan before American forces could come to the rescue. PLA writings refer to American involvement as "intervention of the Strong Enemy."[409] Chinese strategists know that it would not be easy to organize and prosecute the operation and worry that America could enter the war before they had achieved their objective. A brief overview of possible invasion timelines reveals why this is the case.

Taiwanese military intelligence assessments based on internal PLA documents reveal that, in theory, anywhere from one to fifteen days could pass from the onset of hostilities to the Z-Day landings.[410] Military officers in Taiwan generally think four to eight days is more likely.[411] Although the timing cannot be known, Beijing would perhaps have only a week or two to capture Taipei and pacify the rest of the island before American forces could neutralize the area. Of possible force deployments, U.S. aircraft carriers and submarines are the most worrisome possibility from the Chinese perspective. According to the PLA's professional literature, some forms of American support for Taiwan's defenders would begin well before the first shots were fired. Washington would almost certainly share real-time battlefield intelligence with Taipei and send emergency stocks of weapons and equipment to the island. Chinese strategists further anticipate that American bombers could strike military targets early in a cross-Strait war, quite possibly before Z-Day.[412]

Time is a constraint on campaign planners for other reasons. The longer a war with Taiwan dragged on, the more trouble the Communist Party can expect to have on its home front and around the world. The CCP leadership appears to believe that its domestic opponents would take advantage of the war to push their subversive agendas, further "splitting" the nation and "undermining territorial integrity." What's worse, after bearing brutal attacks, Taiwan is expected to exact its revenge by sending agents abroad to support minority groups along China's border areas, helping them foment unrest. Minority groups, religious groups, and "terrorists" could spring to action and begin a campaign to topple the regime.[413]

To deal with these potential threats, PLA writings envision the all-out mobilization of internal security forces. The Chinese army would help keep the domestic situation from spiraling out of control. It is anticipated that the PLA would join the police in conducting "counter-terror" operations. Troops would quell unrest and secure coastal and border regions. The stakes of these missions are portrayed as being sky high. Should any major setbacks occur, China's ability to quickly conquer Taiwan could be sabotaged.[414] Concerns about homeland security are summarized in the following excerpt:

> Ethnic "separatists" forces in our border areas, religious fanatics, and terrorists might join together with foreign forces and take advantage of this window of opportunity to cause trouble and plan terrorist activities. So a decisive campaign would be an effective way to reduce the "chain reaction effect" created by providing others with this chance to intervene, interfere, and influence (our internal affairs).[415]

PLA writings also express concern about the impact a cross-Strait war could have on China's regional prestige and diplomatic position. Neighboring countries that have territorial disputes with China could see a war in the Taiwan Strait as an unparalleled opportunity to push their claims and "make unfounded demands or provoke incidents."[416] Although neighboring countries of concern are not listed by name in PLA documents, the PRC has notable land border disputes with India, Bhutan, and Burma. In the maritime domain, potential challengers include Japan, South Korea, Vietnam, the Philippines, Indonesia, and Malaysia. PLA writings evince concern that India, in particular, could become especially bold if Taiwan's defense plan worked to deter, disable, or even defeat the Chinese military.[417]

Chapter Six

How Taiwan Would Fight

China would have to be stupid to invade Taiwan. It would be about
as smart as getting into a land war in Asia.

—U.S. Army colonel in Taipei

NOTHING matters more to Taiwan's survival as a free country than
overcoming the long-term threat of Chinese invasion. For Taiwan,
defense planning must be a national effort that involves the island's society and its national resources in a way that is generally unseen in the
world's other advanced economies. The Taiwanese people are far from
warlike or naive. They have lived with the shadow of war hanging over
their heads for many decades and place an extraordinary value on peace.
Nonetheless, great care has been taken to make sure that if the worst
were to happen they could marshal enough combat power to secure their
democratic way of life.

Little has been written in English on Taiwan's anti-invasion plan, but
it is fairly well understood in many parts of the Chinese-speaking world.
Some details, of course, are classified and officially nonexistent. Yet the
broad strokes are publically available information on the island, where the
all-out national defense strategy requires millions of people to know what
would be expected of them if the PRC invaded. Like Western European
countries during the Cold War, Taiwan faces an imposing juggernaut

right at its doorstep. The sprawl and density of its cities and the limited land available for maneuver or retreat virtually guarantee that any conflict would impact the whole populace. If war comes, everyone will be involved in some way, and everyone will be expected to contribute however they can.

Size affects strategy. The PRC is the world's largest country by population and fourth largest by territory. China is massive by almost any measure. In contrast, Taiwan is just slightly larger than Belgium, with a population of 23 million people. This asymmetry of size affects how Taiwanese defense strategy is formulated and communicated to the general public. For Taiwan's strategy to work, it must harness every strength available, combining the superior quality of the standing military with the superior size of the reserve forces, while drawing additional power from the island's industrious civilian populace.

Because of the extreme nature of the threat facing Taiwan, defense education is emphasized to a degree that would be unthinkable in most other countries. Nearly every high school and college has uniformed officers stationed on campus to teach courses on military affairs. Bookstores sell a wide selection of relevant materials, including glossy magazines that update readers on recent exercises and weapons deliveries from America. Local internet portals offer an endless array of high-quality studies and papers, published by the MND and easily downloadable. Talking heads on nightly news shows frequently discuss defense issues, their dialogues and debates fed by media outlets that are known for their scathing investigative reports. In addition, the parliament regularly holds rough and tumble public hearings on defense policy.

Taiwan's security authorities have a strong interest in creating an information-rich environment. Every major government office and military base has a school right outside its gates where official dependents study alongside kids from the surrounding neighborhoods. Even assuming Chinese missiles and bombs were to land squarely on their targets (many would not), their impacts would set off indiscriminate fires and send shock waves and debris into surrounding structures. If an enemy attack ever comes, every citizen will be affected, especially those in government jobs, whose families would be at risk and who themselves would likely be imprisoned or shot if they lost the war.

The code name given to Taiwan's national defense plan is the Gu'an Operational Plan.[418] Gu'an can be translated into English as "solid and secure." The purpose of the plan is reportedly to provide an overarching conceptual blueprint for wartime operations and a detailed playbook for defending against anticipated Chinese acts of aggression. Like all such plans, Gu'an is almost certainly founded on fundamental assumptions about the enemy's political intentions and military capabilities, as well as those of allies, partners, and neutrals. These assumptions guide planners in their work by narrowing the range of contingencies commanders must certify their forces can handle. Without boundaries in place, operational plans could grow excessive in their requirements, leading to a situation where the military is spread thin in order to be nominally prepared for a wide range of possible threats. Militaries risk growing weak when they fail to focus on their most critical threats and do not cultivate areas of core competency.

The Gu'an Plan is centered on the worst-case scenario: full-scale invasion. Since 1949, ROC military strategists have regarded the possibility of a Communist Chinese amphibious operation to be the foremost threat facing their nation. Their basic assumption is that the PLA could use a mix of navy and civilian ships to attempt to land around one million men in an all-out attack. This is certainly not China's only possible course of action, but it is by far the most common theme seen in PLA doctrinal writings, operational studies, and training handbooks. It is also the single most dangerous scenario threatening Taiwan's survival, since only a successful invasion would guarantee enemy takeover. The main objectives of the Gu'an Plan are to convince the Chinese not to invade Taiwan and to defeat an invasion if deterrence fails.

For the PRC to actually invade Taiwan, a lot of seemingly improbable things would first have to happen. The PLA Central Military Commission in Beijing would have to convince itself that its Joint Island Attack Campaign could be well executed, and then convince the CCP's civilian leadership the same. In addition, the Politburo Standing Committee would have to decide that the campaign would likely have acceptable political, economic, and social costs. The Gu'an Plan seeks to influence the Chinese calculus, making sure the perceived costs of invasion would be too high for China's leaders to seriously consider. If they attacked regardless of the risks, the anti-invasion plan is designed so that Taipei could drag Beijing into a long war of attrition, delaying amphibious assault and/or occupation until the Chinese high command either collapsed under the strain, or the military retreated after suffering humiliating losses.

Other options for enemy use of force are studied and considered, but they have less saliency for defense planning. While the PRC could forego invasion and attempt to defeat Taiwan using a blockade and/or bombing campaign, this possibility is viewed by military planners as markedly less dangerous. Taiwanese strategists know well that a long duration military operation is an unattractive option. Practically speaking, it would be hugely complex due to local weather patterns, and for much of the year the PLA's ships and planes would struggle to operate in the Taiwan Strait. The political, economic, and diplomatic drawbacks would each be considerable as well. By its very nature, a blockade and/or bombing campaign would have to drag on for a long time to produce results. It is assumed that the negative factors for China would almost certainly become unbearable long before Taiwan had been starved or burned into submission.

Taiwanese strategists assess that PLA doctrine favors a minimal warning, rapid invasion campaign that employs deception and surprise to land on the island and overrun Taipei, securing the government's capitulation before American-led coalition forces could decisively engage. Internal Chinese military writings reveal that a short duration, all-out blockade and bombing operation should be anticipated before the massed landing attempts. As an alternative to invasion, PLA writings indicate that a prolonged, but intermittent and low intensity, blockade and bombing operation could be used to apply pressure—but only if Beijing's objective fell far short of annexation. For these reasons, the blockade and bombing threat is very much secondary to the invasion threat.

The Gu'an Plan is reportedly designed to be flexible and continually updated. Changes and inputs are made to it when there is newly available intelligence on the PLA, when Taiwanese forces receive new equipment and capabilities, or when units are downsized or restructured. Lessons learned from exercises and training are used to modify the anti-invasion plan. It is tested multiple times per year in field deployments, live-fire drills, and computer simulated command post exercises. These war games put it into simulated action.[419] Natural and man-made disasters can have similar and far less artificial effects.

One major test of Taiwan's response system came on the evening of June 27, 2015, when tragedy struck a seaside water park outside Taipei. The Formosa Fun Coast in Bali was hosting a theme dance party that night, featuring colored corn starch thrown into the air in the style of a Hindu festival. As the revelry was heating up, the powder suddenly ignited, creating a horrific fireball that caused over 500 casualties. Most were severe burn victims, who found themselves trapped on a fiery dance stage or inside a drained-out wave pool. The explosion instantly triggered defense early warning nets. Unbeknownst to the party goers, they were raving in one of Taiwan's most dangerous potential invasion zones, an area heavily monitored by the military in case of Chinese attack.

The deadly fireball led national authorities to activate emergency procedures originally designed for the defense of greater Taipei. Rapid reaction units, having regularly practiced deployments to the area before, quickly arrived on scene and had a triage station and evacuation operation set up in record time. Rescue units included a joint force of army, navy, marine, reserve command, and military police teams, who won high praise from the media for their speed and professional demeanor during the chaos. While tasked with defending the capital region from invasion, that night the ROC military handled a different type of man-made disaster. The Gu'an Plan and the military units assigned to execute it were put to the test, and they passed with flying colors.[420]

Taiwan's anti-invasion plan nonetheless has its critics. Some American experts have asserted that Gu'an is too ambitious and demands too much of the ROC military. In their minds, the goal of the plan should be to, "hole up and hold out until the cavalry arrives."[421] Their thinking is informed by the history of allied war planning in Asia, especially with Japan and

South Korea, both of whom have American troops permanently based in their countries. However, in the absence of a formal defense treaty, Taiwanese strategists are unwilling to emulate Tokyo and Seoul, placing their country's survival at the mercy of American decision makers.

The Gu'an Plan is designed so that the armed forces of Taiwan are prepared for the three worst-case scenarios they might one day confront. In the first scenario, China invades and the U.S. "cavalry" never shows up. In the second, the Americans arrive on the battlefield too late to make a difference. In the final scenario, the Americans deploy in good time, but are routed by overwhelming PLA surprise attacks. These scenarios, though seemingly unlikely, could be catastrophic for Taiwan. Precautions are therefore made to guard against an overreliance on America's superior military capabilities and good intentions.[422]

Taiwanese defense planners cautiously and prudently assess that ROC military forces have to be prepared to defend their own country, without any international help. Coercive blockade and bombing campaigns, although more probable than all-out invasion, are not at the forefront of their thinking. Military planners assume that no Taiwanese government elected into being would ever capitulate as the result of intimidation. In their minds, economic devastation and limited combat would never be sufficient to force them to surrender. If the Chinese Communists want to take Taiwan, they will have to actually invade and occupy the entire country because the defenders will fight to the bitter end to preserve their freedom.[423] Having outlined the basic assumptions that guide Taiwanese strategists, let us now turn to some of the details of their anti-invasion plan.

Phase One: Mobilization and Force Preservation

Publically available materials indicate that Taiwan's war plan likely has three major phases of operations, each of which is specifically designed to counter the three main phases of the PLA's Joint Island Attack Campaign. The first phase aims to prepare for PLA surprise attacks. Reservists would be mobilized to fortify the island, and high value assets bunkered down. The second phase of the plan envisions launching joint task forces out to engage and destroy Chinese amphibious fleets before they could strike. The last phase of the plan calls for surviving Taiwanese units to fight along the coast to repel invasion and defend the homeland. If necessary, homeland defense forces would fall back into the major population centers and mountains to fight a prolonged series of sieges and counterattacks.

Mobilization and force preservation begins once Taiwan's government receives unambiguous warning of an impending attack. At this point, the president would confer with her cabinet and the leaders of parliament. She would then announce a state of emergency and declare a limited period of marital law.[424] Classified legal procedures have reportedly been drawn up to bring Taiwan's latent strength alive and turn the government into a highly organized war machine. These secret procedures are reviewed, updated, and tested at least once every year to certify that the process, if necessary, could be carried out swiftly in very stressful circumstances. As soon as the president gave the order, Taiwan's military could elevate readiness levels and go to a war footing.[425]

According to Taiwanese sources, force preservation in the invasion scenario would probably begin with the president, her cabinet and parliamentary leaders being moved to deep underground vaults, sealed into a system of secret command complexes that are capable of housing thousands of essential personnel under the earth's surface. They might also disperse to safe houses and hide sites. Surrounding them would be a layered phalanx of ROC marines, military police, and special service bodyguards, entrusted with their protection. It seems probable that certain key decision makers would avoid meeting in person to ensure that the entire government could not be knocked out by a single sinister blow.[426]

Fleets of armored fighting vehicles and bullet-proof sedans housed in locations around Taipei are assigned the mission of moving selected personnel from place to place. Special tunnel systems are also thought to exist for moving them across the capital unseen. In wartime, bunkers and mobility operations are often the first lines of defense. Decoys and other deception measures would be instituted to confuse enemy agents. Individuals of interest, routinely monitored but left free to go about their business, would be rounded up in counterintelligence dragnets and put under lock and key. In some cases, known Chinese agents could be fed false information, used as pawns in high stakes deception operations.

With the top leaders secured, the priority order of business would be to call up the reserves. Taiwan maintains one of the largest and most sophisticated reserve systems in the world, allowing the military in the supreme emergency to call upon the services of more citizen-soldiers than the entire PLA could ever to hope land on the island. Two and a half million Taiwanese men of military age are registered. Almost another million citizens of all ages, both male and female, have signed up to be civil defense workers. Government employees, health care professionals, and private contractors form a large block of wartime support personnel. Truck and bus driver unions, construction companies, and fishing associations all have their members and their machines registered. Even temples and churches are in the war reserve system. Many patriotic religious groups plan to feed and shelter troops at their rustic mountain retreats.[427]

Mobilization would reportedly commence with alerts flashing urgently across television channels, internet and social media pages, and radio broadcasts. Personal devices would beep, chirp, vibrate, and ring, signaling incoming calls and text messages. Military bases, police stations, fire stations, and hospitals would start to go into high gear. The Cabinet Office (Executive Yuan) and MND Reserve Command would light up in a surge of activity. Government personnel would scramble out to post notices at schools, parks, and other public spaces. Sirens would sound and public service announcements would echo across Taiwan's immense mass transit systems.

Once the emergency alert goes out, normal daily activities will cease across the nation as men of military age, in batches numbering in the hundreds of thousands, are called in for military service. Schools would close down, with young children likely sent out of the cities to stay with elderly relatives in the countryside. Plans call for high school and university students to be gathered into combat support groups, tasked with assisting air defense, medical, communications, and police operations. Assuming there would be enough time, the primary danger zones in greater Taipei, Taoyuan, Tainan, and elsewhere would be evacuated by the military, with all non-essential civilian personnel moved to shelter areas via a system of special access roads. Dozens of pre-surveyed refugee camp sites are scattered across rural areas in the island's hinterlands. Neighborhoods likely to soon become warzones would be cleared out, becoming as much as possible the sole domains of military and paramilitary units.[428]

Taiwan's reservists reportedly could be brought into action rapidly. The emergency mobilization plan assumes that some 200,000 to 300,000 men would muster within the first 24 hours. According to the plan, the bulk of the reserve force would be mobilized in 72 hours, with over two million military personnel at their duty stations or on standby. Taiwan's defense planners are cautious, assuming that only 80 percent would show up on time. Some men might be away on travel, or they might be sick, or attending urgent family business. Others might lose their nerve and flee the country, or be waylaid by unforeseeable circumstances. The vast majority would obey the law, do their duty, and fight.[429]

Tests of the emergency mobilization system are performed every year at randomized locations across Taiwan and the outer islands to see how well it works. Men know that they have been called up when they see their unit's code name and number on the news. These simulations offer great hope. Year after year, they indicate that around 97 percent of a local reserve brigade will muster on time (they are generally given less than 24 hours). Nonetheless, war planners assume the actual situation would be far worse. False messages could go out online, or the power grid might go down, forcing military police units to drive around towns with bullhorns to call up reserve units. In some circumstances, military police officers may have to go door to door with name lists, something they are reportedly well prepared to do. After years of testing and tweaking, there is a high degree of confidence that the mobilization system would work even in the most stressful conditions the enemy could create.[430]

Activated reservists would not have to travel far. Most citizen-soldiers in Taiwan, like national guardsmen and militia units in other countries, are assigned the task of defending their own hometowns, virtually guaranteeing that they would fight much harder than an invading enemy. Once reservists arrived to their nearby armories and marshaling stations, they would be issued weapons, ammunition, and equipment. Most would be sent to the firing ranges for three to seven days, where they would refresh their training. Others would almost immediately be sent to work on construction teams, their mission to erect fortification networks along the coasts and around other key points. Taiwan is reported to have amassed sea mines, landmines, and beach obstacles, which are piled up in coastal bunkers and ready to deploy quickly in an emergency. As of 2015, the military was estimated to have over 7,000 sea mines of all types, stored in at least four naval armories. The navy trains to have over half of these mines sown in dense underwater arrays around the invasion beaches within fourteen hours, with the rest used for other missions or held in reserve.[431] In case naval mine-laying ships were sabotaged or sunk, hundreds of fishing boats in the reserve system are to be outfitted for filling in.[432] No solid estimate exists regarding the number of landmines and obstacles that are available for the beaches, but they are depicted as vast in number.[433]

PLA sources devote considerable attention to Taiwan's coastal fortification and defense capabilities. They ruefully note that Taiwan's military does not deploy minefields and obstacle networks in peacetime, except in a highly limited fashion during exercises, in order to ensure that operational security is maintained. If the locations and layouts of Taiwan's beach defenses could be studied over time with overhead satellite reconnaissance, Chinese military analysts apparently feel they would be in a better position to develop countermeasures for defeating them.[434] Secrecy is not the only reason the ROC military waits for a wartime emergency. The nature of its planned coastal defense system is such that it would pose a serious threat to normal sea traffic.

According to PLA assessments, Taiwan has the ability to rapidly establish an elaborate and lethal coastal defense system, holding every type of amphibious vessel in the Chinese fleet at risk of destruction. It is assessed that this system would be comprised of an interlocking series of minefields and obstacles at sea. The minefields would reportedly be laid in a series of large belts, established along the best lines of approach to the invasion beaches. It is envisioned that the outer fields could start somewhere on the eastern side of the Taiwan Strait middle line (or Davis Line), which runs approximately 60 miles from Taiwan's western shores. Minefields in the Strait would, in theory, be laid about six to eight miles across, comprised of moored contact mines, drifting contact mines, and large bottom mines scattered across a broad area to block the deep water passes.[435]

The anticipated minefields would be relatively thin far from Taiwan and thicker the closer to shore one got. They could be planted with a special focus on pre-surveyed anchorage areas off the coast, where the PLA would launch small landing craft and amphibious tanks, unloading them from their mother ships for the final sprint to the beach. These waters are expected to be sown with belts of death, each row of mines five to seven miles long, when measured from west to east. Another mine belt could be around two miles across, made up of small and medium-sized bottom mines laid in tight clusters a few miles off the coast, where PLA gunboats otherwise could sit and shell the shore.

Naval minefields, it is believed, would create kill boxes, trapping and sinking landing ships and their escorts. The threat of mines is psychological as well as physical. Taiwan's planned kill boxes are intended to limit the willingness of Chinese ship captains to maneuver at high speeds outside the slender shipping lanes they considered safe. Vessels traveling in formation along fixed routes at fixed speeds are an easy target. In war, the advantages of dodging randomly across the sea are significant and often vital to a ship's survival. Taiwanese naval mines, deadly in their own right, could make cautious ships vulnerable to being shredded by air attacks or blown to pieces by coastal defense batteries.

PLA texts anticipate that minefields at sea would be followed by beach obstacle systems, emplaced in the shallow waters that begin 300 to 600 feet offshore. These are designed to entangle, rip apart, and incinerate small landing boats full of troops. Taiwan's planned obstacle systems are believed to make use of moored nets, clamshell traps, log cages, steel spikes, sunken truck containers, and mines. The military is believed to have stockpiled 53 gallon oil drums for wartime beach defense. Just prior to invasion, these would reportedly be filled with 220 pounds of TNT, mixed with gasoline, and chained three or four feet below the surface, where they would wait menacingly for Chinese landing craft to touch them off.

Each is estimated to have a lethal blast radius of 100 to 150 feet, killing with shock and shrapnel, and leaving flaming oil slicks in their wake.[436]

Pike obstacles are made of steel bars emplaced at 45 degree angles, each about six feet long and weighing 150 pounds. These would be emplaced in the surf, facing the enemy. It is anticipated that at low tide they would rest entirely on dry land, spaced out in long rows, each around 15 feet apart, looking like forests of black needles protruding from the sand and silt. From the perspective of PLA planners, however, the most horrific beach obstacle facing them would be what they call, "the seawalls of fire."[437] According to Chinese military texts, Taiwan's invasion beaches are protected by secret underwater pipelines, designed for pumping flammables out into the shallows. Just as the first waves of PLA amphibious troops were storming ashore, Taiwanese officers would open pipe values to create a thick film of oil and gasoline. This unstable slick would be lit off by artillery shells and gunfire, creating sheets of fire that could consume the invaders all along the blackened beach lines. In peacetime, oil and gas stores that could be used in this defense system are reportedly kept inside hardened subterranean bunkers at the edge of the Taoyuan plain and elsewhere up and down the coast. Nearby airports and harbors store their own fuel, providing additional supplies for fire making purposes.[438]

Although the full extent of Taiwan's secret pipeline system is unknown, internal Chinese manuals caution PLA tacticians to prepare for the worst and assume that every breakwater and seawall has gas lines embedded that are capable of releasing large jets of flame. To reduce the number of burn deaths, restricted-access PLA handbooks recommend covering amphibious landing craft in fire retardant materials to mitigate the risk of them being engulfed while motoring through the slicks. In theory, the first wave of troops is to be provided with fire protection suits, fire extinguishing equipment, and water cannons. When possible, landing craft crews would be advised to swerve around flaming sea areas, although this could be difficult given the other obstacles. As a consequence, the firewalls are anticipated to be horrific and difficult to escape.[439]

Assuming Chinese skirmishers made it to shore alive, it is anticipated that they would have to fight through a dense interlocking system of beach obstacles, minefields, and coastal fortifications. It is believed that some frontline defense systems could extend over a quarter mile inland. Defensive works are expected to be designed like quilts, with each box one component of a larger patchwork of death, sprawled across the landscape. Chinese military writings depict the envisioned fortification systems as something ugly and medieval, painting dystopian pictures of landmine fields, razor wire nets, spike strips, hook boards, and skin-peeling planks. They envision Taiwanese beaches fortified with gun emplacements, machine gun nests, mortar pits, cement barriers, trenches, and tank traps, with open spaces covered by sharp piles of broken glass and blades of junk metal.

Landmines in the system are anticipated to include both anti-personnel and anti-tank variants, laid out in kill zones designed to trap the attacker between steel hedgehogs wrapped in tangles of barbed wire. Giant "dragon teeth" (complex geometric-shaped, steel-reinforced concrete blocks) would link together with other obstacles in the system to either block pathways off the beach, needed by amphibious tanks and hovercraft, or channel them into minefields and ambush sites where troops with anti-tank rockets and heavy machine guns would be waiting.[440]

Behind Taiwan's landing beaches are low inland areas, pockmarked with countless cement drainage ditches, ponds, salt fields, swamps, and wind-breaks. Here is where Taiwan's army would reportedly establish frontline anti-invasion bases. During the mobilization phase of Gu'an, combat engineers and civilian contractors would fortify these bases and the roads connecting them. Each strongpoint would be protected by barbed wire fences, wire obstacles, spike strips, landmines, anti-tank barrier walls, anti-tank obstacles, and anti-tank trenches. The entire area would be littered with something PLA writings refer to as "glass shard mountains," in addition to bamboo spikes, felled trees, truck shipping containers, and junkyard cars.[441] According to Chinese assessments, Taiwan's beach and coastal defense works will pose an enormous problem for amphibious troops. One excerpt summarizes the challenge as follows: "This wide-area, defense-in-depth obstacle system will increase the difficulty of landing operations. It makes our obstacle clearing mission a giant burden. It makes setting up forward command posts highly difficult and highly risky. It makes the situation ever more complex."[442] This same text goes on to describe how Taiwan's army has greatly altered the coastal landscape in peacetime to make it more defensible in wartime. Examples given include the cultivation of sharp-spine agave plants, cactuses, and thick thorny hedgerows. In addition, military engineers have reportedly constructed water retention areas that can be opened in an emergency to flood low-lying areas, denying them to the enemy.[443]

One PLA source evaluates Taiwan's coastal fortifications as follows:

After decades of battlefield preparation, the Enemy on the Island has constructed a hardened system of central tunnels surrounded by static defensive works, field works, and interlocking coastal bunkers. It faces and looks down on areas of utility for landings. It is a hardened interlocking coastal defense system, which emphasizes single bunkers and groups of bunkers, some that can be seen, some that are hidden, both at forward areas and into the depths of the Island, with obstacles both natural and manmade, and parts both underground and above ground, forming a combined coastal defense system to envelop attackers, launch localized counterattacks, and all-out counterattacks to execute decisive battles along the shore.[444]

Although Chinese military analysts take great pains to warn tactical PLA commanders of Taiwan's lethal beach defenses, their writings are equally pessimistic about what would be waiting farther inland. Taiwan's anti-invasion plan reportedly assigns units to defend fortified key points deep inside the island. Before Z-Day, local air defense teams would dig in to guard landing zones where Chinese paratroopers might fall. Infantry would set up patrols of city streets and rural fields. Military police units would man bridges, tunnels, power stations, water reservoirs, and highway checkpoints. Under their watchful gaze, explosive ordinance specialists would rig tunnels, bridges, and ports with detonation mechanisms.[445]

Taiwan's anti-invasion plan reportedly calls for the defense of all strategic infrastructure that could be of aid to the enemy if captured. In the unlikely event that defense should prove untenable, everything of value is to be demolished, especially large sections of the coastal highway system and the bridges leading into Taipei. Other roads are to be blocked by collapsed buildings, overhead power lines, and trees.[446] According to PLA writings, the plan calls for stringing steel cables between mountain passes, across rivers, and around tall buildings to crash low flying attack helicopters. It is even envisioned that barrage balloons (blimps tethered to the ground with metal cables) could be put in place to defend major cities against low flying aircraft, entangling them, or forcing them to approach via more dangerous routes. These blimps, it is believed, could have small explosives charges attached that would be flung into the sides of ensnared helicopters.[447]

The following PLA study excerpt succinctly captures an official Chinese military view of Taiwan's inland defenses:

> The Island's urban battlefield has undergone many years of buildup. Its defensive deployments are quite complete. All defensive works have been hardened and perfected. Detailed pre-war plans are in place for emplacing obstacles at every critical transportation point from the coast into city depths. When our combat groups are fighting on the Island, these obstacles, which will certainly be emplaced according to their layered defense plan, will cause our army units extreme difficulties in maneuvering.[448]

The same source states that since the 1970s Chinese war planners have regarded Taiwan's elaborate fortification lines as "critical bottlenecks" that needed to be broken through before the island could be conquered. It stresses that a long series of technical studies and exercises have been held in China to develop an approach whereby the PLA would bomb the shore, mine-sweep the sea, clear channels through beach obstacles with combat engineers, and send troops storming into whatever remained armed with flamethrowers and dynamite. But this approach is viewed as sub-optimal and possibly even a receipt for stalemate and repulse. According to this account, the PLA has not yet broken the code on how to quickly get through Taiwan's planned grid of fortifications.[449]

Before Z-Day, while Taiwanese citizen-soldiers and contractors were preparing the battlefield, a much smaller elite would be gearing up: the rapid reaction brigades. The ROC Army has thousands of tanks, self-propelled rocket launchers, artillery guns, and armored fighting vehicles. These outfit specialized armor and mechanized infantry brigades. They are supported by helicopters and special operation groups, and backstopped with marine counter-invasion brigades. The mission of the rapid reaction brigades is to stay hidden at inland sites until the main focal points of enemy invasion are clear. Before landing zones could consolidate, they would converge on and smash into lodgments, making sure enemy forces were not able to secure footholds. Some reservists would report to duty at these brigades in the run-up to war, but not many. They are active duty units, maintained close to full-fighting strength even in peacetime.

Force preservation for the rapid reaction brigades means parking tanks, guns, and ammunition at hide-sites. Hidden caves, tunnels, concrete-covered shelters, and concealed garages dot the countryside. Many units would disperse into civilian infrastructure, where the PLA could not find them even if it had a master copy of Taiwan's defense plan. Helicopters and other large machines would deploy to pre-planned operating areas where the enemy might not expect them, such as factory grounds, university campuses, parks, golf courses, parking lots, and open fields at abandoned construction sites. Lists of pre-surveyed hideouts are kept and ready to be distributed when needed. Many prime sites are never used in exercises in order to maintain their secrecy. Some have been tested in war game maneuvers, but some exist only in the minds of battalion-level commanders, each of whom would have his or her pick of the local terrain.[450]

PLA writings express concern that the main elements of the ROC Army would go to ground across Taiwan's population centers and hinterlands. It is very unlikely that they could be neutralized before Z-Day. Layered air defense shields protect them from close-in overhead reconnaissance and strikes. They would be buried or camouflaged, and so vast in number and widely dispersed that anything other than a long-term concentrated bombing operation against them is likely to prove a waste of effort. The guidance given to PLA commanders is to wait until the invasion begins, and then concentrate on finding tank brigades, in particular, attempting to disrupt their movements after they have come out of hiding and formed up for counterattacks.[451]

Finding and hitting mobile units in the fog of war, however, is acknowledged to be a herculean task, and one which, to be successful, would have to soak up all available intelligence, targeting, and strike assets, drawing them away from amphibious operations just as they were surging to their climax. Presenting the aggressor with hard, confusing, and complex situations, terrible dilemmas, and painful tradeoffs is the hallmark of any good defense plan. From the perspective of Taiwan's ground force generals, force preservation is not the least bit theoretical; it is about surviving a concentrated enemy first strike and husbanding strength for the final struggle to repel invasion.

The mobilization and force preservation phase of the Gu'an Plan is believed to call for the ROC Air Force to bunker down and ride out Chinese missile attacks, making the skies clear shooting ranges for Taiwan's ten batteries of Patriot Advanced Capability-3 missiles, which have the ability to intercept ballistic missiles.[452] To stay alive during the initial onslaught, Patriot launchers would "shoot-and-scoot," not lingering in any one place for long enough to be hit. For defense against cruise missiles and stealthy fighter-bombers, Taiwan has self-built a significant number of Tien Kung "Sky Bow" air defense missiles. At least six batteries of this advanced, long-range missile system are deployed around Taiwan's major operational areas, and up to twelve more batteries are expected by 2024.[453] Units in the field would be fed information from a resilient network of American-made radars and satellites. At the current pace of development, Taiwan's missile shield may be one of the most robust defensive networks of its kind in the world. It offers overlapping fields of fire and the ability to link up and exchange information with American and Japanese ballistic missile defense ships.[454]

For force preservation purposes, Taiwan's defense plan would assign squadrons of the nation's most advanced fighters to enormous "nuclear proof" mountain bunkers on the east coast of Taiwan. There is enough space in Hualien's *Chiashan* "Optimal Mountain" and Taitung's *Shihzishan*

"Stone Mountain" for hundreds of jets. They would likely sit out the early hours of war in vault-like stables, their pilots preparing for counterstrikes. Not all air squadrons are assigned to the mountain depths. Some would sit in dome-like shelters of reinforced concrete and earth. Taiwan has hundreds of hardened hangars spread across its airbases. Unlike the super bunkers in the mountains, they are not capable of surviving the impact of a ballistic missile hit. They can however weather carpet-bombing attacks and near misses, and they prevent secondary explosions when planes nearby are stricken. The sheer number of hardened shelters and hide-sites in Taiwan makes them a challenge for Chinese war planners. Targeting each individually would waste a mountain of precision ordinance because many will be either empty or occupied by a dummy plane.

Further complicating matters for PLA generals, the counter-invasion plan allows for Taiwanese air force commanders to move their squadrons out to the highways. Taiwan is one of the only countries in the world that regularly shuts down sections of its freeway system, turning them into makeshift fighter bases. Exercises to date have involved thousands of participants and hundreds of support vehicles, with all essential personnel and equipment moved out of their home airbases and onto highway runway strips. At least five locations are maintained for this emergency air mission. Taiwan's mainstay F-16, IDF, and Mirage fighters, and E-2 Hawkeye airborne early-warning and control planes, have been certified to land and take off on the highways. The national freeway system was originally designed to support heavy C-130 Hercules transport planes as well, but that prospect has never been tested in peacetime.[455]

Taiwan's large P-3 Orion sub-hunters have not been highway certified, but could operate from civilian airports which might be taken over by the military and used to hide high-value planes. Hangars that housed passenger jets in peacetime, could suddenly find themselves home to planes used for electronic warfare, parachute assault, and maritime patrol. Camouflage, concealment, and deception measures are planned on a large scale. False radio chatter would create a tremendous white noise, blanketing the airwaves and overwhelming targeting designs. PLA satellites that passed overhead could find themselves unable to see anything, or they might be fooled, transmitting images and signals that appeared to be those of real planes, but were not.[456]

There is no guarantee that each action taken would have its intended effect, but considered as a whole, Taiwan's air shield is very likely to thin the herd of incoming missiles, making passive defense measures like hardening, camouflage, concealment, and deception more effective. No one in Taiwan's defense planning circles harbors any illusion that the air force could emerge from ballistic missile and cruise missile attacks in the same fashion it went into them. The PLA has invested enormous resources into preparations for grounding Taiwan's flying service. Early losses are expected to be heavy.[457]

Neither side can be certain before the storm comes that its forecasts will prove true. Steps taken during the mobilization and force preservation stage of the anti-invasion plan are intended to ensure that China would stand little chance of seizing air superiority in the first days of conflict. In the minds of even optimistic PLA planners, the ROC Air Force represents a fleet-in-being, a vague menace whose full strength and wartime role cannot be calculated out of the equation. Only the most foolish of general disregards a mighty air force hiding dispersed and deep in the mountains, waiting to strike out at a time and place of its own choosing.

Taiwan's navy intends to fight shoulder to shoulder with the air force. Unlike the other services, the ROC Navy would not be able to hide its fleet in underground citadels.[458] The counter-invasion plan calls for the fleet to sortie, with ships pulling anchor and pushing out to sea at the earliest warning of impending attack. Regular exercises are held to certify that naval ports could be emptied out in short order.[459] Not all warships could be put into action. Maintenance, repair, and overall schedules preclude all navies from getting their full fleet underway at once. Most consider it a feat just to put one third of their fleet to sea. For Taiwan, the goal is to get well over half of all ships mobilized for battle. The rest would be drained of fuel, unloaded of ordinance, and then towed out of their harbors and scuttled, making each a sunken obstacle to incoming submarines and surface ships. In some cases, warships might have to be exploded in their dry docks and at their piers to forestall capture.[460]

The bulk of the fleet would in this way get out ahead of the first missile attacks, and every ship left behind would perish doing its duty. Task forces at sea would steam to prepared operating areas. Here they would hunt for enemy submarines and ships, harassing or evading whatever they could not readily sink. The east coast of Taiwan, with its wall of mountains, offers deep-water sanctuary areas offshore and wide open spaces for maneuver. Ship groups here would operate under the protective bubble of land-based air defenses and coastal anti-ship missile batteries, which have a force-multiplying effect that increases joint combat power.[461]

In the frigid depths below would be anchored sonar-buoys, capable of alerting ship captains to the approach of enemy vessels through the two principal chokepoints: the waters of the Miyako Strait in the north, between Taiwan and Okinawa, and the Bashi Channel in the south, between Taiwan and the Philippines. At the roof of the South China Sea, Taiwan's Pratas (Dongsha) Island would serve as an additional outpost for monitoring Chinese ship movements. Task forces at sea would operate essentially like those of the ground and air services, dispersing to safe zones to preserve their strength until the enemy's first strikes had subsided. Once the invasion armadas began forming up along the Fujian coast, naval task forces could launch strikes and raids upon them.

Meanwhile, on shore, Taiwanese civilians would be marshaling in support of the coming convulsions. As the strategic situation came unglued and China rushed toward the brink, Taiwanese logistics experts would stockpile food, medicine, and war supplies. Factories would retool and ramp up their production lines to meet wartime needs. Farmers would harvest and store whatever crops they could before their fields become warzones. Fishermen would swap their nets out, replacing them with equipment for laying mines and obstacles. Fuel depots would top off their buried supply chambers. The stock market would close. The Bank of Taiwan and other major financial institutions would inject rivers of cash into emergency spending programs, utilizing foreign reserves long held for just such an emergency.[462]

Declaring a temporary state of martial law in Taiwan would bring the entire society and economy to a frenzied pitch. The defense plan is designed

THE CHINESE INVASION THREAT

to extract every available ounce of national power and to meet the threat.[463] The result would not just transform Taiwan, it would alter the financial fabric of the world. Supply chains everywhere, normally fed by Taiwanese manufactures, would be paralyzed—especially in the areas of advanced computing and electronics. Many routine transactions that are taken for granted would be suddenly become impossible. The effects would ripple into the headquarters of major corporations around the globe. Given the far-reaching and intractable consequences of misreading enemy intentions, Taiwan's government leaders are only going to issue the emergency order to mobilize the entire nation when they are absolutely certain an invasion is imminent. The threat is likely to manifest itself slowly over the course of many months, and it could after all be a bluff intended to set off a false alarm to weaken public confidence in the government, kindle panic, and get Taiwan to reveal some of its preparatory defensive measures. Weeks before Z-Day, Taiwan would most likely begin climbing a mobilization ladder that would allow the president to increase readiness levels in a steady, step-by-step manner in accordance with Chinese actions. The nationwide invasion alarm would almost certainly not be sounded until defense and security professionals handed truly dire warning intelligence to the president and cabinet.[464]

The system is designed with fail-safes. A weak-willed, indecisive, or naive president could dally in a crisis and avoid hard decisions. Certainly, all the options open to them would be painful. They could find that the least painful choice to make before war is to make no choice at all, postponing mobilization for as long as they could. They might also be under American pressure. In Washington, there are likely to be those who would rationalize that all-out mobilization could "provoke" the Chinese, inviting an attack when there was still some slim chance of peace.

Historically, most countries facing invasion tend to wait until the threat is right on top of them before they act.[465] This seems unimaginable in the case of Taiwan, but the defense plan is reportedly flexible enough to account for less than perfect readiness outcomes. In the improbable event of total strategic surprise, the plan could ensure latent strength was rapidly brought to life just as the enemy's missiles started to rain down.

However, fewer defense forces would be mobilized and preserved for the coming battle. Only the most essential ones would be ready for the fight. The dangers to the life of Taiwan in such circumstances could skyrocket. Such is the burden of decision and responsibility that must be borne by the island's elected leaders.

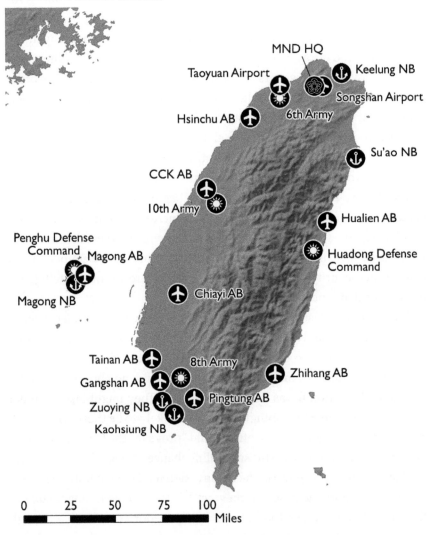

Major Taiwanese military bases

Phase Two: Joint Interdiction

In the joint interdiction phase of Taiwan's anti-invasion plan, ROC military forces would emerge from their bunkers and safe zones to give battle to Chinese amphibious forces before they crossed the Taiwan Strait and stormed the beaches.[466] It is not clear when the military intends to transition to the joint interception phase, but PLA writings assume Taiwanese counterstrikes could begin against their fleets soon after war was initiated. Although many defenders would remain inactive until the aggressor's opening blows were spent, some might engage in combat as soon as the first waves of missiles were fired at them.

Taiwan's missile defense shield would probably be the first to go into action. Launch batteries, sandbagged into mountainside revetments around major cities, would release radiant lines of projectiles high into the upper atmosphere, their warheads racing toward incoming rockets at ultra fast speeds. Supporting them, electronic warfare squadrons would blast the airwaves with carefully tuned beams of electrons, designed to scramble mini-computers imbedded within PLA missile seekers. With luck, some enemy missiles might be lured away from their real targets and driven into decoys. Others might slam harmlessly into rivers, empty fields, or mountains.[467] Billions of defense dollars and countless hours of engineering and training would be put on trial.[468] The verdict would come within minutes. The average Chinese ballistic missile, once fired, takes just seven minutes and twenty seconds to reach Taiwan.[469]

Sharp fighting would light up along the PRC coastline, as Taiwanese artillery guns on the fortress islands came under fire and gave their retorts. In the interest of survival, each side would attempt to knock out the other's gun emplacements first. Some artillery batteries, knowing their time was short, might turn their sights on more profitable mainland targets within range. Taiwanese special operations forces could be infiltrated behind enemy lines to begin their deadly sabotage work. Spymasters in Taipei could send out clandestine signals via number stations to bring long-dormant sleeper agents to life.[470] Submarines and ships, stalking each other in the tense pre-war hours, would begin dueling, the stricken disappearing forever into the black waters below.

It seems unlikely that the entire ROC Air Force would bunker down ahead of the first strike. Some squadrons may be required for combat air patrols. Fighters on strip alert, responsible for the protection of the national capital, might plan to scramble just ahead of the missile storm, clawing their way up to meet any approaching fighter-bombers. Those already on patrol high above would descend on their targets, tearing into them with missiles and cannon fire. In an air war, the large numbers of modern fighter jets available to China would give it a distinct advantage, especially because they would have the initiative. Taiwanese pilots, however, are superior in terms of skill thanks to their robust, American-style training regimes.[471]

When they were joined, losses in aerial engagements would be staggering on both sides. Taiwanese pilots that were shot down might have good prospects of parachuting back into their homeland. The same could not be said of Chinese fliers. It does not seem probable that all Taiwan's many runways could be cratered by missile strikes in the first hours of fighting, but many strips would be wounded and inoperable.[472] Taiwan's rapid runway repair crews are arguably the best trained and equipped in the world, but they would have to stay sheltered with their equipment until the first two or three waves blasted down, lest they risk being caught out on open tarmacs and cut to pieces by Chinese cluster bombs.[473]

To confuse PLA targeting cells, who would be receiving information piped in from satellites, drones, and local spies, Taiwan's airbases would employ their stockpiles of fake debris and use smoke machines to mimic battle damage and obscure observation. False radio chatter would assist with deception operations. Clearing and re-opening airstrips in the dead of night seems to be a favored option. It could allow air squadrons to exit their mountain lairs unseen and jet off into the fray when least expected. Night fighting is a skill emphasized by Taiwan's air force for giving pilots a comparative advantage over their numerically superior adversaries.[474]

It would be operationally unsound and wasteful for Taiwanese air planners to focus their main effort on a war of attrition in the skies. Rather than fight uphill battles against swarms of enemy fighters, they are much more likely to aim at high value surface targets along the Chinese coast. Taiwanese strike groups would speed toward PLA invasion staging areas at low altitude, flying below the radar to avoid detection. Once in range of their targets, they would launch missiles in multi-axis attacks. Assisting them would be electronic jamming planes, cruise missiles, and drones capable of kamikaze-style attacks on shore-based early warning sites. If successful, counterattacks would create widespread chaos and open holes through China's radar networks, knock-out the command centers that orchestrate each sector's air defense operations, and paralyze the system.

The soft underbelly of any amphibious operation against Taiwan would be the window of time after war was initiated, when Chinese armadas were loading assault troops and their equipment. It is imagined that Taiwan, in the final countdown to Z-Day, would launch a well-knit campaign of air and missile attacks to gut the aggressor at the very moment its ships were sprawled out along the shore and being fed. The PLA's professional literature summarizes their understanding of Taiwan's interdiction operations as follows:

> The Enemy on the Island emphasizes cross-Strait maneuvers to execute suppression operations, mainly in the form of air raids. Landing troops will be easily stricken by enemy assaults while moving, assembling, and boarding ships. The Enemy on the Island emphasizes suppression operations every step of the way, placing particular importance on engaging in firepower raids against important targets including the assembly areas on the land and at sea for the landing troops and the landing ships, and ports, docks, airports, ground transportation nodes, road infrastructure, and missiles.[475]

Some fighters would be armed with Taiwan's self-built Wan Chien (Ten Thousand Swords) joint standoff weapon. This is a heavy, air-launched missile designed to engage ground targets from outside the effective ranges of Chinese air defenses. These missiles work by gliding stealthily through air defense nets, raining down sub-munitions on enemy targets. According to reports, each bomblet is capable of punching through a solid foot of concrete. Because they are fired at great distances, they increase the survivability of Taiwanese fighters and minimize their losses.[476]

Other fighter jets would be armed with Harpoon and Maverick missiles, which are designed for precision air-to-surface strikes against tactical targets including ships, harbor facilities, fuel storage sites, ground transportation infrastructure, and tanks. Different than joint standoff weapons, these missiles require jets to get close to their targets before firing, making missions more risky for the pilots. Taiwan is believed to have a plan for tightly interwoven raids and strikes in the form of missiles hurled great distances across the sea. Only once China's air defenses had been degraded could fighter groups shred apart the armadas.[477]

Taiwan has a considerable arsenal of self-made, truck-mounted cruise missiles for striking operationally and strategically significant targets in the depths of China. The ROC Air Force also maintains elite fighter squadrons for a potential Doolittle-style raid in retaliation for PLA missile attacks. Their mission would be to demonstrate to Beijing that all of China is vulnerable to Taiwanese attacks. Pilots selected for this mission are said to "punch a one-way ticket" because the odds of coming home are low. To increase striking range, speed, and payload, plans for deep interdiction apparently call for pilots to bailout after servicing their targets or crash their aircraft into secondary targets after all their munitions were exhausted. In addition, Taiwan is believed to maintain a modest inventory of indigenous ballistic missiles for strategic strikes on targets deep in China.[478]

Whether or not any of Taiwan's long-range counterstrike capabilities would be used in anger is likely to depend a great deal on Taipei's wartime strategic calculations. If American support was viewed as sufficient to ensure Taiwan's survival, deep interdiction would likely be held in abeyance. On the other hand, if the strategic picture looked desperate, and Taiwan was heavily bombed and tightly blockaded and about to be invaded, retaliatory attacks on political targets in Beijing and Shanghai could be conducted. Because of the distances involved, this could only be on a small scale compared with what the PRC was doing to Taiwan from nearby Fujian and Guangdong. Yet it would almost certainly be judged as good to hit back, raise the stakes, and defy the aggressor. Taiwan's president would have no better option for impressing and disturbing the Chinese political leadership, making Taiwanese wrath and willpower perfectly clear to them before they took the plunge across the Strait.

If the PLA armadas put to sea, concerted naval attacks on them would begin. After many years of research, testing and refinement, Taiwan has developed a system of coastal defense missiles for sinking the main ships of the Chinese amphibious fleet. The *Hsiung Feng* (Brave Wind) anti-ship missile is larger and faster than almost any other weapon of its kind in the world. Many of its operational characteristics are classified, but it's believed to have a range of 60–250 miles (depending on variant) and the ability to impact targets at supersonic speeds. It is widely deployed on Taiwan's warships and fast missile boats, and can be launched from inside shore-based bunkers and truck launchers.[479]

According to PLA assessments, *Hsiung Feng* anti-ship missiles have advanced warheads allowing them to fly over the horizon and lock onto visible targets selected from databases loaded with known enemy ship characteristics. They are reportedly programmed to differentiate between ship group types, attacking known PLA amphibious formations first, then amphibious support groups, then irregular formations (when no better target can be acquired). Large amphibious assault ships, loaded with helicopters and located at the center of formations, are the priority. If these could not be found, warheads would be commanded to strike Chinese aircraft carriers, destroyers, or frigates. If these were not found, then missiles would obliterate smaller warships, like minesweepers. In the event that automated target selection systems were jammed, the computer fail-safe mode would kick-in, directing missiles to hit large ships, not small ones, concentrated groups, not dispersed ones, and leading ships, not rear echelon ones.[480]

Taiwan has a network of hardened anti-ship missile bases that allows for overlapping fields of fire against approaching armadas. These missile bases give Taiwan the ability to "control the sea from the land." Bases near Tamsui and Keelung, and on Dongyin Island, protect against hostile Chinese warships approaching from the northwest. Bases in Kaohsiung and on Xiao Liuqiu (Lamay) Island protect the southwest approaches. A missile base on Siyu Island in the Penghus covers the central area of the Taiwan Strait; and a base south of Hualien protects Taiwan's east coast. Since fixed positions known to the enemy are in peril of being knocked out by precision munitions, Taiwan fields hard-to-find truck launchers, guaranteeing that a steady stream of steel would meet the invader. In peacetime, truck launch batteries are garrisoned at concealed locations. In wartime, they would motor to wherever they were needed.[481]

Taiwanese strategists recognize that their navy does not have the resources to match the Chinese ship-for-ship or submarine-for-submarine. However, that does not necessarily mean Taiwan would lose control over its surrounding waters in the opening days of war. Taiwan's anti-invasion plan calls for using a missile-centric strategy to deny Chinese fleets access to its territorial waters. The concept of operations appears sound because Taiwan has home-built the advanced systems needed to see and strike an invasion force from great distances. It also appears sound because Taiwanese planners have decided they would not wait for heavily loaded troop transport ships to get close to the invasion beaches before turning them into giant steel coffins.

Joint interdiction operations would open with strikes on PLA ship groups at their coastal embarkation points. If raids failed to significantly disable or delay the enemy's amphibious plan, waves of strikes would be hurled against the armadas as they put to sea and steamed toward Taiwan. Attacks would grow in intensity as Chinese ships crossed the centerline and steamed into minefields and prepared kill boxes. It is envisioned that the battle would crescendo decisively off of Taiwan's coastline. In recent years, the live-fire iteration of the Han Kuang national defense exercises have publically demonstrated how the military would defend against an invasion of the Penghu Islands. During one such drill, a joint force unleashed a spectacular series of missiles, rockets, artillery, mines, decoys and jammers at the simulated invasion fleet. The result was that not a single "Red" infantryman made it to shore.[482] Taiwanese planners know that only by refusing to cede the initiative do they stand a chance of keeping their country's heavily populated western coastline from becoming a horrific battlefield.

It cannot be known in advance when Taiwan's surviving naval task forces would steam out of their safe zones and into the Strait to enter the fray. Chinese analysts seem to assume naval attacks might be launched on their fleets at anytime, although they seem far more concerned about air raids. The protective shield provided by the PLA's own coastal defense batteries is such that Taiwanese naval strategists are likely to judge it better to wait and spring the trap once the armadas are far from the Chinese coast. One approach that might be considered would be to keep all large surface ships out of the Strait, allowing the entire area to become an open target range for coastal missile batteries, attack jets, helicopter gunships, and stealthy fast attack craft. Once these had done their maximum damage, Taiwan's fleet could steam in at whatever time and place was judged to be the most advantageous. In practice, however, it seems likely that the navy could be anxious to engage earlier to gain its fair share of glory. Sinking the PLA armadas is principally a naval mission. The brother services have supporting roles to play, but their supreme missions are elsewhere.

In the event that long- and medium-range interdiction failed to halt advancing ship formations, Taiwan's surviving defense force would begin attacking Chinese ships as they anchored and disgorged troops into hover-craft, amphibious tanks, and landing craft. Attack helicopters would have a leading role to play in striking more distant offshore disembarkation points.[483] The forward anchorage points are approximately ten miles from shore, placing thousands of exposed and vulnerable infantry and sailors within artillery range.[484] Taiwan's ground forces plan to be waiting for them with mobile rocket launchers and large artillery guns perched on coastal hills. They would spray fire on Chinese ships approaching from over the horizon.[485]

Perhaps the most notable capability in Taiwan's arsenal for attacking enemy forces as they approach is the *Ray-Ting* 2000 (Thunderbolt 2000), a wheeled multiple-launch rocket system. Rockets have longer ranges and considerably larger payloads when compared to traditional artillery, but they can be relatively inaccurate and slow to reload. To overcome this, the *Ray-Ting* 2000 combines rockets into tubes that can fire volleys simultaneously. They have guided munitions, with shotgun-like projectiles filled with tens of thousands of ball bearings. They are anticipated to create macabre kill zones around the anchorage sites and along amphibious lines of approach.[486] If long-range interdiction failed to turn back the attack, Taiwanese tanks, armored fighting vehicles, and infantry would greet Chinese invaders up close on the beaches with murderous firepower.[487]

Sequence of Joint Interdiction Operations

PLA assembling and loading amphibious ships along PRC coast	
Interdicting Forces	**Potential Targets**
Surface-launched cruise missiles (HF-2E)	Strategic (politically sensitive) targets, command posts, power grid
Fighter jets (F-16, IDF) armed with joint standoff weapons, Harpoon missiles, Maverick missiles, etc.	Airfields, docked ships, ground transportation infrastructure (rail and road bridges), logistics (fuel depots), radars
Ballistic missiles (Yun Feng, TK-B)	Strategic (politically sensitive) targets, command posts, power grid
Special operations forces (frog-men)	Harbor facilities, radars, command posts, bridges
Anti-radiation drones	Early warning radars

PLA crossing the Taiwan Strait	
Interdicting Forces	**Potential Targets**
Anti-ship missiles (Harpoons, HF-2, HF-3) launched from aircraft, ships, subs, land bases	Large amphibious assault ships, escort vessels, mine sweepers
Anchoring and disembarking troops	
Interdicting Forces	**Potential Targets**
Multiple launch rocket systems (RT-2000)	Amphibious assault ships, escort vessels, mine sweepers, hovercraft, helicopters
Attack helicopters (AH-1W Super Cobras)	
Fighter jets (F-16, IDF, Mirage, F-5)	
Frigates (Perry, Knox, Layette class)	
Stealth corvette (Tuo-Chiang class)	
Missile boats (Kuang Hua VI class)	
PLA approaching coast in landing craft	
Interdicting Forces	**Potential Targets**
Artillery (203mm, 155mm, 105 howitzers, 120mm mortars)	Landing craft, amphibious tanks
Attack helicopters (AH-64E Apaches)	
Multiple launch rocket systems (Kung Feng IV)	

PLA storming the beaches and moving inland	
Interdicting Forces	**Potential Targets**
Heavy tanks (M60A3, M48H)	
Armored fighting vehicles (M48A3, M42, CM-32 "Clouded Leopard")	
Infantry with anti-tank missiles (FGM-148 Javelin, etc.)	Landing craft, amphibious tanks, bulldozers, officers, combat engineers, infantry
HUMVEE with anti-tank missiles (BGM -71 TOW, etc.)	
Snipers	
Gun emplacements, machine gun nests, mortar pits, grenade launchers	

This table is notional and for illustrative purposes only. Based on available ROC military and PLA assessments.

Phase Three: Homeland Defense

In the seemingly impossible event that everything else failed to stop the invasion and Chinese troops actually began landing in force, Taiwan's generals would turn to their defense plan's final chapter. The homeland defense phase of the Gu'an Plan is designed to crush amphibious forces at the water's edge and wipe out airborne troops on their landing zones. In this phase, any surviving air force planes and naval ships would join army artillery and helicopter units in lethal volleys against landing ships. Infantry would defend fortified beaches, airbases, and ports, while rapid reaction units enveloped and smashed into enemy lodgments. The full weight of Taiwan's superior ground force, including elite army and marine units, would finally come into action on well-prepared home grounds.[488]

It cannot be known by anyone what would actually happen on Z-Day. Nonetheless, the ROC Army has planned it out in fine detail. It is assessed that the first wave of Chinese tanks and troops landed on their assigned beach sectors would likely be spread out in small battalion sized pockets, each around 500 men strong. They would be showered with artillery shells and hit with mechanized counterattacks, which would probably commence 40–60 minutes after they had slogged ashore, or just as they were about to break through beach obstacles and penetrate the perimeters of frontline bases. It is expected that bloody battles would continue for hours, as units struggled for mastery over the shore and the nearby terrain. If Taiwanese forces were unable to push landing forces back into the sea, they would regroup at fortified bases and try again, encircling and destroying amphibious tanks and firing down the beaches from the flanks.[489]

Second wave counterattacks would be launched in the afternoon or at dusk, after it was clear where the main thrusts of Chinese landings were concentrated. These are envisioned to be larger, continuous, and multi-directional assaults on beachheads. They would be directed by the ROC Army's local theater headquarters, who would direct armor and mechanized brigades against long coastal stretches, now likely to be held by division sized units, each around 10,000 men.[490] Assuming the interior roads were passable, additional brigades would at this point arrive from other theaters, pouring on the scene to reinforce any counterattacks that got bogged down. Meanwhile, a giant joint force would be gearing up for the big night fight.

If needed, Taiwan's anti-invasion plan reportedly envisions third wave counterattacks, which would be the supreme and final event of the war. It is assumed the Chinese might be able to defend their footholds throughout Z-Day, stabilizing beach landing areas and expanding into nearby airports and seaports. This could allow them to bring forces ashore throughout the tumultuous day. As night grew deeper, the landing troops, having fought all daylong after a harried crossing the night before, would feel their energy drain away. Equipment could start to run low. More reinforcements might be brought ashore in the dark, but the tempo of offloading operations would have to slow. Any light that was turned on would become a homing beacon for artillery guns perched in the surrounding mountains. Mines and obstacles would still be littered everywhere, making coastal movement in the dark perilous. The tides would be changing again and again, and perhaps the weather too.

In the early morning hours of Z+1, the shadowy scene would light up with explosions and flares. It is anticipated that strategic rapid reaction units (the 66th and 99th Marine brigades), armor, self-propelled artillery, and helicopter gunships would come streaming down out of the hills and the cities, followed by multitudes of infantrymen, who would wash over the invaders like a human tsunami.[491] Airborne assault troops would drop right on top of the astonished enemy, landed by parachute or Blackhawk helicopter. Special forces teams, highly proficient at night fighting, would plunge behind PLA lines from the land, air, and sea. Others would emerge from tunnels and urban hide-sites. Fighter jets, ships, and submarines that had survived to this point in the conflict would now converge on the soft flanks of the landing zones. Ships anchored offshore and beached along the coast would be torn apart. Ammunition and fuel drums piled on the beaches would be blown up in garish eruptions of flame and smoke.[492]

By dawn, it is anticipated that the war would have surged to its culmination point. PLA command posts ashore and afloat would likely be shattered, Chinese tanks, artillery pieces, and air defense guns everywhere smoldering wrecks. Mass casualties, with entire units driven back into the sea and drowned, some consumed by the toxic smoke of burning chemical plants and tank farms, others surrendered and captured. Ships sunk in vast numbers, the lucky ones limping wounded back to their home ports. Havoc would reign across southeastern China. Communications blackouts across the mainland would follow, purges in Beijing, the possibility of an impending regime change.

This is one way the invasion could end. There are others. If the Chinese attacks prior to Z-Day were devastating enough, Taiwan's president, political advisors, and high command (the General Staff Department at the MND) could be dead, or cut off in isolated bunkers and unable to communicate. If the theater-level command bunkers and mobile brigade command posts were also neutralized, no one could organize the counterattacks. Fighting would be localized and disjointed. If there were no surviving helicopters and jets, and no ships and submarines left, and the roads were rendered impassable to tanks and armored vehicles, the landing zones would be safe. PLA divisions could continue swarming ashore. Taiwanese special operations forces could make sharp attacks, backed up by masses of local infantry, but the enemy would probably have helicopter gunships and ground attack fighters over their heads, raking them with cannon fire and missiles. During daylight hours, the defenders would also be at the mercy of warship guns and bombers.[493]

In this nightmare scenario, the anti-invasion plan envisions a grueling war of attrition, which would commence amidst the rubble of cement buildings, through fragmented factories and residential neighborhoods. If Taiwan's ground forces were not able to achieve their objective of winning a decisive battle along the shore, they would fall back onto prepared defensive lines running across cities and mountains. These control the transportation arteries and bottlenecks. As citizen-soldiers fell back, they would demolish bridges, tunnels, supply depots, fuel stores, airport tarmacs, and anything else that might be of aid to the enemy. They would move and regroup within one fortified network after the next, steeling themselves for a marathon of fierce and drawn out battles. They would fight without control over the air or seas, but on familiar terrain that is highly favorable to the defense.[494]

The objective at this stage of operations would be to prevent the PLA from conquering key inland points around the island, while protecting rear area sanctuaries so that reinforcements could marshal and move to the front. The Taiwanese army would fight, move, wait; fight, move, wait. As the aggressor ground his way closer to the capital, some defenders would hideout and fight from underground metro lines, or subterranean parking garages, or from under bridge overpasses.[495] Others would fight in the streets, moving from one building to the next, others outside in the jungle and hills.[496] All of them hoping and praying that the Americans (and/or the Japanese) used their superior air and naval firepower to seal off the Strait, strangling the PLA's lifelines to Taiwan.[497]

According to one former defense minister, the Gu'an Plan apparently estimates that the ROC military would be able to hold out unassisted for at least 30 days. Other Taiwanese defense ministers have posited that American forces would have to arrive at Taiwan's side sooner—within 21 to 28 days, or even in as little as two weeks. They argue that, though highly improbable, it is possible everything might go awry for defenders in the first days of fighting. The political and military leadership might be neutralized, air control lost, and morale subsequently shattered. It is not clear if the notional clock on this grim thought experiment would begin ticking on Z-Day or when pre-invasion hostilities commenced. The latter seems much more probable.[498] Not everyone in Taiwan's defense community assumes American military assistance is critical to victory, and some generals are optimistic they could handle the invasion on their own. Most Taiwanese military officers, however, believe that they would need American air and naval support. Nonetheless, they are highly confident in their ability to resist and repulse invasion on the ground alone, if necessary.[499]

ROC military research teams have used advanced modeling techniques to simulate a worst-case invasion scenario. In one computer war game, they assumed the PLA could have complete mastery over the electromagnetic, air, and sea domains 12 days into the onset of hostilities. They further assumed that on Z-Day the PLA could land three group armies (105,000 men) at multiple points along Taiwan's west coast (apparently at Taoyuan, Taichung, and Tainan), paving the way for a huge follow-on wave of troops to land. They also assumed that the ROC Army suffered pre-war defense cuts, and China achieved complete strategic surprise, which meant the reserve forces were not mobilized before Z-Day. Finally, they assumed that the transportation grid was paralyzed by bombing, so defense units could not move up or down the island to reinforce each other. These assumptions left the Taiwanese side a meager force of 98,000 troops, divided between three isolated theaters of operations. Despite embracing remote possibilities, their simulations nonetheless found that in 17 out of 18 trial runs, the defense was able to repulse invasion by Z+8. In the 18th trial, northern

Taiwan was lost on Z+45, after a grueling fight, but central and southern Taiwan held fast.[500]

Modeling and simulation can only do so much. Operational researchers and army officers in Taiwan warn that war gaming is neither reliable nor predictive. Urban warfare, in particular, is so complex that it defies modeling and crashes military-grade supercomputers. The unending exponential multiplication of variables over time simply overwhelms software. Just to play through Z+1 requires that analysts make leaps of faith and dumb down their coding. In truth, it is unknowable in advance how things would really play out. How long could the outer island perimeter and the Penghus hold? How severe might the blockade and bombing be? How many days would it last? After that, how many divisions could the PLA really land on Z-Day and the days following? How long could the PLA sustain its operations ashore? How long might defenders stand against a full-scale invasion if the Americans never showed up? Would the Japanese enter the war and conduct fleet and air actions or assist Taiwan in other ways? Would the democracies of the world join the fight to save Taiwan, or would they cower in fear?

Taiwanese military analysts have scrutinized the possibilities open to the invader. If the enemy landed on Taiwan, they predict he would probably not be able to stay for long. For their part, PLA theorists, in full recognition of the complex problems facing campaign plans, hope their ground forces could move fast to achieve a decisive victory on the island, but worry the war would drag on for a protracted period of time. Taiwan's government and military, in their eyes, will probably be fiercely resolved when the crunch comes and fight courageously to the bitter end.[501]

If the impregnable fortress of Taiwan was actually breached, the contextual peculiarities of the situation would decide what happened next. As much would depend on luck and determination as on plans and preparation. More than anything else, the prospects of war and peace, invasion and survival, hinge on what the United States and its allies do in the years ahead.

Chapter Seven
American Strategy in Asia

I will prevent disease whenever I can, for prevention is preferable to cure.

—Hippocratic Oath

THERE is an odd defect in the human mind that allows people living under an enormous dam to suffer little anxiety as the reservoir behind it gradually fills to the brim and the concrete walls crack from the mounting force. In such circumstances, most people will go about their daily business. The specter of sudden catastrophe will remain unthinkable to them, if only because it has not yet happened—as if the ravages of time were positive evidence instead of something to worry about. In the aftermath, the same defect will cause survivors of disaster to blame it all on the trigger event, the unforeseen engineering flaw or earthquake or storm that finally burst the dam and brought the water crushing down. People naturally ignore that unhappy reality: all dams break sooner or later if they are not strengthened.

Like people living under a slowly failing dam, many observers of the Taiwan Strait flashpoint are convinced that disaster will not strike as long as no trigger event occurs. Of these, the most frequently mentioned is a formal Taiwanese declaration of *de jure* independence. Proximate causes of war, while dramatic and easily seen, are unimportant when the situation is structurally unstable and the political problems intractable. In situations such as this one, violent conflict may eventually become unavoidable no matter what Washington and Taipei do. Attempts to appease Beijing are at least as likely to encourage aggression as those aimed at providing Taiwan with international recognition. Sooner or later, the dam is probably going to surrender to the pressure and break.

The Taiwan Strait has separated two countries, China (PRC) and Taiwan (ROC), since 1949. The fissures between them have grown over time and will continue to grow. For a long time, both Beijing and Taipei falsely claimed that there was only one China in the world and they were the sole legal representative of it. Only one side now maintains that position. To resolve the issue, China has engaged in an arms race on a vast scale, while the United States, distracted by events elsewhere in the world, has allowed its defenses to stagnate in the Pacific. American leaders have done little to address the fact that China's main strategic objective is to conquer Taiwan, something that would give Beijing hegemony over East Asia and the Western Pacific. If nothing major changes, if the United States continues conducting business like everything was fine, the dangers will continue to rise. They will rise to the point where the slightest push could set off a chain of events that unleashes seven decades of pent-up aggression.

The trigger could very well be an accident or innocent act, something calculated as benign but perceived as hostile. It may go down in history as an infamous event, or it may not be understood what exactly happened. Like the case of World War I, the true cause may be debated for a century and still undecided. Defense plans are for times of madness like these, but they are of limited utility by themselves. It is important to be ready when the dam bursts—that is what this book so far has attempted to address—but far better would be to figure out how to strengthen the dam and lower the pressure. That is what this chapter is about.

While few are comfortable admitting it, the United States and China are firmly entrenched in what will likely be a long and intense strategic competition for dominance over the Pacific Rim.[502] American strategists Andrew Marshall, Robert Kaplan, and Aaron Friedberg each began foretelling of this great power struggle well over a decade ago.[503] They were quick to recognize that there are strong forces underpinning the U.S.-PRC rivalry. Events have proven their foresight. In February 2016, then Secretary of Defense, Ashton Carter, announced that great power competition has reemerged as the Pentagon's top priority and would define the next twenty-five years.[504] That same month, the Commander of the Pacific Command, Admiral Harry Harris, warned the Senate Armed Services Committee that China seeks hegemony in East Asia.[505]

Their candid assessments came as a surprise to many. It has been taboo to speak of competition with China in an honest and open way in Washington power circles. What they said was nonetheless quite appropriate and strategically healthy. The first step of dealing with a highly sensitive global problem is admitting it exists. In the nuclear age, avoiding conflict between great powers is absolutely essential, and the weight of evidence suggests that nothing is more likely to invite war than covering up uncomfortable truths. Obsequiousness and silence in the face of coercion could only validate Beijing's behavior.

The political systems and national interests of the United States and PRC stand in fundamental opposition to each other. America is an imperfect democracy, but it nonetheless is an inspiration to people everywhere who yearn for the freedom and dignity that come from having a representative government, independent legal system, and market economy. In contrast, all power in China is monopolized by the Communist Party, an unelected political organization which has a troubling history.[506] The State Department's annual report on human rights makes it clear that China's government is a deeply authoritarian regime, and one that continues to oppress the Chinese people.[507]

The CCP compounds its governance failures by forgoing moves toward a genuine market economy and stifling innovation. For all its much celebrated reforms, China's economy is still largely run by CCP-controlled corporations, making it a mercantilist country, not a capitalist one.[508] China treats the American-led international economic order with contempt, bending or breaking all the rules when it comes to trade and finance, and stealing what it cannot create. According to authoritative studies, much of China's economic power stems from its ability to lure foreign business elites with promises of access to an immense market. Once the hook is set, state industries routinely pocket American companies' investments, siphon off their intellectual property, and undercut their market competitiveness.[509]

It is not China's disquieting political or economic practices that will ensure sustained competition over the coming years. American presidents, pragmatic by nature, will generally seek to paper over ideological differences for expediency's sake. It is the CCP that is at the root of the problem.[510] China's leadership has recently stoked tensions with Japan, South Korea, and the Philippines, all American treaty allies; provoked border clashes with India, a democracy and security partner; and enabled nuclear missile proliferation amongst North Korea, Pakistan, and Iran.[511] Track records tell a compelling story. That is why credit scores (remarkably accurate predictions of future financial behavior) rely entirely on historical data points. Beijing's track record indicates that a growing number of geostrategic issues could result in a clash between America and China.

Washington's attempts to cooperate with CCP leaders and shape China into a responsible stakeholder have foundered and will continue to achieve little. Elites in Beijing view the United States as hostile to their revanchist interests, and they will continue to compete regardless of foreign gestures of goodwill.[512] Anti-American pathologies have long plagued Chinese decision-making, but conditions have grown considerably worse under the current General Secretary of the CCP, Xi Jinping.[513] His cognitive failures appear to include a paranoid reading into American actions, hawkish ideology, and departures from reality.[514] Making matters worse, Chairman Xi has engaged in a brutal campaign to purge his peers within the party elite. The collective leadership model cultivated in the 1980s by Deng Xiaoping, while profoundly flawed, at least had checks and balances for restraining radical decision-making. Those internal constraints are now gone, a development attended by immense risks.

The U.S. government has failed to develop and dedicate the resources needed for the broad collection, translation, analysis, and dissemination of Chinese writings and speeches. As a consequence, Washington has only a limited understanding of the official Chinese worldview, and even less knowledge of what is going on inside China's halls of power. In the absence of understanding, too many Americans assume that the PRC operates basically like the United States, when in fact it is profoundly different in all the ways that matter: politically, economically, and militarily.[515] This is why Chinese behavior so often puzzles Western observers, and this is why, despite the long-time reluctance to officially admit it, strategic competition is here to stay.

Past as Prologue

To better see the shape of things to come, we must first look to the past. Prior to America's entrance into World War II, the nation had much reason to fear Nazi Germany and Imperial Japan, but isolationism meant there were few actual flashpoints. Only an enemy attack on American soil, realized at Pearl Harbor, could drag the country into war. In contrast, the Cold War featured a rapid expansion of American security commitments and interests abroad. Far-flung standoffs and proxy wars ranged from the Korean Peninsula to Berlin, from Cuba to Vietnam, and from Afghanistan to Grenada. When the Soviet Union collapsed in 1991, the world became a much safer place for the United States and other democracies. Great power conflict and the attendant specter of nuclear war no longer seemed threatening simply because no other country had the military wherewithal to compete. After a twenty-year military buildup, China now confronts America with a new rivalry and new flashpoints around which to organize strategic efforts.

Of all the powder kegs out there, the potential for a war over Taiwan is by far the largest and most explosive.[516] China has made clear that its primary external objective is attaining the ability to apply overwhelming force against Taiwan during a conflict, and if necessary destroy American-led coalition forces.[517] Chinese strategists focus on Taiwan because CCP elites are insecure. They view the island's government as a grave threat to their grip on power. Taiwan is anathema to them because it serves as a beacon of freedom for ethnically Chinese people everywhere.[518] Consequently, the PLA considers the invasion of Taiwan to be its most critical mission, and it is this envisioned future war that drives China's military buildup.[519]

Understanding any Taiwan Strait war scenario requires some myth-busting. It has become conventional wisdom that Taiwan will eventually be pulled into China's orbit by cross-Strait trade entanglements.[520] In spite of the power disparity that exists, Taipei's close ties with Washington means that it does not have to bow to coercion from the authorities in Beijing, economic or otherwise.[521]

Nor is America likely to sell Taiwan out, another remarkably popular myth.[522] The American commitment to Taiwan is articulated in U.S. Public Law 96-8, the Taiwan Relations Act.[523] This legal instrument is founded on bedrock judgments of national interest. While it is true that there are those in Washington who have convinced themselves that Taiwan cannot prevail in a protracted contest with its giant neighbor across the Strait, they are making an unwise assumption, both for Taiwan's sake and the sake of America's own security. Every professional strategist since Admiral Chester Nimitz and General Douglas MacArthur has recognized that Taiwan is a center of gravity in the Asia-Pacific.[524] The island sits astride the world's busiest maritime and air superhighways, right in the middle of the first island chain, a defensive barrier keeping Chinese military power in check.[525]

America does not covet Taiwan as a base for its soldiers, sailors, marines, and airmen, but it does require that the island remain in the hands of a friendly government. If Taiwan were lost, Japan, South Korea, and the Philippines would become vulnerable to naval blockades and air assaults. For this reason, and many others, any Chinese attempt to gain control of Taiwan would almost certainly be regarded as an attack on the vital interests of the United States, and therefore repelled by any means necessary, including the use of force.

While China's expansionism in the South China Sea has dominated the discourse on the PRC's rise and brought its naval threat into sharp relief, it is the threat to Taiwan that will most likely keep the Pentagon awake at night in the years ahead.[526] The RAND Corporation, the venerable defense think tank that helped guide America's strategic competition with the Soviet Union, has repeatedly warned of the challenge PLA modernization poses to America, especially in a Taiwan conflagration.[527] The

ROC military still maintains an array of potent capabilities, but its overall combat power risks being eclipsed by China's rapid buildup, increasing the likelihood of future aggression.[528] Barring a dramatic reduction in Taiwan's self-defense capabilities or a general reversal of American military power in Asia, the direct defense of Taiwan will remain a credible strategy for the foreseeable future—but only if leaders in Washington and Taipei can work more closely together.[529]

According to RAND, China's investments into space and cyberspace weaponry, conventional ballistic missiles and cruise missiles, and stealthy submarines and fighters all make it more conceivable that America could lose the next war, or at the very least fail to deter it, a strategic defeat in its own right. Maintaining a favorable balance of power in the Taiwan Strait will therefore be essential for the prevention of catastrophe.[530] The destructive potential of China's growing military strength means that even though America and coalition partners are likely to emerge from any future war over Taiwan victorious, they would still wish more had been done to keep the conflict from occurring in the first place.

Thinking Ahead

The question of how to best deter Chinese aggression against Taiwan will be hotly debated in the years ahead and rightfully so; peace and prosperity in Asia and beyond are riding on America's ability to address this challenge. Some scholars have entertained notions of abandoning Taiwan, coldly trading it away for other ends as if it were a stack of poker chips.[531] Their views, however, will be ignored by policymakers in Washington who recognize that the dispute between China and Taiwan cannot be separated from the larger geopolitics of the region, and that there is an underlying confluence of U.S.–Taiwan interests.[532]

Taiwan is critical not only for its location, but also for its shared liberal values and its position as a key trading partner.[533] Chinese diplomats in Washington often assert that China is big and Taiwan is little, and therefore constructive relations with China matter more and it is in the American interest to compromise on Taiwan. When it comes to freedom, human rights, and quality of government, Taiwan towers over China. Experience has shown senior American policymakers time and time again that nations that share democratic values are the best partners and worth defending. Common values generate common interests, which are the basis for making a common cause in addressing global challenges.

Taiwan has intrinsic value as a responsible member of the international community. It is also America's tenth largest trading partner, ahead of Saudi Arabia, Italy, and Brazil.[534] The Taiwanese excel when it comes to researching, designing, and manufacturing the advanced technology that drives much of America's economy. Integrated circuits (or microchips) are the brains of our handheld devices and computers. The global chip-making business as we know it was invented by Taiwan in the 1980s and the high-tech island nation still occupies a strong position on the global supply chain. Today China is rapidly catching up, something that poses a serious threat to the security of the world's hardware.[535] America needs Taiwan as a "Silicon Shield," keeping the technology of tomorrow from being controlled and corrupted by an adversary.[536]

Washington has long suffered from a lack of strategic clarity, unsure of what is needed to compete effectively against China or even whether there is a real competition underway. Ever since the early 1970s, many American foreign policy elites have taken it for granted that the PRC was of supreme importance and that Washington needed Beijing's cooperation, first as a counterweight to the USSR, then for market access, and more recently as a partner on global issues ranging from North Korea to terrorism and from proliferation to climate change. This view is especially pronounced among those who embrace the notion that America is in decline and authoritarian China is going to prevail over the long run. From their perspective, the best the United States can do is make a "grand bargain" from a position of weakness that would limit China's ascendency to its own sphere of interest, much like detente tried (and failed) to do with the Soviet Union.[537] American presidents, influenced by these defeatist views, have sometimes gone to great lengths to appease China's communist leadership. The tendency to overvalue the strategic importance of U.S.-China relations is something that unnecessarily weakens

Washington's bargaining power with Beijing, and undermines efforts to formulate long-term strategy.

America's relatively sanguine approach to China's emergence as a strategic competitor is increasingly difficult to reconcile with events. Over the past decade the PRC has offered numerous indicators that trouble is lurking ahead, each of which has been minimized or ignored in the name of positive Sino-American relations. One of the first wake-up calls came on January 11, 2007, when China shot a ballistic missile into a target satellite in low earth orbit.[538] This missile test was followed by several others, all which clearly demonstrated China's intention to weaponize space and neutralize the eyes and ears of American military power in a conflict.[539] Another warning came in 2010, when China deployed the world's first anti-ship ballistic missile, a weapon apparently capable of targeting aircraft carriers, the queens of America's fleet.[540] Many other unsettling developments, both diplomatic and military, followed over the course of the next several years.[541]

A startling number of American "China Hands" have turned a blind eye to these developments, and instead have clung to the false hope that mutual economic interdependence, military-to-military exchanges, and favorable diplomatic treatment could build trust and socialize China, enticing it into becoming a responsible stakeholder. They often emphasize the risks of inadvertent conflict and rapid escalation if their policy prescriptions are not followed. However, none of their recommendations, which have been tested to the limit of prudence in recent years, have dulled China's ruthless competitive instincts. If anything, examples of American risk aversion and compromise have only emboldened Beijing to push farther and harder.[542]

Recognizing the gathering storm ahead, Kurt Campbell, then Assistant Secretary of State for East Asia, spearheaded the pivot to Asia strategy in the first years of the Obama administration.[543] The pivot, or "rebalance" as it became known, was warmly welcomed by America's allies and partners in Asia. As part of the effort, the Pentagon publically rolled out its new Air-Sea Battle Office, which generated excitement among those who recognized fresh operational concepts were needed for dealing with China's growing military threat.[544] The excitement was short-lived. Then-President

Obama shuffled his cabinet in early 2013, and things began unraveling. The new foreign policy team, characterized by a strong focus on the Middle East, Europe, and climate change, allowed the much-anticipated strategy to gather dust on the drawing board. Asia policy, and especially Taiwan policy, fell to the wayside.[545]

In 2015, several major strategic setbacks occurred. First, the PRC created a giant archipelago of artificial islands in the South China Sea, claiming the entire area as a virtual province of China. This shocking development disrupted ongoing attempts to apply international legal mechanisms to settle disputes and weakened the defensive positions of Brunei, Indonesia, Malaysia, Philippines, Taiwan, and Vietnam.[546] Next, it was revealed that Chinese intelligence agents had penetrated sensitive computer systems and compromised the identities (including fingerprints) of over twenty million Americans who either worked for the federal government or had family members who did. The military, intelligence, and contractor communities lost untold reams of confidential information on their most precious asset: people.[547] Not long after, Chairman Xi held a jingoistic military parade in Beijing, rolling out a number of new weapons systems, including an intermediate-range ballistic missile capable of attacking the United States territory of Guam, a strategic hub in the Western Pacific.[548]

Selected Chinese Provocations, 2005–2015

Anti-Seccession Law (March 2005)
Actors: PRC, Taiwan, USA
China passes a law aimed to "legalize" a military attack on Taiwan (and the United States) if its vaguely defined "red lines" are crossed.

First Joint Sino-Russian Military Exercise (August 2005)
Actors: PRC, Russia
China and Russia stage their first joint military exercise since the Cold War, "Peace Mission 2005," an event that appeared to simulate an assault on Taiwan.

Anti-Satellite Missile Test (January 2007)

Actors: PRC, USA, others

China successfully carries out test of an anti-satellite missile, creating massive debris cloud endangering the International Space Station and U.S. intelligence satellites.

USNS Impeccable Incident (March 2009)

Actors: PRC, USA

Chinese maritime forces harass an unarmed U.S. ocean surveillance ship in international waters.

Anti-Ship Ballistic Missile Deployment (Late 2010)

Actors: PRC, USA

China's strategic rocket force deploys the world's first anti-ship ballistic missile, a weapons system designed for targeting ships, including U.S. aircraft carriers.

Stealth Fighter Test (January 2011)

Actors: PRC, USA

China unveils stealth fighter prototype during visit of then-U.S. Defense Secretary Robert Gates to Beijing.

Scarborough Reef Occupation (April–July 2012)

Actors: PRC, USA, Philippines,

China illegally occupies a reef near the Philippines after failing to abide by U.S.-negotiated deal to end standoff in the area.

Air Defense Identification Zone Declaration (November 2013)

Actors: PRC, Japan, USA, Taiwan, South Korea

China declares an intrusive air defense identification zone in the East China Sea without prior notification of other parties.

USS Cowpens Incident (December 2013)

Actors: PRC, USA

Chinese warship unsuccessfully attempts to collide with U.S. guided missile cruiser in international waters.

Spy Ship Incident at RIMPAC Exercises (July 2014)
Actors: PRC, USA, others
Chinese naval intelligence-gathering ship arrives uninvited to U.S.-led Rim of the Pacific naval exercises near Hawaii despite participation of other PRC ships.

Island Building in South China Sea (Spring 2015)
Actors: PRC, USA, others
China begins rapid buildup of artificial islands in the South China Sea, militarizing the international maritime sovereignty dispute.

Security Clearance Data Hack (June–July 2015)
Actors: PRC, USA
Chinese intelligence hack into security clearance files of over 22 million Americans revealed.

Military Parade in Beijing (September 2015)
Actors: PRC
China conducts large-scale military parade in Beijing, unveiling DF-26 "Guam Killer" ballistic missile, and other advanced nuclear-capable delivery vehicles.

Confidence in American leadership has declined among allies and partners across the Asia-Pacific as a result of Beijing's actions and Washington's inactions. While the Bush and Obama administrations developed some excellent talking points, not enough was actually done to adapt to changing facts on the ground. Strong rhetoric and weak execution is a toxic mix. It hit Taiwan especially hard because Taipei has no other security partners to turn to for help, and its threat-environment is the most stressing. Taiwanese officials discovered to their chagrin that Washington was unwilling to sell them new fighter jets, tanks, drones, and destroyers.[549] Even diesel-electric submarine technology, promised in 2001, proved out of reach.[550] The White House, fearful of rousing Beijing's ire, instead offered Taiwan equipment of the type provided to Mexico.[551] Adding insult to injury, the Taiwanese looked on in astonishment as U.S. Navy ships made port calls up and down the Chinese coast, then sailed around Taiwan at full steam as if it were a failed state, not a flourishing and friendly democracy.[552]

The landslide results of the 2016 presidential and legislative elections in Taipei are telling. The citizens of Taiwan chose Dr. Tsai Ing-wen, who is widely viewed as tough on China and friendly to America, and therefore more likely to secure a better future relationship with Washington.[553] At the same time, they also chose the Democratic Progressive Party whose policy platform calls for a more robust indigenous defense industry as a pragmatic hedge against continued American dysfunction.[554] Taiwan's government wants to arm itself and will do so whether its long-standing ally feels it can help or not. Its resolve is likely to mean that the island, largely ignored for the past two decades, will soon be at the forefront of American geostrategic thinking. If the contest of the century is to be waged between the United States and China for primacy in the Pacific, Taiwan will be at the center of the action.

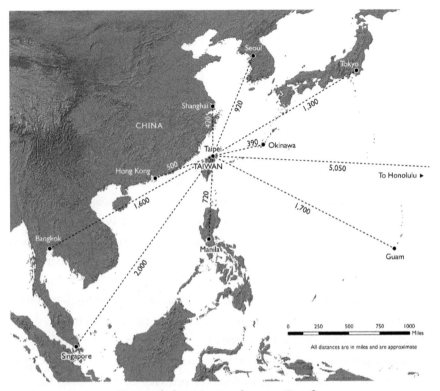

Taiwan's location in the west Pacific

Broad Contours of Strategy

Going forward, one of the central problems for U.S. foreign policy in Asia is that Taiwan, a democracy located in a crucial geostrategic location, could be invaded. The question every political leader and military officer from Washington to Honolulu, and Tokyo to Canberra should be asking themselves is, "What would we do in the event of a Chinese invasion of Taiwan?" An even more important question might be, "Are we on a path that makes this high-end conflict more or less appealing to China? Can we prevent Beijing from breaking the peace?"

It is not enough for American strategists to think about whether or not they could fight and win a war. They must also think about how their adversary thinks about war so they can effectively induce him or coerce him away from it, to do things to make it less tempting. Because this problem is unlikely to go away and will only get more acute over time, it is essential to think in terms of a competitive strategy. American foreign policy works best when it is goal-oriented and sustainable for the long run. At the current time, it is neither. Insufficient effort has been put into creating a strategic vision for the future of Asia that benefits America's national interests.

The United States has been slow to acknowledge and accept that the PRC is its main strategic rival and the most dangerous source of instability in the world today. It is essential that the approach to Asia begins to reflect the fundamentally competitive nature of U.S.-China relations, including in the spheres of politics, economics, and defense.[555] An improved policy toward China in the future might consist of three primary pillars: external resistance to Chinese expansionism, especially as it relates to Taiwan, Japan, South Korea, and the Philippines; internal pressure to weaken the CCP and peacefully nudge China toward democracy; and purposeful negotiations on the basis of reciprocity.

Washington should seek to deter Chinese expansionism by competing effectively in a sustained manner with Beijing in all international arenas, but particularly in the overall balance in the Asia-Pacific. This geographical region is a priority for the American national interest. Maintaining a favorable balance of power should be the main focus of American policy toward China. However, nothing would benefit Beijing more than to get Americans to forbid their allies and partners from reaping the benefits of trade with China in exchange for security guarantees. It would be a mistake to turn the entire situation into a black and white choice between rivals. Demanding that everyone take sides in a polarized region would place great strain on America's diplomatic relationships. Rather, Washington's strategy should be to use political, economic, and military instruments of power to help free peoples pursue their destinies and dreams however they see fit and to support them as they resist Chinese pressure.

American policy should aim to support the process of political change in China, moving Beijing toward a more pluralistic political system. The power of the CCP must be steadily constrained by institutional checks and balances if China is to peacefully evolve to become a responsible democracy that plays a positive role in the world. China's intransigence has resulted from nothing America has done or failed to do. Rather, it is rooted in the nature of the regime. In the foreseeable future, there is nothing America could compromise on that might change the fact that China's leaders have to approach Washington as an enemy. Only their narrative of victimization and struggle gives them the basis for concentrating all authority into their own hands, denying self-determination to the Chinese people, and maintaining an oppressive system in the absence of an appealing ideology. By treating the United States as a rapacious, hostile force bent on undermining China's rightful rise, they can justify the infliction of suffering on ordinary people and demand unreasonable sacrifices from them. This, in turn, advances their goals of achieving security for themselves, their families, and their regime, in precisely that order. American leaders should consider whether or not they are inadvertently helping to support this rival system and strengthening its ability to engage in aggression.

An improved policy could be to engage China in negotiations to attempt to reach agreements only when they protect and enhance well-defined American interests. Pursuing open-ended dialogues, summits, and state visits for the sake of unclear objectives like "trust-building" unnecessarily gives the Chinese political leverage and wastes finite government resources and energies that would be better spent elsewhere. When exchanges and negotiations do occur, it is important that they are purposeful and consistent with the principle of strict reciprocity. To expect that concessions might be reciprocated and agreements honored is to be naive and to ignore decades of foreign policy history.

The United States must develop ways to communicate clearly that unacceptable Chinese behavior will incur costs that would significantly outweigh any of Beijing's hoped-for benefits. This is foundational to the implementation of American strategy in Asia, and continued peace and stability. China's leaders must clearly recognize that only genuine restraint in their behavior will bring the possibility of achieving future peace and prosperity. Washington would be well advised to continue to modernize

THE CHINESE INVASION THREAT

its military, both nuclear and conventional, to show both the Chinese and regional allies and partners that America is resolved to stand firmly in its commitments to the causes of peace, prosperity, and self-determination, and never accept a continued erosion of its military power. Calculations of possible war outcomes in all possible scenarios must always be so unfavorable to Chinese leaders that they do not perceive any incentive to initiate an attack. Elevating the role of Taiwan in U.S. strategy would likely prove to be the single most effective means of signaling resolve and purpose, diminishing the likelihood of a potentially cataclysmic regional conflict.

What would robust support for Taiwan look like? Setting aside the issues of "one China" or *de jure* Taiwan independence, Washington could assert that its official position is that: "The status of Taiwan remains to be determined, by peaceful means. The objective reality is that Taiwan's democratic government exists, and our policy is to treat Taiwan with respect and dignity, and provide it more international space." Under such a framework, the U.S. government could continue to maintain unofficial relations with Taiwan, and gradually normalize diplomatic contacts over time. Incrementally improving bilateral relations between Washington and Taipei is the best available way to avoid military confrontation with China while advancing the American interest in securing Taiwan from hostile takeover.

In the Taiwan Strait context, political and military issues are woven together so tightly that it is nearly impossible, and rarely advisable, to separate them. Washington's failure to think critically about its Taiwan policy over the past two decades has created a situation where American defense professionals are poorly equipped to make recommendations to their Taiwanese friends regarding what they ought to do to defend their homeland. ROC military officers dedicate their entire careers to the study and improvement of Taiwan's defense. In contrast, even those officials at the Pentagon, the American Institute in Taiwan, and the Pacific Command, who well understand the military situation at the tactical level of warfare, cannot coherently articulate thoughts regarding the strategic dimensions of the conflict.[556] Making any political-military analysis significantly more difficult, the Chinese have large forces of capable officers conducting bilingual propaganda, surveillance, misinformation, truth denial, and history manipulation operations.[557] Media reports on Taiwan defense issues, as a result, are notoriously misleading for American readers unable to assess motives or even the original sources.

Rethinking the Balance

Chinese propaganda, like a Potemkin village, is only effective when its target audience is either unaware of the farce or plays along and forgoes peeking behind the facade. To induce fear and obedience, the Chinese will often threaten to do things to their adversaries that are not politically or militarily feasible. They will intimidate with capabilities they do not have and feign self-confidence when little actually exists. As such, it is exceedingly difficult to truly understand the strategic balance in cross-Strait relations.

The most outstanding weaknesses of the PLA are often overlooked by American strategists, who tend to focus heavily on defense budgets, weapons ranges, equipment numbers, and other factors that can be easily quantified and compared. The annual Pentagon report to Congress on Chinese military power is a good example of this tendency. In recent years, it has painted a picture of a situation dire for the defense of Taiwan.[558] This picture is misleading because it focuses on the quantifiable at the expense of qualitative factors. Moreover, it only offers a detailed examination of the PLA's capabilities and not those of the ROC military, whose capabilities would be the ones to beat. If you build up the reputation of one fighter, but say little to nothing of the capabilities of their opponent, then you are painting a distorted picture that makes the described fighter more impressive since he is not being compared to anyone else in any meaningful way.[559] A better starting point when assessing the cross-Strait balance would be to take an unvarnished look at the two main actors involved.

The PLA is the armed wing of a political organization, the CCP, and not a normal professional military. It has no meaningful allies or partners. North Korea is unlikely to assist the Chinese to invade Taiwan. Pyongyang, with its own destabilizing behavior, is far more likely to continue serving as a mere distraction. The Chinese army must help defend land borders with fourteen sovereign states, few of which are closely aligned with Beijing, and many of which are unstable. Perhaps more importantly, militaries do not exist independent of their home nations. China's authoritarian system distorts reason, undermines bonds of trust, and relies on fear to sustain itself. The entire political structure is ridden with corruption, and the economic model is unsustainable. The PLA has made remarkable strides over the past two decades in the face of enormous challenges. But its foundation, human capital, is still weak.

The ROC Armed Forces, on the other hand, are a professional military, and they are bolstered by the best fighting force on the planet, the U.S. military. Taiwan has no land borders to patrol and is surrounded by rough waters that greatly augment its defense. It enjoys low levels of corruption because of its watchdog media and dynamic parliamentary system. The armed forces draw strength from a stable society and sustainable economic system. Their homeland is a prosperous, democratic country with an innovative, hard-working populace. Taiwan's troops are positioned on favorable terrain, both human and geographic. Taiwan's principal danger is not from within. The same cannot be said of China, where CCP leaders appear to believe their army could at any time snap and revolt.

China's war planning community is at a significant intellectual disadvantage. PLA officers must limit themselves to the study of past cases that are deemed politically acceptable. They learn nothing from failure, which is a far greater teacher than success. An example of this tendency can be found in their professional literature, where only wildly successful amphibious operations are examined. The World War II landings in North Africa, Sicily, and Normandy are clear favorites, alongside more recent assaults on Grenada and the Falklands. The American experience in the Pacific theater and the Allied landings at Dieppe and Anzio are nowhere to be seen in the PLA's writings. Costly and controversial past battles are censored even in restricted-access documents.

Censorship makes itself plain in other places inside their writings. Internal documents and technical studies fail to acknowledge the possibility of sustaining a real defeat. Everything that might happen on Taiwan is described as being inevitable. They never address the cardinal question that every good officer must face: If my Plan A fails, what is my Plan B? Heavy and costly frontal attacks with insufficient forces are what they appear to envision, but this is obscured by euphemisms and flowery rhetoric. Taiwan's strategists, however, have the advantage of coming from an open society and professional military culture. They study history to the full and ask themselves hard questions all the time.[560]

If that were the end of the story, there would be little to fear from the Chinese military. Unfortunately, the situation is far more complex. Taiwan is a country which is not treated like a country. Its diplomatic isolation, a result of poor policy choices in both Washington and Taipei, has deepened in recent years as a result of Chinese efforts to erase the existence of the island from the international consciousness. The fundamental security threat facing Taiwan is political in nature, not military, but politics affects the military balance because strategic choices like limiting arms sales and bilateral exercises can directly and negatively impact battlefield outcomes.

Recommendations

The United States will find it difficult to maintain a favorable balance against the PRC over the long run unless it reevaluates its policy and begins to integrate Taiwan into its strategy. For its part, Taiwan will not be able to ensure its security unless it is able to get more support from America. Peace and stability in the Taiwan Strait turn on whether or not Washington and Taipei can improve their bilateral political, economic, and military relationships. Progress undoubtedly can be made, with a bit of diplomatic ingenuity, while maintaining a formal, but unofficial relationship. Achieving official government-to-government relations should be the long-term goal. It is strategically unsound and morally indefensible for America not to diplomatically recognize a democracy and capable partner. Ideals, of course, oftentimes must be tempered with pragmatism. It is imperative to evolve policy in a steady and incremental fashion to avoid sudden and destabilizing countermoves from China.

The United States should focus on new initiatives which reflect the objective reality that Taiwan currently exists as a free and sovereign state. Since 1979, the most tangible manifestation of Taiwan's international political legitimacy has been American arms sales. However, since 2006, the United States has developed a pattern of freezing arms sales for long periods of time out of deference to Beijing. Multiple administrations have bought into the narrative that frequent, high-quality arms sales are too provocative to China. This policy has damaged America's credibility as a reliable security partner. It has also undermined Taiwan's negotiating position with China. Whether or not top-tier weapons systems like advanced fighter jets and stealthy diesel submarines could alone turn the tide at the tactical level of warfare is debatable and cannot be known until there is a war. At the strategic level, however, these systems would be valuable for bolstering Taiwan's defense. Their positive political effects would be immediate and undeniable, greatly bolstering confidence and morale in Taiwan.

It would be unwise for the U.S.–Taiwan military and security relationship to continue being so heavily dependent upon arms sales alone. Resiliency in any relationship is not found by creating single points of failure. The U.S. president and his top advisors should conduct regular exchanges with their Taiwanese counterparts, in person and on the phone. Taiwan should be invited to participate in activities such as international maritime events and negotiations over territorial disputes. U.S. military commanders, especially those at the two-star and above rank with significant joint experience, should regularly visit Taiwan from the Pentagon, Pacific Command, and Seventh Fleet. In a crisis, it will be imperative that they are able to provide the White House with military judgments that are informed by actual knowledge of the local terrain. The highest-ranking U.S. defense official serving in Taiwan should be a general, not a colonel, as was the case from the 1950s to the 1970s.

Other efforts to demonstrate support for Taiwan's government are possible and would be important components of a closer military and security relationship. Reciprocal ship visits, bilateral exercises, and defense industrial cooperation should all be positively considered. Taiwan's capable military should be allowed to work side-by-side with the U.S. military in conducting humanitarian and disaster relief operations, counter-terror operations, and cyber operations. Taiwan played an important and positive, but thankless, role in responding to reconstruction in Afghanistan, the nuclear disaster in Japan, Typhoon Haiyan in the Philippines, and Ebola in Africa. Much more can and should be done to make sure that Taiwan's future efforts are closely coordinated with those of the U.S. military.

Taiwan, for its part, has every right to be wary and cautious when dealing with China. It is now clear to Taipei that Beijing will never accept Taiwan's sovereignty and allow it to enjoy the international position in the world it deserves. The PRC has shown it will not hesitate to use every tool at its disposal, including economic links and cultural exchanges, to undermine Taiwan's government. The strongest and most enduring friend Taiwan has is the United States. Given the competing challenges that Washington is grappling with at home and around the world, Taipei is right to continue highlighting its concerns and its desire for a better bilateral relationship. Closer ties are needed.

As for defense matters, it might be thought that some small profit could be gained from an analytical overview of available Chinese writings. By knowing what the potential adversary plans to do, one may know where he might be best countered; and by knowing what he fears, one knows what weaknesses, real or imagined, to exploit. Several conclusions can be drawn from those PLA writings that have been analyzed in this book. The following briefly lays out three.

First, Taiwan's development of counterstrike capabilities seems to have significantly impacted PLA planning. On both the strategic and operational battlefields, joint interdiction capabilities have a strong effect.[561] It would be unwise for Taiwan to reduce its capacity to conduct strikes far across the Taiwan Strait. To the contrary, Taiwan should probably expand its stockpiles of long-range mobile missiles, fighter aircraft, rocket artillery, and drones, and consider deploying the most survivable of them close to PRC territory.

Second, engineering projects to harden and fortify island groups in the Taiwan Strait, especially Kinmen, Matsu, and the Penghus, appear to have successfully added a degree of complexity to PLA war plans. By creating forward bastions for intelligence collection and counterstrike in the Strait, the ROC military has made it more difficult for Chinese generals to imagine a fast and easy campaign to land on Taiwan proper. In the same vein, efforts to construct fortification lines and deeply buried underground facilities on the main island appear to have shaken the PLA's confidence that it could actually purchase an invasion campaign at an acceptable price, especially when defense works are combined with camouflage, concealment, deception, force dispersal, sheltering, and rapid repair.[562]

Third, Taiwanese electronic warfare capabilities for protecting command, control, communications, computer, intelligence, surveillance, and reconnaissance platforms, while denying them to the enemy, are critical. PLA writings make it clear that the first targets of their attack would be Taipei's eyes and ears in order to affect an information blackout. They demonstrate a widely held belief that victory is not possible for them if their forces do not control the electro-magnetic spectrum at every stage of the conflict. At the same time, Chinese officers view themselves as reliant upon information and communications capabilities, especially vulnerable satellites. The ROC military should continue efforts to make sure PLA commanders will not have unimpeded access to their satellites in a war. Chinese demands for intelligence on Taiwan, including intelligence derived from space assets, apparently still outstrip collection and analysis capabilities.[563]

When it comes to studying the threat posed by the PLA, both Taiwanese and American strategists have to overcome mirror imaging, a problem which plagues analysis the world over and must be avoided to the greatest extent possible. It is too easy to forget that reality and facts are things that are arbitrary and subjective. The same situation will often be perceived in radically different ways by those in opposing governments, each with their own personalities, experiences, organizational logics, politics, cultures, and sub-cultures. Strategic mistakes happen this way, often with tragic outcomes. The good news is that PLA officers only rarely underrate the challenges posed by the ROC military. Assuming that the civilians who sit on the all-powerful CCP Politburo Standing Committee listen to their military advisors, no invasion of Taiwan is going to be seriously contemplated as a viable option for many years to come. To understand why, one needs only to review the foundational beliefs that run throughout internal Chinese military documents.

One major assumption is that Taiwan's defenders are unlikely to ever give up. The Chinese military establishment nurtures hope that an interlocking combination of psychological warfare, subversion, electronic attack, bombing, and blockades might compel Taiwan's government to break and surrender. This would allow them to conquer and occupy the island cheaply. However, their assumption is that Taiwan's military will fight to the death to defend their cherished freedoms and democratic way of life. For this reason, Chinese troops must be prepared to invade Taiwan and face the traumas of urban warfare, mountain warfare, and colonial occupation.

Another major assumption is that the United States will almost certainly intervene. From the Chinese perspective, Taiwan occupies a critical geostrategic location. Whoever controls this island controls East Asia and the West Pacific. They believe it is widely recognized around the world that Taiwan is the high ground that will decide the outcome of the U.S.-PRC strategic competition. They take it for granted that the "Strong Enemy" and "World Hegemon" will not allow it to fall into their hands easily. PLA writings assume that America will help defend Taiwan, and they express concern that this might result in a great power war which would unhinge the CCP regime. Given their expressed fears, it seems unlikely that China would resort to invading Taiwan if it did not have some reasonable prospect that the United States could be deterred or sufficiently delayed from acting to secure its interests in Asia.

The next major assumption, which relates to the first two assumptions, is that a rapid and decisive war is imperative. PLA strategists recognize that China will have the luxury of choosing when, where, and how to invade. There is little that Taiwan could do to force the invasion before China had a chance to build up requisite forces. However, once the course of action had been decided upon and all the pieces were in place, amphibious operations would have to be launched suddenly to catch Taiwan off-guard. The objective would be to astonish and destroy Taiwan's government before the Americans could gather sufficient resolve to spoil their landings. Achieving surprise and rapid results would be critical, but they are viewed by PLA experts as highly unlikely.

These basic assumptions are foundational to the invasion scenario alone. They do not account for other possibilities, including a long and drawn-out stalemate. Rather than invade, China could opt to engage in a war of nerves that played out over the course of years or even decades. This should be considered more probable than invasion, especially if the correlation of forces continues to confront Chinese leaders with the prospect of a prohibitively costly and uncertain war. American strategists should prepare for the worst case, while using all instruments of national power to prevent conflict and secure a brighter future in Asia.

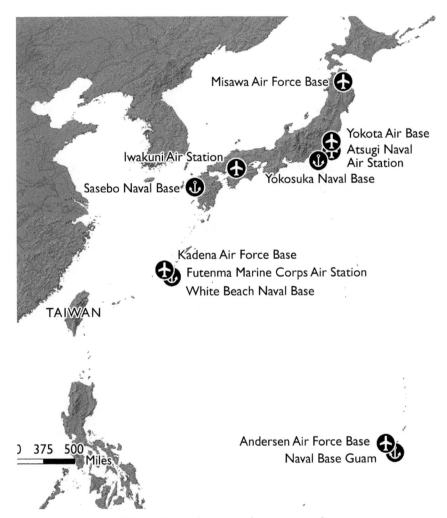

Misawa Air Force Base

Yokota Air Base
Atsugi Naval
Air Station
Iwakuni Air Station
Yokosuka Naval Base
Sasebo Naval Base

Kadena Air Force Base
Futenma Marine Corps Air Station
White Beach Naval Base

TAIWAN

0 375 500
Miles

Andersen Air Force Base
Naval Base Guam

U.S. military bases in the west Pacific

Chapter Eight
What Lies Ahead?

People always tell me how Taiwan is losing and China is winning. I don't understand this opinion.... You have two countries, Taiwan, capitalist, democratic, prosperous, and you have China, communist, autocratic, poor.

—U.S. President Bill Clinton

Regimes planted by bayonets do not take root.

—U.S. President Ronald Reagan

IT may be fairly observed that, in some ways, American foreign policy in Asia has evolved in an absurd fashion. Over the past two decades, Taiwan has become a vibrant full-fledged democracy, only to be treated like an international pariah state. Today, American diplomats are forbidden from recognizing Taiwan's ROC flag and calling the Taiwanese people and government by their proper names. At the same time, the PRC has become more authoritarian, only to be treated as if it were a respectable and even indispensable member of the community of nations. American policymakers have shown a remarkable deference to Beijing's cross-Strait interests.

As a consequence of this unnecessary, self-imposed policy choice, an entire generation of young Americans has been brought up believing that such is the natural order of things and it is somehow right and good that the principle of self-determination be denied to the Taiwanese people, who are being "provocative" every time they attempt to chart their own path. Too many people in too many places have resigned themselves to the perpetuation of a bizarre status quo in which might makes right. An amoral idea has been locked into the collective mind of American policy. Taken to its logical conclusion, a continued policy of accommodation would curse future generations in East Asia to live in a perpetual state of vulnerability and fear.

Already the situation in the Taiwan Strait is severe, but the emerging threat has not passed beyond the capabilities of the defending side, nor will it in the near future. There are even indications that trends in precision strike technology could provide Taiwan with a significant advantage. Missile and sensor technology developments could make it next to impossible for China to invade. In any event, it is not certain that Beijing will have the sustained economic strength required to continue its military buildup. If it does, the PLA would still have to break the defenders on their home island or lose a war because no elected government in Taipei is likely to surrender without a ferocious fight.

Taiwan's greatest danger is the possibility of a concentrated Chinese attempt to rapidly push an enormous invading force across the Strait. This threat has faced Taiwan for decades, and it is worsening over time. Dialogue, exchanges, and trade agreements with China will not save the Taiwanese from it. The CCP in recent years has focused on advancing its security interests at the expense of Japan and South Korea to the north, and the Philippines and Vietnam to the south, but its primary objective has always been Taiwan. Undoubtedly, the danger to Taiwan is being aggravated by the PLA's naval and air activities in the East China Sea, the Philippine Sea, and the South China Sea. The continued buildup of forces along the Chinese seaboard close to Taiwan should be the highest point of concern. It is an unmistakable sign that the CCP's intentions have not been changed by goodwill visits and improved cross-Strait trade.

There is every reason to expect that Taiwan, with American help, can meet the threat it faces. The ROC military may be incapable of interdicting small PLA raids of commandos raced across on fast hovercraft, but it is almost unimaginable that a force of several hundred thousand troops could be transported across the sea and maintained for more than two or three days against Taiwan's superior ground forces. As long as Taiwan's air force and navy exist—even if they are reduced only to fleets in being— they provide a powerful partner to the army and marines in preventing amphibious landings and would take a terrible toll against an invader.[564]

Although Taiwan is likely to suffer grievous losses in the first few days of attacks before the PLA invasion began, it appears well prepared to preserve sufficient strength for the final battle. Taiwanese invest- ments into long-range missiles make their air force and navy more lethal now than they have ever been. Surviving Taiwanese fighter jets would probably inflict a loss ratio of two or even three to one against inferior Chinese pilots when fighting above the adverse conditions of the Strait. Moreover, many Taiwanese pilots, even shot down, would crash land or parachute into home territory and would be able to get back into the fight. It is possible that Taiwanese air and naval forces may maul their adversaries so badly in the first days of war that the CCP leadership finds an invasion too costly.[565]

Chinese jet and ship numbers, of course, are far larger than those of the defending forces, but not so much larger as to deny the president of Taiwan a reasonable chance of wearing the enemy down after some days or weeks of mortal struggle around the Strait. Taiwan's leaders would almost certainly not sit passively and watch their cities bombed and burned. Missiles, rockets, and glide bombs could be launched from the island to strike continually at the PRC's critical nodes. These engagements might devastate any PLA ability to assemble an adequate invasion force at its staging areas.[566] Taiwanese soldiers and civilians will likely stand up to bombing and blockades every bit as well as their enemy, but probably better because their society is far more cohesive. Pollution, corruption, and injustice tear at China's social fabric every day. In any event, the fighting would be bitter for both sides once China initiated the war. All available information indicates that the PLA is deeply concerned by Taiwanese missile capabilities.

In the end, if the invasion operation was actually launched, it must be remembered that Taiwanese ground forces would be fighting in their homeland. They would be on familiar ground, inside prepared urban and mountain terrain that greatly advantages the defense. They have an enormous reserve force and would operate on internal lines of communications. These strengths would be further augmented by a supportive and grateful populace in the throes of war. Self-defense units would muster at temples, schools, and stadiums, and utilize local trucks and buses for clandestine transportation.[567] While Taiwan is hardly a Spartan society, the government has worked hard to keep its troops welcome at the local level. The land forces would be numerically superior at every possible amphibious landing beach, and far better motivated to win.

Therefore, it should be anticipated that whatever number of PLA troops could be dropped from the air or landed from sea would either be captured or killed. They would serve as an example to those who might try to follow. Taiwan, no doubt, must expect new forms of attack, including assassinations and attempts to bring special forces and mechanized forces quickly across the Strait, and race them toward the capital.[568] The ROC military is preparing to deal with these threats to the extent they can be foreseen.[569] No one can accurately predict the course of a bloody, life-and-death struggle like this one. It would be unprecedented in the modern history of amphibious and island warfare. If the Chinese attempt the ultimate act of aggression, Taiwan should certainly enter the war with confidence that it can defend its shores and cities better than the enemy can attack them.

There are compelling reasons behind Taiwan's resolve not to allow the nation to share the fate of Tibet and become a police state. Taiwanese soldiers, sailors, airmen, marines, and military police would have every reason to fight on to the end. The stakes for them would be so much higher than for their enemies. Respect for international law and shared values would probably draw the United States, Japan, Australia, and other democracies to Taiwan's side. Even in the highly unlikely event that Taiwan's northwestern and southwestern coastal defenses were overwhelmed and the major population centers were lost, the military could seal itself into a series of mountain redoubts in the island's eastern half that have been prepared at the cost of billions of dollars and decades of engineering.[570] These could enable Taiwan's leaders to continue the war. Along with American efforts to sustain it, the government could survive until the authorities in Beijing broke under the strain.

In the face of these facts, the Chinese propaganda system has for many years churned out a steady line, arguing that the doom of Taiwan is already sealed and annexation is a simple matter of time. Recent history has clearly shown this to be a spurious claim, falsified by events far beyond Beijing's control. Taiwan's democracy has never been stronger than it is today. But great political and military convulsions may very well be impending. A nuanced understanding of the PLA's strategy, doctrine, and war plan is essential. In the event of conflict, it would suit the Chinese military to keep outside eyes off their internal studies, so that foreigners have no means of informing themselves of the actual situation. Americans and their allies, being denied the truth, would be at the mercy of assertions.

The reality is that there is little justification for accepting any Chinese voice claiming their right to rule Taiwan, their right to engage in hostile acts of aggression against Taiwan, their right to attack Americans and others who came to Taiwan's defense, and their ability to actually succeed in these tasks. The future of Asia will be somber, with the great achievements of Chinese civilization diminished, until the CCP gives up its revanchist dreams and embraces political plurality, rule of law, and respect for individual rights. In that sense, Taiwan is a far-reaching test case, whose results, if lasting peace can be secured, will shine rays of hope. On the other hand, if Beijing breaks the peace, a darkness will fall over the Pacific. The fate of Taiwan touches upon the fortunes of so many.

If the public statements of Chairman Xi and the unified writings of his military experts are any indication, the Taiwan Strait may become the scene of world-shaking events in the years ahead. China's centralized and officially approved internal writings on Taiwan run contrary to universal values. They espouse the idea of hostile takeover and the rule of an authoritarian minority by fear, force, and misrepresentation. China's military doctrine is offensive and destabilizing. PLA texts are anti-American and opposed to the benign world order that Washington created at such great costs after World War II. It would be dangerous for any military to follow such lines of thinking. Given the immense consequences in the case of China, it could be catastrophic.

The PRC has been shown much goodwill by the United States over the past four decades and given many opportunities to rise and succeed as an equal great power. Countless foreign hands have reached to pull China out of the misery of famine and chaos that was orchestrated by the CCP authorities after they took over in 1949. It is disappointing to see so much hard work squandered and so much hope squelched. But American policymakers would be unwise to ignore the trend lines and the backsliding going on right in front of their eyes, and foolish to think this new world of uncertainties does not demand hard choices and self-questioning.

Events await across the years ahead, and it cannot be known at the present time how things will play out and what the implications of future actions will be. What can be known, and is documented in this book, is that China is preparing for amphibious operations against Taiwan. The invasion of Taiwan, unlike other Chinese war planning scenarios, would be the largest and most complex in the PLA's history. Every domain of modern combat would be engaged to the full. The plan to invade Taiwan is likely to hinge upon landing a severe blow against the United States, delaying it from unleashing full fury until it is too late to change the final outcome. The stakes and the risks are unparalleled.

There could very well occur a crisis in the Taiwan Strait that does not result in bloodshed. The options available to China's leaders for applying coercion, a form of violence that is more mental than physical, are numerous and restricted only by the limits of their imaginations. Even more pathways exist for brinksmanship and intimidation that are mixed with small acts of war. The PLA could seize distant Taiwanese islands, or fire salvos of ballistic missiles at their home island, or attempt some form of blockade. Beijing has many means for ratcheting up tensions to test Taiwan's resolve. Taiwan, quite naturally, has developed some ways of striking back to humiliate the Communist Party leadership in return. Both sides have guns for firing warning shots at the other.

It must be recognized that China's leaders have a first mover advantage. In politics and war, great benefits are accorded to the side on the offensive. They have the initiative and can attack at the time and place and manner of their own choosing. They can keep pushing forward until someone else takes the initiative away, something that often takes strenuous effort to do and cannot be ensured in advance. China enjoys a growing asymmetry of power over Taiwan in many respects. The time has long passed when Taiwan could compete in a conventional arms race. Nonetheless, it would be wrong to ignore the most obvious and important factor, the role played by American power and influence, which favors Taiwan. The long-standing partnership between Washington and Taipei gives Taiwan's defenders a qualitative advantage that Chinese military officers do not regard lightly.

It is quite possible that Taiwan's military could resist invasion and force the Chinese to de-escalate even before the United States arrived to the fight. It is at least equally possible that the credible threat of American military intervention would cause Beijing to back down and cut its losses in a crisis, before it had achieved its objectives. PLA writings make clear that what China's leading thinkers fear most is a war against Taiwan and the United States combined. They dread what that would mean in terms of domestic instability. They regard their military and political prospects in that eventuality to be dire. From their perspective, Taiwan is a hard enough nut to crack all on its own.

Timely American intervention, almost certainly alongside the other Pacific democracies of Japan and Australia, is a nightmare for Chinese war planners, and very possibly could occur in ways they have not thought of. However, it must be remembered that the decision to risk great power war and invade Taiwan would not be the PLA's to make. Civilian authorities in the system would be responsible for deciding war policy, and they would be less clear about the risks involved. Finding generals with the courage to speak truth to civilian power is hard enough in democracies where they are protected by the law. It must be thought far rarer still or virtually nonexistent in authoritarian countries like China where delivering bad news can cost a man far more than his next promotion.

Making matters more dangerous, recent purges within China's military will almost certainly reinforce the ingrained tendency to avoid provoking top-level ire. The PLA has been known to cover up unfavorable truths even during periods when Beijing was less harsh. PLA leaders are the stars of a Leninist system that advances political loyalists and family insiders at the cost of weeding out talented professional warriors. The implications of this are that whereas mid-level officers in the field may understand the folly of invasion, senior military leaders in Beijing may buy into their own propaganda or ignore unwelcome facts that emerge before them. In the current environment, it seems highly improbable that Chairman Xi and his top advisors are going to be told anything they do not want to hear.

CCP elites are likely to conclude at some point in the coming few years that their chances of gaining control over Taiwan by peaceful means have been exhausted. Nothing the regime does can reverse the swelling majority of Taiwanese who hold as self-evident that Taiwan is its own country, and cross-Strait relations are actually state-to-state relations. China's coercive power will almost certainly prove sufficient to avoid an outright move by Taiwan's government toward *de jure* independence. This type of independence is generally defined to mean changes to Taiwan's constitution and flag, which would end the Republic of China and the myth, however tenuous, that Taiwan belongs to China. Taiwan's likely approach, no matter how cautious and pragmatic, will offer Beijing little solace. The CCP is not seeking the continuation of the "status quo" and cross-Strait peace and stability. Their goal is the annexation of Taiwan.

Once it becomes clear in Beijing power circles that some use of force is required to close this vital issue on terms favorable to the regime, then the question they might ask could be: What type of force should we use to achieve our desired end state? Past experience has shown that acts of aggression only harden the Taiwanese against the notion of unification and drive them farther away from China's grip. Beijing's leaders will likely find that they have three basic options. The first is that they could ignore the problem and make only symbolic gestures, while hoping something changes in their favor in the future. The second is that they could engage in small-scale acts of aggression to weaken Taiwanese resolve over time in a long drawn-out standoff. The third is that they could attempt an invasion and occupation of Taiwan. Given prevailing conditions, the third option would be the least probable and most dangerous to all concerned. Plans and preparations for it will continue nonetheless.

No military leader in the PLA is likely prepared to recommend the invasion plan or want to take responsibility for it. There appears to be a broad agreement that although no major operation to cross the Taiwan Strait could take place in the near future, all preparation for mounting it in the greatest strength should continue with the utmost dedication. It is believed that the conditions which would make the invasion of Taiwan a sound and sensible enterprise will take time to reach. The chances of the Chinese launching the operation before everything is ready appears remote.

As PLA experts have studied the facts which present themselves in planning for the invasion of Taiwan, a repellant picture has emerged to their collective military mind. A certain lack of conviction and optimism is apparent to anyone who reads their internal studies. This is covered up by boastful external propaganda, consumed and absorbed as if it were true by many who have it fed to them. The CCP is brilliant at propaganda, but also pragmatic when it comes to issues relating to its own survival. The invasion of Taiwan would run the greatest of risks and is unlikely to be successful if attempted anytime soon. Even in the event that it was attempted sooner than expected and proved more successful than expected, it would bleed China dry physically and materially. Taiwan has little to fear of invasion right now.

Although this is good news, little comfort should be drawn from the knowledge. The PLA's preparations will continue apace and the situation could quickly change. There are many facts that they dwell upon and will try to overcome. The historical experiences of others have shown the Chinese military that landing on a hostile shore in the teeth of defensive air opposition is not a sound military proposition for any army. The inescapable consequence for them is that their amphibious troops cannot be embarked and sailed, let alone disembarked and landed, without first ensuring that Taiwan's air force and navy are decisively crippled and killed. This is something that is difficult to guarantee, and it may very well prove to be impossible given Taiwan's preparations to keep them alive and fighting in a worst-case scenario.

There are few nations on the planet more resilient and ready for an enemy first strike than Taiwan. The island's whole coast has been fortified with Taiwanese engineering diligence for many decades. It would bristle with missiles, rockets, and artillery guns and be covered by protective sea mines, obstacles of every description, landmines, traps, barbed wire entanglements, trenches, and pillboxes. Some of Taiwan's tunnel systems date back to World War II, when the Japanese readied the island for an American invasion that never came. According to the PLA, the labyrinthine underground networks have grown on a vast scale and they are more sophisticated than anything previously imagined. These defenses are elaborate and deadly, if almost entirely invisible in peacetime. They lie in silent wait.

All possible amphibious approaches are surveyed by Taiwanese marines on a yearly basis. After exhaustive study, they know with precision where to expect attack and what the limited possibilities available to the aggressor are. The rugged coastal hills are masses of and alive with bunker complexes. They are home to mobile missile batteries commanding the sea approaches from above, some of which can fire right across the Strait. To attempt a landing in force against these dense fortifications would likely be to test futility and encounter a crushing repulse. Small commando raids could result in fiasco and might do more harm than good to Chinese efforts.

Once alerted, Taiwan's government has the ability to mobilize at least 200,000 to 300,000 reserve troops in 24 hours. Taiwan's full reserve component of two and a half million troops and one million civil defense personnel and contractors could all be ready in short order. They could bolster the regular army to help completely seal off the island for a long siege. They would wait in vast number, ready to meet the invader at every point. After suffering heavy bombardment and strikes on their hometowns, their probable rebuke would be a series of stern blows, shattering the Chinese invasion armadas and any forces that landed.

All that is purely hypothetical now, however, and the invasion threat could manifest itself in ways that go well beyond the military realm. It may happen in ways not currently envisioned, and nobody can know with any certainty what the future will bring. Taiwan appears safe for now, but it will only stay that way over the next decade if sufficient efforts are made across the full spectrum of political, economic, and defense affairs. The work required to maintain Taiwan's defense will be increasingly heavy and hard. It will demand greater harmony of thought between the United States, Taiwan, and Japan. These friendly democracies have all been together through so much over the past several decades, but they nonetheless have very different military cultures and uneven levels of understanding and ability to focus on this problem.

If the United States and Japan can stand together with Taiwan to put combined pressure on China's rulers, peace is very likely to be the reward, and with it unprecedented freedom and prosperity across Asia. If on the other hand they fail, the Chinese military may eventually be able to overwhelm and destroy Taiwan. The means to prevent war and avert defeat are within sight, but the distressing reality is that not enough has been done. Many American leaders, having never lived abroad, cannot conceive of anyone whose views are not more or less within the boundaries of their own. Lacking knowledge of modern Chinese history and of the dangers inherent in its authoritarian system, they place forward-deployed U.S. forces in a vulnerable position. It is long past time the U.S. military was retooled and refitted for great power conflict.

There is no way to know what will happen in China and how whatever happens will affect everything on the outside. Taiwan is held hostage by the unknown to the extent that it slackens its guard against Beijing's growing offensive power. There are good prospects for deterring Chinese attacks or defeating them if that should become necessary. Taiwan's military has a solid defense plan and stands ready to face the supreme test. War will not come as long as the regime in China judges possible outcomes to be unfavorable and uncertain. Radical decisions could be made, however, and may even become likely if the current trend toward dictatorship continues. The only thing that may be concluded with absolute confidence is that there is no reason for panic and despair in Taiwan, but every reason for vigilance and resolve.

Americans, when considering cross-Strait conflict, would be wise to remember the great strategist Carl von Clausewitz, who famously observed that rationality is fragile in war. The enemies of reason are emotion, friction, and fear, which can quickly turn battles into scenes of purposeless violence and carnage. Though it may seem improbable when viewed in the cool lights of peacetime, crises can rapidly escalate to limited wars, which might turn at any time into something uncontrollable. The Chinese authorities, by planning and preparing to strike Taiwan with exceptionally naked acts of aggression, risk jeopardizing their own security and prosperity. While China's generals would have the initiative against Taiwan on Z-Day, they could only be on the receiving end of the Americans and their allies, who would be free to present them with unpleasant surprises.

This of course assumes that the PRC would not preemptively strike U.S. forces first, an assumption that could be tragically falsified by events. If China did, it would be an act of madness given the predictable magnitude of American wrath. The inescapable conclusion of this book is that the sum of Chinese strategy, doctrine, and war planning for the Taiwan invasion scenario is something likely to prove self-destructive and dangerous. While the theoretical essence of the campaign may appear defensive to the eyes of Chinese strategists, its actual character is wholly offensive and escalatory. It should be repudiated by the entire world, and especially those who seek to advance the cause of human progress.

Appendix I: Five Scenarios

THE invasion threat facing Taiwan is something which has many sides to it and can be little understood without concentrated study. It is a complex problem. The immense numbers of variables involved in the equation defy quick and easy comprehension. Making matters worse, some of the variables, like weather and people, for example, are themselves ever changing. Other variables are less prone to change. The location of Taiwan's capital city, Taipei, and the surrounding mountains and coastline are unmoving. Major pieces of infrastructure that are in place today on both sides of the Taiwan Strait (like ports, airfields, highways, rail lines, tunnels, and bridges) will all be in the exact same place tomorrow. But the capabilities and compositions of forces and machines positioned in or on or under them, or moving over or through them, will change over time. War would take its destructive toll on everything as well, keeping the situation fluid and chaotic.

There are simply too many shifting pieces in the overall picture for accurate prediction to occur. It therefore makes sense to talk about the unknown future in abstract terms and to push forward various possibilities about what the situation might look like, if it was to occur. When dealing with abstractions there often exists a basic human need to fix concrete points on the map and on the clock, even if they are just assumed and imagined. Scenarios can help us think through problems. They take piles of data and turn them into a storyline, much in the way a digital camera fuses pixels of light into a snapshot.

No single image, whatever its brilliance, can illuminate the entire string of events and capture every angle. So too with scenarios. Our minds rarely allow us to see far into the vast expanse of the unknown future, filled as it is with limitless possibilities. We are constrained by our programmed patterns of thought and limited imaginations. For this very reason, scenarios are great to have when facing the future. They feed the mind pictures of scenes that might occur, but also might not, depending on the contextual peculiarities at play and the actions and counteractions taken. Some scenarios are, or may seem, more "realistic" than others, but that is not their purpose. The most important thing they do is allow the mind's eye to see potential problems before they occur. Having seen problems, one can then prepare solutions, or plans, as a hedge against them.

The studies conducted by the PLA suggest to us the questions that would be the most important to explore. Once identified, they will be the basic building blocks for our scenarios. Chinese war planners will certainly take certain essentials into account and use them to construct the answers to their problems. They will just as certainly not share their final designs and conclusions. Rather, they will make every attempt to obscure their intentions behind an impenetrable wall of deception. Internal PLA documents and other writings which may be indicative of doctrine are nonetheless revealing. They provide a good foundation for understanding how the armed wing of the Communist Party might see various options. These should not be confused for the official invasion plan—available materials do not give away vital details—but they are helpful in deciding what to guess at.

To further get a sense of the possibilities open to the PLA's operational planning community, it is essential for us to put ourselves in the other guys' shoes (or boots) and envision different scenarios. We will explore five notional scenarios as they might imagine them. Our five scenarios will, for the most part, stick closely to the fixed assumptions seen in Chinese military writings. These assumptions have been described elsewhere in this book, but have not been melded together in any form. Some of them may seem strange and foreign, but it is important they be recognized.

We are interested in the question of invasion. However unlikely it may seem at the current time, the invasion of Taiwan must be allowed for, thought about, and studied. What follows are five scenarios which walk through variations of it. They should not be considered predictive or realistic. This is merely a thought exercise.

Scenario One: Election Year Shocker

The PRC economy is in deep trouble and the desperate central leadership sees an opportunity to distract public outrage, replacing it with nationalistic fervor. The decision is made to take advantage of Taiwan's presidential election season to launch an invasion and "liberate" the wayward province. None of Taiwan's three presidential candidates is offensive to the rest of the world, or to the Taiwanese electorate, so Beijing plans to employ misinformation to create diplomatic discord, driving a wedge between Taiwan and America, while weakening social unity in Taiwan. Two of the stronger candidates are labeled as "pro-independence" radicals, and pitted against the third, who is seen as more "pro-China".

The PLA's campaign plan calls for invading Taiwan during the spring. Z-Day is set for the first week of April, just after the presidential elections, but before the May 20th inauguration day. Strategic psychological warfare operations are organized and undertaken to ensure that the post-election transition period is racked with social discord and scandal. Pre-invasion air strikes are to start on Z-8. Naval actions are to start on Z-6. In late February, the PLA begins forming up three invasion forces.

The Northern Force assembles around Wenzhou, some 210 miles north of Taiwan. The Northern Force is comprised of major elements of the PLA's 1st Group Army and the 12th Group Army, including an air assault (helicopter) brigade, and two airborne (parachute) divisions from the 15th Airborne Corps. On Z-Day the objective of this force will be to capture and build up the main landing zone at Taoyuan.

The Central Force assembles around Xiamen, 220 miles west of Taipei. It is comprised of the 31st Group Army, including its amphibious armored brigade, and several army aviation (helicopter) regiments, and one Marine brigade. Other division and brigade-sized units from across China, and major portions of the 54th and 20th Group Armies, also move toward the area. The objective of the Central Force is to storm the Kinmen Islands on Z-6, and then to capture a secondary landing zone at Hsinchu on Z-Day. Central Force will also provide second echelon forces after Z-Day to reinforce forces ashore.

The Southern Force assembles around Shantou, 325 miles southwest of Taipei, but only 180 miles from the Penghu Islands and 225 miles from Tainan. It is comprised of major elements of the PLA's 42nd and 41st Group Armies, and one marine brigade. The objective of Southern Force is to serve as both a decoy and a reserve force. On Z-3, two large ship groups from the Shantou area will make threatening maneuvers toward the Penghu Islands and the beaches south of Tainan. Many old ships are expected to be sunk along the way, but they will be packed full of uniformed prisoners with mock military equipment. Fake radio chatter, oil slicks, and debris will mimic the demise of thousands of troops and marines. No actual forces will be landed anywhere. Real Chinese army and marine units will be held in reserve ashore, ready to board ships to reinforce the beachheads at Taoyuan or Hsinchu, as needed.

The invasion plan assumes that the United States will deploy three aircraft carrier groups to the Philippine Sea, augment Marine Corps and Air Force units on Okinawa, and station bomber wings in Guam, Japan, and Alaska. These will not all arrive at once. It is assumed by PLA planners that the buildup will not be complete by Z-Day, and direct U.S. intervention will not be ordered by the American President until Z+15. By that time, they expect that Taipei will have already fallen. The PLA allocates various space warfare, cyber warfare, rocket force, air defense, submarine, and bomber units to the command tasked with handling contingencies that could arise if the United States intervenes earlier or if the assault on Taipei is delayed.

Scenario Two: Hammer and Anvil

A nuclear power plant in central China suffers catastrophic failure during an earthquake, releasing lethal doses of radiation that poisons hundreds of thousands of people and overwhelms medical response teams. This tragic event triggers a sudden outburst of party infighting and a failed coup attempt in Beijing, the underlying causes of which are unclear to the outside. The humiliated and weakened PRC leadership decides to use a war with Taiwan to unite the military and the nation against an external enemy.

The PLA's plan is to employ a hammer and anvil approach. Forces are to land at Taoyuan, Tamsui, and Yilan to smash Taipei between three advancing fronts. Two major amphibious groups are to assemble: one at the harbors around Fuzhou and Pingtan Island, the other at Ningbo, far to the north. Decoy army groups are to be stationed at Xiamen, Quanzhou, and Dongshan to the south. Covert operations will be launched to convince Taiwanese intelligence that the outer islands of Kinmen and Matsu will be attacked, but nothing more.

The plan calls for building forces up slowly, coiling them up like a tight spring. When fully ready, they are to strike with lightning speed and maximum surprise to achieve their military objectives. Late September is chosen for launching the operation, allowing PLA units ample time to sharpen their skills over the spring and summer. A series of training drills and war games is organized to practice the invasion. Hainan Island is used as the main amphibious training ground. Propaganda reports on the war games show marine units capturing two small islands off of the big island of Hainan, furthering the fiction that Taiwan's outer islands are the PLA's real targets.

Acts of sabotage are staged on Kinmen and Matsu. In August, both island groups begin experiencing anomalies in their power grids that result in periodic blackouts. An arsonist on one island burns down several old warehouses. Gangsters attack a jail on another island, killing several officers and releasing all the prisoners back onto the streets. A third outer island is cut off when an approaching oil tanker loses control and crashes into the port, disabling the only pier and polluting the surrounding waters.

The plan will be set in motion on Z-7, when Chinese forces are to launch a concentrated artillery barrage against Taiwan's outer islands, making it look like they are being softened up for invasion. Simultaneous cyber attacks and drone strikes in the Taiwan Strait are to be used to reduce

Taiwanese maritime domain awareness. On Z-2, missile and air strikes are to begin against Taiwan's air defense bases and command bunkers. The next day, hunter killer groups of submarines are to fire swarms of torpedoes into two Taiwanese naval task forces they are stalking, one thirty miles off of Hualien, the other well south of the Penghu Islands. The mission is to sink or scatter as many ships as possible. Naval bomber groups armed with supersonic anti-ship cruise missiles, and escorted by hundreds of fighter jets, are to mop up whatever remains.

Ship landing groups, escorted by dozens of large surface ships, are to approach anchorage sites to the northwest and the east of Taipei the night before Z-Day. To maximize surprise, mine sweeping and obstacle clearing operations will only start a few hours before landing craft are launched. It is recognized, and accepted as unavoidable, that some coastal water zones will still be heavily infested with lethal traps. Heavy bombing runs are to be made against Taiwan's army formations before troops begin hitting the beaches at dawn. Hours before, specially trained commandos will attempt to infiltrate into Taiwan and seize both ends of the Xiangshan Tunnel and the highway system that links the Yilan landing zone to Taipei.

Casualties are expected to be very high for the PLA during the first several days, but it is hoped that if two of the three landing zones surrounding Taipei can be seized and built up, ground troops can execute a "hammer and anvil" attack, slamming into the capital before American forces can decisively intervene. Chinese planners assume, based on recent intelligence reports, that they will have only five to eight days of relatively unimpeded access to the Taiwan Strait. After that it is believed that American stealth fighter-bombers will sortie and flatten their high value logistics bases, and American submarines, laying in wait, will emerge from their hiding places to begin sinking the Chinese fleet. A preemptive strike on U.S. bases in Okinawa and Guam is planned for Z+4 to reduce the ferocity of the expected attacks.

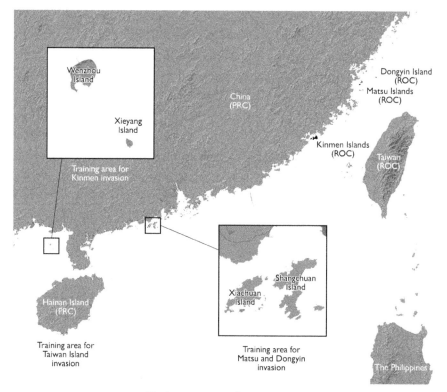

Training areas for invasion

Scenario Three: Stepping Stones

The PRC political establishment is in a tailspin. A pro-democracy hacker group has breached the Great Firewall of China and exposed the Chinese people to incontrovertible evidence showing that communist elites have squandered vast national resources enriching themselves. This corruption is responsible for stagnating the nation's economy and causing high unemployment rates. Incensed students organize protest marches and sit-ins at major college campuses across China. These are suppressed, some violently and with heavy loss of life.

Branding the information breach an act of foreign subversion, a group of ambitious PLA generals convince their political masters to go to wartime footing and curtail international communications into China. Intelligence cannot confirm the location and membership of the hacker group, but many suspect Taiwanese student involvement.

The Beijing authorities, concerned by growing social unrest and unsettled by their shared sense of vulnerability, decide Taiwan's continued experiment with democracy will put their regime in mortal peril unless it is destroyed.

The Chinese military is ordered to employ a conservative stepping-stone approach to the invasion of Taiwan. The plan is to seize the Kinmen Islands first, then to invade the Penghu Islands, and then, if necessary, to land on Taiwan near Taichung. From central Taiwan, the PLA could build up a giant force and drive north to capture Taipei, but it is assumed that this will probably not be necessary. The agreed upon timetable starts operations in March, gradually escalating the scope and scale of conflict through the spring and summer months to increase pressure over time. Taiwan's government, it is hoped, will break before the first week of October, when an all-out invasion push is required to ensure PLA troops can occupy the island before the winter squalls descend on the Taiwan Strait.

Each battle along the way is to be followed by a lull in operations to allow political talks to occur. Taiwan will be issued ultimatums, which, if accepted, would allow the Chinese military to occupy the island at a relatively low cost. If Beijing's demands are not met, the PLA will be better positioned to spring further forward. After every new conquest, China will raise the stakes diplomatically as well, attempting to deter American intervention in a long drawn out international war of nerves.

The campaign is to start with a joint land, air, and sea assault on the Kinmen islands. Planners assume the entire island group will be within their grasp within three days. With Kinmen neutralized, the Penghu Islands will be sprung upon 30 to 45 days later, depending on weather conditions and other factors. The battle for Penghu is expected to be particularly intense, but victory is expected within 10 to 15 days. Once the islands in this group have been taken, they will be turned into a large staging area for the invasion of Taiwan.

Taiwan itself will be left almost completely unscathed until July, when blockades and bombing operations will commence to wear down the defenders. Air and sea operations will be suspended with each passing typhoon, and re-started as soon as the skies clear and the waters settle. If Taipei has not buckled under the weight of the mounting pressure by September, two amphibious groups, staging out of Xiamen and the Penghus, will assail Taichung. It is envisioned that second echelon forces will flow rapidly into central Taiwan after Taichung's harbors and airstrips have been captured and brought to working order.

Scenario Four: Chinese New Year Wildcard

The aging chairman of the Chinese Communist Party—already the strongest and most brutal PRC leader since Mao Zedong—grows increasingly paranoid and obsessed with his exercise of power. Influenced by his extended time as governor of Fujian Province, and suffering from delusions of grandeur, he orders the military to prepare for the invasion of Taiwan. The chairman views taking Taiwan to be his supreme mission and greatest contribution to Chinese history. The PLA Joint Staff leadership, eager to show value after a series of military purges, presents him with five different variations of their carefully crafted war plan.

Of the options presented by the Joint Staff, the chairman selects the boldest: the military plan to take advantage of the Chinese New Year to catch Taiwan by surprise. The timing of the new year holiday is dictated by the traditional Chinese calendar and varies by year, almost always falling between January 22 and February 19. PLA planners know Taiwan's government and military are at their lowest state of readiness during the holiday, with the majority of their personnel on vacation for at least one week. Every year many Taiwanese travel abroad to Japan, Southeast Asia, or North America. Taipei's central government district is always closed for business, and the city becomes considerably less populated for several days. Many residents of the capital have hometowns down south where they spend the holiday.

Traditionally, the holidays affect China's military and government machinery at least as much as Taiwan's. This year will be different. The PLA plan calls for initiating attacks with a relatively small number of specialized units, which will deploy to assembly areas unnoticed amidst the tumult of Chinese New Year holiday. Measures will be taken to ensure Taiwan's intelligence community does not issue an alert. "Terrorist attacks" in Guangdong will be staged to justify certain units moving toward higher states of readiness. A ferry accident south of Shanghai will be arranged to explain large naval movements near Ningbo. To further alleviate potential concerns, Beijing will send out diplomatic and propaganda messages, signaling a positive breakthrough could be ahead in cross-Strait relations.

Z-Day will be set for the first day of the Chinese New Year holiday. Zero Hour will be 3am, when Taipei will be empty and almost everyone in Taiwan is sleeping. A sudden cruise missile strike will knock out command centers and air defense nets around the capital. Bridges and tunnels that connect Taipei to the south will be blown up with ballistic missiles. At 5am paratroopers will drop into major parks downtown and empty golf courses. Helicopter assault units will seize Taipei's Songshan Airport for use as an airhead. Clandestine commando units delivered by submarines and hovercraft will storm ashore near Tamsui to assault the Guandu Army Command, which protects the northern approaches to the capital. In the hours before the attack, a Chinese sleeper cell will poison the water and contaminate the fuel of Taiwan's elite 66th Marine Brigade in the Taipei suburbs to reduce its ability to respond. Another sleeper cell will target Taiwan's Military Police Command leadership.

The plan calls for exploiting the chaos that would follow to launch air raids to sink most of Taiwan's navy in port and destroy the air force's elite fighter wings on the ground. PLA army brigades poised near Fuzhou and on Pingtan Island would cross the Taiwan Strait and push down the Tamsui River or land near the Port of Taipei, depending on the situation. Once the capital is seized, the entire Chinese military will be mobilized and, in a race to see which side can respond faster, China will attempt to move forces into Taipei faster than Taiwan's army can retake the capital.

PLA planners assume that this will be a very high-risk operation. Bad weather could easily throw off the invasion. Taiwan could obtain early warning through its intelligence and counterintelligence networks and foil the plot, turning it all into a political victory. Even if the weather held and surprise was obtained, it seems likely that Taiwan's army would be able to mobilize and figure out a way to push tank columns downtown faster than Chinese commandos could secure the city and receive adequate reinforcements from the mainland. In addition, Taiwan's own paratroopers and helicopter assault forces could swiftly organize counterassaults from the south to regain Taipei.

The advantages of such an attempt nonetheless proves attractive to the CCP Chairman. From his perspective, even if the Chinese New Year plan fails to reach its full potential and the Taipei raid has to be aborted, holiday attacks might still create enough panic and chaos in Taiwan to pave the way for a traditional invasion attempt a few weeks later when the weather improved. The raid would help PLA planners gather valuable experience and information regarding Taiwanese reaction speeds and capabilities. Moreover, the suddenness of this scenario might catch the U.S. military off guard, allowing Chinese propagandists to claim Taiwan was abandoned in its hour of need.

Scenario Five: Split Decision

For murky reasons that historians will argue over for long decades to come, the PRC makes an attempt to conquer Taiwan. In the after light, it appears to some scholars that Beijing may have been motivated by perceptions of American retreat from the world, manifested most clearly by Washington's defense spending cuts and a declared policy of foregoing future security engagements with allies and partners like Taiwan. Other scholars point to Taiwan's stubborn desire to have a seat at the United Nations. A national referendum on this issue is passed by a majority of Taiwanese voters just months prior to the war, eliciting a firestorm of threats from China—although preparations for invasion appear to have begun a year prior. Another school of thought holds that the war was the natural result of a Chinese military-industrial complex run amok.

Whatever the reason, Chinese forces are ordered to take Taiwan. The war plan is to feint north toward Taoyuan where the invasion has long been expected and then go south, landing on the beaches of Tainan and Fangliao to split the island apart. By Z+15, it is expected that everything south of the Chuoshui River will be PRC territory. At this point Chinese forces are to dig in for what may turn out to be a long war of attrition. Meanwhile, massive tonnages of troops and equipment will flow into "liberated" areas through the captured harbor city of Kaohsiung, Taiwan's mega port.

PLA doctrine has traditionally called for the rapid resolution of cross-Strait conflict, but in this case there is little rush because no U.S.-led international rescue force is expected to come to Taiwan's aid. America's growing isolationism has completely altered the region's strategic calculus. The ample time available allows Chinese planners to allot an unprecedented amount of time (45 days) for pre-invasion blockade and bombing operations, ensuring that amphibious forces arrive to find the defender greatly weakened and demoralized. Beijing's political and military circles anticipate that the awesome specter of Chinese military might well tear at Taiwanese willpower and obviate the need for forcible entry operations. Taiwan's president, they are sure, will crack long before the first landing craft rumbles ashore and the first paratrooper drops to ground.

Army generals in front-line Fuzhou, apprised of the latest local intelligence, are far less optimistic than their far-off superiors. They expect Taiwan to go down fighting, possibly with weapons of mass destruction. Concerned that chemical and radiological weapons will be cast upon their vulnerable staging areas and beachheads, PLA commanders at the front intend to purposely delay ground force deployments into theater, elongating the overall timetable so that rocket force, cyber, navy, and air force operations can be brought to fruition.

The operational plan calls for storming Taiwan's two island holdings in the South China Sea, Itu Aba and Pratas, on Z-30, and then next attacking Kinmen on Z-15. Dongshan and Shantou are selected as the main staging areas for the assault on Taiwan. To the north, Pingtan Island and the port of Ningde are also saturated with troops and ships. Their mission will be to confirm Taiwanese assumptions that the Taoyuan plain is the prime target, thereby drawing attention away from the intended point of attack down south.

In the nights before Z-Day, thousands of tanks will be loaded aboard giant roll-on roll-off vessels in Shanghai and Guangdong. They are to arrive on Taiwan Z+10, by which time it is believed major ports in the south will be in hand and fully operational. PLA officers realize that this activity cannot be hidden from the view of enemy agents, known to be locally active. So to confuse Taiwanese intelligence they plan to spread rumors at the dockyards that the tank-loading exercise is merely a ruse designed to spread fear in Taiwan.

On Z-1, a fleet of drone ships on autopilot will drive themselves into the densely knit minefields and obstacle networks along the Taoyuan coast, sacrificing themselves in a vain attempt to clear safe lanes to the beach. At the same moment, hundreds of pilotless 1950's era fighter jets, retooled for the modern battlefield, are programmed to fly themselves like kamikazes into northern Taiwan's air defense nets. Similar acts of deception are to prove rampant on both sides of the Strait and across the entire theater of operations to such an extent that neither side is remotely prepared for what is next to come.

Appendix II: Sources and Methods

WHAT sources and methods were used to produce this book? Where did the research materials come from? Who wrote them and what institutions published them? Why should we think these materials are authoritative or credible? In the following section, I will attempt to address these questions to the greatest extent possible and appropriate.

Given the closed nature of China's military and Beijing's well-known attempts at influencing foreign audiences with propaganda and misinformation, one always has to be cautious when handling Chinese sources. Peter Mattis, in his excellent book, *Analyzing the Chinese Military*, points out that any high-quality analysis of the PLA will strive to be transparent and use authoritative sourcing. Transparent analyses should provide, at a minimum, details on who wrote each source (names and affiliations) and the organizations that published them. They will sometimes also explain to the reader how they assessed the authoritativeness of their sources. Evaluating PLA sources is hard. It requires advanced Chinese language skills, a detailed knowledge of organizational structures and hierarchy, and discernment.

PLA books or technical studies that are written by teams of officer-researchers are more authoritative than those written by one individual (unless that individual sits in an extraordinarily high position in the system, like on the Central Military Commission). Edited volumes published by the National Defense University Press, the Academy of Military Science Press, and the Liberation Army Press tend to be the best. Each military service in

China has its own publishing house. Lantian (Blue Sky) Press, for example, is the official publishing house of the PLA Air Force. Publishers like this one tend to produce more authoritative materials. A Chinese military book is not necessarily authoritative just because is a collaborative effort that was published by an official publishing house, but these conditions certainly make it more likely to be.

In the case of PLA research on Taiwan, one has to be especially cautious with their sources. A good source will generally evince genuine respect for Taiwan's military. It may express concern that the Taiwanese have some strengths which the PLA cannot match. It might even hint that a war with Taiwan could be disastrous for China. This only happens, with extremely few exceptions, inside military-use-only, restricted access, and/ or classified Chinese military writings. Pessimism is a sure sign of a professional military establishment, since military officers have to prepare for the worst to happen. In China, however, it is not politically correct to openly admit serious doubts, especially when Taiwan is concerned.

The quickest way to smoke out a source written by a propagandist is to note tones of derision and undercurrents of Marxist-Leninist-style scientific inevitability. If the source mocks the Taiwanese military and forecasts certain doom for the defenders, it was written by a political officer and/ or intelligence operative with a political motive in mind. Such sources are an advanced persistent threat to good analysis. They are everywhere.

When possible, it is important to use internal studies and teaching materials as sources. Even if flawed, they represent the conventional wisdom of their respective communities. One can safely assume these sources are indicative of official doctrine and have been carefully vetted for "correctness." They tend to be more detailed and candid than other sources. Some are surprisingly blunt.

As a final note, it is essential to confirm sources using other sources, especially when in uncharted territory. Taiwanese military studies can often be used to backstop (or debunk) claims made by Chinese military sources. Both sides go to extreme lengths to study the other. High-quality Taiwanese military books and journals are great for confirming PLA writings. Human subject matter experts with firsthand knowledge are even better. Finding them always requires a combination of two things: time in Taiwan and Washington, and dumb luck. I've been lucky to have had both.

These are the methods I have employed to the best of my limited abilities in writing this book. Now, let's turn to the sources. What follows is a selection of those I found to be the most informative.

Informatized Army Operations
Publisher: National Defense University

Editors:
- Cao Zhengrong is listed as a Senior Colonel with a Ph.D., at the Nanjing Army Command Academy, who is a professor in the Campaign Studies Office.
- Sun Longhai is listed as a Senior Colonel with a Ph.D., at the Nanjing Army Command Academy, who is an associate professor in the Tactical Studies Office.
- Yang Yin is listed as a Senior Colonel, who commands an unidentified provincial military district's logistics department.

Contributing authors:
- Li Zongkun (Senior Colonel, Nanjing Army Command Academy)
- Xu Faguo (Major, Nanjing Army Command Academy)
- Wang Jiaxing (Colonel with a Ph.D., Nanjing Army Command Academy)
- Sun Jianjun (Senior Colonel, Nanjing Army Command Academy)
- Liu Yong (Major, Nanjing Army Command Academy)
- Yi Bangdong (Major, Nanjing Army Command Academy)

Other details: This book was first published in June 2014, and published again in June 2015. It was printed by the Nanjing Army Command Academy. It is marked "Military Internal Distribution" (军内发行) on the back cover and on the back of the first page.

Informatized Joint Operations
Publisher: Liberation Army Press

Editors:
- Cao Zhengrong is listed as a Senior Colonel with a Ph.D., at the Nanjing Army Command Academy, who is an associate professor in the Campaign Studies Office.
- Wu Runbo is listed as a Senior Colonel, at the Nanjing Army Command Academy, who is an associate professor in the Foreign Military Training Materials Translation Office.
- Sun Jianjun is listed as a Major, at the Nanjing Army Command Academy, who is an associate professor in the Campaign Studies Office.

Contributing authors:
- Qu Tiaojun (Senior Colonel, Nanjing Army Command Academy)
- Li Zongkun (Major, Nanjing Army Command Academy)
- Luo Dong (Major, Nanjing Army Command Academy)
- Wang Ning (Senior Colonel, Nanjing Army Command Academy)
- Wang Yulong (Captain, Shenyang Military Region)
- Chen Fei (Captain, Zhenjiang Military Ship Academy).

Other details: The book was first published in June 2006, and published again in August 2008. It was printed by the Jiangsu Province Committee on Innovation. It is marked "Military Internal Distribution" (军内发行) on the back cover and on the back of the first page.

Research on Port Landing Operations
Publisher: National Defense University

Editors:
- Xu Lisheng is listed as a Senior Colonel with Ph.D., at the Nanjing Army Command Academy, who is an associate professor in the Campaign Studies Office.
- Wang Tiaoyong is at the Nanjing Army Command Academy, who directs the library and is an associate researcher. Wang has worked

on over twenty major research projects for the General Staff Department and the Nanjing Army Command Academy.

Contributing authors:

- Li Zongkun
- Chen Wei
- Dong Zhe
- Jiang Haihong
- Yu Guo
- Xu Faguo
- Bai Yinsheng

No details are provided on any of the authors.

Other details: The book was published in May 2015. It was printed by the Nanjing Army Command Academy. It is marked "Military Internal Distribution" (军内发行) on the back cover and on the back of the first page.

Space Information Support Operations

Publisher: National Defense University

Editor:

- Wang Yongping's identity is not listed, but he appears to be an associate professor at the PLA Armament Command Academy and an expert on space support to joint operations.

Contributing authors:

- Zhao Zhongqiang (Associate Professor, National Defense University's Campaign Studies Department)
- Cao Tinghua (Professor, Armament Command Academy)
- Zhang Zhanyue (Professor, Armament Command Academy)
- Tiao Honglin (Associate Professor, Armament Command Academy)
- Yang Zhangshou (Armament Command Academy Ph.D.)
- Two other people are credited as having provided help and guidance:
- Li Zhi (Professor, Armament Command Academy)
- Du Haiqiang (Research Fellow, Academy of Military Science)

Other details: The book was published in May 2014. It is marked "Military Internal Distribution, No Outside Transmission Allowed" (军内发行 不

得外传) on the back cover and on the back of the first page. This book is listed as having required three years of research to complete.

Research on Operational Theory of Army Aviation Troops
Publisher: National Defense University

Editors:
- Zhang Zhiwei appears to be a senior colonel with a Ph.D., at the Nanjing Army Command Academy, and a famous calligrapher and painter within the PLA.
- Huang Chuanxian is not identified.

Contributing authors:
- Liu Tiaozhong
- Zhao Hailing
- Zou Hao
- Jiang Xin
- Jiang Zunwei
- Zhou Xun
- Li Jian
- Li Xiang
- Ke Linmin
- Li Yuming
- Zhang Junqiang
- Liu Yonghong
- Yi Jun

No details are provided on any of them.

Other details: The book was published in March 2014. It was printed by the Nanjing Army Command Academy. It is marked "Military Internal Distribution, No Outside Transmission Allowed" (军内发行 不得外传) on the back cover and on the back of the first page.

Course book on Taiwan Strait Military Geography
Publisher: Academy of Military Sciences Press

Editor:
- Bai Guangwei (no details provided).

Contributing authors
- Li Bo
- Ren Guozheng
- Zhang Lu
- Song Minghai

No details are provided on any of them.

Other details: It was published in September 2013. It is marked "Military Internal Distribution, No Outside Transmission Allowed" (军内发行 不得外传) on the front and back of the first page. It is part of a series of educational materials produced by the Academy of Military Sciences for PLA officers seeking a master's degree.

Informatized Warfare and Psychological Protection
Publisher: People's Military Medical Press

Editor:
- Zhang Qingzhi (no details provided).

Contributing authors
- Li Buqian (Political Officer, General Logistic Department)
- Zhu Feng (Political Officer, General Logistics Department)
- Yan Jin (Professor, Number Two Military Hospital University)
- Mei Qinghai (Professor, Number Four Military Hospital University)
- Zhang Jingping (Associate Professor, Number Four Military Hospital University)
- Guan Peng (Associate Professor, Number Three Military Hospital University)
- Gao Guanghong (General Logistics Command Academy)
- Shen Dahong (Jinan Military Region Logistics Department)

- Cao Wenxian (Director, Nanjing Military Region Logistics Department Health Department)
- Long Ping (Deputy Director, Nanjing Political Academy Training Department)
- Hao Weixue (Director, Nanjing Political Academy Shanghai Branch Psychological Warfare System)
- Xu Dekui (Director, Jinan Military Region's Political Department's Political Warfare Office).

Other details: The book was published in March 2008. It is marked "Military Internal Materials, Store Carefully" (内部资料，注意保存) on the inside of the first page. The research was undertaken as part of the PLA's 11th Five-Year Plan, and carried out over a three-year period. It involved field research in the Jinan and Nanjing military regions.

Appendix III: Order of Battle

PLA Order of Battle

(Probable Major Units in Taiwan Invasion)

Eastern Theater Command

Location: Nanjing, Jiangsu

In wartime Eastern Theater Command may become the Joint Taiwan Attack Command with assets assigned to it from other theater command by the CMC and Joint Staff Department; direct reporting units include: 31st Pontoon Bridge Brigade, 13th Coastal Defense Division; and three coastal defense brigades.

PLA Army Theater HQ

Location: Fuzhou, Fujian

In wartime may become forward joint command post for amphibious assault operations.

12th Group Army

Location: Xuzhou, Jiangsu

May now be designated 71st Group Army; in wartime likely to be responsible for assaults on northern Taiwan; units also include unidentified artillery brigade, air defense brigade, and special operations brigade.

- 34th Mechanized Infantry Brigade (Chuzhou, Anhui)
- 35th Mechanized Infantry Brigade (Xuzhou, Jiangsu)
- 179th Motorized Infantry Brigade (Nanjing, Jiangsu)

1st Group Army
Location: Huzhou, Zhejiang
May now be designated 72nd Group Army; in wartime likely to be responsible for assaults on northern Taiwan; units also include unknown artillery brigade and air defense brigade; likely has brigade equipped with multiple launch rocket system.

- 1st Amphibious Mechanized Infantry Division (Hangzhou, Zhejiang)
- 178th Mechanized Infantry Brigade (location unknown)
- 3rd Motorized Infantry Brigade (Jinhua, Jiangsu)
- 10th Armored Brigade (Suzhou, Jiangsu)
- Long-Distance Artillery Brigade (Wuxi, Jiangsu)
- 5th Army Aviation Brigade (location unknown)

31st Group Army
Location: Xiamen, Fujian
May now be designated 73rd Group Army; in wartime likely to be responsible for assaults on Kinmen, Matsu, Penghu, and possibly northern or central Taiwan; units also include unknown special operations brigade.

- 86th Motorized Infantry Brigade (Fuzhou, Fujian)
- 91st Motorized Infantry Brigade (Zhangzhou, Fujian)
- 92nd Motorized Infantry Brigade (Quanzhou, Fujian)
- 3rd Artillery Brigade (Quanzhou, Fujian)
- 13th Air Defense Brigade (Xiamen, Fujian)
- Amphibious Armored Brigade (Zhangzhou, Fujian)
- 10th Army Aviation Regiment (location unknown)

PLA Navy East Sea Fleet HQ

Location: Ningbo, Zhejiang

In wartime may become main command post for naval support to amphibious assault operations.

- Naval Aviation Unit (Ningbo)
- 4th Naval Aviation Division (Taizhou, Zhejiang)
- 6th Naval Aviation Division (Shanghai)
- 1st Flying Panther Regiment (Yiwu, Zhejiang)
- 8th Frigate Flotilla (Shanghai)
- 3rd Destroyer Flotilla (Zhoushan, Zhejiang)
- 6th Destroyer Flotilla (Zhoushan, Zhejiang)
- 21st Fastboat Flotilla (Ningde, Fujian)
- 5th Landing Ship Flotilla (Shanghai)
- 42nd Submarine Flotilla (Ningbo)
- 22nd Submarine Flotilla (Ningbo)
- 2nd Combat Support Ship Flotilla (Zhoushan, Zhejiang)
- 2nd Radar Brigade (Ningbo)
- 2015 fleet totals:
- 18 diesel-powered attack subs
- 9 destroyers
- 19 frigates
- 6 corvettes
- 14 tank landing ships
- 9 medium landing ships
- 39 missile patrol craft
- 1 fighter division
- 1 mixed air division
- 1 radar brigade

PLA Air Force Theater HQ

Location: Nanjing, Jiangsu

In wartime may become main command post for air support to amphibious assault operations; likely also includes special aviation division.

3rd Fighter Division (Wuhu, Anhui)

- 14th Fighter Division (Zhangshu, Jiangxi)
- 29th Fighter Division (Quzhou, Zhejiang)
- 28th Attack Division (Hangzhou, Zhejiang)
- 10th Bomber Division (Anqing, Anhui)
- SAM Brigade (Quanzhou, Fujian)
- Attack UAV Brigade (Liancheng, Fujian)
- 85th Air Brigade (Quzhou, Zhejiang)
- 8th Anti-Air Artillery Brigade (Shanghai)
- 3rd SAM Brigade (location unknown)
- 3rd Radar Brigade (Shanghai)
- 4th Radar Brigade (Fuzhou, Fujian)
- 12th Radar Brigade (Zhangzhou, Fujian)
- 27th Radar Regiment (Xuzhou, Jiangsu)
- 2016 Air Force totals:
- 3 fighter divisions
- 1 bomber division
- 1 attack division
- 1 SAM brigade
- 3 radar brigades
- 1 radar regiment

PLA Rocket Force Theater HQ (Base 52)
Location: Huangshan, Anhui
May now be designated Base 61; in peacetime, this organization is probably under direct command of CMC and Joint Staff Department in Beijing; in wartime, it is likely to be allocated to Joint Taiwan Attack Command and become main command post for missile support to amphibious assault operations; only missile brigades believed to be armed with conventional ballistic missiles are included.

- 815 Brigade (Shangrao, Jiangxi)
- 817 Brigade (Yong'an, Fujian)
- 818 Brigade (Meizhou, Guangdong)
- 819 Brigade (Ganzhou, Jiangxi)
- 820 Brigade (Jinhua, Zhejiang)

Southern Theater Command

Location: Guangzhou

In wartime Southern Theater Command may become merged into the Joint Taiwan Attack Command with its assets assigned by the CMC and Joint Staff Department.

PLA Army HQ

Location: Nanning, Guangxi

41st Group Army

Location: Liuzhou

May now be designated 75th Group Army; in wartime likely to be responsible for assaults on southern Taiwan.

- 121st Mountain Infantry Brigade (Guilin, Guangxi)
- 122nd Infantry Brigade (Guilin)
- 123rd Mechanized Infantry Division (Guigang, Guangxi)
- Artillery Brigade (Liuzhou, Guangxi)
- Armored Brigade (Guilin)

42nd Group Army

Location: Huizhou

May now be designated 74th Group Army; in wartime likely to be responsible for assaults on southern Taiwan.

- 132nd Infantry Brigade (Wuzhishan, Hainan)
- Artillery Division (Qujiang, Guangdong)
- 124th Amphibious Mechanized Infantry Division (Boluo, Guangdong)
- 163rd Infantry Division (Chaozhou, Guangdong)
- Special Operations Brigade (Guangzhou, Guangdong)
- Long Range Artillery Brigade (Dongguan, Guangdong)
- Air Defense Brigade (Chaozhou)
- Army Aviation Brigade (Sanshui, Guangdong)
- 9th Armored Brigade (Guangzhou, Guangdong)
- Chemical Defense Regiment (Shenzhen, Guangdong)

PLA Navy South Sea Fleet HQ

Location: Zhanjiang, Guangdong

In wartime likely to be responsible for naval support to amphibious assault operations against southern Taiwan.

- 2nd Destroyer Flotilla (Zhanjiang)
- 3rd Combat Support Ship Flotilla (Zhanjiang)
- 6th Landing Ship Flotilla (Zhanjiang)
- 1st Marine Brigade (Zhanjiang)
- 164th Marine Brigade (Zhanjiang)
- 11th Fastboat Flotilla (Haikou, Hainan)
- 2nd Frigate Flotilla (Shantou, Guangdong)
- 9th Destroyer Flotilla (Sanya, Hainan)
- 2nd Submarine Base (Sanya, Hainan)
- 8th Naval Aviation Division (Jialaishi, Hainan)
- 9th Naval Aviation Division (Lingshui, Hainan)
- 3rd Radar Brigade (Haikou)

2015 Fleet Totals:

- 4 nuclear-powered ballistic missile subs
- 2 nuclear-powered attack subs
- 20 diesel-powered attack subs
- 7 destroyers
- 21 frigates
- 8 corvettes
- 3 amphibious transport docks
- 11 tank landing ships
- 7 medium landing ships
- 38 missile patrol craft
- 10,000 marines (approx.)
- 1 fighter-bomber division
- 1 mixed air division
- 1 radar brigade

PLA Air Force Theater HQ

Location: Guangzhou, Guangdong

In wartime may become command post for air support to amphibious assault operations against southern Taiwan.

- 2nd Fighter Division (Suixi, Guangdong)
- 42nd Fighter Division (Nanning, Guangxi)
- 9th Fighter Division (Shantou, Guangdong)
- 44th Fighter Division (Luliang, Yunan)
- 18th Fighter Division (Changsha, Hunan)
- 8th Bomber Division (Leiyang, Hunan)
- 10th SAM Brigade (Guangzhou)
- 1st Radar Brigade (Nanning)
- 19th Radar Regiment (Shantou)
- 20th Radar Regiment (Foshan)

2016 Air Force totals:

- 5 fighter divisions
- 1 bomber division
- 1 radar brigade
- 2 radar regiments
- 1 SAM brigade

PLA Rocket Force Theater HQ (Base 53)

Location: Kunming, Yunnan

May now be designated Base 62; in peacetime, this organization is probably under direct command of CMC and Joint Staff Department in Beijing; in wartime, it is likely to be allocated to Joint Taiwan Attack Command for missile support to amphibious assault operations; only missile brigades believed to be armed with conventional ballistic missiles and cruise missiles are included.

- 821 Brigade (Luzhai County, Guangxi)
- Puning Brigade (Puning, Guangdong)
- Qingyuan Brigade (Qingyuan, Guangdong)

Northern Theater Command

Location: Shenyang

In wartime Northern Theater Command is likely to provide the Joint Taiwan Attack Command with assets (as assigned by the CMC and Joint Staff Department), most of which are likely to be treated as second echelon or strategic reserve forces.

PLA Army Theater HQ
Location: Jinan, Shandong

26th Group Army
Location: Weifang, Shandong
May now be designated 80th Group Army.
- 138th Motorized Infantry Brigade (Yantai, Shandong)
- 199 Motorized Infantry Brigade (Zibo, Shandong)
- 77th Motorized Infantry Brigade (Yantai)
- 8th Armored Brigade (Weifang, Shandong)
- 8th Artillery Brigade (Weifang, Shandong)
- 7th Army Aviation Regiment (Liaocheng, Shandong)
- Air Defense Brigade (Jinan, Shandong)

39th Group Army
Location: Liaoyang, Liaoning
May now be designated 79th Group Army.
- 115th Infantry Brigade (Dalian, Liaoning)
- 116th Mechanized Infantry Division (Anshan, Liaoning)
- 190th Mechanized Infantry Brigade (Benxi, Liaoning)
- 202nd Mechanized Infantry Brigade (Siping, Jilin)
- 203rd Motorized Infantry Brigade (Yingkou, Liaoning)
- 3rd Armored Brigade (Siping, Jilin)
- 7th Artillery Brigade (Liaoyang, Liaoning)
- 9th Army Aviation Brigade (Liaoyang, Liaoning)
- Air Defense Brigade (Liaoyang, Liaoning)
- Special Operations Brigade (Liaoyang, Liaoning)

PLA Navy North Sea Fleet HQ

Location: Qingdao, Shandong

In wartime likely to provide some naval support to amphibious assault operations against northern Taiwan.

- 1st Submarine Flotilla (Qingdao, Shandong)
- 2nd Submarine Flotilla (Qingdao, Shandong)
- 1st Destroyer Flotilla (Qingdao, Shandong)
- Anti-ship Missile Regiment (Qingdao, Shandong)
- 1st Combat Ship Support Flotilla (Qingdao, Shandong)
- Air Defense Brigade (Qingdao, Shandong)
- 12th Submarine Flotilla (Dalian, Liaoning)
- 10th Destroyer Flotilla (Dalian, Liaoning)
- 2nd Air Division (Dalian, Liaoning)
- 5th Air Division (Yantai, Shandong)
- 2015 fleet totals:
- 1 aircraft carrier
- 3 nuclear-powered attack subs
- 19 diesel-powered attack subs
- 7 destroyers
- 12 frigates
- 9 corvettes
- 2 tank landing ships
- 6 medium landing ships
- 18 missile patrol craft
- 1 fighter division
- 1 fighter-bomber division
- 1 special aviation division

PLA Air Force Theater HQ

Location: Shenyang, Liaoning

In wartime likely to provide some air support to amphibious assault operations against northern Taiwan.

- 11th Attack Division (Siping, Jilin)
- 88th Air Brigade (Dandong, Liaoning)

- 90th Air Brigade (Dalian, Liaoning)
- 91st Air Brigade (Tonghua, Jilin)
- 1st Fighter Division (Anshan, Liaoning)
- 21st Fighter Division (Dandong, Liaoning)
- 12th Fighter Division (Weihai, Shandong)
- 5th Attack Division (Weifang, Shandong)
- SAM Brigade (Chengyang, Shandong)
- SAM Brigade (Shenyang)
- Air Defense Brigade (Anshan, Liaoning)

2016 Air Force totals:
- 3 fighter divisions
- 2 attack divisions
- 3 air brigade
- 2 SAM brigades
- 1 air defense brigade

Central Theater Command

Location: Beijing
In wartime the Central Theater Command is likely to provide the Joint Taiwan Attack Command with assets (assigned by the CMC and Joint Staff Department), most of which are likely to be treated as second echelon or strategic reserve forces, with the probable exception of air force paratrooper units.

PLA Army Theater HQ
Shijiazhuang, Hebei
In wartime might provide some army elements to second echelon operations against Taiwan.

54th Group Army
Location: Xinxiang, Henan
May now be designated 83rd Group Army; could serve as second echelon or strategic reserve force.

PLA Air Force Theater HQ.
Location: Beijing
In wartime would likely provide some air support to operations against Taiwan, especially in the form of transport planes for airborne landings

15th Airborne Corp
Location: Xiaogan, Hubei
In wartime the 15th Airborne Corp is likely to be assigned to the Joint Taiwan Attack Command and provide units to support first wave of Taiwan assault.
- 43rd Airborne Division (Kaifeng, Henan)
- 44th Airborne Division (Guangshui, Henan)
- 45th Airborne Division (Wuhan, Hubei)

Taiwan (ROC) Order of Battle

Taiwan (ROC) Army

6th Field Army
Location: Zhongli, Taoyuan
In peacetime, the 6th Field Army oversees the Third Theater of Operations (TO), and area encompassing northern Taiwan. In wartime, the 3rd TO becomes a joint structure with assets assigned to it by the MND General Staff Department.

269th Mechanized Infantry Brigade
Location: Yangmei, Taoyuan
Directly subordinate units: HQ Company, Signal/MI Company, an Anti-Armor Company, an Armored Cavalry Company, Maintenance Company, Combat Engineer Company, and Medical Company. The Armored Cavalry Company is usually composed of a tank platoon with four M41 tanks, a mortar platoon composed of three mortar-equipped M113s, and three ar-

mored cavalry platoons composed of Humvees). Anti-Armor companies come equipped with Javelin and TOW missiles.

- Mechanized Infantry Battalion × 3 (CM21/M113 variants)
- Tank Battalion × 1 (CM11)
- Artillery Battalion × 1 (M114 155mm towed howitzers)

542nd Armored Brigade

Location: Hukou, Hsinchu

Directly subordinate units

- Tank Battalion × 3 (CM11 with reactive armor)
- Mechanized Infantry Battalion × 1 (CM21/M113 variants, V150)
- Artillery Battalion × 1 (155mm M109 SPH)

584th Armored Brigade

Location: Hukou, Hsinchu

Directly subordinate units

- Tank Battalion × 2 (CM11)
- Mechanized Infantry Battalion × 2 (CM21/M113 variants)
- Artillery Battalion × 1 (M109 155mm SPH)

21st Artillery Command

Location: Pingzhen, Taoyuan

- Target Acquisition Company × 1
- Air Defense Battalion × 1 (Avengers)
- 621st Group (A group is a unit smaller than a brigade but larger than a battalion)
- Artillery Battalion × 3
- Rocket Artillery Battalion × 1 (Thunderbolt-2000)
- 622nd Group
- Artillery Battalion × 2 (M109 155mm SPH, M110 203mm SPH, M59 155mm Long Tom)

33rd Chemical Group
Location: Zhongli, Taoyuan
- Reconnaissance/ Decontamination Battalion × 1
- Smoke Battalion × 1

53rd Engineering Group
Location: Bade, Taoyuan
- Combat Engineer Battalion × 2
- Bridge Battalion × 1

73rd Signals Group
Location: Zhongli, Taoyuan
- Network Transmission Company × 1
- Area Communication Battalion × 1
- Communication Support Battalion × 1

153rd Infantry Brigade
Location: Yilan County
- Infantry Battalion × 5
- Artillery Battalion × 1

206th Infantry Brigade
Location: Guanxi, Hsinchu County
- Infantry Battalion × 5
- Artillery Battalion × 1

Guandu Defense Command
Location: Tamsui, New Taipei City
Directly subordinate units same as above, save for the absence of a medical company.
- Mechanized Infantry Battalion × 4 (CM21/M113 variants, M42 Duster, V150, CM32, as well as one tank company per battalion consisting of CM11s)
- Artillery Battalion × 1 (company-sized ceremonial artillery)

Lanyang Defense Command

Location: Sanxing, Yilan County

Directly subordinate units same as the Guandu Defense Command.

- Tank Battalion × 1 (M60A3)
- Mechanized Infantry Battalion × 2 (CM21/M113 variants, possible CM32 variants)

10th Field Army

Location: Xinshe, Taichung

In peacetime, the 10th field army oversees the Fifth Theater of Operations, an area covering the central portion of western Taiwan, including the population centers of Taichung and Chiayi. In wartime, the 5th TO becomes a joint structure with assets assigned to it by the MND General Staff Department.

586th Armored brigade

Location: Houli, Taichung

Directly subordinate units

- Tank Battalion × 2 (M60A3)
- Mechanized Infantry Battalion × 2 (CM21/M113 variants, CM32 variants)
- Artillery Battalion × 1 (M109 155mm)

234th Mechanized Infantry Brigade

Location: Dali, Taichung

Directly subordinate units

- Mechanized Infantry Battalion × 3 (CM32 variants, CM21/M113 variants)
- Tank Battalion × 1 (M60A3)
- Artillery Battalion × 1 (M114 155mm towed howitzer)

58th Artillery Group

Location: Shengang, Taichung

- Target Acquisition Company × 1

- Air Defense Battalion × 1 (Avengers)

626th Artillery Group
- Artillery Battalion × 3 (M110 203 mm SPH, M114 155mm towed howitzer, M109 155 mm SPH)
- Rocket Artillery Battalion × 1 (Thunderbolt-2000)

52nd Engineering Group
Location: Taiyang, Taichung
- Combat Engineer Battalion × 2
- Bridge Battalion × 1

36th Chemical Group
Location: Daya, Taichung
- Reconnaissance/ Decontamination Battalion × 1
- Smoke Battalion × 1

74th Signals Group
Location: Xinshe, Taichung
- Network Transmission Company × 1
- Area Communication Battalion × 1
- Communication Support Battalion x1

302nd Infantry Brigade
Location: Wuri, Taichung
- Infantry Battalion × 5
- Artillery Battalion × 1

104th Infantry Brigade
Location: Wuri, Taichung
- Infantry Battalion × 5
- Artillery Battalion × 1

257th Infantry Brigade
Location: Dalin, Chiayi
- Infantry Battalion × 5
- Artillery Battalion × 1

8th Field Army
Location: Qishan, Kaohsiung
In peacetime, the 8th Field Army oversees the Fourth Theater of Operations (TO), an area encompassing the southern portion of Taiwan's west coast, including the population centers of Tainan and Kaohsiung. In wartime, the 4th TO becomes a joint structure with assets assigned to it by the MND General Staff Department.

333rd Mechanized Infantry Brigade
Location: Wanluan, Pingtung
Directly subordinate units
- Mechanized Infantry Battalion × 3 (CM32 variants, V150, CM21/M113 variants)
- Tank Battalion × 1 (CM11)
- Artillery Battalion × 1 (M114 155mm towed howitzer)

564th Armored Brigade
Location: Alian, Kaohsiung
Directly subordinate units (armored cavalry company has CM32 variants)
- Tank Battalion × 2 (CM11)
- Mechanized Infantry Battalion × 2 (CM21/M113 variants)
- Artillery Battalion × 1 (M109 155 mm SPH)

43rd Artillery Command
Location: Dashu, Kaohsiung
- Target Acquisition Company × 1
- Air Defense Battalion × 1 (Chaparral)

624th Group
- Artillery Battalion × 3 (M110 203mm SPH, M114 155mm towed howitzer, M109 155mm SPH, M59 155mm Long Tom, M115 203mm towed howitzer)
- Rocket Artillery Company × 1 (Thunderbolt-2000)

54th Engineering Group
Location: Yanchao, Kaohsiung
- Combat Engineer Battalion × 2
- Bridge Battalion × 1

39th Chemical Group
Location: Qishan, Kaohsiung
- Reconnaissance/ Decontamination Battalion × 1
- Smoke Battalion × 1

203rd Infantry Brigade
Location: Guantian, Tainan
- Infantry Battalion × 5
- Artillery Battalion × 1

Huatung Defense Command
Location: Hualien
Responsible for the defense of eastern Taiwan. Oversees the Second Theater of Operations in peacetime. Serves as a last line of defense.

Hualien Defense Team
Location: Hualien
Directly subordinate units same as previous, with the exception of a chemical warfare company and a military police platoon.
- Tank Battalion × 1 (M60A3, as well as one mechanized infantry company equipped with CM21/M113 variants)
- Mechanized Infantry Battalion × 1 (CM21/M113 variants)

- Mixed Artillery Battalion × 1 (M114 155mm towed howitzer, M101 towed howitzer 105mm)

Taitung Defense Team
Location: Taitung
Directly subordinate units limited to the HQ company, a signal/MI company, an armored cavalry company, and a combat engineer company.
- Mechanized Infantry Battalion × 2 (CM21/M113 variants)
- Mixed Artillery Battalion × 1

Penghu Defense Command
Location: Magong City
Responsible for the defense of the Penghu island chain. Oversees the First Theater of Operations. Serves as forward line of defense.
Penghu Defense Team
- Mechanized Infantry Battalion × 1 (CM21/M113 variants, one tank composed of M60A3)
- Armored Cavalry Battalion × 1
- Mixed Artillery Battalion × 1 (M114 155mm towed howitzer, M101 105mm towed howitzer)

Kinmen Defense Command
Location: Greater Kinmen
Responsible for the defense and Kinmen and its surrounding islands and islets. In the event of conflict, it is tasked with damaging and slowing down the PLA invasion force to buy time for defense preparation in Penghu and Taiwan proper.

Kinmen Defense Command
Location: Greater Kinmen
Directly subordinate units include a HQ company, a Signal/MI Company, a Combat Engineer Company, a Support Company, and a MP Platoon.
- Mixed Air Defense Artillery Company × 1

- Mixed Field Artillery Battalion × 1 (M1 240mm towed howitzer, M115 towed howitzer 203mm, 155mm Long Tom towed howitzer, M101 105mm towed howitzer, 120mm mortars)

Kinmen Defense Team
Location: Greater Kinmen
- Tank Battalion × 1 (M60A3, with one mechanized infantry company composed of CM21/M113 variants)
- Mechanized Infantry Battalion × 1 (CM21/M113 variants)

Lieyu Defense Team
Location: Lieyu Island (Lesser Kinmen)
- Mechanized Infantry Company × 1
- Mixed Artillery Company × 1

Matsu Defense Command
Responsible for the defense of Matsu. In the event of conflict, it is tasked with damaging and slowing down the PLA invasion force to buy time for defense preparation in Penghu and Taiwan proper.

Matsu Defense Command
Directly subordinate units include a HQ Company, a Signal/MI Company, a Combat Engineer Company, an Air Defense Company, and a Rocket Platoon (unconfirmed equipment, but probably Thunderbolt-2000)

Nangan Defense Team
Location: Nangan, Matsu
- Mixed Artillery Company
- Mechanized Infantry Company
- Infantry Company

Beigan Defense Team
Location: Beigan, Matsu
- Mixed Artillery Company

- Mechanized Infantry Company
- Infantry Company

Juguang Defense Team
Location: Juguang, Matsu
- Mixed Artillery Company
- Mechanized Infantry Company
- Infantry Company

Dongyin Defense Command
Location: Dongyin
Responsible for the defense of Dongyin. Role similar to that of forces on Matsu and Kinmen. Separate from Matsu Defense Command due to isolation and distance.

Dongyin Defense Team
Location: Dongyin
Directly subordinate units include a HQ Company, a Support Company, a Signal/MI Company, a Combat Engineer Company
- Mixed Air Defense Artillery Company × 1 (possibly under the Mixed Artillery Battalion)
- Infantry Battalion × 1 (includes one mechanized infantry company equipped with CM21/M113 variants)
- Mixed Artillery Battalion × 1 (81 mm mortar, M101 105mm towed howitzer, 120mm mortar, M115 203mm towed howitzer, 20mm anti air cannon)

Aviation and Special Forces Command
Location: Longtan, Taoyuan
Responsible for army aviation and special operations community.

Special Service Company
Location: Liangshan, Pingtung (?)
Elite counterterrorism unit, similar to U.S. Army Delta Force.

Army 101st Amphibious Reconnaissance Battalion (Frogman Unit)
Location: Detachments spread across Taiwan's outlying islands, with head-quarters based at Liaoluo Bay, Kinmen
- 1st Reconnaissance Company (Kinmen)
- 2nd Reconnaissance Company (Penghu)
- 3rd Reconnaissance Company (Nangan)
- 4th Reconnaissance Company (Dongyin)

Air Transport Battalion
Location: Guiren, Tainan
- CH-47SD × 8 (possibly one with Aviation Training Command)

Tactical Reconnaissance Group (UAV unit equipped with 32 Chung Shyang II UAVs)
Location: Taitung
- 1st Tactical Reconnaissance Squadron (Taiping, Yangmei)
- 2nd Tactical Reconnaissance Squadron (Shenkang, Taichung)
- 3rd Tactical Reconnaissance Squadron (Kaohsiung)

601st Air Calvary Brigade
(under 3rd TO in wartime)
Longtan, Taoyuan
- Attack Battalion × 2 (Apache AH-64E)
- Reconnaissance/Search Battalion × 1 (OH-58D)
- Utility/Transport Battalion × 1 (UH-1H, UH-60)

602nd Air Cavalry Brigade
(under 5th TO in wartime)
Location: Xinshe, Taichung
- Attack Battalion × 2 (AH-1)
- Reconnaissance/Search Battalion × 1 (OH-58D)
- Utility/Transport Battalion × 1 (UH-1, UH-60)

Aviation Training Command
(under 4th TO in wartime)
Location: Guiren, Tainan
- AH-1W, OH-58D, UH-1H, TH-67A, UH-60D
- Training Battalion × 2
- Cadet Battalion × 1

Army Special Operations Command
Location: Longtan, Taoyuan
- Special Operations Battalion × 5

Taiwan (ROC) Navy

124th Flotilla
Location: Zuoying
- *Kangding*-class (*Lafayette*) frigates × 6

131st Flotilla
Location: Keelung
- Ching Chiang-class missile patrol ship × 12
- Kuang Hua VI-class missile boat × 31
- Tuo Chiang-class catamaran corvette × 1 (up to 12 planned)

146th Flotilla
Location: Magong
- Cheng Kung-class (Perry) guided missile frigates × 8

151st Flotilla
Location: Zuoying
- Newport-class tank landing ships × 2
- Anchorage-class dock landing ship × 1
- Chung Hai-class tank landing ships × 7 (including one amphibious command ship)
- Wu Yi-class fast combat support ship × 1

- Pan Shi-class fast combat support ship × 1

168th Flotilla

Location: Su'ao

- Chi Yang-class (Knox) frigates × 6
- Oliver Hazard Perry-class frigates × 2 (entering service in 2017)
- Keelung-class (Kidd) destroyers × 4

192nd Flotilla

Location: Zuoying

- Yung Yang-class (Agile) minesweepers × 3
- Yung Feng-class mine hunters × 4
- Yong Jing-class (Osprey) coastal mine hunters × 2

256th Squadron

Location: Zuoying

- Hai Shih-class (Tench) × 2
- Hai Lung-class (Zwaardis) × 2

Naval Anti-Submarine Aviation Group

Location: Hualien AFB

- 701st and 702nd Squadrons (18 S-70C(M), 8 MD500 Defenders)

Anti-Ship Missile Group

(Hsiung Feng missiles)
Various locations

Northern defense

- 1st Squadron—Keelung
- 3rd Squadron—Tamsui
- 5th Squadron—Dongyin

Southern defense

- 2nd Squadron—Pingtung

- 4th Squadron—Kaohsiung

Penghu defense
- 6th Squadron—Penghu

Eastern defense
- 7th Squadron—Hualien

Taiwan (ROC) Navy Marine Corps

66th Marine Brigade
Location: Guishan District, Taoyuan
Assigned to northern Taiwan in 2005 to defend Taipei against potential PLA decapitation strikes. Operates under 3rd TO.
Directly subordinate units
- Mechanized Infantry Battalion × 3 (CM21/M113 variants)
- Tank Battalion × 1 (M60A3)
- Artillery Battalion × 1 (M109 155mm SPH)

99th Marine Brigade
Location: Kaohsiung
Responsible for the defense of Kaohsiung. Serves as strategic counterattack brigade. Operates under the 4th TO.
Directly subordinate units
- Mechanized Infantry Battalion × 3 (CM21/M113 variants)
- Tank Battalion × 1 (M60A3)
- Artillery Battalion × 1 (M109 155mm SPH)

ROCMC Air Defense Group
Location: Various locations, headquartered in Zuoying, Kaohsiung
Formerly the 77th Marine Brigade. Dissolved and repurposed for naval base defense in 2013.
- Base Security Battalion × 2 (Military Police units under Marine Corps control)

- Air Defense Battalion × 1 (Chaparral)

Amphibious Armor Group
Location: Zuoying, Kaohsiung
Amphibious armor element of the marines. Assets deployed with both marine brigades.
- Amphibious Transport Squadron × 4 (AAV7, LVT5)
- Amphibious Artillery Squadron × 2 (LVT5)

Amphibious Reconnaissance and Patrol Unit
Location: Unknown
- Reconnaissance Company × 3
- Marine Special Service Company × 1 (Taiwanese Navy SEALs)
- Underwater Demolition Company × 1

Wuqiu Garrison Group
Location: Wuqiu Islets, Kinmen Island Chain
- Garrison Company × 2 (M114 155mm howitzer, M1011 105mm howitzer)
- Air Defense Detachment X 1 (40mm AAA)

Taiwan (ROC) Air Force

499th Tactical Fighter Wing
Location: Hsinchu Airbase
Responsible for defense of Taipei area and 24/7 strip alerts for enforcing ADIZ.

41st Tactical Fighter Group
- Mirage 2000-5

42nd Tactical Fighter Group
- Mirage 2000-5

48th Training Group
- Mirage 2000-5

427th Tactical Fighter Wing
Location: Ching Chuan Kang Airbase (CCK, Taichung)
Responsible for defense of northern and central Taiwan.

7th Tactical Fighter Group
- F-CK-1 IDF

28th Tactical Fighter Group
- F-CK-1 IDF

Testing and Evaluation Squadron
- F-CK-1 IDF

455th Tactical Fighter Wing
Location: Chiayi Airbase
Responsible for defense of central and southern Taiwan, air rescue, and strategic counterattacks.

21st Tactical Fighter Group
- F-16 A/B

22nd Tactical Fighter Group
- F-16 A/B

23rd Tactical Fighter Group
- F-16 A/B

Air Rescue Group (Seagulls)
- S-70C-1 Bluehawk × 13
- S-70C-6 Bluehawk × 3
- EC225 Super Puma Mk2/15 × 3

443rd Tactical Fighter Wing

Location: Tainan Airbase

Responsible for defense of southern Taiwan, strategic counterattacks, and 24/7 strip alerts for enforcing ADIZ.

1st Tactical Fighter Group

- F-CK-1 IDF

3rd Tactical Fighter Group

- F-CK-1 IDF

9th Tactical Fighter Group

- F-CK-1 IDF

401st Tactical Combined Wing

Location: Hualien Airbase

Responsible for intelligence gathering, strategic counterattacks, and 24/7 strip alerts for enforcing ADIZ.

17th Tactical Fighter Group

- F-16 A/B

26th Tactical Fighter Group

- F-16 A/B

27th Tactical Fighter Group

- F-16 A/B

12th Tactical Reconnaissance Group

- RF-5E Tigereye (5 or less)
- RF-16 (8 or less)

737th Tactical Combined Wing
Location: Zhihang Airbase (Taitung)
Responsible for training

44th Tactical Fighter Group
- F-5E

45th Tactical Fighter Group
- F-5E

46th Tactical Fighter Group
- F-5E

439th Combined Wing
Location: Pingtung Airbase
Responsible for intelligence gathering, airborne assault, electronic warfare, anti-submarine warfare, and maritime patrol

10th Air Transport Group
- C-130H × 19

20th Electronic Warfare Group
- C-130HE × 1
- E-2 Hawkeye × 6

Air Force Anti-Submarine Group
- S-2T × 11 (retiring in 2017)
- P-3 Orion × 12

Taiwan (ROC) Air Defense Missile Command

Strategic Counterstrike Missile Group
(Actual name unknown)
Location: Unknown, probably MND HQ

Responsible for strategic counterstrikes with road mobile (and possibly silo-based) ballistic missiles and land attack cruise missiles

641st Battalion, 1st Company
Location unknown
- Possibly Hsiung Feng IIE cruise missiles

641st Battalion, 2nd Company
Location unknown
- Possibly Hsiung Feng IIE cruise missiles

642nd Battalion, 3rd Company
Location unknown
- Possibly Hsiung Feng IIE cruise missiles

642nd Battalion, 1st Company
Location unknown
- Possibly Hsiung Feng IIE cruise missiles

642nd Battalion, 2nd Company
Location unknown
- Possibly Hsiung Feng IIE cruise missiles

642nd Battalion, 3rd Company
Location unknown
- Possibly Hsiung Feng IIE cruise missiles

606 Missile Defense Group
Location: Location unknown, probably MND HQ
Responsible for defense against ballistic missiles and cruise missiles

631st Battalion, 1st Company
Linkou District, New Taipei
- PAC-2/Config 3

631st Battalion, 2nd Company
Xindian District, New Taipei
- PAC-2/Config 3

631nd Battalion, 3rd Company
Nangang District, New Taipei
- PAC-2/Config 3

632nd Battalion, 1st Company
Renwu District, Kaohsiung
PAC-3

632nd Battalion, 2nd Company
Pingtung Airbase
- PAC-3

632nd Battalion, 3rd Company
Xinhua District, Tainan
- PAC-3

633rd Battalion, 1st Company
Taiping District, Taichung
- PAC-3

633rd Battalion, 2nd Company
Ching Chuan Kang Airbase
- PAC-3

633rd Battalion, 3rd Company
Chiayi Airbase
- PAC-3

Training/Reserve Unit (actual unit name unknown)
Location unknown, probably Taoyuan area
- PAC-3

608 Missile Air and Missile Defense Group
Location: Location unknown, probably MND HQ
Responsible for defense against air threats and some ballistic missiles

611th Battalion, 1st Company
Sanzhi District, New Taipei
- Tien Kung 2/possibly 3 SAM

611th Battalion, 2nd Company
Dongyin Islands
- Tien Kung 2/possibly 3 SAM

611th Battalion, 3rd Company
Dadu Township, Taichung
- Tien Kung 2/ possibly 3 SAM

612th Battalion, 1st Company
Alian Township, Kaohsiung
- Tien Kung 2/ possibly 3 SAM

612th Battalion, 2nd Company
Linyuan Township, Kaohsiung
- Tien Kung 2/possibly 3 SAM

612th Battalion, 3rd Company
Penghu Islands
- Tien Kung 2/ possibly 3 SAM

621st Battalion, 1st Company
Su'ao Township, Yilan County
- Hawk SAM (all HAWK batteries will be replaced with Tien Kung 3 systems by 2024)

621st Battalion, 2nd Company
Jinshan District, New Taipei
- Hawk SAM

621st Battalion, 3rd Company
Tamsui District, New Taipei
- Hawk SAM

621st Battalion 4th Company
Zhunan Township, Miaoli
- Hawk SAM

621st Battalion 5th Company
Luzhu Township, Taoyuan
- Hawk SAM

623rd Battalion, 1st Company
Penghu Islands
- Hawk SAM

623rd Battalion, 2nd Company
Jiali District, Tainan
- Hawk SAM

623rd Battalion, 3rd Company
Baozhong Township, Yunlin County
- Hawk SAM

623rd Battalion, 4th Company
Xiaogang District, Kaohsiung
- Hawk SAM

625th Battalion, 1st Company
Zhiben, Taitung
- Hawk SAM

625th Battalion, 2nd Company
Meilunshan, Hualien
- Hawk SAM

141st Air Defense Artillery Group
Location: Various locations—for example, the 302nd Battalion's 1st company and the 501st Battalions 2nd Company are responsible for defending the SRP installation at Leshan
Responsible for point defense of airfields and radar sites.
- 302nd ADA Battalion, with Oerlikon 35mm twin cannons and the Skyguard air defense system
- 303rd ADA Battalion, with Oerlikon 35mm twin cannons and the Skyguard air defense system
- 501st ADA Battalion, with Tien Chien-1 missiles and the Antelope air defense system

142nd Air Defense Artillery Group
Location: Various locations
Responsible for point defense of airfields and radar sites
- 301st ADA Battalion, with Oerlikon 35mm twin cannons and the Skyguard air defense system
- 502st ADA Battalion with, Tien Chien-1 missiles and the Antelope air defense system

Taiwan (ROC) Military Police

202nd Military Police Command
Location: Taipei
Responsible for the defense of the Taipei city during wartime.
- 211st MP Battalion, which defends the Presidential Office Building
- 228th MP Artillery Battalion, 120mm guns
- 229th MP Battalion, which supposedly protect the General Staff's Joint Command Center
- 239th MP Armored Battalion (V150, CM32 variants), which is responsible for evacuating the president and other important government officials in wartime
- 332nd MP Battalion, which is responsible for defending the Presidential Residence
- Various regional MP offices

203rd Military Police Command
Location: Taichung
- Various regional MP offices

204th Military Police Command
Location: Kaohsiung
- Various regional MP offices

205th Military Police Command
Location: Taoyuan
- Various regional MP offices

Ministry of National Defense Orderly Battalion MP element
Location: Taoyuan
- MP Company × 1

6th Field Army MP element
Location: Taoyuan

- MP Company × 1

8th Field Army MP element
Location: Kaohsiung
- MP Company × 1

10th Field Army MP element
Location: Taichung
- MP Company × 1

Kinmen Defense Command MP element
Location: Kinmen
- MP platoon × 1

Marine Corps Air Defense Group MP element
Location: Various
- Base Security Battalion × 2

Air Force Headquarters MP element
Location: Various
- MP detachment × 12

Sources available from author by request.

Selected Bibliography

Chinese Books

Academy of Military Sciences' Strategic Research Department (editors). *Science of Military Strategy* (战略学). Beijing: Academy of Military Sciences, 2013.

Bai Guangwei (editor). *Course Book on Taiwan Strait Military Geography* (台海军事地理教程). Beijing: Academy of Military Sciences Press, 2013.

Cao Zhengrong, Sun Longhai, and Yang Yin (editors). *Informatized Army Operations* (信息化陆军作战). Beijing: National Defense University Press, 2014.

Cao Zhengrong, Wu Runbo, and Sun Jianjun (editors). *Informatized Joint Operations* (信息化联合作战). Beijing: Liberation Army Press, 2008.

Gao Defu (editor). *Military Forces Informatization* (军队信息化). Beijing, Liberation Army Press, 2007.

Guo Ming (editor). *Course Book on the Art of Special Operations* (特种作战学教程). Beijing: Academy of Military Sciences Press, 2013.

Hu Guoqiao (editor). *Research on Army Aviation Tactics* (陆军航空兵战术研究). Beijing: PLA General Staff Department Army Aviation Department, 2013.

Huang Bingyue, Wu Shaofeng, and Zhou Zhichao (editors). *Research on Command Systems for Amphibious Fleet Operations* (两栖作战编队 指 挥体系研究). Beijing: Academy of Military Sciences Press, 2013.

Jiang Yanyu (editor). *A Military History of Fifty Years in the Taiwan Area 1949-2006* (台湾地区五十年军事史 1949-2006). Beijing: Liberation Army Press, 2013.

Li Qingshan (editor). *Taiwan Military Exercises* (台军演习). Shenyang: Baishan Press, 2008.

Li Zhiguang and Yuan Shuyou (editors). *China's Military Geography* (中国 军事地理). Beijing: Encyclopedia of China Publishing, 2008.

Liu Haijiang and Li Zhiyuan (editors). *Research on Joint Combat Thought* (联合战术思想研究). Beijing, Lantian Press, 2012.

Liu Xing (editor), *Air Defense and Space Defense Information Systems and Their Integrated Technologies* (防空防天信息系统及其一体化技 术). Beijing: National Defense Industry Press, 2009.

Ning Sao (editor). *2006-2008 Research Report on Taiwan Strait Situation* (2006-2008年台海局势研究报告). Beijing: Jiuzhou Press, 2006.

Shen Shaoying and Zhang Yingzhen (editors). *Research on Foreign (and Taiwan) Militaries' Army Training* (外台军陆军军事训练研究). Shiji-azhuang: Liberation Army Press, 2006.

Wang Yongping (editor). *Space Information Support Operations* (空间信息 支援作战). Beijing: National Defense University Press, 2014.

Xiong Fen and Zuo Jiayue (editors). *China Port Authority Yearbook 2014* (中国口岸年鉴2014). Beijing: China Port Authority Press, 2014.

Xu Lisheng and Wang Tiaoyong (editors). *Research on Port Landing Operations* (港口登陆作战研究). Beijing: National Defense University Press, 2015.

Yang Pushuang (editor). *The Japanese Air Self Defense Force* (日本航空自 卫队). Beijing: Lantian Press, 2013.

Yuan Wenxian (editor). *Course Book on Joint Campaigns and Information Operations* (联合战役信息作战教程). Beijing: National Defense University, 2009.

Zhang Qingzhi (editor). *Informatized Operations and Psychological Protec-tion* (信息化战争心理防护). Beijing: People's Military Medical Press, 2008.

Zhang Zhiwei, and Huang Chuanxian (editors). *Research on Operational Theory of Army Aviation Troops* (陆军航空兵作战理论研究). Beijing: National Defense University Press, 2014.

Zhang Yuliang (editor). *The Science of Campaigns* (战役学). Beijing: National Defense University Press, 2007.

Zhao Feng (editor). *The Taiwan Military's 20 Year Transformation* (台军20年转型之路). Beijing: National Defense University Press, 2015.

Zhou Zhihuai (editor). *Taiwan in 2013* (台湾2013). Beijing: Jiuzhou Press, 2014.

Zhou Zhihuai (editor). *Taiwan in 2008* (台湾二〇〇八). Beijing: Jiuzhou Press, 2009.

Chinese Journal Articles

Cai Junfeng and Mei Sijun, "Design of Protective Storage for Ordinance to be Carried during Amphibious Strait Crossing and Island Landing Operations (渡海登岛作战弹药两栖携行防护装具设计)," *Packaging Engineering Journal*, March 2015, pp. 140–143.

Chen Songhui, Qiu Hongli, and Du Hu, "Research and Analysis on an Amphibious Formation's Comprehensive Landing and Assault Capabilities (两栖编队综合登陆突击能力的分析研究)," *Ship Electronic Engineering Journal*, No. 5, 2014, pp. 34–37, 64.

He Libo and Song Fengying, "Preliminary Examination of Mao Zedong's Military Thought on Sea-Crossing and Island Landing Operations (毛泽东渡海登陆作战军事思想初探)," *Henan Social Science Journal*, January, 2004, p. 40.

Huang Guangyan, et al., "Method for Assessing Effects of Joint Anti-Runway and Area Blockading Sub-munitions (反跑道与区域封锁子母弹联合对封锁效能的评估方法)," *Journal of Ballistics*, March 2013, p. 46.

Jia Ziying, Chen Songhui, and Wen Rui, "Analysis of Troop Unit Effectiveness During Systemized Landing Operations Based on Data Field

(基于数据场的登陆作战体系兵力编组效能分析)," *Command Control & Simulation Journal*, Vol. 36, No. 6, December 2014, pp. 92–95.

Jiang Zengrong, et al., "Numerical Modeling of Blast Depth Influence on Destruction Effects of Penetrating Warhead (炸点深度对侵爆战斗布摧伤效果影响数值模拟)," *Acta Armamentarii Journal*, April 2010, pp. 28–31.

Li Jun and Zhang Qi, "Research on How to Optimize the Deployment of Artillery Forces for Offensive Combat against Offshore Islands Based on FCE (基于ＦＣＥ对近岸岛屿进攻战斗炮兵部署优化研究)," *Ship Electronic Engineering Journal*, December 2012, pp. 43–47.

Li Yong, et al., "Simulation and Calculation Research on Terminal Course-Correcting Submunitions' Airfield Runway Blockade Probability (末修子母弹对机场跑道封锁概率计算仿真研究)," *Journal of System Simulation*, Vol. 18, No. 9, 2006, pp. 2397–2400.

Liu Hongkun, "Analysis of Our Tank Companies' Offensive Operational Capabilities against Combat Vehicles on the Island (坦克连对岛上战车排进攻作战能力分析)," *Fire Control and Command Control Journal*, September 2006, pp. 64–66, 78.

Liu Runcai, et al., "Analysis and Modeling of Communications Environment during Landing Operations (登陆作战中的通信环境分析与建模)," *Sichuan Ordinance Studies Journal*, December 2010, pp. 63–65.

Liu Zengyou, et al., "Deployment Method of Vessel and Equipment Support Forces for Joint Operations against Offshore Islands (近岸岛屿联合作战船艇装备保障力量部署方法)," *Ordinance Industry Automation Journal*, April 2010, pp. 58–62.

Lu Hui and Zheng Huaisheng, "Thoughts on the Experience of the Sea-Crossing and Landing Operations against Dengbu Island (登步岛渡海登陆作战经过与思考), *PLA Military History Journal*, No. 3, 2007, pp. 21–25.

Shen Zhihua, "The CCP's Taiwan Attack Campaign: Policy Changes and Limiting Factors, 1949–1950 (中共进攻台湾战役的决策变化及其制约因素，1949-1950), *Social Science Research Journal*, No. 3, 2009, pp. 48–49.

Song Jian, "Risk Assessment on Camouflaging a Landing Campaign (登陆战 役伪装风险评估), *Journal of Computer and Digital Engineering*, Vol. 41, No. 8, 2013, pp. 1232–1234.

Tang Hongsen, "Discussing the Taiwan Strait Standoff and the Battle of Dengbu (论登步之战与台海对峙)," *Zhejiang Studies Journal*, No. 2, 2012, pp. 59–68.

Tao Guiming, et al., "Modeling the Order of Surface to Surface Missile Strikes on Airfields (地地导弹打击机场排序模型)," *Computer and Information Technology Journal*, February 2013, pp. 12–14.

Wang Dazhong, et al., "Initial Evaluation of Ship Fire Support Effectiveness and Fire Distribution during Landing Operations (登陆作战中舰艇 火力支援效能及分配模型初探)," *Ship Electronic Engineering Journal*, No. 2, 2010, pp. 32–34, 44.

Wang Yinlai, Chen Songhui, and Jia Ziying, "Analysis of Troops Unit Effectiveness During Landing Operations Based on Complex Networks (基于复杂网络的登陆作战兵力编组效能分析)," *Fire Control & Command Control Journal*, Vol. 39, No. 8, August 2014, pp. 87–90.

Yan Feilong and Jia Ziying, "Airborne Landing Operation Target Selection Method Based on Complex Networks (基于复杂网络的机降作战 目标选择方法)," *Fire Control & Command Control Journal*, April 2014, pp. 38–41.

Yang Fengshou and Hu Xiaoyun, "Infantry Unit Landing Operations Decision Plan Evaluation based upon Improved Three Marker Method (基于三标度改进方法的步兵分队登陆作战决心方案评价)," *Command, Control, and Simulation Journal*, December 2009, pp. 48–51.

Yin Jun and Bao Zhan, "Thinking on Campaign Simulation Based on Military Concept Modeling Method (关于战役模拟军事概念建模方法论的 思考)," *Military Operations Research and Systems Engineering Journal*, September 2012, pp. 35–38.

Zhao Yiping, "Taiwan Strait Attack Strategy: The Beginning and End of Planning and Preparation for Taiwan Liberation Operations just as New China was Established (台海攻略：新中国成立前后解放台湾作战计划与准备始末)," *PLA Military History Monthly*, No. 1, Issue 130, January 2005, pp. 10–17.

Taiwanese Books

Chen Ching-lin (editor). *All-Out National Defense Education: Defense Mobilization* (全民國防教育防衛動員). New Taipei City: Wun Ching Developmental Publishing, 2013.

Chen Ching-lin, Hwuang Zheng-yi, and Kuo Wen-liang (editors). *All-Out National Defense Education* (全民國防教育). New Taipei City: Wun Ching Developmental Publishing, 2010.

Kuo Nai-ri (editor). *The Unseen War in the Taiwan Strait* (看不見的台海戰爭). Xizhi, Taipei County: Kaoshou Zhuanye Press, 2005.

Kuo Wen-liang (editor). *National All-Out Defense Education: National Defense Technology.* (全民國防教育國防科技). New Taipei City: New Wun Ching Developmental Publishing, 2014.

Lin Chong-bin (editor). *Calculating the Taiwan Strait: The Strategic Situation in the Strait in the New Century* (廟算台海：新世紀海峽 戰略態勢). Taipei: Chinese Council of Advanced Policy Studies, 2002.

Republic of China (R.O.C.) Ministry of National Defense. *National Defense Report 2015* (國防報告書). Taipei: Ministry of National Defense, 2015.

Republic of China (R.O.C.) Ministry of National Defense. *National Defense Report 2013* (國防報告書). Taipei, Taiwan: Ministry of National Defense, 2013.

Republic of China (R.O.C.) Ministry of National Defense. *Republic of China 2013 Quadrennial Defense Review.* Taipei: Ministry of National Defense, 2013.

Taiwanese Journal Articles

Chang Hsueh-chang, "Discussion on Military Police Missions in Wartime (戰時憲兵任務之探討)," *ROC Military Police Command Journal*, No. 80 (June 2015), pp. 25–40.

Chang Kuo-ta, "Research on Application of Advanced Infantry Platoon Firepower in Urban Defense (精進進步兵排城鎮防禦火力運用之研析)," *ROC Army Infantry Journal*, No. 257, 2016, pp. 1–18.

Chang Sheng-Kai and Tseng Chen-yang, "Analysis of Chinese Communist Mine-laying Operations off Taiwan's East Coast (中共對我東岸海域布雷行動之研析), *ROC Navy Journal*, No. 49, Vol. 4 (August 1, 2015), pp. 132–140.

Chang You-ching, "Research on Combat Engineer Support in River Crossings during Defense Operations-The Case of the Third Theater of Operations and the Tamsui River (防衛作戰中工兵支援渡河作業之研究—以第三作戰區淡水河爲例)," *ROC Army Combat Engineer Journal*, No. 147, 2015, pp. 1–24.

Chang Zong-Tsai, "Research on Tactics and Techniques of Communist Military 'Decapitation Operations' through the lens of the U.S. Military's 'Operation Neptune Spear' (共軍'斬首行動'戰術戰法- 以美軍'海神之矛行動'研析)," *Journal of ROC Aviation and Special Forces Command*, No. 56, 2012, pp. 10–12.

Chen Chiu-yang, "Analyzing Application of Electronic Warfare Techniques in Taiwanese Urban Warfare using of other Countries' Experiences (從各國經驗探討我城鎮戰中電子戰應用作爲之研析)," *ROC Army Combat Engineer Journal*, No. 147, 2015, pp. 1–20.

Chien Yi-jian and Ong Ming-hui, "Research on Armor Brigade Counterattack Operations during Defense Operations-The Case of a Suitable Landing Area (防衛作戰中裝甲旅反擊之研究 -以適宜登陸地區 爲例)," *ROC Armor Journal*, No. 240, July 2015, pp. 15–42.

Chu Bih-wei, "The Communist Military's Amphibious Operational Thought and Platform Developments (共軍兩棲作戰思維與載台發展)," *ROC Navy Journal*, No. 47, Vol. 1 (February 1, 2013), pp. 120–129.

Fung Chiu-kuo, "Research on Military Value of Urban Underground Infrastructure (城鎮地下設施軍事價值之研究)," *ROC Army Infantry Journal*, No. 256, 2015, pp. 1–22.

Hsiao Ing-li and Wu Kuang-chung, "Research on American and Japanese Pacific Island Combat during World War Two: Examples from Okinawa, Iwo Jima, and Formosa (第二次世界大戰美，日太平洋 島嶼作戰之研究-以沖繩島，硫磺島及台灣爲例)," *ROC Army Journal*, Vol. 51, No. 543 (October 2015), pp. 102–123.

Hsieh Chih-Peng, "Research on the Communist Military's New Campaign Guidance (共軍新時期戰役指導之研究)," *ROC Army Journal*, No. 50, Vol. 536 (August 2014), pp. 35–50.

Hsieh You-teng, "Research and Analysis on Army Development of 'Asymmetric Operations' Capabilities (陸軍發展「不對稱作戰」能力之研析), *ROC Army Journal*, No. 524, August 2012, pp. 88–98.

Hsu Chi-po and Chen Jun-hung, "Discussion on Taiwan's Highway Bridges and Their Military Support Levels (本島公路橋樑與軍用載重等級之探討)," *ROC Army Combat Engineer Journal*, No. 142, 2013, pp. 1–16.

Hsu Niu, "Analysis of Ray-Ting 2000 Multiple Launch Rocket System Application and Operational Effects During Attacks on Anchorage Areas (雷霆2000多管火箭系統運用於泊地攻擊作戰效能之研析)," *ROC Artillery Forces Journal*, No. 171, 2015, p. 10.

Hsu Yi-Lien, "Homeland Defense Integrated Land-Air Operations: Research on Application of Army Aviation Units (國土防衛地空整體作戰：陸航部隊運用之研究)," *ROC Army Journal*, No. 49, Vol. 529 (June 2013), pp. 23–37.

Huang Tai-Chi, "Insights from the Okinawa Campaign for ROC Counterlanding Operations and Artillery Unit Force Preservation (沖繩島戰役對我反登陸作戰砲兵部隊戰力保存之啓示)," *ROC Army Artillery Journal*, No. 170 (2015), pp. 8–23.

Huang Wei, "What Joint Service Command Officers Should Understand about Fire Support and Coordination (聯合兵種指揮官應了解之火力支援協調作爲)," *ROC Army Journal*, No. 52, Vol. 546, April 2016, pp. 83–98.

Kao Zhi-yang, "Record of U.S. Military Forces Formerly Stationed in Taiwan (駐台美軍曾經的記錄)," *Defence International*, April 2011, pp. 88–95.

Lan Jong-Sheng, "Xi Jinping's Strong Military Dream: Discussing Plans for Rocket Force Buildup (習近平強軍夢: 論火箭軍建軍規劃)," *ROC Army Journal*, No. 52, Vol. 548 (August 2016), pp. 120–121.

Lieu Ching-jong, "Examining the Application of Mechanized Infantry in Future Defense Operations (機步部隊在未來防衛作戰運用之探討), *ROC Army Journal*, Vol. 49, No. 529, June 2013, pp. 4–22.

Lieu Ching-jong, "Research on War Zone Unit Modularization for Homeland Defense (國土防衛中 作戰區部隊模組化之研究)," *ROC Reserve Force Journal*, April 2011, pp. 17–33.

Lieu En-kuang, "Briefing on Mechanized Mine-Laying Systems-Sharp Weapons for Countering Enemy Mobility Operations (反機動作戰利器—機械布雷系統簡介)," *ROC Army Combat Engineer Journal*, No. 146, 2015, pp. 1–21.

Lieu Shien-Chu, "Discussion on Chinese Communist Submarine Threat to Taiwan and Their Blockade Capabilities (中共潛艦對台威脅及對 封鎖能力探討)," *ROC Navy Journal*, No. 46, Vol. 4 (August 1, 2012), pp. 56–74.

Lin Sheng-jie, "Discussion on Combat Engineer Units Application of Robots in Support Missions during Urban Warfare Operations (城鎮戰中工 兵部隊運用機器人直行支援任務之探討), *ROC Combat Engineer Journal*, No. 144, 2014, pp. 1–20.

Lin Zhe-chun, "Discussion on Defense Operations in Urban Infrastructure with Support of Defense Combat Engineers (防衛作戰城鎮設施防 工兵支援之探討)," *ROC Combat Engineer Journal*, No. 144, 2014, pp. 1–23.

Liu Ta-sheng, Menq Jau-yan, Chang Cheng-chang, and Chen Shian-Ruei, "Study on the Homeland Defense Operations Deployment of Seacoast Brigades (國土防衛海岸守備旅兵力配置之研究)," Conference paper presented at the *16th Annual Joint National Defense Management College and National Armaments Management College Seminar*, 2009, pp. 2–13.

Luo Zhen-jun, "Joint Surface Defense: Analyzing the Application of Special Operations Units in Urban Areas (聯合地面防衛--以城鎮地區運 用特種作戰部隊爲分析對象)," *ROC Army Aviation and Special Operations Forces Journal*, No. 56, 2012, pp. 1–18.

Ma Li-te and Chang Nan-Zong, "Analysis of Communist China's New Type Amphibious Transports and the Communist Military's Landing Operation Models (中共新型兩棲載具對共軍登陸作戰模式的研析)," *ROC Navy Journal*, February 2013, p. 80.

Pan Shih-Yeong and Shen Qi-lin, "Analysis of the Chinese Communist's Amphibious Landing Combat Force (中共兩棲登陸戰力之研析)," *ROC Navy Journal*, No. 46, Vol. 3 (June 1, 2012), pp. 69–84.

Su Mao-Hsien, "Discussing Future Operational Concepts of Communist Military's Application of Special Operations Units During Attack on Taiwan (淺談未來共軍攻台運用特種作戰部隊作戰構想)," *ROC Army Aviation and Special Forces Journal*, Vol. 57, 2013, pp. 22–29.

Sun Chi-dao, "Military Applications of Taiwan's Fishing Boats (台灣漁船與軍事應用)," *ROC Navy Journal*, August 2014, pp. 95–108.

Sun Shu-hwua, "Responding to Chinese Communist Urban Warfare Operations Against Taiwan—the Case of Army Aviation Units (中共對我城鎮作戰之因應之道—以陸航部隊為例)," *ROC Army Aviation and Special Forces Journal*, No. 56, 2012, pp. 1–15.

Tsai Cheng-chang, "Weapons for Suppressing Enemy Air Defenses — Discussion on Process of Surface Unit Fire Support Operations (制壓敵防空武力—地面部隊火協作業程序探討)," *ROC Artillery Forces Journal*, No. 169, 2015, pp. 47–64.

Tsai Ho-Hsun, "Research on the Communist Military's Division Landing Operations (共軍師登陸作戰之研究)," *ROC Army Journal*, Vol. 50, No. 537, October 2014, p. 61.

Tsai Ho-Hsun, "Research on the Communist Military's Joint Landing Campaign (剖析共軍聯合登陸戰役)," *ROC Army Journal*, Vol. 50, No. 537, October 2012, pp. 35–49.

Unattributed, "Han Kuang Exercise 32 Series 1: ROC Army 5th Support Department at the Fulcrum (漢光32號演習系列1--陸軍五支部前 支點)," *Defence International*, No. 385, September 2016, pp. 32–34.

Unattributed, "Han Kuang Exercise 32 Series 2: Key Node Hsuehshan Tunnel Blockade Drill (漢光32號演習系列2：關節要點雪山封阻作業)," *Defence International*, No. 385, September 2016, pp. 36–40.

Unattributed, "Reserve Mobilization: Counterattack after Tamsui Raid and Taipei Port Attack (後備動員淡水反突擊台北港反擊), *Defence International*, No. 362, October 2014, pp. 36–43.

Unattributed, "Penghu Wude Joint Counter Amphibious Exercise (澎湖五德聯信聯合反登陸操演)," *Defence International*, May 2013, pp. 32–40.

Wang Cheng-Fang, "Assessment of the Communist Military's Missile Threat to Taiwan's Theater-Level Underground Command Posts (共

軍導彈 對我作戰區級地下指揮所威脅之評估)," *ROC Army Engineer Journal*, Vol. 145, 2014, pp. 2–6.

Wang Chung-fung, "Discussion and Analysis on Combat Engineering Support to Force Preservation Actions (探討工兵支援戰力保存作 爲 之研析)," *ROC Army Combat Engineer Journal*, No. 146, 2015, pp. 1–28.

Wang Chung-fung, "Discussion on Various Types of Blast Door Designs by Overpressure Level (探討各類型爆壓下防爆門之設計)," *ROC Army Combat Engineer Journal*, No. 144, 2014, pp. 1–27.

Wang Hsin-lee, "Research and Analysis on the ROC's 'Three Lines of Defense' National Security Strategy (我國國家安全「三道防線」 的戰略研析)," *ROC Reserve Force Journal*, No. 84, October 2012, pp. 108–132.

Wang Hsiu-Hung, "Analysis of Communist China's Landing Craft Air Cushion Vehicle Developments and Military Applications (中共軍用 氣墊登陸艇發展與軍用之研析)," *ROC Army Journal*, No. 52, Vol. 548 (August 2016), pp. 83–103.

Wang Wei-hsien and Ong Ming-hui, "Discussion on History, Development, and Application of Communist Military's Amphibious Armored Assault Vehicle for Landings (共軍兩棲裝甲戰斗車輛發展歷程與 運用上陸 之探討)," *ROC Army Journal*, No. 52, Vol. 546 (April 2016), pp. 53–54.

Wu Ding-an, "Discussion on ROC Military Beach Obstacle Enterprise in Light of Chinese Communist's 'Mission Action 2013' Exercise, Landing Tactics, and Platforms (從中共 '使命行動2013' 演習之 登陸戰法與輸具探討我軍灘岸阻絕作爲)," *ROC Army Combat Engineer Journal*, No. 147, 2015, pp. 1–23.

Wu Qi-han, "Research on Engineering Unit Obstacle Clearing Capabilities during Communist Military Landing Operations (共軍登島作戰工程兵突擊破障能力與我 反制作爲之研究)," *ROC Army Combat Engineer Journal*, March 2008, pp. 1–28.

Wu Kuang-chang, "Discussion on Integration and Application Model of AH- 64D Attack Helicopter and Joint Defense Operations (AH-64D 攻擊 直升機於聯合防衛作戰之整合與運用模式探討)," *ROC Aviation and Special Forces Journal*, No. 56, 2012, pp. 1–18.

Wu Qi-lun and Huang Zhen-ge, "Analyzing Application and Effects of Smart Mines (智能地雷運用效益之研析)," *ROC Army Combat Engineer Journal*, No. 142, 2013, pp. 1–18.

Wu Qi-yu, "Analyzing the Application and Effects of HESCO Bastions (組合式掩體運用效益之研析)," *ROC Army Journal*, No. 52, Vol. 545 (February 2016), pp. 111–126.

Wu Qi-yu, "Research on Executing Surf Zone Mining Operations with Combat Engineer Units (工兵部隊執行激浪區布雷作業之研究)," *ROC Army Combat Engineer Journal*, No. 147, 2015, pp. 24–27 (of 30).

Yan Chung-yi, "Insights for Our Military on Counter-landing Operations from the Battle of Iwo Jima (硫磺島戰史對國軍反登陸作戰之啓示)," *ROC Navy Journal*, December 2015, pp. 108–117.

Yang Hou-sheng, "Analyzing the Operational Effectiveness of the Communist Military's Type ZLT-05 Amphibious Assault Artillery Vehicle (共軍ZTL-05型兩棲攻擊跑車作戰效能之研析), *ROC Army Infantry Journal*, No. 258, 2016, pp. 1–24.

Yang You-hung, "Research into Communist Military's Joint Island Landing Offensive Campaign Capabilities (共軍聯合島嶼進攻戰役能力研究)," *ROC Reserve Force Journal*, No. 88, October 2013, p. 109.

Yeh Chien-Chung and Chen Hong-diao, "Evaluating Infantry Unit Urban Warfare Training (步兵部隊城鎮作戰訓練之探討)," *ROC Army Journal*, No. 537, October 2014, pp. 23–34.

English-language Books

Blasko, Dennis J. *The Chinese Army Today: Tradition and Transformation for the 21st Century.* New York: Routledge, 2012.

Bush, Richard C. *Uncharted Strait: The Future of China-Taiwan Relations.* Washington, D.C.: Brookings Institution Press, 2013.

Bush, Richard C, and Michael E. O'Hanlon. *A War Like No Other: The Truth About China's Challenge to America.* Hoboken, New Jersey: John Wiley & Sons, Inc. 2007.

Bush, Richard C. *Untying the Knot: Making Peace in the Taiwan Strait.* Washington, D.C.: Brookings Institution Press, 2005.

Campbell, Kurt M. *The Pivot: The Future of American Statecraft in Asia.* New York: Hachette Book Group. Inc., 2016.

Chase, Michael S. *Taiwan's Security Policy: External Threats and Domestic Politics.* Boulder, Colorado: Lynne Rienner Publishers, Inc., 2008.

Churchill, Winston S. *The Second World War: Closing the Ring.* Cambridge, Massachusetts: Riverside Press, 1951.

Clausewitz, Carl Von (Edited and Translated by Michael Howard and Peter Paret). *On War.* Princeton, New Jersey: Princeton University Press, 1976.

Cliff, Roger. *China's Military Power: Assessing Current and Future Capabilities.* New York: Cambridge University Press, 2015.

Cliff, Roger, Mark Burles, Michael S. Chase, Derek Eaton, and Kevin L. Pollpeter. *Entering the Dragon's Lair: Chinese Antiaccess Strategies and Their Implications for the United States.* Arlington, Virginia: RAND Corporation, 2007.

Cole, Bernard D. *The Great Wall at Sea: China's Navy in the Twenty-First Century* (Second Edition). Annapolis, Maryland: Naval Institute Press, 2010.

Cole, Bernard D. *Taiwan's Security: History and Prospects.* New York: Routledge, 2006.

Cole, J. Michael. *Black Island: Two Years of Activism in Taiwan.* Taipei, Taiwan: Createspace Publishing, 2015.

Dikotter, Frank. *Mao's Great Famine.* New York: Walker & Company, 2010.

Elleman, Bruce A. *High Seas Buffer: The Taiwan Patrol Force, 1950–1979.* Newport, Rhode Island: Naval War College Press, 2015.

Erickson, Andrew S. (editor). *Chinese Naval Shipbuilding.* Annapolis, Maryland: Naval Institute Press, 2016.

Erickson, Andrew S. *Chinese Anti-Ship Ballistic Missile (ASBM) Development: Drivers, Trajectories and Strategic Implications.* Washington, D.C.: The Jamestown Foundation, 2013.

Finkelstein, David M., and Kristen Gunness (editors.). *Civil-Military Relations in Today's China: Swimming in a New Sea.* Armonk, New York: M.E. Sharpe, 2007.

Fisher, Richard D. Jr. *China's Military Modernization: Building for Regional and Global Reach.* Westport, CT: Praeger Security Studies, 2008.

Friedberg, Aaron L. *A Contest for Supremacy: China, America, and the Struggle for Mastery in Asia*. New York: W.W. Norton & Company, 2011.

Gaddis, John Lewis. *The Cold War: A New History*. New York: The Penguin Press, 2005.

Grabo, Cynthia M. *Anticipating Surprise: Analysis for Strategic Warning*. Washington, D.C.: Defense Intelligence Agency, 2002.

Greenfield, Kent Roberts (editor). *Command Decisions*. Washington, D.C.: Center of Military History, United States Army, 1960.

Hallion, Richard P, Roger Cliff, and Phillip C. Saunders. *The Chinese Air Force: Evolving Concepts, Roles, and Capabilities* (editors). Washington, D.C.: National Defense University Press, 2012.

Hart, Liddell B.H. *Strategy* (Second Revised Edition). New York: Meridian Press, 1991.

Heginbotham, Eric, et al. (editors). *The U.S.-China Military Scorecard: Forces, Geography, and the Evolving Balance of Power 1996–2017*. Arlington, Virginia: The RAND Corporation, 2015.

Kamphausen, Roy, and David Lai (editors), *The Chinese People's Liberation Army in 2025*. Carlisle, PA: The Army War College Press, 2015.

Kamphausen, Roy, David Lai, Andrew Scobell (editors), *Beyond the Strait: PLA Missions Other Than Taiwan*. Carlisle, PA: Strategic Studies Institute, 2009.

Kamphausen , Roy, and Andrew Scobell (editors.), *Right-Sizing the People's Liberation Army: Exploring the Contours of China's Military* (Carlisle, PA: Strategic Studies institute, 2007.

Krepinevich, Andrew, and Barry Watts. *The Last Warrior: Andrew Marshall and the Shaping of Modern American Defense Strategy*. New York: Basic Books, 2015.

Krepinevich, Andrew F. *7 Deadly Scenarios: A Military Futurist Explores War in the Twenty-First Century*. New York: Bantam Books, 2010.

Li Xiaobing. *A History of the Modern Chinese Army*. Lexington, KY: University Press of Kentucky, 2007.

Marolda, Edward J. *Ready Seapower: A History of the U.S. Seventh Fleet*. Washington, D.C.: Naval History & Heritage Command, 2012.

Mattis, Peter. *Analyzing the Chinese Military: A Review Essay and Resource Guide on the People's Liberation Army.* Middletown, Delaware: Createspace Publishing, 2015.

McGregor, Richard. *The Party: The Secret World of China's Communist Rulers.* New York: Harper Perennial, 2010.

Miller, Edward S. *War Plan Orange: The U.S. Strategy to Defeat Japan, 1897–1945.* Annapolis, Maryland: Naval Institute Press, 1991.

Minnick, Wendell (editor). *Chinese Rocket Systems: Multiple Launch Rocket Systems Brochures.* Middletown, Delaware: Createspace Publishing, 2016.

Minnick, Wendell (editor). *Chinese Fixed-Wing Unmanned Aerial Vehicles: Product Brochures.* Middletown, Delaware: Createspace Publishing, 2016.

Montgomery, Evan Braden. *In the Hegemon's Shadow: Leading States and the Rise of Regional Powers.* Ithaca, New York: Cornell University Press, 2016.

Mulvenon, James, and David Finkelstein (editors). *China's Revolution in Doctrinal Affairs: Emerging Trends in the Operational Art of the Chinese People's Liberation Army.* Alexandria, Virginia: CNA Corporation, 2005.

Murray, Williamson and Rochard Hart Sinnreich (editors). *Successful Strategies: Triumphing in War and Peace from Antiquity to the Present.* Cambridge, United Kingdom: Cambridge University Press, 2014.

Navarro, Peter. *Crouching Tiger: What China's Militarism Means for the World.* Amherst, New York: Prometheus Books, 2015.

Pillsbury, Michael. *The Hundred-Year Marathon: China's Secret Strategy to Replace America as the Global Superpower.* New York: Henry Holt and Company, 2014.

Pollpeter, Kevin, and Kenneth W. Allen (editors). *The PLA as an Organization: Reference Volume v2.0.* Fairfax, VA: Defense Group Inc. 2015.

Rigger, Shelley. *Why Taiwan Matters: Small Island, Global Powerhouse.* New York: Rowman & Littlefield Publishers, Inc., 2011.

Romberg, Alan D. *Rein In at the Brink of the Precipice: American Policy Toward Taiwan and U.S.—PRC Relations.* Washington, D.C.: The Henry L. Stimson Center, 2003.

Roy, Denny. *Taiwan: A Political History.* Ithaca, New York: Cornell University Press, 2003.

Scobell, Andrew, Arthur S. Ding, Phillip C. Saunders, and Scott W. Harold (editors). *The People's Liberation Army and Contingency Planning in China*. Washington, D.C.: National Defense University Press, 2015.

Scobell, Andrew, David Lai, and Roy Kamphausen (editors). *Chinese Lessons from Other People's Wars*. Carlisle, PA: Strategic Studies Institute, 2011.

Shambaugh, David. *Modernizing China's Military: Progress, Problems, and Prospects*. Berkeley, California: University of California Press, 2002.

Spector, Ronald H. *Eagle Against the Sun: The American War with Japan*. New York: Vintage Books, 1985.

Suettinger, Robert L. *Beyond Tiananmen: The Politics of U.S.-China Relations 1989–2000*. Washington, D.C.: Brookings Institution Press, 2003.

Wortzel, Larry M. *The Dragon Extends its Reach: Chinese Military Power Goes Global*. Dulles, VA: Potomac Books, 2013.

Notes

Chapter One: Why Invade Taiwan?

1. See *Annual Report to Congress: Military and Security Developments Involving the People's Republic of China* (Washington, D.C.: Department of Defense, 2016), p. 5.

2. See *The Science of Military Strategy* 战略学 (Beijing: Academy of Military Sciences, 2013), pp. 198–200; "The One-China Principle and the Taiwan Issue," *The Central People's Government of The People's Republic of China, 2000*; and "Full text of Anti-Secession Law," *People's Daily,* March 14, 2005, at http://english.peopledaily.com.cn/200503/14/print20050314_176746.html.

3. Of many examples, see Cao Zhengrong, Sun Longhai, and Yang Yin (eds.), *Informatized Army Operations* 信息化陆军作战 (Beijing: National Defense University Press, 2014), pp. 109–112. *The Science of Military Strategy* 战略学 (Beijing: Academy of Military Sciences, 2013), pp. 198–200; Liu Haijiang and Li Zhiyuan (eds.), *Research on Joint Tactical Thought* 联合战术思想研究 (Beijing, Lantian Press, 2012), p. 156; Cao Zhengrong, Wu Runbo, and Sun Jianjun (eds.), *Informatized Joint Operations* 信息化联合作战 (Beijing: Liberation Army Press, 2008), pp. 143–144; and Zhang Yuliang (ed.) *Science of Campaigns* 战役学 (Beijing: National Defense University Press, 2007), p. 293.

4. See Sydney J. Freedberg Jr. and Colin Clark, "Threats from Russia, China Drive 2017 DoD Budget," *Breaking Defense*, February 2, 2016, at http://breakingdefense.com/2016/02/russia-china-drive-2017-budget/; Andrew Krepinevich and Barry Watts, *The Last Warrior: Andrew Marshall and the Shaping of Modern American Defense Strategy* (New York: Basic Books, 2015), pp. 227–246; Aaron L. Friedberg, *A Contest for Supremacy: China, America, and the Struggle for Mastery in Asia* (New York: W.W. Norton & Company, 2011); and Robert Kaplan, "How We Would Fight China," *The Atlantic*, June 2005, pp. 49–64.

5. December 7, 1949, is the date that the ROC government officially re-established its capital in Taipei. See Bruce A. Elleman, *High Seas Buffer: The Taiwan Patrol Force, 1950–1979* (Newport, Rhode Island: Naval War College Press, 2012), p. 10.

6. Among various sources, see Zhu Feng, "Why Taiwan Really Matters to China," *China Brief*, Vol. 4, Issue 19, September 30, 2004, at http://www.jamestown.org/single/?no_cache=1&tx_ttnewstt_news=3680#.U5dMf-fldXxY; Richard C. Bush, *Untying the Knot: Making Peace in the Taiwan Strait* (Washington DC: Brookings Institution Press, 2005); Alan Wachman, *Why Taiwan? Geostrategic Rationales for China's Territorial Integrity* (Stanford, CA: Stanford University Press, 2007); and Robert D. Kaplan, "The Geography of Chinese Power," *Foreign Affairs*, May/June 2010, at http://www.foreignaffairs.com/articles/66205/robert-d-kaplan/the-geography-of-chinese-power.

7. For a good resource on contemporary dynamics in Northeast Asia, see Donald S. Zagoria, "NCAFP Visit to Taipei, Beijing, Seoul and Tokyo: October 13–27, 2015," *National Committee on American Foreign Policy*, at https://www.ncafp.org/ncafp/wp-content/uploads/2016/01/2015-NCAFP-Asia-Trip-Report.pdf.

8. See *Annual Report to Congress: Military and Security Developments Involving the People's Republic of China* (Washington, D.C.: Department of Defense, 2016), at http://www.defense.gov/Portals/1/Documents/pubs/2016 China Military Power Report.pdf. See also *Science of Military Strategy* 战略学 (Beijing: Academy of Military Sciences, 2013), pp. 198–200.

9. "The One-China Principle and the Taiwan Issue," *The Central People's Government of The People's Republic of China, 2000*; and "Full text of Anti-Secession Law," *People's Daily*, March 14, 2005, at http://english.people-daily.com.cn/200503/14/print20050314_176746.html.

10. Tseng Wei-chen and Chen Wei-han, "Unification support dives: poll," *Taipei Times*, July 26, 2015, at http://www.taipeitimes.com/News/taiwan/archives/2015/07/26/2003623930.

11. See Ian Bremmer, "5 Statistics That Explained the World This Week," *Politico*, March 2, 2014, at http://www.politico.com/magazine/story/2014/03/statistics-that-explained-the-world-this-week-104088; and Yuan-kang Wang, "Taiwan Public Opinion on Cross-Strait Security Issues: Implications for U.S. Foreign Policy," *Strategic Studies Quarterly*, Summer 2013, p. 100, available online at http://homepages.wmich.edu/~ymz8097/articles/wang_taiwan public opinion.pdf.

12. Fang-Yu Chen, Wei-Ting Yen, Austin Horng-en Wang, and Brian Hioe, "The Taiwanese see themselves as Taiwanese, not as Chinese," *Washington Post*, January 2, 2017, at https://www.washingtonpost.com/news/monkey-cage/wp/2017/01/02/yes-taiwan-wants-one-china-but-which-china-does-it-want/?utm_term=.7bc908f3504c.

13. Alison Hsiao, "No such thing as the '1992 Consensus': Lee Teng-hui," *Taipei Times*, May 3, 2015, at http://www.taipeitimes.com/News/front/archives/2015/05/03/2003617348.

14. For one of best assessments to this effect, see Robert D. Kaplan, "The Geography of Chinese Power," *Foreign Affairs*, May/June 2010, at http://www.foreignaffairs.com/articles/66205/robert-d-kaplan/the-geography-of-chinese-power.

15. Michael Thim, "Why Removing Taiwan Strait Missiles is Not the Real Issue," *Ketagalan Media*, November 20, 2015, at http://www.ketagalanmedia.com/2015/11/20/why-removing-taiwan-strait-missiles-is-not-the-real-issue/; Stephen Young, "Pageantry without a hint of real substance," *Taipei Times*, November 10, 2015, at http://www.taipeitimes.com/News/editorials/archives/2015/11/10/2003632092; and Wang Yu-chung, "Ma talks peace deal with China," *Taipei Times*, October 18, 2011, at http://www.taipeitimes.com/News/front/archives/2011/10/18/2003516029.

16. Author's discussion with ROC government officials in Taipei, 2016.

17. For an excellent resource and background on the Sunflower Movement, see J. Michael Cole, *Black Island: Two Years of Activism in Taiwan* (Taipei, Taiwan: Createspace Publishing, 2015).

18. See *Republic of China 2013 National Defense Report* 中華民國一〇二年國防報告書2013 (Taipei, Taiwan: Ministry of National Defense, 2013), p. 56. See also Michael Gold and Ben Blanchard, "Taiwan says China could launch successful invasion by 2020," *Reuters*, October 9, 2013, at http://www.reuters.com/article/us-taiwan-china-idUSBRE99809020131009. MND reporting was further backed up by a series of authoritative, but not widely disseminated, Chinese military studies on the invasion of Taiwan. These show that PLA strategists and operational planners undertook a series of internal operational studies on the invasion of Taiwan around the year 2012. While these studies did not result in published books until 2014 and 2015, MND presumably knew that these research efforts were underway. Xi Jinping, as then-Vice Chairman of the CMC, presumably also knew.

19. Ibid.

20. See Douglas Paal, "China, the U.S. and the Coming Taiwan Transition," *The Diplomat*, December 29, 2015, at http://thediplomat.com/2015/12/china-the-u-s-and-the-coming-taiwan-transition/; and "Assumption in US, China of Tsai victory, Glaser says," *Taipei Times*, September 11, 2015, at http://www.taipeitimes.com/News/taiwan/archives/2015/09/11/2003627457.

21. Luo Tian-bin, "Communist Military Holds Repeated Landing Exercises Ahead of May 20 Inauguration (520前 共軍頻頻登陸演習)," *Liberty Times*, May 18, 2016, http://news.ltn.com.tw/news/focus/paper/990759; and "Sword Pointed at Taiwan? PLA Exercise Held in Zhangzhou, Fujian (劍指台灣？解放軍福建漳州軍演)," *Apple Daily*, December 23, 2015, http://www.appledaily.com.tw/realtimenews/article/new/20151223/759559.

22. See Alan Romberg, "Tsai Ing-wen Takes Office: A New Era in Cross-Strait Relations," *China Leadership Monitor*, No. 50, June 22, 2016, at http://www.stimson.org/sites/default/files/file-attachments/Tsai-Ing-wen-Takes-Office-New-Era-Cross-Strait-Relations.pdf; and Richard Bush, "Tsai's inauguration in Taiwan: It could have been worse," *Brookings Institute*,

May 23, 2016, at http://www.brookings.edu/blogs/order-from-chaos/posts/2016/05/23-tsai-ing-wen-inauguration-taiwan-bush.

23. *Informatized Army Operations*, pp. 109–119.

24. Ibid. pp. 119–121.

25. See J. Michael Cole, "Unstoppable: China's Secret Plan to Subvert Taiwan," *The National Interest*, March 23, 2015, at http://nationalinterest.org/feature/unstoppable-chinas-secret-plan-subvert-taiwan-12463; and Mark Stokes and Russell Hsiao, *The People's Liberation Army General Political Department: Political Warfare with Chinese Characteristics* (Arlington, VA: Project 2049 Institute, October 2013), at http://nationalinterest.org/feature/unstoppable-chinas-secret-plan-subvert-taiwan-12463.

26. See Cao Zhengrong et al. (eds.), *Informatized Army Operations*, pp. 119–121. For background, see Thomas J. Christensen, "Coercive Contradictions: *Zhanyixue*, PLA Doctrine, and Taiwan Scenarios," in James Mulvenon and David Finkelstein (eds.), *China's Revolution in Doctrinal Affairs: Emerging Trends in the Operational Art of the Chinese People's Liberation Army* (Alexandria, VA: Center for Naval Analyses CNA Corporation, 2002), pp. 317–321.

27. J. Michael Cole, "Chinese Propaganda: Coming Soon to a Conference Near You," *The Diplomat*, September 23, 2015. This assertion is also based on the authors private discussions with graduate students, university professors, and think tank researchers in Boston, Princeton, San Diego, and Washington, D.C., from 2015–2017.

28. Ibid. See also the respective testimonies of Michelle Van Cleave, John Costello, David Major, Peter Mattis, and Mark Stokes before the *U.S.-China Economic and Security Review Commission*, June 9, 2016, at http://www.uscc.gov/Hearings/hearing-chinese-intelligence-services-and-espionage-operations.

29. For example, see Richard Bush, "Taiwan's security policy," *The Brookings Institution*, August 3, 2016, at https://www.brookings.edu/articles/taiwans-security-policy/.

30. For details see Shirley A. Kan, *Taiwan: Major U.S. Arms Sales Since 1990* (Washington D.C.: Congressional Research Service, March 2014), pp. 42–47, at http://www.fas.org/sgp/crs/weapons/RL30957.pdf.

31. While the list is long, one of the most notable examples is retired U.S. Navy Admiral, Bill Owens, "America must start treating China as a friend," *Financial Times*, November 17, 2009, at http://www.ft.com/intl/cms/s/0/69241506-d3b2-11de-8caf-00144feabdco.html.

32. See Yuan-kang Wang, "China's Growing Strength, Taiwan's Diminishing Options," *Brookings Institute Paper*, November 2010, at http://www.brookings.edu/research/papers/2010/11/china-taiwan-wang; Ralph Jennings, "Taiwan Resisting China's Most Ambitious Plans For Stronger Ties," *Voice of America*, February 13, 2014, at http://www.voanews.com/content/taiwan-resisting-chinas-most-ambitious-plans-for-stronger-ties/1850454.html; and Jonathan Adams, "Chinese compete for 'worst tourist' label," *Global Post*, July 13, 2009, at http://www.globalpost.com/dispatch/china-and-its-neighbors/090711/chinese-tourist-taiwan.

33. *Informatized Army Operations*, p. 112.

34. *Informatized Joint Operations*, pp. 143–144.

35. Ibid. See also *Science of Campaigns*, p. 293.

36. While often translated as "motherland," in Chinese this is written in the paternalistic *Zuguo* (祖国).

37. Of many examples, see *Informatized Army Operations*, p. 112.

38. Ibid.

39. Ibid., p. 113.

40. Ibid.

41. Bai Guangwei (ed.), *Course Book on the Taiwan Strait's Military Geography* 台海军事地理教程 (Beijing: Academy of Military Sciences Press, 2013), pp. 56–58.

42. Ibid., pp. 56–57.

43. Ibid., pp. 57–58.

44. Yang Pushuang (ed.), *The Japanese Air Self Defense Force* 日本航空自卫队 (Beijing: Air Force Command College, 2013) pp. 190–191.

45. *Course book on Taiwan Strait Military Geography*, p. 58.

46. *Science of Military Strategy*, pp. 198–200; and *Science of Campaigns*, p. 293.

47. *Informatized Army Operations*, p. 113.

48. Richard C. Bush and Michael E. O'Hanlon, *A War Like No Other: The Truth About China's Challenge to America* (Hoboken, New Jersey: John Wiley & Sons, 2007).

49. David Shambaugh appears to be one of the first American "China Hands" to recognize and record this phenomenon. See his book, *Modernizing China's Military: Progress, Problems, and Prospects* (Los Angeles, CA: University of California Press, 2002), pp. 307–311.

50. This is a complex but diminishing problem that appears to be especially pronounced among the older generation of American "China Hands" who generally spent less time in China, developed less proficiency in Chinese, were few in number, and divided themselves into easily defined camps. The younger generation, in contrast, is a larger and better educated (if less experienced) group, which is generally more open to a plurality of viewpoints. For an excellent assessment of the American PLA-watching community, see Peter Mattis, *Analyzing the Chinese Military: A Review Essay and Resource Guide on the People's Liberation Army* (Middletown, DE: Createspace Publishing, 2015).

51. In China, cruise missile is written *xunhang daodan* (巡航导弹). In Taiwan, it is written *hsun-yi fei-dan* (巡弋飛彈).

Chapter Two: An Evolving Flashpoint

52. Zhao Yiping, "Taiwan Strait Attack Strategy: The Beginning and End of Planning and Preparation for Taiwan Liberation Operations just as New China was Established (台海攻略：新中国成立前后解放台湾作战计划与准备始末)," *Junshi Lishi* (Military History Monthly), No. 1, Issue 130, January 2005, p. 10. See also Zhao Yiping, "Early Liberation, Operational Planning for Attacking Taiwan (解放初期的攻台作战计划)," *Juece Tansuo* (Policy Research and Exploration Journal), 2005 (2).

53. Lu Shizhong, "1949–1950: The Chinese Communists' Preparations to Attack Taiwan and America's Gamesmanship Behind the Scenes (1949-1950：中共准备攻台背后与美国的博弈)," *People's Daily*, December 27, 2013; and Zhao Yiping, "Taiwan Strait Attack Strategy," p. 11.

54. In Chinese, their names are written 粟裕 and 张震, respectively.

55. Zhao Yiping, "Taiwan Strait Attack Strategy," p. 11. See also He Libo and Song Fengying, "Preliminary Examination of Mao Zedong's Military Thought on Sea-Crossing and Island Landing Operations (毛泽东渡海登陆作战军事思想初探)," *Henan Shehui Kexue* (Henan Social Science Journal), January, 2004, p. 40.

56. Zhao Yiping, "Taiwan Strait Attack Strategy," p. 12.

57. Zhao Yiping, "Taiwan Strait Attack Strategy," p. 12.

58. For an outstanding study in this pivotal event, see Maochun Miles Yu, "The Battle of Quemoy: The Amphibious Assault that Held the Postwar Military Balance in the Taiwan Strait," *Naval War College Review*, Spring 2016 (Vol. 69, No. 2), pp. 91–107.

59. Zhao Yiping, "Taiwan Strait Attack Strategy," p. 16.

60. Tang Hongsen, "Discussing the Taiwan Strait Standoff and the Battle of Dengbu (论登步之战与台海对峙)," *Zhejiang Xuekan* (Zhejiang Journal), No. 2, 2012, pp. 59–68; and Lu Hui and Zheng Huaisheng, "Thoughts on the Experience of the Sea-Crossing and Landing Operations against Dengbu Island (登步岛渡海登陆作战经过与思考), *Junshi Lishi* (Military History Journal), No. 3, 2007, pp. 21–25.

61. Zhao Yiping, "Taiwan Strait Attack Strategy," p. 17.

62. Ibid.

63. Ibid., p. 14.

64. Ibid., p. 15.

65. Ibid., p. 16.

66. Ibid., pp. 16–17.

67. Ibid., p. 17.

68. Zhao Yiping, "Taiwan Strait Attack Strategy," p. 17.

69. Zhao Yiping, "Taiwan Strait Attack Strategy," p. 17.

70. Lu Shizhong, "1949–1950: The Chinese Communists' Preparations to Attack Taiwan and America's Gamesmanship Behind the Scenes (1949-1950：中共准备攻台背后与美国的博弈)," *People's Daily*, December 27, 2013.

71. Zhao Yiping, "Taiwan Strait Attack Strategy," p. 11. See also Lu Shizhong.

72. Zhao Yiping, "Taiwan Strait Attack Strategy," p. 15.

73. Zhao Yiping, "Taiwan Strait Attack Strategy," p. 15.

74. Zhao Yiping, "Taiwan Strait Attack Strategy," p. 15.

75. Zhao Yiping, "Taiwan Strait Attack Strategy," pp. 12–15.

76. Ibid.; and Lu Shizhong.

77. Ibid.

78. Zhao Yiping, "Taiwan Strait Attack Strategy," p. 13.

79. Shen Zhihua, "The CCP's Taiwan Attack Campaign: Policy Changes and Limiting Factors, 1949–1950 (中共进攻台湾战役的决策变化及其制约因素, 1949-1950), *Shehui Kexue Yanjiu* (Social Science Research Journal), No. 3, 2009, pp. 48–49.

80. "Traitor to Chinese Communism: Cai Xiaogan (中共叛徒蔡孝乾)," *Phoenix News Net*, January 21, 2013, at http://news.ifeng.com/history/zhongguoxiandaishi/detail_2013_01/21/21426217_0.shtml.

81. Ibid.; and "Cai Xiaogan, Chinese Communist General Secretary for Taiwan Operations, Betrayed Taiwan Underground Party Organizations, Entire Army Annihilated (中共台湾书记蔡孝乾叛变台地下党组织全军覆没), *Sohu News*, May 26, 2014, at http://history.sohu.com/20140526/n400044379.shtml.

82. Ibid.

83. Ibid. and Shen Zhihua, "The CCP's Taiwan Attack Campaign: Policy Changes and Limiting Factors, 1949–1950 (中共进攻台湾战役的决策变化及其制约因素, 1949-1950), *Shehui Kexue Yanjiu* (Social Science Research Journal), No. 3, 2009, p. 49.

84. Note that many of the Communist agents who evaded capture in the ROC's 1950 roundup eventually wound up in Hong Kong, where they established new centers of underground work which reportedly continue operating to this day. See Mark Stokes and Russell Hsiao, *The People's Liberation Army General Political Department: Political Warfare with Chinese Characteristics* (Arlington, VA: Project 2049 Institute, October 2013), p. 8.

85. Shen Zhihua, "The CCP's Taiwan Attack Campaign: Policy Changes and Limiting Factors, 1949–1950 (中共进攻台湾战役的决策变化及其制约因素, 1949-1950), *Shehui Kexue Yanjiu* (Social Science Research Journal), No. 3, 2009, p. 49.

86. Ibid.

87. Shen Zhihua claims that additional troops were allotted to Su Yu's invasion force in June 1950. Zhao Yiping writes that more troops were

not assigned. However, he seems to suggest that the issue was under consideration when the Korean War broke out.

88. Zhao Yiping, "Taiwan Strait Attack Strategy," p. 14.

89. Zhao Yiping, "Taiwan Strait Attack Strategy," p. 14; and Shen Zhihua, p. 50.

90. Zhao Yiping, "Taiwan Strait Attack Strategy," p. 17.

91. Winston S. Churchill, *The Second World War: Closing the Ring* (Cambridge, Massachusetts: Riverside Press, 1951), p. 87.

92. Ibid. p. 575. See also, Ronald H. Spector, *Eagle Against the Sun: The American War with Japan* (New York: Vintage Books, 1985), pp. 418–420.

93. Phelim Kyne, "Operations CAUSEWAY: The Invasion that never was," *China News*, August 10, 1997, accessible online at https://sites.google.com/site/operationcauseway/.

94. Ibid.

95. Ibid.

96. See Robert Ross Smith, "Luzon Versus Formosa" in Kent Roberts Greenfield (ed.), *Command Decisions* (Washington, D.C.: Defense Department Army Center of Military History, 1960), pp. 461–477.

97. Xiaobing Li, *A History of the Modern Chinese Army* (Lexington, KY: University Press of Kentucky, 2007), p. 127.

98. Quote drawn from Bernard D. Cole, *Taiwan's Security: History and prospects* (New York: Routledge, 2006), p. 17.

99. Edward J. Marolda, *Ready Seapower: A History of the U.S. Seventh Fleet* (Washington, D.C.: Naval History and Heritage Command, 2012), pp. 33–35; and Bruce A. Elleman, *High Seas Buffer: The Taiwan Patrol Force, 1950–1979* (Newport, Rhode Island: Naval War College Press, 2012); and Bernard D. Cole, *Taiwan's Security*, p. 18.

100. See Kao Zhi-yang, "Record of U.S. Military Forces Formerly Stationed in Taiwan (駐台美軍曾經的記錄)," *Quanqiu Fangwei Zazhi* (Defence International), No. 320, April 2011, pp. 88–95; and *American Footsteps in Southern Taiwan: Our People in a Defining Era* (Kaohsiung: Sun Yat-Sen America Center, 2010), p. 75.

101. Survey and Mapping Bureau of the PLA General Staff Department, *China's Military Geography* 中国军事地理 (Beijing: Encyclopedia of China Publishing House, 2008), p. 577.

102. Elleman, pp. 60–61.

103. Ibid. pp. 59–62.

104. Ibid., pp. 62–70; and Marolda, pp. 40–42.

105. Elleman, pp. 99–102.

106. The following discussion on the Second Taiwan Strait Crisis draws from, Cole, *Taiwan's Security*, p. 23; Marolda, pp. 49–51; and Elleman, pp. 99–102.

107. See Shelley Rigger, *Why Taiwan Matters: Small Island, Global Power-house* (New York: Rowman & Littlefield Publishers, Inc., 2011).

108. See Richard McGregor, *The Party: The Secret World of China's Communist Rulers* (New York: Harper Perennial, 2010); Frank Dikotter, *Mao's Great Famine* (New York: Walker & Company, 2010); and Yang Jisheng, *Mubei: Zhongguo Liushi Niandai Da Jihuang Jishi* Tombstone: A Record of the Great Chinese Famine of the 1960s (Hong Kong: Cosmos Books, 2008).

109. Of many excellent sources on the PLA, see Mark Cozad, "The PLA and Contingency Planning," in Andrew Scobell, Arthur S. Ding, Phillip C. Saunders, and Scott W. Harold (eds.), *The People's Liberation Army and Contingency Planning in China* (Washington, D.C.: National Defense University Press, 2015), pp. 15–32; and Dean Cheng, "Chinese Lessons from the Gulf Wars," in Andrew Scobell, David Lai, and Roy Kamphausen (eds.), *Chinese Lessons from Other People's Wars* (Carlisle, PA: Strategic Studies Institute, 2011), 153–199. For further background, see David M. Finkelstein and Kristen Gunness (eds.), *Civil-Military Relations in Today's China: Swimming in a New* Sea (Armonk, New York: M.E. Sharpe, 2007); and James Mulvenon and David Finkelstein (eds.), *China's Revolution in Doctrinal Affairs: Emerging Trends in the Operational Art of the Chinese People's Liberation Army* (Alexandria, VA: Center for Naval Analyses CNA Corporation, 2002).

110. For background, see and Richard Bush, *Untying the Knot: Making Peace in the Taiwan Strait* (Washington DC: Brookings Institution Press, 2005); and Alan D. Romberg, *Rein In at the Brink of the Precipice: American Policy*

Toward Taiwan and U.S.-PRC Relations (Washington, D.C.: The Henry L. Stimson Center, 2003).

111. For details on the crisis, see Robert L. Suettinger, *Beyond Tiananmen: The Politics of U.S.-China Relations 1989–2000* (Washington, D.C.: Brookings Institution Press, 2003), pp. 200–263; Robert S. Ross, "The 1995–1996 Taiwan Strait Confrontation: Coercion, Credibility, and the Use of Force," *International Security*, Vol. 25, No. 2 (Fall 2000), pp. 87–123. .

112. Ibid.

113. See Wen Dong-Ping (聞東平), *The Intelligence War Now Underway* 正在進行的諜戰 (New York: Mirror Books, 2009); and Guo Nairi (郭乃日), *The Unseen War in the Taiwan Strait* 看不見的台海戰爭 (Xizhi, Taiwan: Gaoshou Publishing, 2005).

114. Ibid.

115. For background on PLA modernization, see Richard P. Hallion, Roger Cliff, and Phillip C. Saunders, *The Chinese Air Force: Evolving Concepts, Roles, and Capabilities* (Washington, D.C.: National Defense University Press, 2012); Phillip C. Saunders, Christopher D. Yung, Michael Swaine, and Andrew Nien-Dzu Yang (eds.), *The Chinese Navy: Expanding Capabilities, Evolving Roles* (Washington, D.C.: National Defense University Press, 2011); Roy Kamphausen, David Lai, Andrew Scobell, *Beyond the Strait: PLA Missions Other Than Taiwan* (Carlisle, PA: Strategic Studies Institute, 2009); and Roy Kamphausen and Andrew Scobell (eds.), *Right-Sizing the People's Liberation Army: Exploring the Contours of China's Military* (Carlisle, PA: Strategic Studies institute, 2007).

116. For background, see Cliff, Roger. *China's Military Power: Assessing Current and Future Capabilities* (New York: Cambridge University Press, 2015); Roy Kamphausen and David Lai (eds.), *The Chinese People's Liberation Army in 2025* (Carlisle, PA: The Army War College Press, 2015); Eric Heginbotham, et al., *The U.S.-China Military Scorecard: Forces, Geography, and the Evolving Balance of Power, 1996–2017* (Washington, D.C., RAND Corporation, 2015), at http://www.rand.org/pubs/research_reports/RR392.html; Peter Navarro, *Crouching Tiger: What China's Militarism Means for the World* (Amherst, New York: Prometheus Books, 2015); Larry M. Wortzel, *The Dragon Extends its Reach: Chinese Military Power Goes Global* (Dulles,

VA: Potomac Books, 2013); and Richard D. Fisher Jr., *China's Military Modernization: Building for Regional and Global Reach* (Westport, CT: Praeger Security Studies, 2008).

Chapter Three: Warning Signs

117. The most notable example is U.S. Naval War College professor, William Murray, who assumes Taiwan would be completely surprised by a Chinese attack. See William S. Murray, "Revisiting Taiwan's Defense Strategy," *Naval War College Review*, Summer 2008, pp. 13–38. For a more nuanced analysis, see Jim Thomas, John Stillion, and Iskander Rehman, *Hard ROC 2.0: Taiwan and Deterrence Through Protraction* (Washington, D.C.: Center for Strategic and Budgetary Analysis, 2014).

118. Cynthia M. Grabo, *Anticipating Surprise: Analysis for Strategic Warning* (Washington, D.C.: Defense Intelligence Agency, 2002), pp. 3–4, available online at http://www.ni-u.edu/ni_press/pdf/Anticipating_Surprise_Analysis.pdf.

119. Ibid.

120. Ibid.

121. Ibid.

122. See National Security Bureau, R.O.C., "Policy Guidelines," at http://www.nsb.gov.tw/En/En_index01.html, accessed October 24, 2016.

123. See Ian Easton and Randall Schriver, *Standing Watch: Taiwan and Maritime Domain Awareness in the Western Pacific* (Arlington, Virginia: Project 2049 Institute, December 2014), p. 15; and Ian Easton, *Able Archers: Taiwan Defense Strategy in an Age of Precision Strike* (Arlington, Virginia: Project 2049 Institute, September 2014), pp. 30–31.

124. See MND, *National Defense Report 2015* 國防報告書 (Taipei: Ministry of National Defense, 2015), p. 112.

125. See Ian Easton, Mark Stokes, Cortez Cooper, and Arthur Chan, *Transformation of Taiwan's Reserve Force* (Arlington, VA: RAND Corporation, 2017), p 11.

126. For example, see J. Michael Cole, "The Spies Are Coming! The Spies Are Coming To Taiwan!" *The Diplomat*, January 22, 2015, http://thediplomat.com/2015/01/the-spies-are-coming-the-spies-are-coming-to-taiwan/; and Peter Mattis, "China's Espionage Against Taiwan (Part 1), Analysis of Recent Operations," *China Brief*, November 7, 2014, p. 7, at https://jamestown.org/wp-content/uploads/2014/11/China_Brief_Vol_14_Issue_21_2.pdf. See also Peter Mattis, "Chinese Human Intelligence Operations Against the United States," *Testimony before the U.S.-China Economic and Security Review Commission*, June 9, 2016, available online at http://www.uscc.gov/sites/default/files/Peter Mattis_Written Testimony060916.pdf.

127. For example, see Luo Tianbin, et al., "China's State Media Accuses Taiwan Spies of Recruiting Chinese Students (中國官媒控台諜策反中生)," *Ziyou Ribao* (Liberty Times), October 28, 2014, pp. A1–A3; and Wendell Minnick, "The Men in Black: How Taiwan spies on China," *Asia Times*, February 26, 2004, at http://www.atimes.com/atimes/China/FB26Ad05.html.

128. See Wen Dong-Ping, *The Intelligence War Now Underway* 正在進行的諜戰 (New York: Mirror Books, 2009); and Guo Nairi (郭乃日), *The Unseen War in the Taiwan Strait* 看不見的台海戰爭 (Xizhi, Taiwan: Gaoshou Publishing, 2005). See also Wendell Minnick, "Spook Mountain: How U.S. Spies on China," *Asia Times*, March 6, 2003 at http://www.atimes.com/atimes/China/EC06Ad03.html; and Wendell Minnick, "Taiwan-US Link Up on SIGINT," *Jane's Defence Weekly*, January 24, 2001, at https://www.fas.org/irp/news/2001/01/jdw-taiwan-sigint.html.

129. See Xu Lisheng and Wang Zhaoyong, *Research on Port Landing Operations* 港口登陆作战研究(Beijing: National Defense University, 2015), pp. 37–38.

130. Unless where otherwise noted, the following section draws from Chen Qing-lin (ed.), *National Defense Education: Defense Mobilization* 全民國防教育防衛動員 (New Taipei City: New Wun Ching Development Publishing, 2013), pp. 36–39; and Li Qingshan (ed.), *Taiwan Military Exercises* 台军演习(Shenyang: Baishan Publishing, 2008), pp. 185–187.

131. For an illuminating study on how a command group might be organized and structured in an non-invasion scenario, see Mark A. Stokes, "Employment of National-Level PLA Assets in a Contingency: A Cross-

Strait Conflict as Case Study," in Andrew Scobell, Arthur S. Ding, Phillip C. Saunders, and Scott W. Harold (eds.), *The People's Liberation Army and Contingency Planning in China* (Washington, D.C.: National Defense University Press, 2015), pp. 135–147.

132. For an illustrative example, see "Authorities eavesdrop on social media chat of Chinese military brigade's wives," *South China Morning Post*, April 6, 2015, at http://www.scmp.com/news/china/article/1757560/authorities-eavesdrop-social-media-chat-chinese-military-brigades-wives.

133. For details on PLA mobilization, see Dean Cheng, "Converting the Potential to the Actual: Chinese Mobilization Policies and Planning," in Andrew Scobell, Arthur S. Ding, Phillip C. Saunders, and Scott W. Harold (eds.), *The People's Liberation Army and Contingency Planning in China* (Washington, D.C.: National Defense University Press, 2015), pp. 107–134.

134. Specific offshore locations where increased PLA activity is anticipated include Pingtan Island, Nanri Island, Dongshan Island, and Nan-ao Island. See Chang Zong-Tsai, "Research on Tactics and Techniques of Communist Military 'Decapitation Operations' through the lens of the U.S. Military's 'Operation Neptune Spear' (共軍'斬首行動'戰術戰法--以美軍'海神之矛行動'研析)," *Journal of ROC Aviation and Special Forces Command*, No. 56, 2012, p. 11.

135. These include airbases at: Fuzhou, Longxi, Denghai, Liancheng, Xingning, Chong'an, Longtian , Hui'an, (Taizhou) Luqiao, Weixian, Xincheng, Zhangqiao, Hangzhou, Daishan, Jiaxiang, Shanghai, Nanjing, Guangzhou, Haikou, Wazhuo, and Shuimen.

136. For an illustrative example, see Adam Minter, "Flight Delayed in China? Blame the Military," *Bloomberg*, September 1, 2015, at https://www.bloomberg.com/view/articles/2015-09-01/flight-delayed-in-china-blame-the-military.

137. See Chang Zong-Tsai, p. 11.

138. See Alan D. Romberg, *Rein In at the Brink of the Precipice: American Policy Toward Taiwan and U.S.-PRC Relations* (Washington, D.C.: The Henry L. Stimson Center, 2003), p. 168.

139. *Informatized Joint Operations*, p. 251.

140. For background on China's nuclear warhead management system, see Mark A. Stokes, "China's Nuclear Warhead Storage and Handling System," *Project 2049 Institute Occasional Paper*, March 12, 2010, at http://www.project2049.net/documents/chinas_nuclear_warhead_storage_and_handling_system.pdf.

141. For more on this, see *Informatized Army Operations*, pp. 130–131. See also Jeffrey Lin and P.W. Singer, "Chinese Cargo Ships Get the Military Option," *Popular Science*, June 23, 2015, at http://www.popsci.com/chinese-cargo-ships-get-military-option.

142. For excellent background on the PRC's shipbuilding industry, see Andrew S. Erickson, *Chinese Naval Shipbuilding: An Ambitious and Uncertain Course* (Annapolis, MD: Naval Institute Press, 2016).

143. See Wang Yongping, et al. (eds.), *Space Information Support Operations* 空间信息支援作战 (Beijing: National Defense University, 2014), pp. 199–201.

144. Ibid., p. 201.

145. Ibid., pp. 159–162.

146. In addition, it should be expected that unmanned aerial vehicles and submarines, including unmanned underwater vehicles, could also be used for supplementing manned reconnaissance missions near Taiwan. Chinese cyber espionage and reconnaissance efforts for intelligence-gathering and preparation of the battlefield would probably increase at this point as well. In addition, Chinese "patriotic hackers" might at this or a later point start to engage in "cyber disruption" through DDoS attacks, etc. The author is indebted to Elsa Kania for these points.

147. For background, see Peter Mattis, "A Guide to Chinese Intelligence Operations," War on the Rocks, August 18, 2015, at https://warontherocks.com/2015/08/a-guide-to-chinese-intelligence-operations/; and Peter Mattis, "The Analytic Challenge of Understanding Chinese Intelligence Services," *Studies in Intelligence*, Vol. 56, No. 3 (September 2012), pp. 47–57, at https://www.cia.gov/library/center-for-the-study-of-intelligence/csi-publications/csi-studies/studies/vol.-56-no.-3/pdfs/Mattis-Understanding Chinese Intel.pdf.

148. See Mark Stokes and Russel Hsiao, *The People's Liberation Army General Political Department: Political Warfare with Chinese Characteristics* (Arlington, VA: Project 2049 Institute, October 2013).

149. *Informatized Army Operations*, pp. 120–121.

150. See J. Michael Cole, "China Intensifies Disinformation Campaign Against Taiwan," *Taiwan Sentinel*, January 19, 2017, at https://sentinel.tw/china-disinformation-tw/; and J. Michael Cole, "Chinese Propaganda: Coming Soon to a Conference Near You," *The Diplomat*, September 23, 2015, at http://thediplomat.com/2015/09/chinese-propaganda-coming-soon-to-a-conference-near-you/.

151. As an illustrative example, China used a non-official backchannel to make nuclear threats against the U.S. during the Taiwan Strait Missile Crisis. See *A War Like No Other: The Truth About China's Challenge to America*, pp. 1–2.

152. See *Informatized Joint Operations*, p. 250.

153. For example, see Chang Hsueh-chang, "Discussion on Military Police Missions in Wartime (戰時憲兵任務之探討)," *ROC Military Police Command Journal*, No. 80 (June 2015), pp. 34–40; and Chang Zong-Tsai, pp. 10–12.

154. Authors discussions with ROC military subject matters experts .

155. *Informatized Army Operations*, pp. 120–121.

156. See *Informatized Joint Operations*, p. 225; and Guo Ming (ed.), *Course Book on the Art of Special Warfare Operations* (Beijing: Academy of Military Science Press, 2013), 184.

157. Ibid. For details on the legal procedures involved in declaring an emergency, see Chang Hsueh-chang, "Discussion on Military Police Missions in Wartime," pp. 25–34.

158. See Li Daguang, "Latest Secrets Revealed on Deception during the Normandy Landing Campaign (诺曼底登陆战役欺骗的最新揭秘)," *Junshi Shilin* (Military History Facts), No. 4, 2011, pp. 41–46; Ji Guangzhi, Liu Shunping, and Zhang Zhiwei, *Camouflaged Landing Campaigns* 登陆战役伪装 (Beijing: Academy of Military Science Press, 2003), op cit.; and Zhang Wei, Zhang Guangming, and Liu Yaxing, "Insights from the Application of Stratagems during Normandy Landing Campaign (诺曼底登

陆战役的谋略运用及其启示), *Junshi Shilin* (Military History Facts), No. 1, 2001, pp. 3–6.

159. *Informatized Army Operations*, p. 115.

160. Note that Blasko also points out mobilization could be used to signal intentions as part of a deterrence strategy, and operational and tactical surprise might still be possible if military deception measures are successful. See Dennis J. Blasko, "The PLA Army/Ground Forces," in Kevin Pollpeter and Kenneth W. Allen (eds.), *The PLA as an Organization: Reference Volume v2.0* (Fairfax, VA: Defens Group Inc. 2015), p. 259.

161. *Informatized Joint Operations*, p. 225.

162. Ibid.

163. See *Course Book on Special Warfare Operations*, 184.

164. See *Informatized Joint Operations*, p. 223.

165. Ibid.

166. *Informatized Army Operations*, p. 130.

167. Ibid., pp. 140–142.

168. Ibid., p. 142.

169. Zhang Zhiwei and Huang Chuanxian (eds.), *Research on Operational Theory of Army Aviation Troops* 陆军航空兵作战理论研究 (Beijing: National Defense University Press, 2014), p. 94.

170. *Informatized Army Operations*, p. 146. See also *Research on Operational Theory of Army Aviation Troops*, p. 85.

171. *Informatized Army Operations*, p. 147.

172. Song Jian, "Risk Assessment on Camouflaging a Landing Campaign (登陆战役伪装风险评估), *Jisuanji yu Shuzi Gongcheng* (Journal of Computer and Digital Engineering), Vol. 41, No. 8, 2013, pp. 1232–1234.

173. Unless otherwise noted, the following section draws from Chen Qinglin (ed.), *National Defense Education: Defense Mobilization* 全民國防教育防衛動員 (New Taipei City: New Wun Ching Development Publishing, 2013), pp. 36–42; and Chen Qing-lin, Hwuang Zhen-yi, and Kuo Wen-liang (eds.), *National Defense Education* (全民國防教育) New Taipei City: New Wun Ching Development Publishing, 2010, pp. 185–191.

Chapter Four: China's War Plan

174. Major PLA sources for the following discussion include: *Informatized Army Operations*, pp. 109–215; *Research on Port Landing Operations*, pp. 36–160; *Space Information Support Operations*, pp. 143–212; *Research on Operational Theory* of *Army Aviation Troops*, pp. 80–202 ; and *Informatized Joint Operations*, pp. 208–235. Taiwanese sources include: Tsai Ho-Hsun, "Research on the Communist Military's Division Landing Operations (共軍師登陸作戰之研究)," *ROC Army Journal*, Vol. 50, No. 537, October 2014, pp. 60–78; Hsieh Chih-Peng, "Research on the Communist Military's New Campaign Guidance (共軍新時期戰役指導之研究)," *ROC Army Journal*, No. 50, Vol. 536 (August 2014), pp. 35–50; and Yang You-hung, "Research into Communist Military's Joint Island Landing Offensive Campaign Capabilities (共軍聯合島嶼進攻戰役能力研究)," *ROC Reserve Force Journal*, No. 88, October 2013, pp. 88–109.

175. See *Informatized Army Operations*, pp. 109–110; and Hsieh Chih-Peng, "Research on the Communist Military's New Campaign Guidance (共軍新時期戰役指導之研究)," *ROC Army Journal*, No. 50, Vol. 536 (August 2014), pp. 44–45.

176. See *Informatized Joint Operations*, p. 156; and Chen Yue-Yang, "Analysis of Chinese Communist Army's Electronic Warfare Developments (中共陸軍電子戰發展之研析)," *ROC Army Journal*, No. 49, Vol. 528 (April 2013), pp. 58–64.

177. *Informatized Joint Operations*, pp. 156–157.

178. Ibid.

179. Ibid.

180. Ibid.; and Lan Jong-Sheng, "Xi Jinping's Strong Military Dream: Discussing Plans for Rocket Force Buildup (習近平強軍夢: 論火箭軍建軍規劃)," *ROC Army Journal*, No. 52, Vol. 548 (August 2016), pp. 120–121; and Wang Cheng-Fang, "Assessment of the Communist Military's Missile Threat to Taiwan's Theater-Level Underground Command Posts (共軍導彈對我作戰區級地下指揮所威脅之評估)," *ROC Army Combat Engineer Journal*, Vol. 145, 2014, pp. 2–6. See also, Ian Easton, "Able Archers:

Taiwan's Defense in an Age of Precision Strike," *Project 2049 Institute Occasional Paper*, September 2014, pp. 3–14.

181. Ibid.

182. *Informatized Joint Operations*, p. 180. See also *Space Information Support Operations*, p. 147.

183. In addition to above sources, see Su Mao-Hsien, "Discussing Future Operational Concepts of Communist Military's Application of Special Operations Units During Attack on Taiwan (淺談未來共軍攻台運用特種作戰部隊作戰構想)," *ROC Army Aviation and Special Forces Journal*, Vol. 57, 2013, pp. 22–29.

184. *Informatized Joint Operations*, p. 179.

185. Ibid., p. 157.

186. Ibid., p. 158.

187. Ibid. p. 160. For a detailed Taiwanese assessment of the role of Chinese submarines in a blockade, see Lieu Shien-Chu, "Discussion on Chinese Communist Submarine Threat to Taiwan and Their Blockade Capabilities (中共潛艦對台威脅及對封鎖能力探討)," *ROC Navy Journal*, No. 46, Vol. 4 (August 1, 2012), pp. 56–74.

188. *Informatized Joint Operations*, p. 159.

189. Ibid., pp. 160–161. For a detailed Taiwanese assessment, see Chang Sheng-Kai and Tseng Chen-yang, "Analysis of Chinese Communist Mine-laying Operations off Taiwan's East Coast (中共對我東岸海域布雷行動之研析), *ROC Navy Journal*, No. 49, Vol. 4 (August 1, 2015), pp. 132–140.

190. *Informatized Joint Operations*, p. 163.

191. Ibid., pp. 160–161.

192. Ibid., p. 161.

193. Ibid., p. 158.

194. Ibid., p. 159.

195. Ibid. pp. 159–160.

196. *Space Information Support Operations*, pp. 166–167.

197. Ibid., p. 169.

198. Ibid., p. 170.

199. The PLA's naval armadas and task forces would have their own dedicated SATCOM lines throughout the pre-invasion battle, with satellites

providing admirals at sea with links to all their dispersed ships. In wartime, the PLA would also theoretically attempt to build a navy-to-air force tactical communications network. In practice, however, there are concerns that this satellite communications system would not work, apparently because it is assumed the rival services would be unable to work well together. See *Space Information Support Operations*, pp. 171– 172.

200. Ibid., pp. 173–174.

201. *Informatized Army Operations*, pp. 122–123.

202. For background, see Mark A. Stokes, "The Chinese Joint Aerospace Campaign: Strategy, Doctrine, and Force Modernization," in James Mulvenon and David Finkelstein (eds.), *China's Revolution in Doctrinal Affairs: Emerging Trends in the Operational Art of the Chinese People's Liberation Army* (Alexandria, VA: Center for Naval Analyses CNA Corporation, 2002), pp. 221–305. For a recent PLA source, see *Space Information Support Operations*, pp. 159–162.

203. *Informatized Joint Operations*, p. 179. See also *Space Information Support Operations*, pp. 146–147.

204. *Informatized Joint Operations*, p. 180.

205. *Informatized Joint Operations*, pp. 224–225. Note that the PLA has built a full-scale model of Taiwan's Presidential Office. This reportedly has been hit in live-fire exercises with cruise missiles that targeted the president's desk. While unclear, that test may have occurred in 2013–2014. More recently, the Presidential Office model has been used to train Chinese ground forces in close quarters combat. See J. Michael Cole, "Chinese PLA Simulates 'Attack' on Taiwan's Presidential Office," *The Diplomat*, July 22, 2015; Lo Tien-pin and Jake Chung, "China simulates attack on Presidential Office," *Taipei Times*, July 23, 2015, page one; and Victor Robert Lee, "Satellite Imagery: China Staging Mock Invasion of Taiwan," *The Diplomat*, August 9, 2015.

206. Note that PLA writings do not refer to ROC government organizations by their official titles. Instead, they refer to them as the "enemy's principal brain organizations, where strategic political, economic, and military problems are decided." See *Informatized Joint Operations*, p. 180.

207. *Informatized Joint Operations*, pp. 180–181.

208. *Space Information Support Operations*, p. 157.

209. *Informatized Joint Operations*, pp. 180–181.

210. Ibid. .

211. Ibid.

212. Ibid.

213. Ibid., p. 182.

214. *Research on Operational Theory* of *Army Aviation Troops*, p. 166.

215. *Informatized Joint Operations*, p. 182.

216. Ibid., p. 184.

217. Ibid.

218. Ibid., pp. 183–185. See also *Space Information Support Operations*, p. 148.

219. *Informatized Joint Operations*, p. 185.

220. Ibid.

221. Ibid, p. 162.

222. *Space Information Support Operations*, p. 174.

223. *Informatized Army Operations*, pp. 115–116

224. *Space Information Support Operations*, p. 175.

225. *Informatized Army Operations*, pp. 109–112, and 115.

226. Ibid., p. 115.

227. Ibid, p. 116.

228. See *Informatized Army Operations*, pp. 196–215; and *Informatized Joint Operations*, p. 198. See also Li Jun and Zhang Qi, "Research on how to Optimize the Deployment of Artillery Forces for Offensive Combat against Near Coastal Islands Based on FCE (基于ＦＣＥ对近岸岛屿进攻战斗炮兵部署优化研究)," *Jianchuan Dianzi Gongcheng* (Ship Electronic Engineering Journal), December 2012, pp. 43–47; and Liu Zengyou, et al., "Shipping and Equipment Support Force Deployments for Joint Operations against Offshore Islands (近岸岛屿联合作战船艇装备保障力量)," *Binggong Zidonghua* (Ordnance Industry Automation Journal), April 2010, pp. 58–62.

229. *Course book on Taiwan Strait Military Geography*, pp. 166–167.

230. "Geographic Location," *Wuqiu Township Office Website*, at http://web.kinmen.gov.tw/Layout/sub_B/AllInOne_en_Show.aspx-?path=6370&guid=47592e10-2854-4eaf-876b-26d579bda533&lang=en-us.

231. *Course book on Taiwan Strait Military Geography*, pp. 172–173.

232. *Informatized Joint Operations*, p. 198.

233. *Informatized Army Operations*, pp. 210–211.

234. Ibid., p. 208.

235. Ibid., pp. 211–213.

236. See *Informatized Army Operations*, pp. 111–113, 196–201, and 204–205; and *Informatized Joint Operations*, pp. 187–188; and 198.

237. Ibid.

238. Ibid.

239. Ibid.

240. See *Course book on Taiwan Strait Military Geography*, pp. 166–177.

241. *Research on Operational Theory* of *Army Aviation Troops*, pp. 105–135.

242. Ibid., pp. 116–118. Note that the main island of Kinmen is anticipated to be the most difficult to capture. It is described as having two major defensive lines that protect a central stronghold area located around the highest point of elevation. The central bunker complex reportedly serves as the island's last redoubt. It is believed to be connected to points across the island by long tunnels. Other offshore islands are thought to have one defensive line backed up by a stronghold. Some islands, including Kinmen, are thought to have natural sea caves which have been created over centuries by pounding waves and then expanded by Taiwan's army engineers. These caves are viewed as places where fresh supplies and troops could be clandestinely brought in at night from the sea and where fast missile boats could safely hide.

243. Ibid., p. 121.

244. Ibid., pp. 120–121.

245. *Informatized Army Operations*, p. 210.

246. Ibid.

247. Ibid., p. 209.

248. Ibid, p. 210.

249. Ibid.

250. Ibid., p. 215.

251. See *Informatized Army Operations*, pp. 127–164; *Informatized Joint Operations*, pp. 186–207; and *Space Information Support Operations*, pp.

188–212. See also *Research on Operational Theory* of *Army Aviation Troops*, pp. 80–104.

252. *Informatized Army Operations*, p. 154.

253. *Informatized Army Operations*, p. 155; and *Informatized Joint Operations*, p. 199.

254. *Informatized Army Operations*, p. 155; *Informatized Joint Operations*, p. 199; and *Space Information Support Operations*, pp. 207–208.

255. *Space Information Support Operations*, pp. 191–199.

256. *Informatized Joint Operations*, p. 200.

257. See *Informatized Army Operations*, p. 155.

258. Ibid., p. 156.

259. Ibid.; and *Informatized Joint Operations*, p. 200. See also Chen Song-hui, Qiu Hongli, and Du Hu, "Research and Analysis on an Amphibious Formation's Comprehensive Landing and Assault Capabilities (两栖编队综合登陆突击能力的分析研究)," *Jianchuan Dianzi Gongcheng* (Ship Electronic Engineering Journal), No. 5, 2014, pp. 34–37, 64.

260. *Informatized Joint Operations*, p. 201; and *Research on Operational Theory* of *Army Aviation Troops*, p. 81.

261. Dennis J. Blasko, *The Chinese Army Today* (New York: Routledge, 2012), pp. 49–50.

262. *Informatized Army Operations*, p. 156; and *Informatized Joint Operations*, p. 200.

263. Tsai Ho-Hsun, "Research on the Communist Military's Division Landing Operations (共軍師登陸作戰之研究)," *ROC Army Journal*, Vol. 50, No. 537, October 2014, p. 67. For excellent studies on the PLA's amphibious order of battle, see Pan Shih-Yeong and Shen Qi-lin, "Analysis of the Chinese Communist's Amphibious Landing Combat Force (中共兩棲登陸戰力之研析)," *ROC Navy Journal*, No. 46, Vol. 3 (June 1, 2012), pp. 69–84. See also, Chu Bih-wei, "The Communist Military's Amphibious Operational Thought and Platform Developments (共軍兩棲作戰思維與載台發展)," *ROC Navy Journal*, No. 47, Vol. 1 (February 1, 2013), pp. 120–129.

264. *Informatized Army Operations*, p. 156; and *Informatized Joint Operations*, pp. 200–201.

265. Ibid.

266. *Informatized Army Operations*, p. 157. See also Liu Runcai, et al., "Analysis and Modeling of Communications Environment during Landing Operations (登陆作战中的通信环境分析与建模)," *Sichuan Binggong Xueshu* (Sichuan Ordinance Studies), December 2010, pp. 63–65.

267. *Informatized Army Operations*, pp. 157–158.

268. *Informatized Army Operations*, p. 159; and *Informatized Joint Operations*, p. 201.

269. *Informatized Joint Operations*, pp. 201–202. See also Wang Dazhong, et al., "Initial Evaluation of Ship Fire Support Effectiveness and Fire Distribution during Landing Operations (登陆作战中舰艇火力支援效能及分配模型初探)," *Jianchuan Dianzi Gongcheng* (Ship Electronic Engineering), No. 2, 2010, pp. 32–34, 44.

270. This draws from studies conducted by the PLA Navy's schoolhouse for amphibious operations, which used high-powered computer simulations to find the best composition of a beach assault battalion. These studies found that an optimal Chinese amphibious unit would have a blend of amphibious tanks, amphibious assault vehicles outfitted with mortars and heavy machine guns, and infantry equipped with machine guns, anti-tank weapons, and air defense missiles. They assumed notional assault battalions would have three infantry companies, three amphibious assault vehicle/tank companies, one air defense company, and one anti-tank company. Ideally, each assault team would be supported by four helicopter gunships providing close air support. See Jia Ziying, Chen Songhui, and Wen Rui, "Analysis of Troop Unit Effectiveness During Systemized Landing Operations Based on Data Field (基于数据场的登陆作战体系兵力编组效能分析)," *Zhihui Kongzhi yu Fangzhen* (Command Control & Simulation Journal), Vol. 36, No. 6, December 2014, pp. 92–95; and Wang Yinlai, Chen Songhui, and Jia Ziying, "Analysis of Troops Unit Effectiveness During Landing Operations Based on Complex Networks (基于复杂网络的登陆作战兵力编组效能分析)," *Huoli yu Zhihu Kongzhi* (Fire Control & Command Control Journal), Vol. 39, No. 8, August 2014, pp. 87–90. Note that both studies received the PRC's National Social Science Grant for Military Study Programs (12GJ003-127). See also Yang Fengshou and Hu Xiaoyun, "Infantry Unit Landing Operations Decision Plan Evaluation based upon

Improved Three Marker Method (基于三标度改进方法的步兵分队登陆作战决心方案评价)," *Zhihui Kongzhi Yu Fangzhen* (Command, Control, and Simulation Journal), December 2009, pp. 48–51.

271. *Informatized Army Operations*, pp. 160–161.

272. Ibid. pp. 160–162. For a remarkably detailed discussion on PLA amphibious attacks against Taiwan's ports, see Xu Lisheng and Wang Zhaoyong (eds.), *Research on Port Landing Operations* 港口登陆作战研究(Beijing, National Defense University Press, 2015), pp. 36–70; and Yan Feilong and Jia Ziying, "Airborne Landing Operation Target Selection Method Based on Complex Networks (基于复杂网络的机降作战目标选择方法)," *Huoli Yu Zhihui Kongzhi* (Fire Control and Command Control), April 2014, pp. 38–41.

273. *Informatized Army Operations*, p. 162.

274. Ibid., p. 163.

275. Ibid. See also Wang Yongping, p. 210. See also Liu Hongkun, "Analysis of our Tank Companies' Offensive Operational Capabilities against Combat Vehicles on the Island (坦克连对岛上战车排进攻作战能力分析)," *Huoli Yu Zhihui Kongzhi* (Fire Control and Command Control), September 2006, pp. 64–66, 78.

276. *Informatized Army Operations*, p. 164.

277. *Informatized Army Operations*, p. 164. Cai Junfeng and Mei Sijun, "Design of Protective Storage for Ordinance to be carried during Amphibious Strait Crossing and Island Landing Operations (渡海登岛作战弹药两栖携行防护装具设计)," *Baozhuang Gongcheng* (Packaging Engineering), March 2015, pp. 140–143.

278. *Space Information Support Operations*, pp. 210–211.

279. Note, for example, that while the 2008 version of *Informatized Joint Operations* offers a mere two pages of discussion on this topic, books like *Joint Army Operations* and *Research on Operational Theory* of *Army Aviation Troops*, which were last published in 2015 and 2014, respectively, dedicate entire chapters to a post-Zero Day fight on Taiwan.

280. *Informatized Army Operations*, p. 188.

281. *Informatized Army Operations*, p. 188.

282. *Research on Operational Theory of Army Aviation Troops*, p. 172; *Research on Port Landing Operations*, p. 33;

283. *Informatized Army Operations*, pp. 188–189.

284. Ibid.

285. Ibid., p. 190.

286. Ibid., p. 189.

287. *Research on Port Landing Operations*, p. 42.

288. *Informatized Army Operations*, p. 190.

289. Ibid., pp.190–191.

290. Ibid., pp. 192–193.

291. *Informatized Army Operations*, p. 194; and *Course Book on the Art of Special Operations*, p. 184.

292. *Informatized Army Operations*, p. 194.

293. Ibid., p. 195.

294. *Informatized Army Operations*, p. 195; and *Informatized Joint Operations*, pp. 234–235.

295. *Informatized Army Operations*, p. 195.

296. Ibid.

297. *Port Landing Operations*, p. 29.

298. *Informatized Joint Operations*, pp. 234–235.

299. *Informatized Army Operations* , p. 195.

300. *Informatized Joint Operations*, pp. 234–235.

301. For example, see *Course Book on the Taiwan Strait's Military Geography*, pp. 57–58; and *The Japanese Air Self Defense Force*, pp. 190–191.

Chapter Five: Planning Problems

302. It must be noted that the PLA would also be limited by its budget. How much money would it have available? How many material resources could be pulled over from the civilian economy? How would financial and other resources be managed and channeled into the war effort? When it comes to financial matters, however, almost nothing specific is known. China's military economy is extraordinarily opaque and difficult to assess. One former Taiwanese vice president, Wu Den-yih, has stated that an invasion of Taiwan would probably cost the PRC somewhere between 30 trillion to 50 trillion U.S. dollars. It is not known how he reached this figure,

but it may have been derived from intelligence assessments Taiwan has conducted. See Alison Hsiao, "PRC would pay dearly for taking Taiwan, Wu says," *Taipei Times*, January 25, 2017, at http://www.taipeitimes.com/News/taiwan/archives/2017/01/25/2003663766.

303. In practice, this would mean reducing CCP political interference in military matters, not just in operations, but in selection and promotion, as well as in education and training. Examples from the PRC's past as well as the civil-military experiences of other militaries, both Communist and Fascist, show that reduced political interference results in improved capabilities, at least man-for-man. Political interference may have its benefits, but only if the PLA wanted to do relatively simple (think human wave) tactics that result in high causality rates for its own forces. The author is indebted to Ian McCaslin for this point.

304. See MND's Chinese-language website portal titled, "Military Periodicals (軍事刊物)," at http://www.mnd.gov.tw/Publish.aspx?Prod=軍事刊物&Title=軍事刊物&style=軍事刊物&s=1.

305. *Informatized Army Operations*, pp. 140–141.

306. *China's Military Geography*, p. 351. See also *Informatized Army Operations*,

p.133.

307. "Han Kuang Exercise 32 Series 2: Critical Node Hsuehshan Tunnel Blockade Operation (漢光32號演習系列2--關節要點雪山封阻作業)," *Quanqiu Fangwei Zazhi* (Defence International), No. 385, September 2016, pp. 36–40;

"Reserve Mobilization: Counterattack after Tamsui Raid and Taipei Port Attack (後備動員淡水反突擊台北港反擊), *Quanqiu Fangwei Zazhi* (Defence International), No. 362, October 2014, pp. 37–38.

308. According to Taiwanese studies, the options open to the Chinese for landing on the west coast are especially limited by giant mudflats stretching between the cities of Taichung and Tainan. The high tide and low tide waterlines in this extremely flat and shallow area are approximately two to three miles apart, making it treacherous for amphibious operations. Lin Chang-Sheng, "Chinese Communist Amphibious Landing Forces for Taiwan Strait War (中共台海戰爭兩棲登陸軍力)," in Lin Chong-bin,

Calculating the Taiwan Strait: The Strategic Situation in the Strait in the New Century 廟算台海：新世紀海峽戰略態勢 (Taipei: Chinese Council of Advanced Policy Studies, 2002), pp. 405–406.

309. *Informatized Army Operations*, p. 115.

310. *Course book on Taiwan Strait Military Geography,* p. 83.

311. Ibid.

312. Author's discussions with Taiwanese defense authorities.

313. Author's discussion with Colonel Andrew Drake (USMC).

314. Author's discussions with Taiwanese defense authorities.

315. Wu Qi-yu, "Research on Executing Surf Zone Mining Operations with Combat Engineer Units (工兵部隊執行激浪區布雷作業之研究)," *ROC Army Combat Engineer Journal*, No. 147, 2015, pp. 24–27 (of 30); and Wu Ding-an, "Discussion on ROC Military Beach Obstacle Enterprise in Light of Chinese Communist's 'Mission Action 2013' Exercise, Landing Tactics, and Platforms (從中共【使命行動2013】演習之登陸戰法與輸具探討我軍灘岸阻絕作爲)," *ROC Army Combat Engineer Journal*, No. 147, 2015, pp. 14–18 (of 23). See also Ma Li-te and Chang Nan-Zong, "Analysis of Communist China's New Type Amphibious Transports and the Communist Military's Landing Operation Models (中共新型兩棲載具對共軍登陸作戰模式的研析)," *ROC Navy Journal*, February 2013, p. 80.

316. See *Research on Operational Theory* of *Army Aviation Troops*, pp. 82–88

317. *Informatized Joint Operations*, pp. 202–203.

318. *Informatized Joint Operations*, p. 203.

319. *Informatized Army Operations*, p. 115.

320. *Informatized Army Operations*, p. 166.

321. *Course book on Taiwan Strait Military Geography,* p. 83. For ROC Military assessments, see Wang Hsiu-Hung, "Analysis of Communist China's Landing Craft Air Cushion Vehicle Developments and Military Applications (中共軍用氣墊登陸艇發展與軍用之研析)," *ROC Army Journal*, No. 52, Vol. 548 (August 2016), pp. 83–103; and Chang You-ching, "Research on Combat Engineer Support in River Crossings during Defense Operations--The Case of the Third Theater of Operations and the Tamsui River (防衛作戰中工兵支援渡河作業之研究—以第三作戰區淡水河爲例)," *ROC Army Combat Engineer Journal*, No. 147, 2015, pp. 1–24.

322. *Course book on Taiwan Strait Military Geography,* p. 83. For Taiwanese sources, see Wang Wei-hsien and Ong Ming-hui, "Discussion on History, Development, and Application of Communist Military's Amphibious Armored Assault Vehicle for Landings (共軍兩棲裝甲戰斗車輛發展歷程與運用上陸之探討)," *ROC Army Journal,* No. 52, Vol. 546 (April 2016), pp. 53–54; and Chien Yi-jian and Ong Ming-hui, "Research on Armor Brigade Counterattack Operations during Defense Operations--The Case of a Suitable Landing Area (防衛作戰中裝甲旅反擊之研究 --以適宜登陸地區爲例)," *ROC Armor Journal,* No. 240, July 2015, pp. 15– 42.

323. Of many assessments to this effect, see Chang You-ching, "Research on Combat Engineer Support in River Crossings during Defense Operations--The Case of the Third Theater of Operations and the Tamsui River (防衛作戰中工兵支援渡河作業之研究—以第三作戰區淡水河爲例)," *ROC Army Combat Engineer Journal,* No. 147, 2015, pp. 5–18. See also, *Course book on Taiwan Strait Military Geography,* p. 70.

324. After Taoyuan, the Chuoshui River delta and the areas around Tainan are described as the next-most suitable locations for amphibious landings because they offer sandy beaches and flat open spaces for engaging tanks in maneuver warfare. Texts note, however, that non-traditional landing operations would be required. This is a reference to the huge mudflats that dominate the coast, especially at the Chuoshui River mouth. Located some 230 miles south of Taipei, the Chuoshui river is Taiwan's largest. It picks up silt along the steep sloops of the central mountain range and discharges extraordinary mounds of it into the Taiwan Strait. Hovercraft, hydrofoils, and sea skimmers could cross the shallows here, but few other vessels could avoid being beached in the attempt. See *Course book on Taiwan Strait Military Geography,* p. 83.

325. Indeed, in the absence of suitable beaches near Taichung, the ROC Military assumes that the PLA may try irregular landings at the Dajia River delta and plans accordingly. See Chang You-ching, "Research on Combat Engineer Support in River Crossings during Defense Operations--The Case of the Third Theater of Operations and the Tamsui River (防衛作戰中工兵支援渡河作業之研究—以第三作戰區淡水河爲例)," *ROC Army Combat Engineer Journal,* No. 147, 2015, pp. 2–4.

326. *Taiwan Strait Military Geography*, pp. 196–205.

327. For an excellent Taiwanese assessment, see Lin Zhe-chun, "Discussion on Defense Operations in Urban Infrastructure with Support of Defense Combat Engineers (防衛作戰城鎮設施防工兵支援之探討)," *ROC Army Combat Engineer Journal*, No. 144, 2014, pp. 1–23.

328. See "Han Kuang Exercise 32 Series 2: Key Node Hsuehshan Tunnel Blockade Drill (漢光32號演習系列2：關節要點雪山封阻作業), "*Quanqiu Fangwei Zazhi* (Defence International), No. 385, September 2016, pp. 36–40.

329. *Informatized Army Operations*, p. 133.

330. *Course book on Taiwan Strait Military Geography*, p. 59. *Research on Port Landing Operations*, pp. 16–23.

331. *China's Military Geography*, p. 337.

332. *Course book on Taiwan Strait Military Geography*, p. 67.

333. *China's Military Geography*, p. 394.

334. This of course does not account for the Himalayan and Pamir mountains in southwestern China.

335. *Course book on Taiwan Strait Military Geography*, p. 63.

336. Author's discussions with local residents in Magong City and elsewhere on the Penghu Islands, May 2008.

337. See *Research on Port Landing Operations*, p. 19; and Liu Haijiang and Li Zhiyuan (eds.), *Research on Joint Tactical Thought* 联合战术思想研究 (Beijing: Lantian Press, 2012), pp. 141–142.

338. *Course book on Taiwan Strait Military Geography*, p. 59.

339. Bai Guangwei (ed.), *Course book on Taiwan Strait Military Geography*, p. 60.

340. Ibid.

341. See *Informatized Army Operations*, p. 147; and *Research on Port Landing Operations*, pp. 17–18.

342. Ibid. Note that the latter source asserts that the PLA's amphibious landings on Jintang Island were a success in large part because the tides were carefully studied beforehand and the attacking commander chose to hit the beaches on a high tide day (October 3, 1949). In contrast, the landing attempt on Kinmen later that same month failed because the commander

ignored the tides and attempted to land when the tides were receding. This greatly hindered his operations and contributed to a total defeat.

343. *Research on Port Landing Operations*, p. 17.

344. See Ganning Zeng, Jianyu Hu, Huasheng Hong, and Yiquan Qi, "Numerical Study on M2 Tidal System in the Taiwan Strait," *Procedia Environmental Sciences*, 12 (2012), pp. 702–707. Note that the researchers are affiliated with the PRC State Key Laboratory of Satellite Ocean Environmental Dynamics (Hangzhou), the PRC State Key Laboratory of Marine Environmental Science (Xiamen), and the PRC State Key Laboratory of Tropical Marine Environmental Dynamics (Guangzhou).

345. Author's discussions with Taiwanese locals in New Taipei City, Kaohsiung, and Hengchun.

346. *Course Book on Taiwan Strait Military Geography*, p. 60; *Research on Port Landing Operations*, pp. 20–21; and *Research on Joint Tactical Thought*, pp. 141–142.

347. *Informatized Army Operations*, pp. 133–134.

348. Ibid., p. 140.

349. Ibid., pp. 141–142.

350. *Course Book on Taiwan Strait Military Geography*, p. 60.

351. Ibid.

352. Ibid., p. 59.

353. Ibid.

354. See *Informatized Army Landing Operations*, p. 133. Note that an added danger of this approach would be that preparing for an invasion and then not being able to launch it due to bad weather conditions would tip China's hand to Taiwan, the U.S., and the rest of the world, signaling that the PLA was actually going invade Taiwan and would likely try again the next opportunity the weather allowed. Given the time lag between suitable weather and other factors, a scenario like this could be problematic for Chinese invasion plans, as it might result in the U.S. becoming much closer to Taiwan and more involved in its defense, as happened after every Taiwan Strait Crisis. The author is indebted to Ian McCaslin for this point.

355. See *Research on Port Landing Operations*, pp. 19–23; *Course Book on Taiwan Strait Military Geography*, p. 59; and *Research on Joint Tactical Thought*, pp. 141–142.

356. See Dennis J. Blasko, "The PLA Army/Ground Forces," in Kevin Poll-peter and Kenneth W. Allen (eds.), *The PLA as an Organization: Reference Volume v2.0* (Fairfax, VA: Defens Group Inc. 2015), pp. 244–245; and Kenneth W. Allen, Dennis J. Blasko, and John F. Corbett, Jr., "The PLA's New Organizational Structure: What is Known, Unknown, and Speculation," *China Brief*, February 4, 2016, at http://www.jamestown.org/single/?tx_ttnewstt_news=45069&no_cache=1#.VoNWo-RrMgs.

357. For a dated but still relevant study, see Lin Chang-Sheng, "Chinese Communist Amphibious Landing Forces for Taiwan Strait War (中共台海戰爭兩棲登陸軍力)," in Lin Chong-bin, *Calculating the Taiwan Strait: The Strategic Situation in the Strait in the New Century* 廟算台海：新世紀海峽戰略態勢 (Taipei: Chinese Council of Advanced Policy Studies, 2002), pp. 394–395.

358. Dennis Blasko, *The Chinese Army Today*, p. 50; and author's discussions with ROC Military subject matter experts.

359. See "PLA Doubles Size of Amphibious Mechanized Infantry Division," *Want China Times*, January 5, 2015, at http://stt.soundthetrumpet.ca/media/?m=0&id=25664. See also Franz-Stefan Gady, "China Just Doubled the Size of Its Amphibious Mechanized Divisions," *The Diplomat*, January 9, 2015, at http://thediplomat.com/2015/01/china-just-doubled-the-size-of-its-amphibious-mechanized-infantry-divisions/.

360. For example, a low estimate might assume for two amphibious mechanized infantry divisions capable of attacking with 6,000 troops apiece, two special forces groups capable of attacking with 1,000 commandos each, three helicopter regiments capable of attacking with 1,000 light infantry each, and one armored brigade with 3,000 personnel. Such a force would have a total of 20,000 combat troops. A high-end estimate might assume the PLA could field four amphibious mechanized infantry divisions with 12,000 troops apiece, two special forces groups with 3,000 commandos each, three helicopter regiments with 3,000 light infantry each, and one armored brigade with 5,000 personnel. Such a force would have a total of

68,000. Assumptions would vary depending on numbers of trained and equipped combat troops (as opposed to administrative personnel), fully mobilized unit sizes, pre-invasion force attrition, transportation limitations, and many other factors that affect unit size and availability.

361. Kenneth W. Allen, "PLA Air Force Organizational Reforms: 2000–2012," in Kevin Pollpeter and Kenneth W. Allen (eds.), *The PLA as an Organization: Reference Volume v2.0* (Fairfax, VA: Defens Group Inc. 2015), p. 322.

362. Dennis Blasko, *The Chinese Army Today*, p. 103.

363. For background, see Dennis J. Blasko, "PLA Amphibious Capabilities: Structured for Deterrence," *China Brief*, August 19, 2010, at https://jamestown.org/program/pla-amphibious-capabilities-structured-for-deterrence/; and Chia-Shin Wu, "The Assessment of Communist China's Threat to Launch Amphibious (or Sea-Air-Land) Invasion against Taiwan," *Taiwan Defense Affairs*, Vol. 4, No. 3 (Spring 2004), p. 76.

364. The author is indebted to Dennis Blasko for this point.

365. The most important of the PLA's approximately 17 ship groups for the invasion of Taiwan would be the one based at Dongshan Island, which regularly trains for supporting amphibious operations. Others are mostly used for logistics, with some reconnaissance and amphibious roles, and have landing craft that are unsuitable for crossing the Taiwan Strait. Dennis J. Blasko, "The PLA Army/Ground Forces," in Kevin Pollpeter and Kenneth W. Allen (eds.), *The PLA as an Organization: Reference Volume v2.0* (Fairfax, VA: Defens Group Inc. 2015), p. 239.

366. Dennis Blasko, *The Chinese Army Today*, pp. 94–100; and Lin Chang-Sheng, p. 394.

367. Note that in addition to other bases, there are several significant shipbuilding yards in the Shanghai area. The Jiangnan shipyard currently produces advanced destroyers, frigates, submarines, and large support vessels. The Hudong shipyard produces frigates and supply ships. The Honghua shipyard has been a major supplier of amphibious warfare ships, and Qiuxin makes minesweepers. It should be assumed they would all be cranking out massive numbers of amphibious landing craft and other needed vessels before and during the invasion. See Andrew Erickson, *Chinese Naval Ship Building*; and Bernard Cole, *The Great Wall at Sea*, p. 74

368. Nan Li, "The People's Liberation Army Navy as an Evolving Organization," in Kevin Pollpeter and Kenneth W. Allen (eds.), *The PLA as an Organization: Reference Volume v2.0* (Fairfax, VA: Defens Group Inc. 2015), p. 286.

369. Ibid., p. 279

370. Ibid., pp. 287–288.

371. Ibid., p. 280.

372. Ibid., pp. 278, 285

373. *People's Liberation Army Air Force 2010* (Wright-Patterson Air Force Base: National Air and Space Intelligence Center, 2010), p. 25.

374. Mark Stokes, "China's Air Defense Identification System: The Role of PLA Air Surveillance," *Project 2049 Institute*, May 9, 2014, pp. 4–5, at http://www.project2049.net/documents/Stokes_China_Air_Defense_Identification_System_PLA_Air_Surveillance.pdf.

375. *Annual Report to Congress, Military and Security Developments Involving the People's Republic of China 2016*, p. 32.

376. Mark Stokes, "China's Air Defense Identification System: The Role of PLA Air Surveillance," pp. 4–5.

377. Among many excellent sources, see Michael S. Chase, Daniel Yoon, and Mark Stokes, "The People's Liberation Army Second Artillery Force as an Organization," in Kevin Pollpeter and Kenneth W. Allen (eds.), *The PLA as an Organization: Reference Volume v2.0* (Fairfax, VA: Defense Group Inc. 2015), pp. 356–362; and Mark Stokes, "Expansion of China's Ballistic Missile Infrastructure Opposite Taiwan," *Asia Eye, Project 2049 Institute*, April 18, 2011, at http://blog.project2049.net/2011/04/expansion-of-chinas-ballistic-missile.html.

378. Murray Scot Tanner, "China's People's Armed Police Force Leadership, Command, and Organization in the Wake of the 2009 PAP Law," in Kevin Pollpeter and Kenneth W. Allen (eds.), *The PLA as an Organization: Reference Volume v2.0* (Fairfax, VA: Defense Group Inc. 2015), pp. 378–379.

379. Dennis Blasko, *The Chinese Army Today*, pp. 109–111.

380. Dennis Blasko, *The Chinese Army Today*, pp. 111–113.

381. For excellent background on the maritime militia, see Andrew S. Erickson and Conor M. Kennedy, "China's Maritime Militia," *CNA Corpo-

ration, March 7, 2016, pp. 22–28, at https://www.cna.org/cna_files/pdf/Chinas-Maritime-Militia.pdf.

382. *Informatized Joint Operations*, p. 172

383. *Informatized Joint Operations*, p. 176.

384. *Informatized Army Operations*, p. 167. For a ROC Military source confirming this, see Wang Chung-fung, "Discussion and Analysis on Combat Engineering Support to Force Preservation Actions (探討工兵支援戰力保存作爲之研析)," *ROC Army Combat Engineer Journal*, No. 146, 2015, pp. 1–28.

385. *Informatized Army Operations*, p. 112.

386. *Informatized Army Operations*, p. 127.

387. *Informatized Army Operations*, pp. 127–128.

388. *Informatized Army Operations*, p. 128.

389. Zhao Feng (ed.), *The Taiwan Military's 20 Year Transformation* 台军20年转型之路 (Beijing, National Defense University Press, 2015), p. 171.

390. See "Taiwan Spends 30 Billion to Build Missile Defense Net: Second Phase has Runway Repair and Camouflage to Trick Enemy 第二階段搶修跑道 偽裝欺敵 台砸三千億 建導彈防禦網, *Sing Tao Daily*, September 6, 2010, at http://news.singtao.ca/calgary/2010-09-06/taiwan1283761644d2712081.html. For further details see *Able Archers: Taiwan Defense Strategy in an Age of Precision Strike*, p. 55.

391. *Informatized Army Operations*, pp. 123–124.

392. Ibid.

393. Ibid., p. 131.

394. Ibid., p. 129.

395. Ibid., p. 131.

396. Ibid., pp. 131–2.

397. *Informatized Army Operations*, p. 131.

398. Ibid., p. 124.

399. Ibid., pp. 141–144, 150–157.

400. Zhang Qingzhi, et al. (eds.), *Informatized Warfare and Psychological Protection* 信息化战争心理防护 (Beijing, The People's Military Medical Press, 2008), p. 113.

401. Ibid.

402. Ibid., p. 114.

403. Ibid.

404. Ibid., pp. 114–115.

405. Ibid., p. 116.

406. Ibid., p. 117.

407. Ibid., p. 118.

408. Ibid.

409. *Informatized Army Operations*, p. 113.

410. Tsai Ho-Hsun, "Research on the Communist Military's Division Landing Operations (共軍師登陸作戰之研究)," *Lujun Xueshu Shuangyue Kan* (Army Studies Bimonthly), Vol. 50, No. 537, October 2014, p. 69; and Wang Yunlei and Wang Guangyuan, *Guidebook on Operational Calculations* (作戰計算指南) Beijing, Blue Skies Press, 2013, p. 47 (op cit.). Note that Blue Skies Press (蓝天出版社) is the official publishing house of the PLA Air Force.

411. Author's discussions with ROC military subject matter experts.

412. *Informatized Army Operations*, p. 125.

413. Ibid, p. 113.

414. Ibid.

415. Ibid., p. 115.

416. Ibid., p. 115.

417. *Research on Joint Tactical Thought*, p. 156.

Chapter Six: How Taiwan Would Fight

418. In Chinese, the Gu'an Operational Plan is written: 固安作戰計劃. See "ROC Military 2016 'Hang Kuang 32' Exercise Live Fire Training Regulations (國軍105年"漢光32號"演習實兵演練規劃)," *ROC Ministry of National Defense Website*, posted August 19, 2016.

419. Lauren Dickey, "Taiwan's Han Kuang Exercises: Training for a Chinese Invasion One Drill at a Time, *China Brief*, Vol. 15, Issue 18 (September 16, 2015), at https://jamestown.org/program/taiwans-han-kuang-exercises-training-for-a-chinese-invasion-one-drill-at-a-time/.

420. "The Gu'an Operation Plan! National Military Forces Arrived to Assist at Formosa Fun Coast within Half Hour (固安作戰計畫！國軍半小時內抵八仙支援)," *Yahoo News*, June 28, 2015. For a description of a previous exercise in the Port of Taipei area, see "Reserve Mobilization: Counterattack after Tamsui Raid and Taipei Port Attack 後備動員淡水反突擊台北港反擊, *Quanqiu Fangwei Zazhi* (Defence International), No. 362, October 2014, pp. 36–43.

421. Author's discussions with U.S. military subject matter experts.

422. Author's discussions with U.S. and ROC military subject matter experts.

423. Author's discussions with ROC military subject matter experts.

424. For a brief descriptions of how mobilization and force preservation fit into Taiwan's overall defense strategy, see *Republic of China 2011 National Defense Report* 中華民國2011國防報告書(Taipei: Ministry of National Defense, 2011), pp. 85, 168–173; and *Republic of China 2013 Quadrennial Defense Review* (Taipei: Ministry of National Defense, 2013), pp. 33, 60–61. Military education course materials offer a far more detailed picture. For example, see *Defense Mobilization* 防衛動員 (Taipei: Ministry of National Defense Political Warfare Bureau, December 2011).

425. Note that some aspects of the law are necessarily vague and subject to parliamentary approval to prevent it from being abused by a would-be dictator. See Chang Hsueh-chang, "Discussion on Military Police Missions in Wartime (戰時憲兵任務之探討)," *ROC Military Police Command Journal*, No. 80 (June 2015), pp. 34–40

426. Ibid.; and Chang Zong-Tsai, "Research on Tactics and Techniques of Communist Military 'Decapitation Operations' through the lens of the U.S. Military's 'Operation Neptune Spear,'" pp. 10–12.

427. Dual-use civilian assets in the war reserve system include 10,000 fixed facilities, 2,000 pieces of heavy machinery, 300 fishing boats, 60 aircraft, and 50 large ships. See Easton, Stokes, Cooper, and Chan, p. 17.

428. Author's discussion with ROC military subject matter experts.

429. Author's discussion with ROC military subject matter experts.

430. Author's discussions with ROC military subject matter experts.

431. According to the ROC military's mine-laying doctrine, if it is assumed that all of the 14 most suitable invasion beaches' surf zones were mined at 90% density, then 4,788 total mines would be required. The standard shallow-water minefield would be four kilometers long and 150 meters wide. They would be laid by LCUs and, where necessary, Type-V and Type-M inflatable boats with outboard motors. See Wu Qi-yu, "Research on Executing Surf Zone Mining Operations with Combat Engineer Units (工兵部隊執行激浪區布雷作業之研究)," *ROC Army Combat Engineer Journal*, No. 147, 2015, pp. 1–30.

432. Taiwan's reserve system reportedly includes 71 CT-6 fishing boats and around 230 CT-5 fishing boats, which are required to report to their naval duty stations within 24 hours of an emergency mobilization order. Within 72 hours, they are to be refitted with specialized equipment and able to carry out mine-laying operations. Ibid., p. 13. See also Sun Chi-dao, "Military Applications of Taiwan's Fishing Boats (台灣漁船與軍事應用)," *ROC Navy Journal*, August 2014, pp. 95–108.

433. Liu En-kuang, "Briefing on Mechanized Mine-Laying Systems--Sharp Weapons for Countering Enemy Mobility Operations (反機動作戰利器—機械布雷系統簡介)," *ROC Army Combat Engineer Journal*, No. 146, 2015, pp. 1–21; and Wu Qi-lun and Huang Zhen-ge, "Analyzing Application and Effects of Smart Mines (智能地雷運用效益之研析)," *ROC Army Combat Engineer Journal*, No. 142, 2013, pp. 1–18.

434. Zhao Feng (ed.), *The Taiwan Military's 20 Year Transformation* 台军20年转型之路 (Beijing, National Defense University Press, 2015), p. 89.

435. Ibid. Unless otherwise noted, the following section is based on this source.

436. Ibid.

437. Ibid

438. Ibid.

439. *Informatized Army Operations*, pp. 147–148.

440. These would presumably include breakwater structures comprised of shaped concrete armor units, such as locally produced variants of Dolos, Xbloc, and Tetrapods. See *Informatized Army Operations*, pp. 147–148, and *The Taiwan Military's 20 Year Transformation*, p. 189.

441. See *Informatized Army Operations*, pp. 147–148, and *The Taiwan Military's 20 Year Transformation*, p. 189.

442. Zhao Feng (ed.), *The Taiwan Military's 20 Year Transformation*, p. 189

443. Ibid. p. 190.

444. *Informatized Army Operations*, pp. 122–123.

445. Author's discussions with U.S. and ROC military subject matter experts in Taiwan. See also Chang You-ching, "Research on Combat Engineer Support in River Crossings during Defense Operations--The Case of the Third Theater of Operations and the Tamsui River (防衛作戰中工兵支援渡河作業之研究—以第三作戰區淡水河爲例)," *ROC Army Combat Engineer Journal*, No. 147, 2015, pp. 1–24.

446. Author's discussions with U.S. and ROC military subject matter experts in Taiwan. See also Chang You-ching, "Research on Combat Engineer Support in River Crossings during Defense Operations--The Case of the Third Theater of Operations and the Tamsui River (防衛作戰中工兵支援渡河作業之研究—以第三作戰區淡水河爲例)," *ROC Army Combat Engineer Journal*, No. 147, 2015, pp. 1–24.

447. *Research on Operational Theory of Army Aviation Troops*, p. 168.

448. Ibid, p. 167.

449. Ibid, p. 106. According to this source, the notable exception to this rule might be the outer island groups of Kinmen and Matsu, where masses of helicopters and artillery, all in close proximity to their Chinese bases, would give the PLA a sizable advantage.

450. Author's discussions with ROC military subject matter experts; and *Informatized Army Operations* , pp. 122–123; Wu Qi-yu, "Analyzing the Application and Effects of HESCO Bastions (組合式掩體運用效益之研析)," *ROC Army Journal*, No. 52, Vol. 545 (February 2016), pp. 111–126; Wang Chung-fung, "Discussion and Analysis on Combat Engineering Support to Force Preservation Actions (探討工兵支援戰力保存作爲之研析)," *ROC Army Combat Engineer Journal*, No. 146, 2015, pp. 1–28; and Wang Chung-fung, "Discussion on Various Types of Blast Door Designs by Overpressure Level (探討各類型爆壓下防爆門之設計)," *ROC Army Combat Engineer Journal*, No. 144, 2014, pp. 1–27.

451. *Informatized Army Operations*, pp. 132–134, 142–144.

452. Unless otherwise noted, the following section on ROC Air Force plans and capabilities draws from Ian Easton, *Able Archers: Taiwan Defense Strategy in an Age of Precision Strike* (Arlington, VA: Project 2049 Institute, September 2014), pp. 47–56; and Ian Easton, "Taiwan, Asia's Secret Air Power," *The Diplomat*, September 25, 2014, at http://thediplomat.com/2014/09/taiwan-asias-secret-air-power/.

453. "Taiwan to spend HK$19 billion on home-made missile defense against Beijing," *South China Morning Post*, August 30, 2014, at http://www.scmp.com/news/china/article/1581963/taiwan-spend-hk19-billion-home-made-missile-defence-against-beijing.

454. Luo Tien-pin and William Hetherington, "Purchase of U.S. naval system finalized, "*Taipei Times*," January 22, 2017, at http://www.taipeitimes.com/News/front/archives/2017/01/22/2003663563.

455. At the current time, highway runway strips are located at the No. 1 National Freeway's Minsyong section (near Chiayi), the Rende and Madou sections (near Tainan), the Huatan section (near Changhua); and at Jiadong Provincial Highway (near Kaohsiung). Reportedly, other emergency strips may exist on the east coast, but this cannot be confirmed at the current time.

456. For an excellent overview of Taiwanese electronic warfare capabilities, including those for jamming satellites, see Chen Chiu-yang, "Analyzing Application of Electronic Warfare Techniques in Taiwanese Urban Warfare using of other Countries' Experiences (從各國經驗探討我城鎮戰中電子戰應用作爲之研析)," *ROC Army Combat Engineer Journal*, No. 147, 2015, pp. 1–20

457. Author's discussions with ROC military subject matter experts.

458. Unless otherwise noted, the following section on ROC Navy plans and capabilities draws from Ian Easton, *Taiwan's Naval Role in the Rebalance to Asia* (Arlington, VA: Project 2049 Institute, March 2015), at http://www.project2049.net/documents/150303_Easton_Taiwans_Naval_Role_in_the_Rebalance.pdf; Ian Easton and Randall Schriver, *Standing Watch: Taiwan and Maritime Domain Awareness in the Western Pacific* (Arlington, VA: Project 2049 Institute, December 2014), at http://www.project2049.net/documents/141216_Taiwan_Maritime_Domain_Awareness_Easton_Schriver.

pdf; and James Holmes and Toshi Yoshihara, *Defending the Strait: Taiwan's Naval Strategy in the 21st Century* (Washington, D.C.: The Jamestown Foundation, 2011).

459. Author's discussions with ROC military subject matter experts.

460. Author's discussions with ROC military subject matter experts.

461. Author's discussions with ROC military subject matter experts.

462. See "Han Kuang Exercise 32 Series 1: ROC Army 5th Support Department at the Fulcrum (漢光32號演習系列1--陸軍五支部前支點)," *Quanqiu Fangwei Zazhi* (Defence International), No. 385, September 2016, pp. 32–34; and author's discussions with ROC Military subject matter experts.

463. See Ian Easton, Mark Stokes, Cortez Cooper, and Arthur Chan, *Transformation of Taiwan's Reserve Force* (Arlington, VA: RAND Corporation, 2017), pp. 15–23.

464. Author's discussions with ROC military subject matter experts.

465. For background, see Grabo, pp. 38–50.

466. For a brief description of how joint interception fits in with Taiwan's overall defense strategy, see *Republic of China 2011 National Defense Report* 中華民國2011國防報告書 (Taipei: Ministry of National Defense, 2011), p. 89; and *Republic of China 2013 Quadrennial Defense Review* (Taipei: Ministry of National Defense, 2013), p. 39.

467. For an excellent overview of Taiwanese electronic warfare capabilities, including those for jamming missile guidance systems, see Chen Chiu-yang, "Analyzing Application of Electronic Warfare Techniques in Taiwanese Urban Warfare using of other Countries' Experiences (從各國經驗探討我城鎮戰中電子戰應用作為之研析)," *ROC Army Combat Engineer Journal*, No. 147, 2015, pp. 1–20

468. "Taiwan to spend $2.5 billion on anti-missile systems," *Defense News*, August 30, 2014, at http://www.defensenews.com/article/20140830/DE-FREG03/308300024/Taiwan-spend-2-5-billion-anti-missile-systems?odyssey=mod_sectionstories.

469. This assumes for a 600 kilometer range ballistic missile shot along a standard trajectory. Ballistic missiles launched from 300 kilometers away would only take five minutes and thirty seconds. Those with ranges of 1,000 kilometers would take nine minutes and twenty seconds to arrive.

All times are approximate and they assume for standard ballistic missile trajectories. See Liu Xing (ed.), *Air Defense and Space Defense Information Systems and Their Integrated Technologies* 防空防天信息系统及其一体化技术 (Beijing: National Defense Industry Press, 2009), p. 25.

470. See Wendell Minnick, "Chinese Spy Radio?" *Defense News*, April 26, 2010, at http://minnickarticles.blogspot.com/2010/04/chinese-spy-radio.html.

471. This following discussion on ROC Air Force plans and capabilities draws from Ian Easton, *Able Archers: Taiwan Defense Strategy in an Age of Precision Strike* (Arlington, VA: Project 2049 Institute, September 2014), pp. 47–56; and Ian Easton, "Taiwan, Asia's Secret Air Power," *The Diplomat*, September 25, 2014, at http://thediplomat.com/2014/09/taiwan-asias-secret-air-power/.

472. For a Chinese study supporting this assertion, see Tao Guiming, et al., "Modeling the Order of Surface to Surface Missile Strikes on Airfields (地地导弹打击机场排序模型)," *Computer and Information Technology Journal*, February 2013, pp. 12–14.

473. The PLA Strategic Rocket Force has custom-designed its ballistic missile warheads to release bomblets for annihilating Taiwan's sapper teams, and its plans apparently call for staggering missile raids to increase the probability of kill. As such, it seems likely that raids would involve small numbers of missiles raining down at regular intervals to keep airbases closed for as long as possible. For Chinese studies on this issue, see Huang Guangyan, et al., "Method for Assessing Effects of Joint Anti-Runway and Area Blockading Sub-munitions (反跑道与区域封锁子母弹联合对封锁效能的评估方法)," *Dandao Xuebao* (Journal of Ballistics), March 2013, p. 46; Jiang Zengrong, et al., "Numerical Modeling of Blast Depth Influence on Destruction Effects of Runway Penetrating Warhead (炸点深度对反跑道侵爆战斗布撒伤效果影响数值模拟)," *Conference Paper Presented at China's Ninth National Forum on Blast Dynamics*, undated, pp. 175–179; Jiang Zengrong, et al., "Numerical Modeling of Blast Depth Influence on Destruction Effects of Penetrating Warhead (炸点深度对侵爆战斗布撒伤效果影响数值模拟)," *Binggong Xuebao* (Acta Armamentarii Journal), April 2010, pp. 28–31; Li Xinqi and Wang Minghai, "Research on Standard

Problems of Conventional Missile Effects for Blockading Airfield Runways (常规导弹对封锁机场跑道效能准则问题研究)," *Zhihui Kongzhi Yu Fangzhen* (Command Control and Simulation Journal), Vol. 29, No. 4, August 2007, p. 78; Li Yong, et al., "Simulation and Calculation Research on Terminal Course-Correcting Submunitions' Airfield Runway Blockade Probability (末修子母弹对机场跑道封锁概率计算仿真研究)," *Xitong Fangzhen Xuebao* (Journal of System Simulation), Vol. 18, No. 9, 2006, 2397–2400; and Guan Baohua, et al., "Calculation of Terminal Course-Correcting Submunitions' Blockade Probability Against Airfield Runway (末修子母弹对机场跑道封锁概率的计算)," *Dandao Xuebao* (Journal of Ballistics), No. 4, 2005, pp. 22–26.

474. For a detailed PLA perspective on Taiwan's air defense network, see PLA General Staff Department 54th Research Institute, "Compilation of Air Defense Early Warning Information (防空预警资料汇编)," *Informatized War and Information War Information Compilation Series*, No.2. October 29, 2008, p. 34.

475. *Informatized Army Operations*, p. 131.

476. See *Able Archers: Taiwan Defense Strategy in an Age of Precision Strike*, p. 33.

477. See Tsai Cheng-chang, "Weapons for Suppressing Enemy Air Defenses-Discussion on Process of Surface Unit Fire Support Operations (制壓敵防空武力—地面部隊火協作業程序探討)," *ROC Artillery Forces Journal*, No. 169, 2015, pp. 47–64.

478. Author's discussions with United States and ROC military subject matter experts.

479. Mike Yeo, "Taiwan to upgrade indigenous missile capabilities," *Defense News*, February 6, 2017, at http://www.defensenews.com/articles/taiwan-to-upgrade-indigenous-missile-capabilities.

480. *The Taiwan Military's 20 Year Transformation*, p. 187.

481. Ibid. See also Wendell Minnick and Paul Kallender-Umezu, "Japan, Taiwan Upgrade Strike Capability," *Defense News*, May 6, 2013, available at http://rpdefense.over-blog.com/japan-taiwan-upgrade-strike-capability; and

Michal Thim, "Prickly Situation: Taiwan's missile program spurs debate on pre-emptive, porcupine strategies," *Strategic Vision*, Vol. 2, No. 7 (February 2013), p. 18, at http://www.mcsstw.org/web/SV/sv2013-0207.pdf.

482. For a detailed account of the exercise, see "Penghu Wude Joint Counter Amphibious Exercise (澎湖五德聯信聯合反登陸操演)," *Quanqiu Fangwei Zazhi* (Defence International), May 2013, pp. 32 - 40.

483. For an excellent assessment, see Wu Kuang-chang, "Discussion on Integration and Application Model of AH-64D Attack Helicopter and Joint Defense Operations (AH-64D 攻擊直升機於聯合防衛作戰之整合與運用模式探討)," *ROC Aviation and Special Forces Journal*, No. 56, 2012, pp. 1–18.

484. *Informatized Army Operations*, p. 145. Note that anchorage points used by amphibious assault ships carrying helicopters and hovercraft are expected to be much farther in the rear, some 30 miles from Taiwan's coast. The ROC Army has rocket artillery that can reach these points as well.

485. Huang Wei, "What Joint Service Command Officers Should Understand about Fire Support and Coordination (聯合兵種指揮官應了解之火力支援協調作爲)," *ROC Army Journal*, No. 52, Vol. 546 (April 2016), pp. 83–98.

486. See Hsu Niu, "Analysis of Ray-Ting 2000 Multiple Launch Rocket System Application and Operational Effects During Attacks on Anchorage Areas (雷霆2000多管火箭系統運用於泊地攻擊作戰效能之研析)," *ROC Artillery Forces Journal*, No. 171, 2015, p. 10.

487. See Yang Hou-sheng, "Analyzing the Operational Effectiveness of the Communist Military's Type ZLT-05 Amphibious Assault Artillery Vehicle (共軍ZLT-05型兩棲攻擊跑車作戰效能之研析)," *ROC Army Infantry Journal*, No. 258, 2016, pp. 1–24; Wang Wei-hsien and Ong Ming-hui, "Discussion on History, Development, and Application of Communist Military's Amphibious Armored Assault Vehicle for Landings (共軍兩棲裝甲戰斗車輛發展歷程與運用上陸之探討)," *ROC Army Journal*, No. 52, Vol. 546 (April 2016), pp. 53–54; and "Penghu Wude Joint Counter Amphibious Exercise (澎湖五德聯信聯合反登陸操演)," *Quanqiu Fangwei Zazhi* (Defence International), May 2013, pp. 32–34.

488. For a brief description of how homeland defense operations fit into Taiwan's overall defense strategy, see *Republic of China 2011 National*

Defense Report 中華民國2011國防報告書(Taipei: Ministry of National Defense, 2011), pp. 89–91; and *Republic of China 2013 Quadrennial Defense Review* (Taipei: Ministry of National Defense, 2013), p. 38. Note that homeland defense (國土防衛) overlaps with ground defense (地面防衛), but the latter is more limited in scope. For ROC military studies on maximizing the advantages of the home grounds, see Lai Chih-ming, *Research on Optimal Army Force Defense Deployments, Size, and Structure: the Application of Defense Position and Geometry Theory with Quantified Judgment Model* 陸戰防禦兵力部署、規模及結構適切性之研究-定量判定模型結合防禦幾何學之應用 (Taipei: National Defense University Management College Master's Thesis, 2010); Chen Shian-ruei, *Research on the Deployment of Seacoast Defense Brigades: An Application of Quantified Judgment Method Analysis* 海岸守備旅兵力配置之研究-定量判定分析模型應用 (Taipei: National Defense University Management College Master's Thesis, 2008); and Tim C.K. Shen, The Optimal Size and Defensive Location of the Army Force in Northern Taiwan: The Application of Defense Position and Geometry Theory 陸軍北部地區地面部隊規模與部署適切性之研究-防禦部署與幾何圖形理論之應用(Taipei: National Defense University Management College Master's Thesis, 2001).

489. *Informatized Army Operations*, p. 134; see also Chien Yi-jian and Ong Ming-hui, "Research on Armor Brigade Counterattack Operations during Defense Operations--The Case of a Suitable Landing Area (防衛作戰中裝甲旅反擊之研究 --以適宜登陸地區為例)," *ROC Armor Journal*, No. 240, July 2015, pp. 15–42.

490. Ibid.

491. Liu Ching-chong, "Discussion on Application of Mechanized Infantry Units in Future Defense Operations (機步部隊在未來防衛作戰運用之探討)," *ROC Army Journal*, No. 49, Vol. 529 (June 2013), pp. 4–22; and Hsu Yi-Lien, "Homeland Defense Integrated Land-Air Operations: Research on Application of Army Aviation Units (國土防衛地空整體作戰：陸航部隊運用之研究)," *ROC Army Journal*, No. 49, Vol. 529 (June 2013), pp. 23–37.

492. *Informatized Army Operations*, pp. 134–135; and Sun Shu-hwua, "Responding to Chinese Communist Urban Warfare Operations Against Taiwan—the Case of Army Aviation Units (中共對我城鎮作戰之因應

之道—以陸航部隊爲例)," *ROC Army Aviation and Special Forces Journal*, No. 56, 2012, pp. 1–15.

493. Luo Zhen-jun, "Joint Surface Defense: Analyzing the Application of Special Operations Units in Urban Areas (聯合地面防衛--以城鎮地區運用特種作戰部隊爲分析對象)," *ROC Army Aviation and Special Operations Forces Journal*, No. 56, 2012, pp. 1–18.

494. Lin Zhe-chun, "Discussion on Defense Operations in Urban Infrastructure with Support of Defense Combat Engineers (防衛作戰城鎮設施防工兵支援之探討)," *ROC Army Combat Engineer Journal*, No. 144, 2014, pp. 1–23. See also Chen Chiu-yang, "Analyzing Application of Electronic Warfare Techniques in Taiwanese Urban Warfare using of other Countries' Experiences (從各國經驗探討我城鎮戰中電子戰應用作爲之研析)," *ROC Army Combat Engineer Journal*, No. 147, 2015, pp. 1–20; Lin Sheng-jie, "Discussion on Combat Engineer Units Application of Robots in Support Missions during Urban Warfare Operations (城鎮戰中工兵部隊運用機器人直行支援任務之探討), *ROC Combat Engineer Journal*, No. 144, 2014, pp. 1–20; and Hsu Chi-po and Chen Jun-hung, "Discussion on Taiwan's Highway Bridges and Their Military Support Levels (本島公路橋樑與軍用載重等級之探討)," *ROC Army Combat Engineer Journal*, No. 142, 2013, pp. 1–16.

495. Fung Chiu-kuo, "Research on Military Value of Urban Underground Infrastructure (城鎮地下設施軍事價值之研究)," *ROC Army Infantry Journal*, No. 256, 2015, pp. 1–22.

496. Chang Kuo-ta, "Research on Application of Advanced Infantry Platoon Firepower in Urban Defense (精進進步兵排城鎮防禦火力運用之研析)," *ROC Army Infantry Journal*, No. 257, 2016, pp. 1–18.

497. *Informatized Army Operations*, p. 167.

498. Shih Hsiu-chuan, "Taiwan could withstand attack for a month: Yen," *Taipei Times*, March 7, 2014. See also Rich Chang, Lo Tien-pin, and Jake Chung, "Taiwan would not survive month of attack, NSB says," *Taipei Times*, March 11, 2014.

499. Author's discussions with ROC Army officers. See also Hung Che-Cheng, "American Military Observers in Taiwan: Chang-Ching Exercise Exposes ROC Military's Homeland Defense Ops (美軍來觀摩：長青操

演曝光-揭露陸軍國土防衛戰)," *United Daily News*, October 31, 2016, at https://udn.com/news/story/1/2057947.

500. Liu Ta-sheng, Menq Jau-yan, Chang Cheng-chang, and Chen Shi-an-Ruei, "Study on the Homeland Defense Operations Deployment of Seacoast Brigades (國土防衛海岸守備旅兵力配置之研究)," Conference paper presented at the *16th Annual Joint National Defense Management College and National Armaments Management College Seminar*, 2009, pp. 2–13.

501. For example, see *Informatized Army Operations*, p. 167.

Chapter Seven: American Strategy in Asia

502. The following discussion on US-PRC competition draws from the author's, "Strategic Standoff: The U.S.-China Rivalry and Taiwan," *Project 2049 Institute Occasional Paper*, March 2016, at http://www.project2049.net/documents/Strategic Standoff_US_China_Rivalry_Taiwan.pdf.

503. Andrew Krepinevich and Barry Watts, *The Last Warrior: Andrew Marshall and the Shaping of Modern American Defense Strategy* (New York: Basic Books, 2015), pp. 227–246; Aaron L. Friedberg, *A Contest for Supremacy: China, America, and the Struggle for Mastery in Asia* (New York: W.W. Norton & Company, 2011); and Robert Kaplan, "How We Would Fight China," *The Atlantic*, June 2005, pp. 49–64.

504. Sydney J. Freedberg Jr. and Colin Clark, "Threats from Russia, China Drive 2017 DoD Budget," *Breaking Defense*, February 2, 2016, at http://breakingdefense.com/2016/02/russia-china-drive-2017-budget/.

505. Matthew Pennington, "US-China tensions persist despite progress on NKorea," *Associated Press*, February 23, 2016, at http://bigstory.ap.org/article/4e0a8c6d263d4aad897fb5464d4f1f72/top-diplomats-meet-fraught-time-between-us-china.

506. See Richard McGregor, *The Party: The Secret World of China's Communist Rulers* (New York: Harper Perennial, 2010); Frank Dikotter, *Mao's Great Famine* (New York: Walker & Company, 2010); and Yang Jisheng, *Mubei: Zhongguo Liushi Niandai Da Jihuang Jishi* Tombstone: A Record of the Great Chinese Famine of the 1960s (Hong Kong: Cosmos Books, 2008).

507. *China (Includes Tibet, Hong Kong, and Macau) 2014 Human Rights Report* (Washington, D.C.: Department of State, undated) at http://www.state.gov/j/drl/rls/hrrpt/humanrightsreport/index.htm#wrapper. See also Congressional-Executive Commission on China, *2015 Annual Report* (Washington, D.C.: CECC, 2015), at http://www.cecc.gov/publications/annual-reports/2015-annual-report.

508. Robert D. Atkinson and Stephen Ezell, "False Promises: The Yawning Gap Between China's WTO Commitments and Practices," *Information Technology & Innovation Foundation*, September 17, 2015, at https://itif.org/publications/2015/09/17/false-promises-yawning-gap-between-china's-wto-commitments-and-practices; Stephen Ezell, "China's Economic Mercantilism," *Industry Week*, July 24, 2013, at http://www.industryweek.com/public-policy/chinas-economic-mercantilism; Derrick Scissors and Dean Cheng, "Preparing for the New Chinese Government," *China Business Review*, January 1, 2013, at http://www.chinabusinessreview.com/preparing-for-the-new-chinese-government/.

509. Dennis C. Blair and Jon M. Huntsman, Jr. (Chairs), *The IP Commission Report: The Report of the Commission on the Theft of American Intellectual Property* (Washington, D.C.: The National Bureau of Asian Research, 2013), at http://www.ipcommission.org/report/ip_commission_report_052213.pdf.

510. Elbridge Colby and Ely Ratner, "Roiling the Waters," *Foreign Policy*, January 21, 2014, at http://foreignpolicy.com/2014/01/21/roiling-the-waters/.

511. Shirley A. Kan, *China and Proliferation of Weapons of Mass Destruction and Missiles: Policy Issues* (Washington, D.C., Congressional Research Service, 2015), at https://www.fas.org/sgp/crs/nuke/RL31555.pdf; Vivek Raghuvanshi, "India-China Border Talks Make No Headway," *Defense News*, May 23, 2015, at http://www.defensenews.com/story/defense/policy-budget/leaders/2015/05/23/india-china-border-dispute-summit-talks-lac-tibet-pakistan/27601373/; and Patrick M. Cronin, *The Challenge of Responding to Maritime Coercion* (Washington, D.C.: Center for New American Security, September 2014), at http://www.cnas.org/Challenge-Responding-to-Maritime-Coercion#.VusOv-ZrMgs.

512. See Cary Huang, "Xi Jinping goes back to the future," *South China Morning Post*, January 22, 2016, at http://www.scmp.com/news/china/diplomacy-defence/article/1903831/back-future-chinese-president-xi-jinpings-middle-east?edition=international; Alain Guidetti, "The Silk Road, Sand Castles and the US-China Rivalry," *Geneva Centre for Security Policy*, July 2015, at http://www.gcsp.ch/News-Knowledge/Publications/The-Silk-Road-Sand-Castles-and-the-US-China-Rivalry; Liu Mingfu, "The World Is Too Important to be Left to America," *The Atlantic*, June 4, 2015, at http://www.theatlantic.com/international/archive/2015/06/china-dream-liu-mingfu-power/394748/; Curtis Chin, "Xi Jinping's 'Asia for Asians' mantra evokes imperial Japan," *South China Morning Post*, July 14, 2014, at http://www.scmp.com/comment/insight-opinion/article/1553414/xi-jinpings-asia-asians-mantra-evokes-imperial-japan; and Jane Perlez, "Strident Video by Chinese Military Casts U.S. as Menace," *New York Times Sinosphere*, October 31, 2013, at http://sinosphere.blogs.nytimes.com/2013/10/31/strident-video-by-chinese-military-casts-u-s-as-menace/?_r=0.

513. James Griffiths, "Marco Rubio: Xi Jinping 'devestating' for human rights in China," *CNN*, October 8, 2015, at http://www.cnn.com/2015/10/08/world/rubio-congress-china-xi-human-rights/; Edward Wong and Yufan Huang, "Col. Liu Mingfu on the U.S. and China as Rivals," *New York Times Sinosphere*, October 8, 2015, at http://sinosphere.blogs.nytimes.com/2015/10/08/col-liu-mingfu-on-the-u-s-and-china-as-rivals/; and "A very long engagement: Xi Jinping's state visit to Washington will do little to resolve growing tensions," *The Economist*, September 19, 2015, at http://www.economist.com/news/china/21665034-xi-jinpings-state-visit-washington-will-do-little-resolve-growing-tensions-very-long.

514. Michael Pillsbury, *The Hundred-Year Marathon: China's Secret Strategy to Replace America as the Global Superpower* (New York: Henry Holt and Company, 2014), pp. 113–146. See also Dan Blumenthal, "China's discomfort in an American world," *American Enterprise Institute*, October 2015, at https://www.aei.org/wp-content/uploads/2015/10/Chinas-discomfort-in-an-American-world.pdf; Adam Taylor, "Zimbabwean strongman Robert Mugabe wins China's version of the Nobel Peace Prize," *Washington Post*, October 22, 2015, at https://www.washingtonpost.com/news/world-

views/wp/2015/10/22/zimbabwean-strongman-robert-mugabe-wins-chi-nas-version-of-the-nobel-peace-prize/; Adam Taylor, "Yes, Kim Jong Un is receiving an international peace prize," *Washington Post*, August 3, 2015; and "Vladimir Putin in China Confucius Peace Prize fiasco," *BBC News*, November 16, 2011, at https://www.washingtonpost.com/news/world-views/wp/2015/08/03/yes-kim-jong-un-is-receiving-an-international-peace-prize/.

515. Peter Mattis, *Analyzing the Chinese Military: A Review Essay and Resource Guide on the People's Liberation Army* (Middletown, DE: Cre-atespace Publishing, 2015), pp. 1–2; and Amelia Friedman, "America's Lacking Language Skills," *The Atlantic*, May 10, 2015, at http://www.theat-lantic.com/education/archive/2015/05/filling-americas-language-educa-tion-potholes/392876/.

516. See *A War Like No Other: The Truth about China's Challenge to America*.

517. Office of the Secretary of Defense, *Military and Security Developments Involving the People's Republic of China 2015* (Washington, D.C.: Depart-ment of Defense, 2015), pp. 6 & 57–61; and *The PLA Navy: New Capabilities and Missions for the 21st Century* (Suitland, MD: Office of Naval Intelligence, 2015), p. 9.

518. Ian Easton, "The South China Sea is Not Beijing's Next Battlefield," *The National Interest*, September 19, 2015, at http://nationalinterest.org/feature/the-south-china-sea-not-beijings-next-battlefield-13881. See also Michael Martina and Ben Blanchard, "Don't read too much into military drills, China says after Taiwan alarm," *Reuters*, January 22, 2016, at http://www.reuters.com/article/us-china-taiwan-security-idUSKCN0V0oIM.

519. See Victor Robert Lee, "Satellite Imagery: China Staging Mock In-vasion of Taiwan?" *The Diplomat*, August 9, 2015, at http://thediplomat.com/2015/08/satellite-imagery-from-china-suggests-mock-invasion-of-tai-wan/; and Lo Tien-pin and Jake Chung, "China simulates attack on Presi-dential Office," *Taipei Times*, July 23, 2015, at http://www.taipeitimes.com/News/front/archives/2015/07/23/2003623689.

520. Tom Wright and Aries Poon, "Taiwan Grapples With Closer Chi-na Ties," *Wall Street Journal*, December 7, 2014, at http://www.wsj.com/articles/taiwan-grapples-with-closer-china-ties-1418000788; Ricky Yeh,

"Over-Dependence on China will Doom Taiwan," *The Diplomat*, August 26, 2014, at http://thediplomat.com/2014/08/over-dependence-on-china-will-doom-taiwan/; Robert D. Kaplan, "The Geography of Chinese Power," *Foreign Affairs*, May/June 2010, at https://www.foreignaffairs.com/articles/china/2010-05-01/geography-chinese-power; Stephen Nelson, "Falling into China's Orbit," *CBC News*, December 18, 2008, at http://www.cbc.ca/news/world/falling-into-china-s-orbit-1.747292.

521. See Kin W. Moy, "U.S.–Taiwan Relations in a Changing Regional Landscape," *Remarks of Director of American Institute on Taiwan*, September 30, 2015, at https://www.ait.org.tw/en/officialtext-ot1523.html.

522. See John J. Mearsheimer, "Say Goodbye to Taiwan," *The National Interest*, March-April 2014, at http://nationalinterest.org/article/say-good-bye-taiwan-9931; and Thalia Lin, "Don't Say Goodbye to Taiwan," *The National Interest*, February 27, 2014, at http://nationalinterest.org/commentary/dont-say-goodbye-taiwan-9966; and Nat Bellocchi, "Say goodbye to Taiwan, say goodbye to peace," *Taipei Times*, Match 9, 2014, at http://www.taipeitimes.com/News/editorials/archives/2014/03/09/2003585202.

523. *Taiwan Relations Act* (Public Law 96-8 96th Congress), January 1, 1979, at http://www.ait.org.tw/en/taiwan-relations-act.html.

524. See Bruce A. Elleman, *High Seas Buffer: The Taiwan Patrol Force, 1950–1979* (Newport, Rhode Island: Naval War College Press, 2012); Edward J. Marolda, *Ready Seapower: A History of the U.S. Seventh Fleet* (Washington, D.C., Naval History & Heritage Command, 2011), and Robert Ross Smith, "Luzon Versus Formosa" in Kent Roberts Greenfield (ed.), *Command Decisions* (Washington, D.C.: Defense Department Army Center of Military History, 1960).

525. Ibid. See also Robert D. Kaplan, "The Geography of Chinese Power," *Foreign Affairs*, May/June 2010. For an excellent analysis of Chinese perspectives, see Andrew S. Erickson and Joel Wuthnow, "Barriers, Springboards, and Benchmarks: China Conceptualizes the Pacific 'Island Chains,'" *China Quarterly*, January 21, 2016, at http://www.andrewerickson.com/2016/01/barriers-springboards-and-benchmarks-china-conceptualizes-the-pacific-island-chains-firstview-version-of-article-now-available-on-the-china-quarterly-webs/.

526. See, "The South China Sea is Not Beijing's Next Battlefield."

527. See Eric Heginbotham, et al., *The U.S.-China Military Scorecard: Forces, Geography, and the Evolving Balance of Power, 1996–2017* (Washington, D.C., RAND Corporation, 2015), at http://www.rand.org/pubs/research_reports/RR392.html; David A. Shlapak, et al., *A Question of Balance: Political Context and Military Aspects of the China-Taiwan Dispute* (Arlington, VA: RAND Corporation, 2009), at http://www.rand.org/pubs/monographs/MG888.html; and Roger Cliff, et al., *Entering the Dragon's Lair: Chinese Antiaccess Strategies and Their Implications for the United States* (Arlington, VA: RAND Corporation, 2007), at http://www.rand.org/pubs/monographs/MG524.html.

528. See J. Michael Cole, "Taiwan's Master Plan to Defeat China in a War," *The National Interest*, March 31, 2015, at http://nationalinterest.org/feature/taiwans-master-plan-defeat-china-war-12510; and J. Michael Cole, "Five Taiwanese Weapons of War China Should Fear," *The National Interest*, July 8, 2014, at http://nationalinterest.org/feature/five-taiwanese-weapons-war-china-should-fear-10827. See also, *Able Archers: Taiwan Defense Strategy in an Age of Precision Strike*.

529. See Easton and Schriver, *Standing Watch: Taiwan and Maritime Domain Awareness in the Western Pacific*; and Stokes and Hsiao, *The People's Liberation Army General Political Department: Political Warfare with Chinese Characteristics*.

530. Eric Heginbotham, et al.; David A. Shlapak, et al.; and Roger Cliff, et al.

531. For example, see Charles Glaser, "A U.S.-China Grand Bargain? The Hard Choice between Military Competition and Accommodation," *International Security*, Spring 2015, pp. 49–90.; and Lyle J. Goldstein, *Meeting China Halfway: How to Defuse the Emerging US-China Rivalry* (Washington, D.C.: Georgetown University Press, 2015).

532. For example, see Daniel Twining, "The Future of Japan-Taiwan Relations," *American Enterprise Institute*, November 10, 2011, at https://www.aei.org/wp-content/uploads/2012/10/-the-future-of-japantaiwan-relations-strategic-diversification-in-pursuit-of-security-autonomy-and-prosperity_145415896141.pdf.

533. For an excellent assessment of why Taiwan's values matter to U.S. foreign policy interests, see Mark A. Stokes and Sabrina Tsai, *The United States and Future Policy Options in the Taiwan Strait* (Arlington, VA: Project 2049 Institute, February 2016), at http://www.project2049.net/ documents/160130_ ALTERNATE_FUTURE_POLICY_OPTIONS_IN _THE_TAIWAN_STRAIT.pdf.

534. See "Top Trading Partners - December 2016," *United States Census Bureau*, undated, at https://www.census.gov/foreign-trade/statistics/high-lights/toppartners.html.

535. Jeff Demmin, "The business of chip-making," *The Economist*, October 17, 2013, at http://www.economistinsights.com/technology-innovation/ opinion/business-chip-making. See also Doug Young, Unigroup Boosts Taiwan Ties In Global Chip Challenge," *Forbes*, December 14, 2015, at http:// www.forbes.com/sites/dougyoung/2015/12/14/unigroup-boosts-taiwan-ties-in-global-chip-challenge/#330a88822766.

536. For background, see Craig Addison, *Silicon Shield: Taiwan's Protection Against Chinese Attack* (Irving, TX: Authorlink, 2001).

537. See Glaser and Goldstein. For background see, John Lewis Gaddis, *The Cold War: A New History*.

538. Shirely Kan, "China's Anti-Satellite Weapon Test," *CRS Report for Congress*, April 23, 2007, at https://www.fas.org/sgp/crs/row/RS22652.pdf; and Ian Easton, *The Great Game in Space: China's Evolving ASAT Weapons Programs and Their Implications for Future U.S. Strategy* (Arlington, VA: Project 2049 Institute, June 2009), at https://project2049.net/documents/ china_asat_weapons_the_great_game_in_space.pdf.

539. Brian Weeden, "Through a glass, darkly: Chinese, American, and Russian anti-satellite testing in space," *The Space Review*, March 17, 2014, at http://www.thespacereview.com/article/2473/1.

540. Andrew S. Erickson, *Chinese Anti-Ship Ballistic Missile (ASBM) Development: Drivers, Trajectories and Strategic Implications* (Washington, D.C., The Jamestown Foundation, May 2013), at http://www.andrewerickson. com/wp-content/uploads/2014/01/China-ASBM_Jamestown_2013.pdf; and Mark Stokes, *China's Evolving Conventional Strategic Strike Capability: The anti-ship ballistic missile challenge to U.S. maritime operations in the*

Western Pacific and beyond (Arlington, VA: Project 2049 Institute, September 2009), at https://project2049.net/documents/chinese_anti_ship_ballistic_missile_asbm.pdf.

541. For example, see Robert Windrem, "Exclusive: Secret NSA Map Shows China Cyber Attacks on U.S. Targets," *NBC News*, July 30, 2015, at http://www.nbcnews.com/news/us-news/exclusive-secret-nsa-map-shows-china-cyber-attacks-us-targets-n401211; Sam LaGrone, "China Sends Uninvited Spy Ship to RIMPAC," *USNI News*, July 18, 2014, at http://news.usni.org/2014/07/18/china-sends-uninvited-spy-ship-rimpac; Jon Harper, "Chinese warship nearly collided with USS *Cowpens*," *Stars and Stripes*, December 13, 2013, at http://www.stripes.com/news/pacific/chinese-warship-nearly-collided-with-uss-cowpens-1.257478; Madison Park, "Why China's new air zone incensed Japan, U.S.," *CNN*, November 27, 2013, at http://www.cnn.com/2013/11/25/world/asia/china-japan-island-explainer/; Esther Tran Le, "China and Philippines in Standoff Over Resource -Rich Islands," *International Business Times*, April 11, 2012, at http://www.ibtimes.com/china-and-philippines-standoff-over-resource-rich-islands-436190; Elisabeth Blumiller and Michael Wines, "Test of Stealth Fighter Clouds Gates Visit to China," *New York Times*, January 11, 2011, at http://www.nytimes.com/2011/01/12/world/asia/12fighter.html?_r=0.

542. Elbridge Colby and Ely Ratner, "Roiling the Waters" *Foreign Policy*, January 21, 2014, at http://foreignpolicy.com/2014/01/21/roiling-the-waters/.

543. Catherine Putz, "Campbell: The History of the 21st Century Will be Written in Asia," *The Diplomat*, April 15, 2015, at http://thediplomat.com/2015/04/campbell-the-history-of-the-21st-century-will-be-written-in-asia/; Kurt M. Campbell and Ely Ratner, "Far Eastern Promises: Why Washington Should Focus on Asia," *Foreign Affairs*, May/June 2014, at https://www.foreignaffairs.com/articles/east-asia/2014-04-18/far-eastern-promises; Kurt Campbell and Brian Andrews, "Explaining the U.S. 'Pivot' to Asia," *Chatham House*, August 2013, at https://www.chathamhouse.org/sites/files/chathamhouse/public/Research/Americas/0813pp_pivottoasia.pdf; and Hilary Clinton, "America's Pacific Century," *Foreign Policy*, October 11, 2011, at http://foreignpolicy.com/2011/10/11/americas-pacific-century/.

544. See Aaron L. Friedberg, *Beyond Air-Sea Battle: The Debate Over U.S. Military Strategy in Asia* (New York: Routledge , 2014); and Jan Van Tol, *AirSea Battle, A Point of Departure Operational Concept*, (Washington, D.C.: Center for Strategic and Budgetary Assessments, 2010), at http://csbaon-line.org/publications/2010/05/airsea-battle-concept/.

545. Fareed Zakaria, "Whatever happened to Obama's pivot to Asia?" *Washington Post*, April 16, 2015, at https://www.washingtonpost.com/opinions/the-forgotten-pivot-to-asia/2015/04/16/529cc5b8-e477-11e4-905f-cc896d379a32_story.html.

546. "A 'Great Wall of Sand' in the South China Sea," *Washington Post*, April 8, 2015, at https://www.washingtonpost.com/opinions/a-great-wall-of-sand/2015/04/08/d23adb3e-dd6a-11e4-be40-566e2653afe5_story.html; and Derek Watkins, "What China Has Been Building in the South China Sea," *New York Times*, October 27, 2015, at http://www.nytimes.com/interactive/2015/07/30/world/asia/what-china-has-been-building-in-the-south-china-sea.html.

547. Ellen Nakashima, "Hacks of OPM databases compromised 22.1 million people, federal authorities say," *Washington Post*, July 9, 2015, at https://www.washingtonpost.com/news/federal-eye/wp/2015/07/09/hack-of-security-clearance-system-affected-21-5-million-people-federal-authorities-say/; and Ellen Nakashima, "Chinese hack of federal personnel files included security-clearance database," *Washington Post*, June 12, 2015, at https://www.washingtonpost.com/world/national-security/chinese-hack-of-government-network-compromises-security-clearance-files/2015/06/12/9f91f146-1135-11e5-9726-49d6fa26a8c6_story.html. For an excellent study on PLA hackers, see Mark A. Stokes, *The PLA General Staff Department Third Department Second Bureau: An Organizational Overview of Unit 61398* (Arlington VA: Project 2049 Institute, July 2015), at http://www.project2049.net/documents/Stokes_PLA_General_Staff_Department_Unit_61398.pdf.

548. Wendell Minnick, "China's Parade Puts U.S. Navy on Notice," *Defense News*, September 3, 2015, at http://www.defensenews.com/story/defense/naval/2015/09/03/chinas-parade-puts-us-navy-notice/71632918/.

549. Author's discussions with Taiwanese officials.

550. Wendell Minnick, "Taiwan Turning the Screws on Washington's Sub Deal," *Defense News*, December 5, 2015, at http://www.defensenews.com/story/defense/naval/submarines/2015/12/05/taiwan-turning-screws-washingtons-sub-deal/76676188/.

551. Christopher P. Cavas, "US Frigates Approved For Transfer - Finally," *Defense News*, December 19, 2015, at http://www.defensenews.com/story/defense/naval/ships/2014/12/19/navy-frigates-ships-taiwan-china-mexico/20642841/.

552. See Kevin V. Cunningham, "Stetham Arrives in Shanghai to Promote Cooperation with PLA (N) East Sea Fleet," *America's Navy*, November 16, 2015, at http://www.navy.mil/submit/display.asp?story_id=92020; Megan Eckstein, "USS *Blue Ridge* Pulls into Zhanjiang, China for Port Visit," *USNI News*, April 20, 2015, at http://news.usni.org/2015/04/20/uss-blue-ridge-pulls-into-zhanjiang-china-for-port-visit; and Jacob Waldrop, "Blue Ridge Strengthens Cooperation with PLA(N) North Sea Fleet in Qingdao, China," *America's Navy*, August 5, 2014, at http://www.navy.mil/submit/display.asp?story_id=82580.

553. Andrew Browne, "For U.S., Taiwan Vote Changes Calculus over 'One China,'" *Wall Street Journal*, January 19, 2016, at http://www.wsj.com/articles/for-u-s-taiwan-vote-changes-calculus-over-one-china-1453183661; Dan Blumenthal, "Will the 'One China' policy survive the new Taiwan?" *Foreign Policy*, January 19, 2016, at http://foreignpolicy.com/2016/01/19/will-the-one-china-policy-survive-the-new-taiwan/; and Jeremy Page, Jenny W. Hsu, and Eva Dou, "Taiwan Elects Tsai Ing-wen as First Female President," *Wall Street Journal*, January 16, 2016, at http://www.wsj.com/articles/taiwans-historic-election-set-to-test-china-ties-1452925430.

554. Jennifer M. Turner, "DPP Plans to Enhance Taiwan Defense: Prospects and Cross Strait Implications," *China Brief*, January 12, 2016, at http://www.jamestown.org/programs/chinabrief/single/?tx_ttnewstt_news=44973&cHash=8f92be95d5297ca78d025cd5724cdcc6#.VuwGkeZrMgs; and Defense Policy Advisory Committee, *Bolstering Taiwan's Core Defense Industries* (Taipei, Taiwan: New Frontier Foundation, October 2014), at http://english.dpp.org.tw/seventh-defense-policy-blue-paper-released/.

555. The following discussion draws from the model of, "United States National Security Decision Directive Number 75: U.S. Relations with the USSR," *The White House*, January 17, 1983, accessible at https://fas.org/irp/offdocs/nsdd/nsdd-75.pdf. For an excellent discussion on the significance of this strategy document, see Thomas G. Mahnken, "The Reagan administration's strategy toward the Soviet Union," in Williamson Murray and Richard Hart Sinnreich (eds.), *Successful Strategies: Triumphing in War and Peace from Antiquity to Present* (Cambridge, United Kingdom: Cambridge University Press, 2014), pp. 403–430.

556. Author's discussions with American officials and subject matter experts.

557. See Mark Stokes and Russell Hsiao, *The People's Liberation Army General Political Department: Political Warfare with Chinese Characteristics* (Arlington, VA: Project 2049 Institute, October 14, 2013), at http://www.project2049.net/documents/PLA_General_Political_Department_Liaison_Stokes_Hsiao.pdf.

558. Office of the Secretary of Defense, *Military and Security Developments Involving the People's Republic of China 2015* (Washington, D.C.: Department of Defense, 2015), pp. 57–61.

559. The author is indebted to Ian Mccaslin for this point.

560. Of many examples, see Yan Chung-yi, "Insights for Our Military on Counter-landing Operations from the Battle of Iwo Jima (硫磺島戰史對國軍反登陸作戰之啓示)," *ROC Navy Journal*, No. 49, Vol. 6 (December 2015), pp. 108–117; Hsiao Ing-li and Wu Kuang-chung, "Research on American and Japanese Pacific Island Combat during World War Two: Examples from Okinawa, Iwo Jima, and Formosa (第二次世界大戰美，日太平洋島嶼作戰之研究-以沖繩島，硫磺島及台灣爲例)," *ROC Army Journal*, Vol. 51, No. 543 (October 2015), pp. 102–123; Chen Sheng-chang and Jia Chi-hao, "Insights for ROC Army from German Army Defense Operations during Normandy Campaign (諾曼第戰役-德軍防衛作戰對我之啓示)," *ROC Army Journal*, Vol. 50, No. 534 (April 2015), pp. 5–25; and Huang Tai-Chi, "Insights from the Okinawa Campaign for ROC Counter-landing Operations and Artillery Unit Force Preservation (沖繩島戰役對我反登

陸作戰砲兵部隊戰力保存之啓示)," *ROC Army Artillery Journal*, No. 170 (2015), pp. 8–23.

561. See *Informatized Army Operations*, pp. 111–113, 130–132, 196–199. See also *Space Information Support Operations*, pp. 148–149; and *A Military History of Fifty Years in the Taiwan Area*, p. 228.

562. See *Informatized Army Operations*, pp.112, 122–123, 146–148, 177, 183, 198–199; and *A Military History of Fifty Years in the Taiwan Area*, pp. 84, 116.

563. See Cao Zhengrong et al. (eds.), *Informatized Army Operations*, pp. 127–128, 178; and *Space Information Support Operations*, pp. 156–165, 200, 212.

Chapter Eight: What Lies Ahead?

564. For example, see "Penghu Wude Joint Counter Amphibious Exercise (澎湖五德聯信聯合反登陸操演)," *Quanqiu Fangwei Zazhi* (Defence International), May 2013, pp. 32–40.

565. For more on this topic, see *Able Archers: Taiwan Defense Strategy in an Age of Precision Strike*, p. 30; and Easton and Schriver, *Standing Watch: Taiwan and Maritime Domain Awareness in the Western Pacific*.

566. Ibid.

567. For example, see "Reserve Mobilization: Counterattack after Tamsui Raid and Taipei Port Attack (後備動員淡水反突擊台北港反擊), *Quanqiu Fangwei Zazhi* (Defence International), No. 362, October 2014, pp. 36–43.

568. See *Informatized Army Operations*, pp. 172, 190.

569. For example, see Liu Ching-jong, "Examining the Application of Mechanized Infantry in Future Defense Operations (機步部隊在未來防衛作戰運用之探討), *ROC Army Journal*, Vol. 49, No. 529, June 2013, pp. 4–22. At the time of this article the author was a ROC Army LTC serving as the Director of the ROC Infantry Academy's Tactics Group.

570. For example, see Liu Wen-hsiao, "Taiwan's Chiashan Air Force Base: Combat Effectiveness Preservation and Tactics," *Ping-Ch'i Chan-shu T'u-chieh* (Illustrated Guide of Weapons and Tactics), July 2007; and *A Military History of Fifty Years in the Taiwan Area*, p. 84.

Acknowledgements

This book was only possible because I had tremendous help from colleagues, mentors, friends, and family. I owe a special debt of gratitude to the Project 2049 Institute's president and CEO, Randy Schriver, who has long encouraged self-initiated research into understudied (and underfunded) topics. He generously allowed me to use our institute's own resources to pursue this book project. In the think tank world, there is no better leader and no greater gift. Mark Stokes, my research director, deserves special mention. He has been an invaluable source of knowledge and inspiration for nearly a decade. Mark is a fearless analyst and great mentor. It is no exaggeration to say that this book could never have happened if it wasn't for him. My colleague, Rachael Burton, went above and beyond the call of duty in reviewing and copy-editing this book. Rachael is one of the smartest young China-watchers out there and a delight to work with. Randy, Mark, and Rachael have my profound appreciation for creating an office atmosphere where path-breaking scholarship can thrive.

I would like to acknowledge and thank Wendell Minnick, redoubtable foreign correspondent and Asia military expert, for introducing me to the Taiwan defense studies community and shepherding my early interest in cross-Strait security issues. He reviewed the manuscript, guided me through the publishing process, and provided the cover image.

I am grateful to Peter Mattis, Matt Hallex, Ian McCaslin, and Elsa Kania, who all took time out of their busy schedules to provide expert reviews and comments on various drafts of the manuscript, making for a greatly improved final cut. In addition, Logan Ma tirelessly collaborated with me to produce order of battle charts for the ROC military. It is an honor to work with such dedicated analysts.

Several individuals and organizations hosted me along the way for public conferences and private workshops, including Jan val Tol (CSBA), Denise Der (OSD Strategy), Rick Fisher (IASC), and Jeff McKitrick (Scitor). They gave me the opportunity to brief initial drafts in Washington. Major General Chen Chia-Sheng (MND) and Richard Bitzinger (RSIS) did the same in Taipei and Singapore, respectively.

My friends David An, Dennis Blasko, Amy Chang, J. Michael Cole, Zack Cooper, Emily David, Andrew Erickson, Russell Hsiao, Tetsuo Kotani, Tiffany Ma, Oriana Skylar Mastro, Sam Mun, Craig Murray, Barry Scott, Sabrina Tsai, and Aaron Weinberg all provided much needed sounding boards, while offering their expert critiques.

My grandfather, William F. Murphy (USMC), provided a generous grant which supported a last-minute research trip to Taiwan, needed for finishing this book. He was an infantryman in the Second Marine Division, who made several combat landings in World War II and was thankful that Formosa was not one of them. I am grateful beyond words for his contributions to our family and our nation.

As a final note, I would like to acknowledge and thank the many anonymous military officers, intelligence professionals, diplomats, soldiers, sailors, airmen, and marines I was fortunate enough to meet in Taiwan, Penghu, Kinmen, Guishan Island, Ishigaki, Okinawa, Yokosuka, Tokyo, Washington, and Williamsburg. They all had better and more important things to do, but generously took the time to talk to me about their work and share their perspectives. Their judicious contributions are much appreciated.

If you liked the book, the credit belongs to those listed above. If you disagreed and/or saw mistakes, I am entirely responsible, not only for the translations, analysis, and findings presented, but also for the style in which they were presented. I would warmly welcome your corrections and feedback. My email is: easton@project2049.net.

About the Project 2049 Institute

The Project 2049 Institute seeks to guide decision makers toward a more secure Asia by the century's mid-point. Located in Arlington, Virginia, the organization fills a gap in the public policy realm through forward-looking, region-specific research on alternative security and policy solutions. Its interdisciplinary approach draws on rigorous analysis of socioeconomic, governance, military, environmental, technological and political trends, and input from key players in the region, with an eye toward educating the public and informing policy debate.

About the Author

Ian Easton is a research fellow at the Project 2049 Institute. He previously was a visiting fellow at the Japan Institute for International Affairs (JIIA) in Tokyo, and a China analyst at the Center for Naval Analyses (CNA Corporation). His research has been featured in the *New York Times*, the Associated Press, Reuters, *U.S. News & World Report*, *Newsweek Japan*, and many other media outlets in the United States and Asia. Ian has testified before the U.S.-China Economic and Security Review Commission and given lectures at the U.S. Naval War College, Japan's National Defense Academy, and Taiwan's National Defense University.

Lightning Source UK Ltd.
Milton Keynes UK
UKHW020802061020
371100UK00019B/1846

9 781788 691765